by Stephen L. Nelson, MBA, CPA

WILEY

Wiley Publishing, Inc.

Quicken® 2007 For Dummies®

Published by
Wiley Publishing, Inc.
111 River Street
Hoboken, NJ 07030-5774

www.wiley.com

Copyright © 2006 by Wiley Publishing, Inc., Indianapolis, Indiana

Published by Wiley Publishing, Inc., Indianapolis, Indiana

Published simultaneously in Canada

No part of this publication may be reproduced, stored in a retrieval system or transmitted in any form or by any means, electronic, mechanical, photocopying, recording, scanning or otherwise, except as permitted under Sections 107 or 108 of the 1976 United States Copyright Act, without either the prior written permission of the Publisher, or authorization through payment of the appropriate per-copy fee to the Copyright Clearance Center, 222 Rosewood Drive, Danvers, MA 01923, (978) 750-8400, fax (978) 646-8600. Requests to the Publisher for permission should be addressed to the Legal Department, Wiley Publishing, Inc., 10475 Crosspoint Blvd., Indianapolis, IN 46256, (317) 572-3447, fax (317) 572-4355, or online at http://www.wiley.com/go/permissions.

Trademarks: Wiley, the Wiley Publishing logo, For Dummies, the Dummies Man logo, A Reference for the Rest of Us!, The Dummies Way, Dummies Daily, The Fun and Easy Way, Dummies.com, and related trade dress are trademarks or registered trademarks of John Wiley & Sons, Inc. and/or its affiliates in the United States and other countries, and may not be used without written permission. Quicken is a registered trademark of Intuit, Inc. All other trademarks are the property of their respective owners. Wiley Publishing, Inc., is not associated with any product or vendor mentioned in this book.

For general information on our other products and services, please contact our Customer Care Department within the U.S. at 800-762-2974, outside the U.S. at 317-572-3993, or fax 317-572-4002.

For technical support, please visit www.wiley.com/techsupport.

Wiley also publishes its books in a variety of electronic formats. Some content that appears in print may not be available in electronic books.

Library of Congress Control Number: 2006929465

ISBN-13: 978-0-470-04600-5

ISBN-10: 0-470-04600-7

Manufactured in the United States of America

10 9 8 7 6 5 4 3 2 1

1O/SS/QY/QW/IN

WILEY

About the Author

Stephen L. Nelson is a CPA in Redmond, Washington. Nelson has an under-graduate degree in accounting, a master of business administration degree in finance, and a master of science degree in taxation. He's spent more than two decades helping individuals and businesses manage their finances — usually, in part, by better use of computer systems such as Quicken. More recently, he's worked as a sole proprietor. When he wasn't doing CPA-type work, he served as controller of a small, 50-person computer software company, and then as a book publisher.

As corny as it sounds, Steve truly enjoys writing books that make using personal computers easier and more fun. In fact, a substantiated rumor that appeared first in *The Wall Street Journal* says Steve has written more than 150 computer books.

Steve is the best-selling author on the Quicken product. In fact, Wiley recently tallied up Steve's *Quicken For Dummies* sales — and lo and behold if we haven't printed more than one million copies!

Author's Acknowledgments

The editorial folks are Kevin Kirschner (the project editor), Heidi Unger (the copy editor), and Bob Woerner (the acquisitions editor). Thanks go to David Ringstrom for his technical assistance and superb attention to detail. Thanks also to the composition staff.

Publisher's Acknowledgments

We're proud of this book; please send us your comments through our online registration form located at www.dummies.com/register/.

Some of the people who helped bring this book to market include the following:

Acquisitions, Editorial, and Media Development

Project Editor: Kevin Kirschner

Acquisitions Editor: Bob Woerner

Copy Editor: Heidi Unger

Technical Editor: David H. Ringstrom

Editorial Manager: Kevin Kirschner

Media Development Manager: Laura VanWinkle

Media Development Supervisor: Richard Graves

Editorial Assistant: Amanda Foxworth

Cartoons: Rich Tennant (www.the5thwave.com)

Composition Services

Project Coordinator: Tera Knapp

Layout and Graphics: Andrea Dahl, Lauren Goddard, Stephanie D. Jumper, Heather Ryan, Alicia B. South

Proofreaders: Leeann Harney, Jessica Kramer, Techbooks

Indexer: Techbooks

Publishing and Editorial for Technology Dummies

Richard Swadley, Vice President and Executive Group Publisher

Andy Cummings, Vice President and Publisher

Mary Bednarek, Executive Acquisitions Director

Mary C. Corder, Editorial Director

Publishing for Consumer Dummies

Diane Graves Steele, Vice President and Publisher

Joyce Pepple, Acquisitions Director

Composition Services

Gerry Fahey, Vice President of Production Services

Debbie Stailey, Director of Composition Services

Contents at a Glance

Table of Contents

Part V: The Part of Tens299

Chapter 17 : (Slightly More Than) Ten Questions I'm Frequently Asked about Quicken301

Chapter 18: (Almost) Ten Tips on How Not to Become a Millionaire ..311

Chapter 19: (Almost) Ten Troubleshooting Tips321

Introduction

· ·

You aren't a dummy, of course. But here's the deal: You don't have to be some sort of technogeek or financial wizard to manage your financial affairs on a PC. You have other things to do, places to go, and people to meet. And that's where *Quicken 2007 For Dummies* comes in.

In the pages that follow, I give you the scoop on how to use Quicken 2007 Premier for Windows, without a lot of extra baggage, goofy tangential information, or misguided advice.

About This Book

This book isn't meant to be read from cover to cover like some Dan Brown page-turner. Rather, it's organized into tiny, no-sweat descriptions of how to do the things you need to do. If you're the sort of person who just doesn't feel right not reading a book from cover to cover, you can, of course, go ahead and read this thing from front to back.

I can recommend this approach, however, only for people who have already checked the TV listings. There may, after all, be an *X-Files* rerun on.

How to Use This Book

I always enjoyed reading those encyclopedias my parents bought for my siblings and me. I could flip open, say, the *E* volume, look up *elephants,* and then learn just about everything I needed to know about elephants for a fifth-grade report: where elephants live, how much they weigh, and why they eat so much.

You won't read anything about elephants here, but you can use this book in the same way. If you want to learn about something, look through the Table of Contents or Index and find the topic — printing checks, for example. Then flip to the correct chapter or page and read as much as you need or enjoy. No muss. No fuss.

If you want to find out about anything else, just repeat the process.

What You Can Safely Ignore

Sometimes I provide step-by-step descriptions of tasks. I feel very bad that I have to do this. So to make things easier for you, I highlight the tasks with bold text. That way, you'll know exactly what you're supposed to do. I also often provide a more detailed explanation in regular text so that you can skip the regular text that accompanies the step-by-step descriptions if you already understand the process.

Here's an example that shows what I mean:

1. **Press Enter.**

 Find the key that's labeled Enter. Extend your index finger so that it rests ever so gently on the Enter key. In one sure, fluid motion, press the Enter key using your index finger. Then release the key.

Okay, that's kind of an extreme example. I never go into that much detail. But you get the idea. If you know how to press Enter, you can just do that and not read further. If you need help — say with the finger depression part or something — just read the nitty-gritty details.

Can you skip anything else? Let me see now. . . . You can skip the paragraphs with the Technical Stuff icons next to them. See the "Special Icons" section later in this Introduction for an example of the Technical Stuff icon. The information I stick in those paragraphs is really only for those of you who like that technical kind of stuff.

What You Should Not Ignore (Unless You're a Masochist)

Don't skip the Warnings. They're the text flagged with the picture of the nineteenth-century bomb. They describe some things you really shouldn't do.

Out of respect for you, I'm not going to put such stuff in these paragraphs as "Don't smoke." I figure that you're an adult. You can make your own lifestyle decisions.

So I'll reserve the Warnings for more urgent and immediate dangers — things akin to "Don't smoke while you're filling your car with gasoline."

Three Foolish Assumptions

I assume just three things:

- ✔ You have a PC with Microsoft Windows 95, 98, Me, 2000, NT, XP, or Vista.
- ✔ You know how to turn it on.
- ✔ You want to use some flavor of Quicken 2007.

The Flavors of Quicken

Okay. I lied in the previous section. I'm going to assume one more thing: You own or somehow have access to a copy of Quicken.

You may be interested to know that Quicken comes in several versions. It doesn't really matter which one of the several versions you have. Each version works in basically the same way, and this book applies to all of them. But because each version has a few unique features, you may find that your screen doesn't look exactly like the screens shown in this book. You may, for example, have a few buttons that you don't see in the figures I show you. Don't worry if this happens. It probably means that you're working with a different version than I am.

Just to let you know, I used the Premier version to write this book. You can tell this because at the top of some of the figures, Quicken 2007 Premier appears in the title bar. If you have a different version, those title bars bear the name of the version you're using.

How This Book Is Organized

This book is organized into six mostly coherent parts.

Part I: Zen, Quicken, and the Big Picture

Part I covers some up-front stuff you need to take care of. I promise I won't waste your time here. I just want to make sure that you get off on the right foot.

Part II: The Absolute Basics

This second part of the book explains the core knowledge you need to know in order to keep a personal or business checkbook with Quicken: using the checkbook, printing, reporting on your finances, using online banking, balancing your bank accounts, and using the Quicken calculators.

Some of this stuff isn't very exciting compared to *Dr. Phil* — which really is a good show, isn't it? — so I'll work hard to make things fun for you.

Part III: Home Finances

Part III talks about the sorts of things you may want to do with Quicken if you're using it at home: credit cards, loans, mutual funds, stocks, and bonds. You get the idea. If you don't ever get this far — hey, that's cool.

If you do get this far, you'll find that Quicken provides some tools that eliminate not only the drudgery of keeping a checkbook, but also the drudgery of most other financial burdens.

While I'm on the subject, I also want to categorically deny that Part III contains any secret messages if you read it backward.

Part IV: Serious Business

The "Serious Business" part helps people who use Quicken in a business.

If you're pulling your hair out because you're using Quicken in a business, postpone the hair pulling — at least for the time being. Read Part IV first. It tells you about preparing payroll, tracking the amounts that customers owe you, and other wildly exciting stuff.

Part V: The Part of Tens

By tradition, a *For Dummies* book includes "The Part of Tens." It provides a collection of ten-something lists: ten answers to frequently asked questions about Quicken, ten ways not to become a millionaire, and ten tips for troubleshooting Quicken when you encounter a problem.

Part VI: Appendixes

It's an unwritten rule that computer books have appendixes, so I include two. Appendix A gives you a quick-and-dirty overview of Windows for those new to the world of Windows. Appendix B is a glossary of key business, financial, and computer terms.

Conventions Used in This Book

To make the best use of your time and energy, you should know about the following conventions I use in this book.

When I want you to type something, such as **Hydraulics screamed as the pilot lowered his landing gear**, I put it in bold letters. When I want you to type something that's short and uncomplicated, such as **Hillary**, it still appears in bold type.

By the way, with Quicken, you don't have to worry about the case of the stuff you type (except for passwords, which are case sensitive). If I tell you to type **Hillary**, you can type **HILLARY**. Or you can follow e. e. cummings's lead and type **hillary**.

Whenever I describe a message or information that you see on the screen, I present it as follows:

```
Surprise! This is a message on-screen.
```

Special Icons

Like many computer books, this book uses icons, or little pictures, to flag things that don't quite fit into the flow of things. *For Dummies* books use a standard set of icons that flag little digressions, such as the following:

This icon points out nerdy technical material that you may want to skip (or read, if you're feeling particularly bright).

Here's a shortcut to make your life easier.

This icon is just a friendly reminder to do something.

And this icon is a friendly reminder *not* to do something . . . or else.

Where to Next?

If you're just getting started, flip the page and start reading the first chapter.

If you have a special problem or question, use the Table of Contents or the Index to find out where that topic is covered and then turn to that page.

Part I
Zen, Quicken, and the Big Picture

The 5th Wave By Rich Tennant

"Sometimes I feel behind the times.
I asked my 11-year old to set up
Quicken for my business, and he
said he would, only after he sets
up Quicken for his lemonade stand."

In this part . . .

When you go to a movie theater, some prerequisites are necessary for the show to be truly enjoyable. And I'm not referring to the presence of Angelina Jolie or Will Smith on the screen. Purchasing a bucket of popcorn is essential, for example. One should think strategically both about seating and about soda size. And one may even have items of a, well, personal nature to take care of — such as visiting the little boys' or girls' room.

I mention all this stuff for one simple reason: To make getting started with Quicken as easy and fun as possible, you have to complete some prerequisites, too. And this first part of *Quicken 2007 For Dummies* talks about these sorts of things.

Chapter 1

Setting Up Shop

· ·

In This Chapter

▶ Installing Quicken

▶ Touring Quicken

▶ Setting up your bank (or other) accounts if you're a first-time user

▶ Retrieving existing Quicken data files

· ·

*I*f you've never used Quicken, begin here. This chapter tells you how to install Quicken (if you haven't already) and how to start the program for the first time. You also find out how you go about setting up Quicken accounts to track banking activities — specifically, the money that goes into and out of a checking or savings account.

If you've already begun to use Quicken, don't waste any time reading this chapter unless you want the review. You already know the stuff it covers.

By the way, if you have Windows, I assume that you know a little bit about it. Now, you don't have to be some sort of expert. Shoot, you don't even have to be all that proficient. You do need to know how to start Windows applications (such as Quicken). It also helps immensely if you know how to choose commands from menus and how to enter stuff into windows and dialog boxes. If you don't know how to do these kinds of things, flip to Appendix A. It provides a quick overview of how you work in Windows. Read the stuff in the appendix, or at least skim it, and then come back to this chapter.

When I say Windows, I mean a recent version of Windows — something Microsoft is either currently selling or has sold in the last few years. Quicken 2007 won't run on Windows 3.1, so if you want to run the latest version, I'm afraid it's time to upgrade.

Installing and Starting Quicken

You install Quicken the same way that you install any program in Windows. If you already know how to install programs, you don't need any help from me. Stop reading here, do the installation thing, start your newly installed Quicken program, and then start reading the next section, "Finishing Setup If You've Used Quicken Before."

If you need help installing Quicken, here are the step-by-step instructions. Installing Quicken from a CD-ROM is as easy as one, two, three, four:

1. **Insert the CD-ROM into the CD-ROM drive.**

 In a short amount of time, Quicken should display the Quicken 2007 installation window. I'm not going to show this window in a figure. There's really nothing on the window to talk about. The window just reads Welcome.

 Note: If nothing happens when you put the CD-ROM into the CD-ROM drive, don't panic! First, try removing the CD and then putting it in again. If Windows still doesn't recognize the CD, you need to *tell* Windows that it should install your Quicken program. In many versions of Windows (but not necessarily with your version), you do this with the Windows Control Panel by using a tool called Add/Remove Programs. To do this, refer to your Windows user guide or a good book about your version of Windows (such as *Windows XP For Dummies,* 2nd Edition, written by Andy Rathbone and published by Wiley).

2. **Click Next.**

 Quicken then displays a window that asks you a few questions:

 • The first question is whether you accept the Quicken license agreement.

 • The next question asks where you want to install Quicken. You should accept the installation's program suggestion. (The installation program suggests a Quicken subfolder in your Program Files folder.)

 • The next question — an implicit question really — asks whether it's okay to uninstall the previous version of Quicken if there is a previous version of Quicken installed on your computer. You may also be asked if it's okay with you if it gets any program updates.

3. **Answer these questions by clicking the appropriate buttons. Click Next to move to the next question. Then click the Install Now button when you answer the last question.**

 Quicken installs itself. This process takes a few minutes. Along the way, you see several other screenfuls of messages, including marketing information about the features new to Quicken and some progress reports on the installation itself.

When in doubt about some installation option, just accept the default suggestion by pressing Enter.

After the installation is complete, Quicken displays an `installation complete` message.

4. Click Done.

Congratulations. You're done.

After you install Quicken, you need to start it to finish the setup process. If you told the installation program to launch Quicken 2007, you should see the Quicken program window on your screen. If you didn't tell the installation program to launch Quicken, you need to start Quicken.

The easiest way to start Quicken is to double-click the Quicken shortcut icon that (post-installation) appears on your Windows desktop. The Quicken program window appears, almost like magic.

Quicken might ask if it can download program updates over the Internet. You can just say yes if it asks you this question.

Finishing Setup If You've Used Quicken Before

If you've used a previous version of Quicken, the Quicken program might show option buttons to indicate what you want to do next: Open the found data file. (Alternatively, you can indicate that you want to open some other data file.) You're done. You're ready to begin Quicken-ing.

The Quicken setup process can usually tell if you've used Quicken before. The setup process knows where the Quicken installation program usually puts the Quicken program and data files, and the installation program will look there. If you have used Quicken before but Quicken can't see this, two possibilities exist: The first possibility is that you put the Quicken data file someplace weird. (If that's the case, hopefully, you remember the weird place you hid the Quicken data file. If you can't remember, choose File➪Find Quicken Data File, select the disk you want to search from the Look In box, and click Find. Quicken displays a list of the Quicken data files on the selected disk. For more help with this, you can refer to the section, "The mysterious case of the missing Quicken data files," at the end of this chapter.) The second possibility is that you didn't do anything with the Quicken data file but that the data file has somehow gone missing. (If that's the case, hopefully, you backed up the Quicken data file to a CD or to some other disk from which you can restore the data file.)

Finishing Setup If You Haven't Used Quicken Before

If Quicken can't figure out whether you've used the Quicken program before, it displays the welcome message shown in Figure 1-1.

Figure 1-1: The Getting Started With Quicken 2007 window.

If you have used Quicken before, select the I Am Already A Quicken User option button. Quicken then displays another Getting Started With Quicken 2007 window that asks whether you want to open a Quicken file located on this computer, restore a Quicken data file you've backed up to CD or disk, or start over and create a new data file, as shown in Figure 1-2.

Figure 1-2: Another Getting Started With Quicken 2007 window.

If you indicate that you want to open another Quicken data file located on the computer, Quicken displays a dialog box that asks where that file is. If you indicate that you want to grab a backup copy of the Quicken file, Quicken displays a dialog box that asks where that file is. Presumably, if either of these situations is your case, you'll know where the data file or backup copy of the data file is.

At the very end of this chapter in the section, "The mysterious case of the missing Quicken data files," I describe how you can locate and open a Quicken data file.

If you haven't used Quicken before, Quicken asks if it's okay to use the default location for the data file (you should agree to this) and then it automatically sets up a data file for you (you don't need to worry about it). After the data file is set up, Quicken starts the Quicken New User Setup (see Figure 1-3). This setup process walks you through the steps for setting up Quicken. (You can find out much more on this process in the next section.)

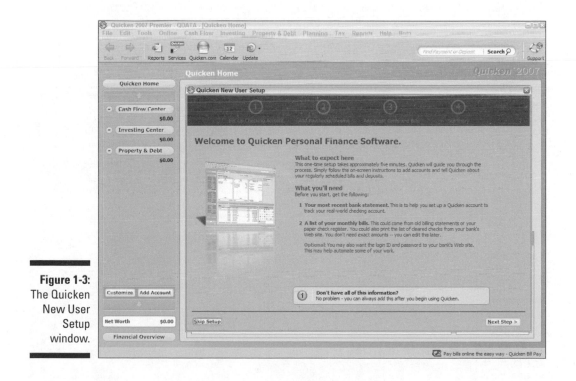

Figure 1-3:
The Quicken
New User
Setup
window.

Running the Quicken New User Setup

Okay. Here's the deal. The Quicken New User Setup walks you through a three-step process that asks about your banking, about your income, and about your regular bills. (You walk through the steps by clicking the Next Step button in the lower-right corner of the window.)

Describing your banking

The "describe your banking" step asks you to provide information about your bank account and its current balance. Figure 1-4 shows the window that collects the first part of this information, but just so you don't get confused, here are the precise steps you take:

1. **Identify the financial institution — usually a bank — by typing your institution's name into the text box provided.**

 As you type, Quicken displays a list of financial institutions that match what you've typed so far. The more you type, the shorter the list of possible matching institutions. If you see your bank or whatever listed, select it. When you click Next, Quicken displays the next Quicken New User Setup window, as shown in Figure 1-5.

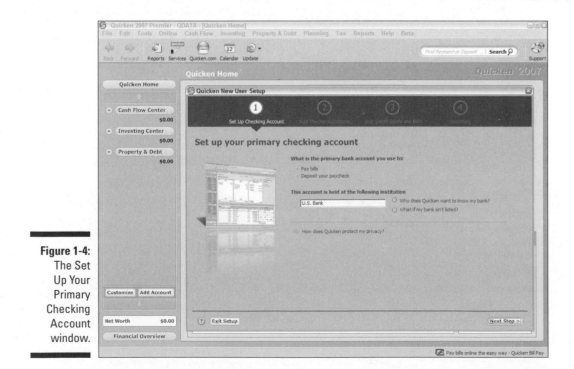

Figure 1-4: The Set Up Your Primary Checking Account window.

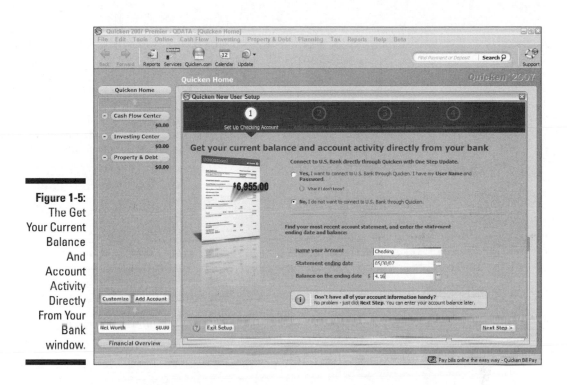

Figure 1-5:
The Get
Your Current
Balance
And
Account
Activity
Directly
From Your
Bank
window.

2. **Tell Quicken whether you want to use the online setup for your account or manually set up your account.**

 I'm going to suggest, because you're just starting out, that you set up your account manually. You have plenty of time later on to find out how online banking works. (Online banking is really cool, though. See Chapter 6 for more information.) To indicate that you'll manually set up your account, select the No button. Note that Quicken may not get into this online banking stuff if Quicken can tell that your bank doesn't support online banking.

3. **Tell Quicken the name you want to use for the checking account.**

 You do so by typing a name in the Name Your Account text box, as shown in Figure 1-5. By the way, you can be as general or as specific as you want. But remember, brevity is a virtue; be as concise as you can. The reason is that Quicken uses your account name to label stuff within the Quicken window and on Quicken reports. If you use a long account name, the name may not always fit on reports and screens.

4. **Enter the ending bank statement date by referring to your bank statement.**

 When Quicken asks for the ending statement date, enter the date of your last bank statement. Enter the date in *MM/DD/YYYY* fashion.

"Geez, Steve," you're now saying to yourself, "what's *MM/DD/YYYY* fashion?" Okay. Here's an example: If your bank statement is dated May 30, 2007, type **05/30/2007**, or you can type **5/30/2007**.

5. **Enter the ending bank statement balance by referring to your bank statement.**

 This balance is whatever appears on your bank statement. This balance is also the amount of money in your account on the date you begin your financial record keeping. If you have $4.16 in your checking account, type **4.16** into the Balance On The Ending Date text box.

6. **After you type the bank statement balance, click the Next Step button to continue moving through the New User Setup.**

Describing your income

The second step in the new user setup? Describing any regular income that you receive (such as a paycheck) and any regular deposits you make into your bank account (see Figure 1-6). To provide this information, you *could* enter the name of the payor into the Company Name box. You *could* describe the type of payment using the Category box and *could even* give the amount of the regular payment using the Take-Home Pay box.

Figure 1-6:
The Add My Deposits And Other Income window.

But you know what? You can also just skip this "Add my deposits and other income" step if you're lazy (like me) or if you don't actually have a regular source of income (also like me).

In fact, I'm going to recommend you skip this step. Seriously.

Describing your outgo

The third step in the new user setup requires you to describe your regular bills and expenses — things like the rent or your mortgage, cell phone charges, and your ever-increasing cable TV bill (see Figure 1-7). To provide this expense information, you *could* (again, if you're really anal) enter the name of the company you're paying into the Name box and the payment amount into the Average Payment box or the Average Amount box. But you know what? Good grief! This setup stuff is getting way too complicated for me. Let's just skip this step, too. We can deal with it later on. (No reason to make this more complicated than we have to.)

You'll need to click the Next Step button a couple more times, click Finish, and then — viola! — Quicken displays the Quicken Home window (see Figure 1-8).

Figure 1-7:
The Add Regular Bills And Expenses window.

TIP

The best way to get started

Quicken wants you to use your last bank statement to set up the bank account you track. This way, your financial records synchronize with the bank's records when you start using Quicken.

But I want to suggest something slightly different to you. Go back further than just to the beginning of the previous month (which is what you do when you use your last bank statement). Go back to the beginning of the year and use the last bank statement of the previous year — even if it's now several months after the beginning of the year. Now, I'm not trying to waste your time. But let me point out two big advantages to having a complete year's data in

Quicken: Tracking and tallying your tax deductions will be a snap, and planning your finances will be easier. When you enter the activity, be sure to enter any outstanding checks or deposits from the prior period with their correct dates also. That way, they are there to check off when you do your first reconcilement.

Going back to the beginning of the year isn't as hard as you may think. Quicken provides a bunch of tools to help you enter several months' worth of data in a very short time, as you can see in this chapter and in the two or three that follow.

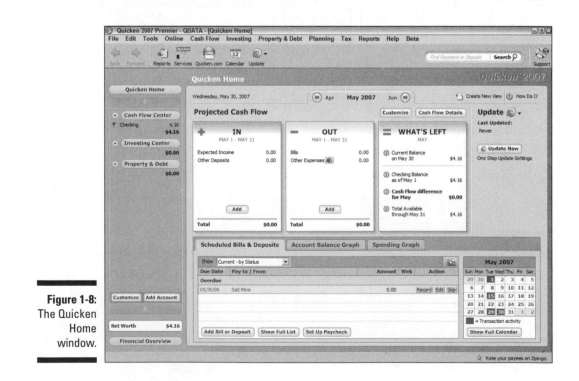

Figure 1-8:
The Quicken Home window.

Now I need to explain something here. The Quicken New User Setup assumes that you're going to set up almost everything you need or will ever need in Quicken all at once and in the beginning. You can do that if you want, but that's not my suggestion (er, obviously). I say, heck, keep it simple. You can easily add stuff later, when you want it. Sound okay? (I do explain how to set up this other stuff in other chapters.)

My reasoning for this suggestion is that I'd like you to have some experience working with Quicken before you go hog-wild. Focus first on those personal accounting tasks that you absolutely will want to perform. This approach gets you started working with Quicken — happily, productively, and successfully — from day one. If you want to do more in a week or a month or a year, great. You can easily do more tasks, and by then, you'll know so much more about Quicken that adding these other tasks will be a snap.

Steve's Overview

You don't need to know much about the mechanics of the Quicken *interface* — the way its windows work — to begin working with Quicken, especially in any chapters in which I cover the basics. I provide plenty of detailed instructions, but I have a couple of quick comments now.

Starting Quicken for the second time

The second time you start Quicken — and every subsequent time — things work pretty much the same way as the first time. Double-click the Quicken icon on your desktop. Or, if you like doing things the hard way, click Start and then choose All Programs⇨Quicken 2007⇨Quicken 2007.

Using Quicken document windows

Quicken doesn't use document windows the way that some other Windows applications do. Quicken basically turns document windows into pages that you leaf through by clicking the window buttons that appear along the left edge of the program window. In Figure 1-8, for example, you see buttons for Cash Flow Center, Investing Center, and Property & Debt. Go ahead and turn back to that page. I'll just wait here for you until you get back.

Navigating with financial activity centers' QuickTabs

Quicken arranges all of its features — whistles, bells, or whatever else you want to call them — into *financial activity centers.* For example, the Cash Flow Center, the Investing Center, and the Property & Debt Center are all financial activity centers. You get the picture. Each of these centers gets its own button. For example, refer to Figure 1-8 for a moment. See the button that's labeled Cash Flow Center?

Quicken lists the features within a financial activity center underneath the financial activity center button. You can collapse and expand this list by clicking the small button that's just to the left of the big financial activity center button. (The small button shows a minus symbol or plus symbol.) You can also jump to a listed feature by clicking the feature — which Quicken calls a QuickTab. For example, see the Cash Flow Center button in Figure 1-8? See the word Checking beneath that button? Checking is a QuickTab, which you can click to quickly jump to the Checking account.

If you're still confused, click the buttons and bits of text in the area of the Quicken window that I'm talking about. You'll clearly see how things work.

Solving Tricky Setup Problems

I want to quickly go over a handful of annoying setup problems new Quicken users may encounter. If you have Quicken set up and are ready to roll, skip this stuff.

Did somebody say Macintosh?

You can use the existing old Quicken files you're working with a new version of Quicken. In fact, if the Quicken installation program can find a version of old Quicken files on your computer, it gives you the option of just skipping all the Quicken New User Setup stuff. In this case, you just begin using your existing files. (I mention this point earlier in this chapter, in fact.)

If you've been using Quicken for Macintosh, however, you have to export your data from the Macintosh before you can read it in the Windows version. And I can think of about a million things more fun to do than exporting Quicken data from a Mac to Windows. See the section in Chapter 17 on importing data from an old accounting system for a brief discussion on the procedure and some suggestions for better ways to spend your time.

The mysterious case of the missing Quicken data files

If Quicken doesn't find the old files, you need to open the specific files. But if you have this problem, you should be able to solve it yourself. What has happened, if you find yourself in this boat, is that you've moved or messed around with the Quicken files using some other program, such as Windows Explorer. If you did that, presumably, you had a reason. And more to the point, you should know where you put the files.

Using the File⇨Find Quicken Files command

You can use File⇨Find Quicken Data Files to select and open your existing Quicken files. Here's how:

1. **Choose File⇨Find Quicken Files from the menu bar by using your mouse.**

 Figure 1-9 shows the Find Quicken Data File dialog box that appears after you choose the command. Quicken uses this dialog box to collect the information it will need to find your lost Quicken data.

Figure 1-9:
The Find Quicken Data File dialog box.

2. **Tell Quicken on which disk the data file is probably stored.**

 Select the disk you want Quicken to search from the Look In list box. Note that you can click the down arrow to the right of the Look In box to display a list of your computer's disks.

 From the list of drives and folders that appears, click the one that stores your Quicken files. Quicken closes the drop-down list box and displays your selection in the list box beneath the Look In box.

3. **Click Find to search the search.**

 Quicken searches the specified disk for Quicken data files. As Quicken finds data files, it adds them to the Data Files Found list box.

4. **Select the correct file from the list box.**

 After Quicken finds the data files stored on the specified disk, select the Quicken data file you know you want.

5. **Click OK after you select the file.**

 Quicken opens the file and displays the active account in the register window. (Quicken also displays its Reminders window to show any unprinted checks or scheduled transactions.)

 Note: If the file you're opening was created in a previous version of Quicken, Quicken converts the data to the Quicken 2007 format.

 Note: If Quicken displays the Quicken Home page rather than the account register, click the bank account name hyperlink beneath the Cash Flow Center button.

Migrating from Microsoft Money

Suppose that you're moving from Microsoft Money to Quicken. The question of the hour is this: Can you reuse your old or existing Money files in Quicken? The answer is, "Yes, sort of."

You can download a program called Data Converter from the Quicken support Web site. Data Converter converts Microsoft Money data files from Microsoft Money 2003 and later versions to the Quicken 2007 for Windows format.

Practically, however, moving financial information from Quicken to Money or vice versa doesn't seem to work all that well. Transactions seem to get lost. Account balances get messed up. People ruin their lives. Well, maybe that last comment is a slight exaggeration. But, no kidding: Migrating is problematic. If you do want to move from one program to another, I suggest making sure that you have a really good reason for doing so and that you allow yourself enough time to track down and correct any errors.

Chapter 2

Introduction to the Big Picture

● ●

In This Chapter

▶ Distilling Quicken down to its very essence

▶ Setting up additional bank accounts

▶ Adding categories

▶ Removing categories

▶ Modifying categories

▶ Understanding classes

● ●

*B*efore you spend a bunch of time and money on Quicken, you have to understand the big picture. You need to know what Quicken can do. You need to know what you want to do. And, as a practical matter, you need to tell Quicken what you want it to do.

Boiling Quicken Down to Its Essence

When you boil Quicken down to its essence, it does six things:

✔ **It lets you track your tax deductions.**

This feature makes preparing your personal or business tax return easier for you or your poor accountant, Cratchit.

✔ **It lets you monitor your income and outgo either on-screen or by using printed reports.**

Usually, this stuff is great fodder for discussions about the family finances.

✔ **It lets you print checks.**

This device is mostly a timesaver, but it can also be useful for people who are neat freaks.

✔ **It lets you track the things you own (such as bank accounts, investments, and real estate) and the debts you owe (such as home mortgage principal, car loan balances, and credit card balances).**

These things are really important to know.

✔ **It helps you make better personal financial planning decisions about such matters as retirement, your children's future college costs, and your savings and investments.**

I think this stuff is really neat.

✔ **It gives you the opportunity to pay bills electronically and in some cases, even do all your banking electronically.**

This stuff is pretty neat, too. No, let me amend that. Online bill paying and banking is really neat. I do have some minor (very minor) reservations, however, which I discuss in Chapter 6, dealing with online banking in depth.

Tracking tax deductions

To track your tax deductions, make a list of the deductions you want to track. To do so, pull out last year's tax return. Note which lines you filled in. (Perhaps mortgage interest, property taxes, state income taxes, and charitable contributions?) This method works because there's a darn good chance that the tax deductions you claimed last year will also be the tax deductions you'll claim in the future.

I cover the Quicken categories, which you use to track your tax deductions, a little later in this chapter.

Monitoring spending

At our house, we (my wife, Sue, and I, your humble author) use Quicken to monitor our spending on the mundane little necessities of life: groceries, clothing, dog food, cable television, and, well . . . you get the picture. To keep track of how much we spend on various items, we also use the Quicken categories.

If you want to monitor a particular spending category, decide up front what the category should be before you begin recording your data.

Your list of spending categories, by the way, shouldn't be an exhaustive list of superfine pigeonholes, such as *Friday-night Mexican food, Fast food for lunch,* and so on. To track your spending on eating out, one category named something like *Meals* or *Grub* usually is easiest.

In fact, I'm going to go out on a limb. You can probably get away with a dozen categories, more or less:

✔ Car

✔ Clothing

✔ Entertainment and vacation

 ✔ Groceries

 ✔ Household expenses (besides food)

 ✔ Insurance

 ✔ Medical and dental

 ✔ Rent (or mortgage payments)

 ✔ Taxes

 ✔ Utilities (electric, water, cable television)

 ✔ Work expenses

If you want to, of course, you can expand this list. Heck, you can create dozens and dozens of categories. My experience, though, is that you'll probably use only a handful of categories.

Printing checks

You can use Quicken to print checks. This little trick provides a couple of benefits: It's really fast if you have several checks to print, and your printed checks look very neat and darn professional.

To print checks, you need to do just two things. First, look through the check supply information that comes with Quicken and pick a check form that suits your style. Then order the form. (The check forms that come with *remittance advices* — or check stubs — work well for businesses.)

Preprinted check forms aren't cheap. If you're using Quicken at home with personal-style checks (such as those that go in your wallet), using computer checks may not be cost effective. Even if you're using Quicken for a business and you're used to buying those outrageously expensive business-style checks, you'll still find computer checks a bit more expensive.

I'm pretty much a cheapskate, so I don't use printed checks at home (although I do use them in my business). I should admit, however, that I also don't write very many checks.

By the way, I've "checked" around. Although you can order Quicken check forms from other sources (such as your local office supplies store), they're about the same price from Intuit (the maker of Quicken). If you want to order from Intuit, you can refer to the catalog that came in the Quicken packaging. You can also visit Intuit's Web site, Quicken.com (`www.quicken.com`).

One other comment here about printing checks: If you're going to pay bills electronically, you don't need to print checks with Quicken. Oh, sure, you can print checks if you want. But you won't want to. Paying a bill electronically is easier and cheaper than paying a bill with a Quicken-printed check.

Tracking bank accounts, credit cards, and other stuff

You must decide which bank accounts and credit cards you want to track. In most cases, you want to track each bank account you use and any credit card on which you carry a balance.

You may also want to track other assets and liabilities. *Assets* are just things you own: investments, cars, a house, and so on. *Liabilities* are things you owe: margin loans from your broker, car loans, a mortgage, and so on.

Shoot, I suppose that you could even track the things your neighbor owns — or perhaps just those things you especially covet. I'm not sure that this is a very good idea, though. (Maybe a healthier approach is to track just those things that you've borrowed from your neighbor.)

Planning your personal finances

Your computer's computational horsepower makes it the ideal tool for doing complicated calculations. So maybe you're not surprised that Quicken comes with six powerful calculators that let you make smarter borrowing choices, better mortgage-refinancing decisions, more accurate savings and investment calculations, and extremely helpful retirement and college savings calculations.

I believe that these financial planning tools are the most valuable features that Quicken offers. I'm just sorry that I have to wait until Chapter 10 to talk about them.

Banking online

If you want, you can tell Quicken that it should do the work of paying some person or merchant electronically. In other words, at the same time that you describe some check to Quicken — you do so by entering stuff into a window — you can say to Quicken, "I not only want you to record this check for me, I also want you to pay it for me."

If your bank supports online banking, you may also be able to move money between your accounts and get up-to-date statements electronically. Ask your bank for details about this service if you're interested.

To perform this sort of online banking, you need to have an Internet connection, and you need to do a little bit of paperwork. But the Quicken Online Banking features can save you loads of time. And the features are easy to use. Basically, all you do is use Quicken in the usual way — which is what I talk about in the chapters that follow — and then click a couple of extra buttons.

Setting Up Additional Accounts

When you first began working with Quicken — and this may have only been a few minutes ago or several years ago — you were prompted to set up an account. And you probably set up at least a checking account because this is probably your most active bank account. If you want to track any additional accounts — for example, a savings account — you must set them up, too.

Setting up another banking account

To set up an additional checking, savings, or money market account, you give the account a name and then its balance as of a set date. Here's how:

1. **Display the Cash Flow Center by clicking the Cash Flow Center button on the left edge of the window.**

 Quicken displays the Cash Flow Center, shown in Figure 2-1.

Figure 2-1:
The Cash
Flow Center.

2. Click the Add Account button.

The Add Account button appears beneath the Spending & Savings Accounts heading. When you click this button, Quicken displays the Quicken Account Setup dialog box, shown in Figure 2-2.

Figure 2-2:
The first
Quicken
Account
Setup
dialog box.

3. Identify the financial institution and click Next.

To identify where you're banking, enter your institution's name into the This Account Is Held At The Following Institution box.

4. Yet again, identify the financial institution and then click Next.

If you see your bank listed, click its name on the list. If you don't, click the None Of These button, which tells Quicken to use your original name. Click Next.

At this point, Quicken may ask whether you want to set up your account manually or use an online setup. You want to set up your account manually, so make this indication if you're asked. (Quicken typically asks the "manual versus online" question if you select a financial institution that allows for online banking, something I talk about more in Chapter 6.)

5. Select the type of account by clicking one of the account buttons and then click Next.

When Quicken displays the next Quicken Account Setup dialog box, shown in Figure 2-3, tell Quicken which type of account you want to set up by clicking one of the account buttons. I'm assuming that at this point, you want to set up either a checking or savings account. After you identify the account type, click Next.

Figure 2-3:
Another
Quicken
Account
Setup
dialog box.

6. **Name the account and then click Next.**

 Move the cursor to the Account Name text box and type a name in that box. Click Next after you do this. You're almost done.

7. **Enter the account balance date.**

 When Quicken displays the dialog box shown in Figure 2-4, enter the date that you're going to start keeping records for the bank account with Quicken. (Quicken wants you to start your record keeping for an account on a bank statement date because on a bank statement date you have a really good balance from the bank.) Move the cursor to the Statement Date text box and type the month number, a slash, the day number, a slash, and the year number. If you start on May 30, 2007, for example, type **5/30/2007**. Or, if this is way too complicated for you, click the button at the end of the Statement Date text box so that Quicken displays a pop-up calendar. Then click the date. Use the << and >> buttons to move back and forth a month at a time.

Figure 2-4:
The final
Quicken
Account
Setup
dialog box.

Note: If you want to keep your transaction records for tax purposes, of course it makes sense to track whatever accounts you can from the first of the year, assuming that you have all the necessary statements or your own records of all the transactions.

 8. **Click inside the Ending Balance text box and enter the bank account balance.**

 Use the number keys to enter the balance. The folks at Intuit, by the way, really want you to use the balance from your bank statement. If you have terrible financial records — for example, you haven't reconciled your account since Clinton left office — this idea is probably good advice. If you have neat, accurate financial records, go ahead and use your check register balance.

 If you do use the bank statement balance as your starting balance, be sure to enter all the transactions that cleared or will clear after the bank statement balance date. (This should make sense, right? If a check or deposit isn't reflected in the bank statement figure, you must enter it with its correct date into Quicken.)

 9. **Click the Done button.**

 Quicken displays the new account in a register window, as shown in Figure 2-5. I discuss the register window in detail in Chapter 4, but for now, let me just say that this window is the one that you use to keep track of the deposits into and the withdrawals from a bank account.

Figure 2-5:
A register window.

Hey, Quicken, I want to use that account!

In Quicken, you work with one account at a time. The logic is simple: You record income and expenses for a particular account — a specific checking account, savings account, and so on. (You do this by using the register that appeared in Figure 2-5, just for the record.)

You use the Cash Flow Center window (refer to Figure 2-1) to tell Quicken which account you want to work with because Quicken provides clickable hyperlinks (technically called *QuickTabs*) that you can use to move to the account.

To display the Cash Flow Center window, click the Cash Flow Center button. (If you're experiencing a sense of *déjà vu* right now, it's probably because I described these techniques earlier in the chapter, too.) Let me mention that you can also use the Cash Flow menu to get to the Cash Flow Center. To do this, choose Cash Flow⇨Go To Cash Flow Center from the menu bar.

After you display the Cash Flow Center window, select the account you want by clicking the account name. Quicken displays the register window for that account.

Whipping Your Category Lists into Shape

Quicken supplies categories to, well, categorize your spending. For example, you would probably use the Rent category to categorize all the checks you write to pay rent.

The predefined categories list may be just what you want. Then again, it may not. Table 2-1 shows the all-inclusive categories list.

Your categories list may vary slightly from the one shown in Table 2-1. Quicken may customize your starting categories list based on your answers to questions it asks in the Quicken New User Setup. I talk about the Quicken New User Setup briefly in Chapter 1.

Take a minute to look through the categories list. If you find categories you don't need, cross them off the list in the book. You can delete them from Quicken in a minute or so. If you need categories you don't see, add them at the bottom of the list. You can add them in about two minutes or so.

✔ To track a certain income or spending item for income tax purposes — wages, property taxes, and so forth — you need a Quicken category.

✔ To track a certain income or spending item because you're just interested in knowing how much you spend on it (for example, renting DVDs), you need a Quicken category.

✔ To budget by categories (because you need a category for any income or spending item that you want to budget), you need a Quicken category.

Table 2-1	The Category List
Categories	**Descriptions**
Income Categories	
Bonus	Bonus money you receive
Div Income	Dividend income from stocks and mutual funds
Gift Received	Gifts received from generous relatives and friends
Interest Inc	Interest income from bank accounts, CDs, and similar items
Invest Inc	Investment income from, well, investments
Other Inc	Other income that doesn't fit better in some other category
Salary	Salary income
Tax Refund	That check you get back from the taxman if you withhold more than you owe
Unemployment Inc	Unemployment benefits
Expense Categories	
Auto	Automobile expenses
Fuel	Auto fuel
Insurance	Auto insurance
Loan	Auto loan payments
Registration	Auto registration, plates, or license tags
Service	Auto service
Bank Charge	Banking fees
Cash	Miscellaneous cash purchases
Charity	Charitable donations
Charity – Non Cash	Charitable donations made with stuff rather than cash

Categories	Descriptions
Expense Categories	
Clothing	Clothing
Computer	Hmmm. This is suspicious. A category for tracking expenses, such as the money you spent on Quicken.
Credit Card Payment	For when you've said, "charge it."
Dining	Dining out
Education	Education
Entertainment	Entertainment
Gifts Given	Gift expenses
Groceries	Groceries
Home Repair	Repair expenses for the ol' homestead
Homeowner's Fees	Homeowner's association fees
Household	Miscellaneous household expenses
Housing	Housing
Insurance	Insurance
Disability	Disability insurance (in case you or your spouse become disabled)
Home Insurance	Homeowner's insurance
Life Insurance	Life insurance premiums
Interest Expense	Interest expense
IRA Contrib	Individual Retirement Account contribution
Medical	Medical expense
Doctor	Doctor and dental visits
Medicine	Medicine and drugs
Misc	Miscellaneous
Personal Care	Personal expenses (shampoo, soap, and other accoutrements of civilized life)
Recreation	Recreation expense
Rent	Housing rent

(continued)

Table 2-1 *(continued)*

Categories	Descriptions
Expense Categories	
Subscriptions	Subscriptions
Tax	Taxes
Fed	Federal income tax
Medicare	Medicare tax
Other	Miscellaneous taxes
Property	Property tax
SDI	State disability insurance
Soc Sec	Social Security tax
State	State income tax
Utilities	Water, gas, electric, and other stuff like this
Cable TV	Cable television
Garbage and Recycling	Hauling away your junk
Gas and Electric	Gas and electricity
Internet	Internet access fees
Telephone	Telephone
Water	Water
Vacation	Vacation expenses
Lodging	Motel/Hotel costs
Travel	Transportation expense

Subcategories . . . yikes, what are they?

You surely didn't buy Quicken so that you could spend all day Saturday sitting at your computer instead of taking the kids to the zoo. I realize this and want to make Quicken easier for you to use. To do so, I figure I should tell you which Quicken features you can ignore if you're feeling a bit overwhelmed. Subcategories are among those things I think that you can ignore.

"Subcategories?" you ask. "Yikes! What are they?"

Subcategories are categories within categories. If you look at the Taxes expense category in Table 2-1, for example, you'll notice a bunch of categories that follow the Tax category and are slightly indented: Fed (federal tax), Medicare (Medicare tax), Other (miscellaneous taxes), Property, SDI (state disability insurance), Soc Sec (Social Security tax), and State (state tax).

When you use subcategories, you can tag a transaction that pays, for example, taxes; you can further break down this category into subcategories such as federal income tax, Medicare tax, and Social Security tax. If you want to see a list of the ways you've spent your money, Quicken summarizes your spending both by category and, within a category, by subcategory. On a Quicken report, then, you can see this level of detail:

Category	*Expense*
Taxes	
Federal tax	900
Medicare tax	100
Soc Sec tax	<u>700</u>
Total taxes	1,700

No doubt about it, subcategories are useful tools. But they make working with Quicken a little more complicated and a little more difficult. As a practical matter, you usually don't need them. If you want to track a spending category, it really belongs on your list as a full-fledged category. For these reasons, I'm not going to get into subcategories here.

If you get excited about the topic of subcategories later on — after you have the hang of Quicken — you can peruse the Quicken documentation for more information.

If you *do* want to use the Quicken subcategories, don't delete the subcategories shown in Table 2-1. If you *don't* want to use the subcategories, go ahead and delete them. (I tell you how to remove categories in "Removing categories you loathe," later in this chapter.)

Category groups . . . double yikes!

Category groups, which were known as *supercategories* in a previous version of Quicken, combine categories into sets that you can use in reports and in your budgeting. Sure, they're sort of cool, but you don't need to worry about them if you're just starting with Quicken.

If you're dying to know more about category groups, you can refer to the Quicken online help. Quicken Help works like help in other Windows programs. If you don't know Windows all that well — or least not well enough to comfortably use Help — refer to Appendix A.

Four tips on categorization

I have just four tips for categorizing:

- ✔ **Cross off any category you won't use.**

 If you don't pay state income taxes in the state you live in, for example, get rid of the state tax category. Extra, unneeded categories just clutter your list. I think it's great if you can get down to just a handful of categories.

- ✔ **Don't be afraid to lump together similar spending categories.**

 Take your utilities expense, for example. If you pay water, natural gas, electricity, and sewer, why not use a single Utilities category? If you pay different utility companies for your water, natural gas, electricity, and sewer, you can still see what you spend on just electricity, for example, even with a single catchall category for utilities.

- ✔ **Be sure to categorize anything that may be a tax deduction.**

 Categorize educational, medical, and dental expenses; state and local income taxes; real estate taxes; personal property taxes; home mortgage interest and points; investment interest; charitable contributions; casualty and theft losses; moving expenses; unreimbursed employee expenses; and all those vague, miscellaneous deductions. (By the way, the foregoing is a pretty complete list of itemized deductions in the United States at the time this book was written.)

- ✔ **Don't sweat this category stuff too much.**

 In spite of the preceding three tips, don't let these category lists or the work of customizing them scare you. If you want to spend a few minutes cleaning up the list, hey, that's great. If not, or if you're starting to get anxious, just skip ahead to the next chapter.

Ch-ch-changing a category list

You should now be ready to fix any category list problems. Basically, you need to do three things: add categories, remove categories, and change category names and descriptions.

Adding individual categories you'd love to use

Adding individual categories is a snap. Here's all you have to do:

1. **Choose Tools⇨Category List from the menu bar.**

 Quicken displays the Category List window (shown in Figure 2-6). This window lists the categories available and the accounts you've set up. Careful readers may notice that the categories shown in Figure 2-6 include those shown in Table 2-1.

Figure 2-6: The Category List window with the Display Tax Information option checked.

2. **Click the New button on the Category List window.**

 The New button, by the way, is the first button on the lower left. Quicken dutifully displays the Set Up Category dialog box (shown in Figure 2-7). You probably aren't surprised that you use this puppy to describe the new category.

3. **Enter a short name for the category.**

 Move the cursor to the Name text box and type a name. Although you can use up to 15 characters, use as short a name as possible to clearly identify the category. Why? Because you use this category name every time you want to tag a transaction to fall into the category.

Figure 2-7:
The Set Up
Category
dialog box.

4. **Enter a description for the category.**

 Move the cursor to the Description text box and then describe the cate-
 gory. Quicken uses the category description on reports that show the
 category. If you don't add a description, Quicken just uses the category
 name. You don't need a description, obviously, if your category name is,
 well, adequately descriptive.

5. **[Optional] Identify the category group.**

 If you disregarded my earlier suggestion to *not* worry about category
 groups, open the Group drop-down list box and select the appropriate
 group.

6. **Indicate whether the category is an income category or an expense
 category.**

 Select the appropriate Income, Expense, or Subcategory Of option
 button — just click the appropriate button with your furry little friend,
 the mouse. If you've totally blown off my admonition not to use subcate-
 gories just yet, use the dialog box's drop-down list to indicate into which
 income or expense category a new subcategory falls.

7. **Indicate whether the category tracks an amount you will use on an
 input line on next year's tax return.**

 By *line,* I mean the actual tax form line — such as the line on the U.S.
 1040 form that tracks alimony.

 Move the cursor to the Tax-Related check box and then *select the check
 box* if the category is tax-related or *deselect the check box* if the category
 isn't tax-related. Just to clear up any confusion, vacationing in Hawaii
 probably isn't a tax deduction — even if your neighbor promises that it
 is. Then identify the form and line by opening the Tax Line Item drop-
 down list box and selecting one of its entries.

8. Click OK.

Quicken adds the new category to the Category List window (refer to Figure 2-6) and then redisplays the window. Now that you understand the stuff in the Category List window, note that it shows the category name, its type, the notation that a category is tax-related (see the check mark in the Tax column?), and, golly darn, even its description and group. (The tax information appears only if the Display Tax Information box is checked.)

Adding categories from a situational list

Quicken keeps lists of categories that are standard for people in certain situations, including Quicken users who are married, homeowners, real estate investors, and business owners.

To use these situational lists as a source of new categories, follow these steps:

1. Choose Tools⇨Category List from the menu bar.

Quicken displays the Category List window (refer to Figure 2-6).

2. Click the Add From List button.

Quicken displays the Add Categories dialog box (shown in Figure 2-8). This window lists the categories that may be useful in certain situations.

Figure 2-8: The Add Categories dialog box.

3. Select one of the situational lists.

Open the Available Categories drop-down list box — you can do this simply by clicking the box — and select the situational list of categories you want to display: standard, married, homeowner, business, children, investment, or rents and royalties. Quicken displays the categories from the situational list selected.

4. **Select the categories you want to add.**

 While holding down the Ctrl key, click the categories in the Categories list that you want to add. Quicken marks the categories you select with a check. You can, by the way, mark all of the categories shown in the situational list by clicking the Mark All button. You can unmark all of the "marked" categories by clicking the Clear All button.

5. **Add the selected categories.**

 After you mark the categories you want to add, click the Add button. Quicken adds the categories to the Categories To Add list. To complete the addition of the categories, click OK.

Removing categories you loathe

Removing categories takes only a couple of keystrokes. With the Category List window displayed, follow these steps:

1. **Right-click the category you want to remove and then choose the Delete command from the shortcut menu that appears.**

 If there are no transactions in the category, Quicken displays a message that asks you to confirm your decision.

2. **If you want to remove the selected category, click OK.**

 Otherwise, press the Esc key or click the Cancel button.

Changing category names and descriptions

You can change a category name, its type, its description, and its tax-related setting if you later discover you made some mistake, such as misspelling a word in a description.

To do so, follow these steps:

1. **Display the Category List window (refer to Figure 2-6).**

2. **Use the arrow keys or click with your mouse to select the category you want to change and then click the Edit button.**

 Quicken displays a dialog box that has text boxes and option buttons describing the selected category's information: its name, description, type, and tax-related settings.

3. **Make the changes you want by replacing text box contents or changing option button settings. Then click OK to save your changes and return to the Category List window.**

Merging Categories

A quick, related point: See the Merge button at the bottom of the Category List window? If you select a category and then click the Merge button, Quicken displays a Merge Category dialog box, which you use to re-categorize transactions in the selected category. The dialog box provides a drop-down list box you use to select the new category you want to use. The dialog box also provides a check box you can check if you want to delete the category after moving transactions out of it.

Do You Need a Little Class?

Using categories isn't the only way that you can summarize your financial records. Quicken provides a second tool, called *classes,* which also lets you summarize transactions in addition to the way you summarize transactions with categories.

Now typically, classes are not something you need to worry about — especially if you're just using Quicken to regain control over your personal finances. However, classes can be very useful if you're using Quicken in a business or if you're investing in rental real estate.

For these reasons, I want to quickly describe how you set up classes.

To set up a class (or several classes), take these steps:

1. **Display the Class List window.**

 To do this, choose Tools⇨Class List.

2. **Click the New button on the Class List window.**

 Quicken displays the Set Up Class box (shown in Figure 2-9).

Figure 2-9: The Set Up Class dialog box.

3. **Enter a short name for the class.**

 Move the cursor to the Name text box and type a name. Use as short a name as possible to clearly identify the class. You use this class name every time you want to tag a transaction to fall into the class. (If you're using classes to identify real estate rental properties — which is probably their most common use — you might want to use the street name as the class: *Winston* as the class for the duplex on Winston Street, *Roosevelt* as the class for the cottage on Roosevelt Avenue, and so on.)

4. **Enter a description for the class.**

 Move the cursor to the Description text box and then describe the class. Quicken uses the class description on reports that show the class. If you don't add a description, Quicken just uses the class name. You don't need a description, obviously, if your class name is, well, adequately descriptive.

The technical editor, David, (who's also a CPA) wants me to tell you that you should just ignore the Copy Number box. He's probably right.

5. **Click OK.**

 Quicken adds the new class to the Class List window and then redisplays the window. And that is that.

Chapter 3

Maximum Fun, Maximum Profits

. .

In This Chapter

▶ Deciding whether you need a budget

▶ Discovering tips for personal and business budgets

▶ Setting up a budget

▶ Reviewing a budget

. .

I don't think that a budget amounts to financial handcuffs, and neither should you. A budget is really a plan that outlines the way you need to spend your money to achieve the maximum amount of fun or the way a business needs to spend its money to make the most profit.

Should You Even Bother with a Budget?

A *budget,* as you probably know, is a list of the ways you earn and spend your money. If you create a good, workable categories list with Quicken (see Chapter 2), you're halfway to a good, solid budget. (In fact, the only step left is to specify how much you earn in each income category and how much you spend in each expense category.)

Does everybody need a budget? No, of course not. Maybe, at your house, you're already having a bunch of fun with your money. Maybe, in your business, you make money so effortlessly that you really don't plan your income and outgo.

For the rest of us, though, a budget improves our chances of getting to wherever it is we want to go financially. In fact, I'll stop calling it a budget. The word has such negative connotations. I know — I'll call it a *Secret Plan.*

Serious Advice about Your Secret Plan

Before I walk you through the mechanics of outlining your Secret Plan (your budget), I want to give you a few tips.

Your personal Secret Plan

You can do four things to make your Secret Plan more likely to work:

✔ **Plan your income and expenses as a family.**

With this sort of planning, two heads are invariably better than one. What's more, though I don't really want to get into marriage counseling here, a family's budget — oops, I mean Secret Plan — needs to reflect the priorities and feelings of everyone who has to live within the plan. Don't use a Secret Plan as a way to minimize what your spouse spends on clothing or on long-distance telephone charges talking to relatives in the old country. You need to resolve your clothing and long-distance charges issues before you finalize your Secret Plan.

✔ **Include some cushion in your plan.**

In other words, don't budget to spend every last dollar. If you plan from the start to spend every dollar you make, you undoubtedly have to fight the mother of all financial battles: paying for unexpected expenses when you don't have any money. (You know the sort of things I mean — car repairs, medical expenses, or that cocktail dress or tuxedo you absolutely *must* have for a special party.)

✔ **Regularly compare your actual income and outgo to your planned income and outgo.**

This part of your plan is probably the most important and also the part that Quicken helps you with the most. As long as you use Quicken to record what you receive and spend, you can print reports showing what you planned and what actually occurred.

✔ **Make adjustments as necessary.**

When you have problems with your Secret Plan — and you will — you'll know that your plan isn't working. You can then make adjustments, by spending a little less calling the old country, for example.

Two things that really goof up Secret Plans

Because I'm talking about you-know-what, let me touch on a couple of things that really goof up your financial plans: windfalls and monster changes.

The problem with windfalls

Your boss smiles, calls you into his office, and then gives you the good news. You're getting a $5,000 bonus! "It's about time," you think. Outside, of course, you maintain your dignity. You act grateful but not gushy. Then you call your husband.

A Secret Plan for your business

The tips for personal Secret Plans also apply to businesses. But I have two special tips for small businesses using Quicken. (I'm going to write very quietly now so that no one else hears. . . .)

Here's the first secret tip: Visit the BizStats.com Web site at http://bizstats.com. It provides tons and tons of good, interesting business statistics about businesses just like yours!

Here's the second secret tip: Go to the library, ask for the RMA (Risk Management Association) survey, and look up the ways that other businesses like yours spend money. If it doesn't have the RMA survey, see whether it has the Dun & Bradstreet survey or Troy's Almanac of Business and Industrial Financial Ratios survey.

These surveys are really cool:

✔ The **RMA** surveys bank-lending officers, creates a summary of the information these bankers receive from their customers, and publishes the results.

✔ **Dun & Bradstreet** collects and summarizes its own proprietary financial information.

✔ **Troy** (who's actually a business Ph.D.) collects Internal Revenue Service data and publishes the same sort of financial results.

At both the BizStats.com Web site and in the preceding surveys, you can get really useful information about what businesses like yours spend, make, and own. For example, you can look up what percentage of sales the average tavern spends on beer and peanuts, the average profit your CPA makes, and the profit a car dealer makes on the average car sale. (Isn't that all kind of interesting stuff?)

By the way, neither the BizStats.com Web site nor the surveys will actually have a line on the taverns page labeled *beer and peanuts,* for example. It'll be called *cost of goods sold* or some similarly vague accounting term.

Here's what happens next. Bob (that's your husband's name) gets excited, congratulates you, and tells you he'll pick up a bottle of wine on the way home to celebrate.

On your drive home, you mull over the possibilities and conclude that you can use the $5,000 as a big down payment for that new family minivan you've been looking at. (With the trade-in and the $5,000, your payments will be a manageable $300 per month.)

On his way home, Bob stops to look at those golf clubs he's been coveting, charges $800 on his credit card, and then, feeling slightly guilty, buys you the $600 set. (Pretend that you're just starting to play golf.)

You may laugh at this scenario, but suppose that it really happened. Furthermore, pretend that you really do buy the minivan. At this point, you spent $6,400 on a van and golf clubs, and you've signed up for what you're guessing will be another $300-per-month payment.

This turn of events doesn't sound all that bad now, does it?

Here's the problem: When you get your check, it's not going to be $5,000. You're probably going to pay roughly $400 in Social Security and Medicare taxes, and maybe around $1,500 in federal and state income taxes. Other money may be taken out, too, for forced savings plans — such as a 401(k) plan — or for charitable giving. After all is said and done, you get maybe half the bonus in cash — say $2,500.

Now you see the problem. You have $2,500 in cold hard cash, but with Bob's help, you've already spent $6,400 and signed up for $300-per-month minivan payments.

In a nutshell, you face two big problems with windfalls:

 ✔ You never get the entire windfall — yet spending as if you will is quite easy.

 ✔ Windfalls, by their very nature, tend to get used for big purchases (often as down payments) that ratchet up your living expenses. Boats. New houses. Cars.

Regarding windfalls, my advice to you is simple:

 ✔ Don't spend a windfall until you actually hold the check in your hot little hand. (You're even better off to wait, say, six months. That way Bob can really think about whether he needs those new golf clubs.)

 ✔ Don't spend a windfall on something that increases your monthly living expenses without first redoing your budget.

The problem with monster income changes

If your income changes radically, planning a budget becomes really hard. Suppose that your income doubles. One day you're cruising along making $50,000, and the next day you're suddenly making $100,000. (Congratulations, by the way.) I'll tell you what you'll discover, however, should you find yourself in this position: You'll find that $100,000 a year isn't as much money as you may think. (By the way, this business about monster income changes is true no matter what your income level. Like, if you're cruising along making $500,000 and see your income double to $1,000,000, everything I'm saying here still applies.)

Go ahead. Laugh. But for one thing — if your income doubles, your income taxes almost certainly more than quadruple.

One of the great myths about income taxes is that the rich don't pay very much or that they pay the same percentage. But that's not actually true. If you make $50,000 a year and you have an average family, you might pay about $3,000 in federal income taxes. If you make $100,000 a year, you pay about $12,000 a year. So if your salary doubles from $50,000 to $100,000

(or perhaps your spouse gets a good job), your income taxes quadruple, going from $3,000 to $12,000. I don't bring this fact up to get you agitated about whether it's right or fair that you should pay a bunch of any extra income you make in taxes. I bring it up so that you can better plan for any monster income changes you experience.

Another thing — and I know it sounds crazy — you'll find it hard to spend $100,000 smartly when you've been making a lot less. And if you start making some big purchases, such as houses and cars and speedboats, you'll not only burn through a great deal of cash, but you'll also ratchet up your monthly living expenses.

Monster income changes that go the other way are even more difficult. If you've been making, say, $100,000 a year and then see your salary drop to a darn respectable $50,000, it's going to hurt, too. And probably more than you think. That old living-expense ratcheting effect comes into play here. Presumably, if you've been making $100,000 a year, you've been spending it — or most of it.

But other reasons contribute — at least initially — to making a monster salary drop very difficult. You've probably chosen friends (nice people, such as the Joneses), clothing stores, and hobbies that are in line with your income.

Another thing about a monster salary drop is sort of subtle. You probably denominate your purchases in amounts related to your income. Make $50,000, and you think in terms of $5 or $10 purchases. But make $100,000 a year, and you think in terms of $10 or $20 purchases. This observation all makes perfect sense. But if your income drops from $100,000 down to $50,000, you'll probably still find yourself thinking of those old $20 purchases.

So what to do? If you experience a monster income change, redo your Secret Plan. And be particularly careful and thoughtful.

Setting Up a Secret Plan

Okay, now you're ready to set up your budget — er, I mean, Secret Plan.

Introducing the Budget window

To get to the window in which you enter your budget, choose Planning⇨ Budget.

Quicken displays the Setup tab of the Budget window. Click the Automatic button if you want Quicken to create a starting budget using any existing financial data. Otherwise, click the Manual button. After you make this choice, click the Create Budget button.

If you indicate that you want to create an automatic budget by, essentially, recycling your old "actual numbers," Quicken displays the Create Budget: Automatic dialog box, in which you can specify which old actual numbers to use (see Figure 3-1). This window allows you to

✔ **Choose a date range to scan.** Use the From and To boxes to identify the range of dates that span the months or the year you want to use.

✔ **Select a budget method.** Use the Select Budget Method buttons and boxes to indicate how you want Quicken to budget.

- Using average monthly amounts (the default)

- Using the exact monthly amounts

- Using the exact quarterly amounts

✔ **Set your options.** Use the Options check boxes to tell Quicken how to handle rounding and one-time, extraordinary transactions. (By default, Quicken rounds budget amounts to the nearest dollar and does *not* exclude one-time transactions.)

After you describe the automatic budget, click OK.

Figure 3-1:
The Create Budget: Automatic dialog box.

After you indicate that you want a manual budget (if you're creating a manual budget) or after you describe how you want an automatic budget corrected (if you're creating an automatic budget), Quicken displays a dialog box with the message, To complete your budget, click the Choose Categories button; underneath that, the Income tab of the Budget window appears, shown in Figure 3-2.

Figure 3-2:
The Income
tab of the
Budget
window.

You use the Income tab to enter your budget for income amounts and use the Expenses tab to budget for expense amounts. If you want to budget savings, you can enter these by using the Savings tab. (*Budgeted savings,* by the way, are just planned account transfers — money you plan to move, for example, into a savings account.)

Initially, none of the tabs shows categories or accounts, which are what you use for your budgeting. To display categories and accounts, follow these three simple steps:

1. **Click the Choose Categories button so that Quicken displays the Choose Categories dialog box. (Or, if you're looking at the Savings tab, click Choose Accounts so that Quicken displays the Choose Accounts dialog box.)**

2. **Click the Mark All button.**

3. **Click OK.**

Categories or accounts appear along the left edge of the window (see Figure 3-3). Any categories with subcategories (if you have these) contain subtotals for the total inflows and for the total outflows.

Figure 3-3:
Categories
(and sub-
categories)
appear
on the left
side of the
Budget
window.

TIP

To move among the Income, Expenses, and Savings tabs, click the tabs.

In a pane along the right edge of the Budget window, Quicken displays buttons and boxes you use to budget the selected income, expense, or savings amount, which I talk about in the next section.

Entering budgeted amounts

To budget an income or expense amount, select the category and then enter the budget into the amount box or boxes. Use the Method buttons to specify how you want to budget the amount: using an average amount, using different monthly amounts (indicated by marking the Monthly Detail button), or using different quarterly amounts (indicated by marking the Quarterly Detail button). Different Amount boxes appear for different budgeting methods. After you specify your budget amounts, click the Apply button (which is grayed out in Figure 3-4).

As you enter amounts, Quicken updates any subtotals and grand totals that use those amounts.

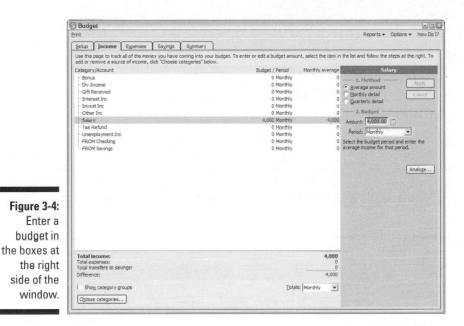

Figure 3-4:
Enter a
budget in
the boxes at
the right
side of the
window.

Reviewing the options

If you click the Options menu, which appears near the upper-right corner of
the Budget window, Quicken displays a menu of several useful commands
and switches:

- ✔ **Save Budget:** Saves a copy of the current budget.

- ✔ **Restore Budget:** Replaces whatever information shows in the Budget
 window with the information contained in the last saved copy of your
 budget.

- ✔ **Show Cents:** Turns on and off the display of cents. This baby is a real
 lifesaver if you need to literally watch your pennies.

- ✔ **Separate View:** Tells Quicken to separate income, expenses, and savings
 budgeting information on separate Income, Expenses, and Savings tabs.
 This is the default view.

- ✔ **Income/Expense View:** Tells Quicken to separate income and expense
 budgeting information on different tabs.

- ✔ **Combined View:** Tells Quicken *not* to separate income, expenses, and
 savings budgeting information on separate tabs.

✔ **Set Up Alerts:** Displays the Alerts Center dialog box, which lets you tell Quicken that it should alert you when your actual spending begins to approach a specified limit (see Figure 3-5).

To use a budget alert

1. Select the Monthly Expenses check box.

2. Select the category you want to monitor.

3. Enter the spending limit into the Spending Limit column.

4. Click Apply and then OK.

✔ **Go to Category List. Displays the Category List window, which lets you add, edit, and delete income and expense categories.**

Figure 3-5:
The Setup tab of the Alerts Center dialog box.

Reviewing your budget

After you enter your budget, click the Summary tab to see a summarized version of your income and expense budgets and a pie chart of your budget (see Figure 3-6). Use the Summary tab's Top Yearly Budget Items drop-down list box to select the budget data you want to plot in the pie chart.

If a careful review of your budget shows things have become, well, rather a mess, you can click the Setup tab and then the Start Over button to, er, start over.

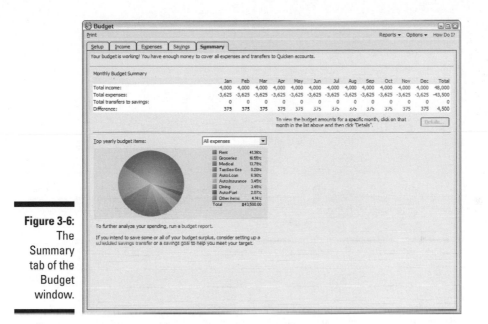

What to do after you enter your budget

After you create your Secret Plan, you don't have to do anything special to save your work. Oh, sure, you can tell Quicken to save your budget by choosing Options⇨Save Budget from the Budget window. But you don't have to. When you leave the Budget window or close it, Quicken automatically saves your work for you.

If you want to revert to the previously saved version of the budget, choose Options⇨Restore Budget from the Budget window.

I talk more about using the budget in later chapters (such as Chapter 7, for example). If you want to print a *hard copy* (computerese for *paper*) of the budget, choose Reports⇨Spending⇨Budget. If you have a printing question, go to Chapter 5.

You're not going to use the Secret Plan for a while. But don't worry; in Chapter 5, I explain how to print reports, including a report that compares your actual spending with, uh, your budget.

Part II
The Absolute Basics

The 5th Wave By Rich Tennant

"So...did you find the money that was missing from the bottom line?"

In this part . . .

Okay, you're ready for the show to start (which is good). This part covers all the nitty-gritty details of using Quicken to keep your personal and business financial records. Whether you're just starting to use the Quicken program or you've just come from Part I, you'll find the stuff covered here dang important — dare I say essential? — to using Quicken in even the most basic way.

Chapter 4

Checkbook on a Computer

• •

• •

*T*his is it. The big time. You're finally going to do those everyday Quicken things: entering checks, deposits, and transfers. Along the way, you also use some of the neat tools that Quicken provides for making these tasks easier, more precise, and faster.

Getting Started

Okay. I'm going to start at the very beginning.

As you start working with Quicken, you probably want to work from the Cash Flow Center (shown in Figure 4-1). "What's the Cash Flow Center?" you may ask. Good question. Basically, it looks and works (sort of) like a Web page that provides clickable hyperlinks to some of the most popular banking and bookkeeping features of Quicken and supplies interesting tidbits of financial trivia.

If you don't see the Cash Flow Center window, you can click the Cash Flow Center button, which appears at the left edge of the Quicken window and is cleverly labeled Cash Flow Center.

A few words about the Quicken Home page

Some people like another starting point to work from — the Quicken Home page. To see the Quicken Home page, click the Quicken Home button, which appears in the top-left corner of the Quicken window and is cleverly labeled Quicken Home. The Quicken Home page is just another starting point from which you move to financial activity centers or account detail windows. You also see a potpourri of hyperlinks that you can use to explore various Quicken features. I don't talk more about it in the pages of this book, but I did want to just mention that the Quicken Home page is worth poking your head around in. And that's all I'm going to say.

Figure 4-1:
The Cash Flow Center window.

Finding Your Checkbook

To enter checkbook transactions, use the Register tab of the Checking window (shown in Figure 4-2). If you can see the bank account you want to work with listed beneath the Cash Flow Center button, you can click it to display that

account's register. If the Cash Flow Center window is displayed, you can also click the bank account's QuickTab hyperlink, which is shown in the Spending & Savings Accounts list area. Finally, if you don't see the account anyplace, you can choose Cash Flow➪Cash Flow Accounts and then select the account you want to work with.

Figure 4-2 shows the account name — Checking — to the left of the Register tab.

The starting balance you specified as part of setting up the account is the first amount that Quicken lists. In Figure 4-2, for example, the starting balance is $4.16. Bummer.

The Download transactions from [name of your bank] information, initially shown at the bottom of the register window, lets you set up an account for online banking or online bill payment. If you want to do this, follow the on-screen instructions. (You can also click the Set Up Online Payment button on the Register tab to set up the account for online banking and bill payment.) If you need help or more information about online banking or bill payment, see Chapter 6. To remove this online services stuff from the window, click the button with the double-chevrons that's to the right of the Download Transactions and Scheduled Transactions tabs.

Figure 4-2:
The Register
tab of the
Checking
window.

Recording Checks

First things first: You can enter checks by using either the Register tab (refer to Figure 4-2) or the Write Checks window, which I describe in Chapter 5.

You use the Register tab for the checks that you don't want to print or pay electronically with Quicken; you use the Write Checks window to enter the checks that you do want to print or pay electronically with Quicken. (This rule isn't etched in stone, but it does make things easier, so it's the rule that I follow.)

Entering a check into the register

Entering a check in the register is a simple matter of describing to whom you wrote the check and how much you paid. Suppose, for example, that you paid $25.50 to the cable television company for your monthly cable service. Here's how you enter this check:

1. **Enter the check date.**

 Move the cursor to the Date field in the next empty row of the register (if it isn't already there) and type the date by using the *MM/DD* format. To enter June 8, 2007, for example, type **6/8**. You usually don't have to type the year because Quicken retrieves the current year number from the little clock inside your computer.

 You can adjust the date in a Date field by using the + and – keys on your keyboard. The + key adds one day to the current date; the – key subtracts one day from the current date.

2. **Enter the check number.**

 Move the cursor (or tab) to the Num field and type the check number. Alternatively, move the cursor to the Num field and then, when Quicken displays a list box of entries (such as ATM, Deposit, EFT, Next Check Number, Print Check, Send Online Payment, and Transfer Funds), select Next Check Number if you want. Quicken then fills in the number with its guess as to the new check number — one more than the last check number you entered. If this guess is right, you can just leave it in place. If it isn't right, type over what Quicken guessed with the correct number or use the + or – key to increase or decrease the check number.

3. **Enter the payee.**

 Move the cursor to the Payee field. Type the name of the person or business you're paying. If the cable company's name is Movies Galore, for example, type **Movies Galore**. (In the future, you can probably select payee names from the Payee list box.)

Interested in online banking and bill payment?

If you want to know more about how online bill payment and banking work, read Chapter 6. For now, just pay attention to how the Quicken register works. Everything you read about in this chapter will help you more easily use the Quicken Online Account Access feature.

4. Enter the check amount.

Move the cursor to the Payment field and type the check amount — **25.50** in this example. You don't have to type the dollar sign, but you do need to type the period to indicate the decimal place and cents.

5. Enter the category.

Move the cursor to the Category field. Quicken displays a drop-down list box of category names from your category list. You can select one of these categories by using the arrow keys or the mouse. Or, if you're the independent type, just type the name yourself. For example, if you use the standard Quicken categories list, you may categorize a payment to your cable company as Utilities:Cable TV. The first part of this entry, Utilities, is the category. The second part, Cable TV, is the subcategory.

If you go with the typing approach and you're not a superfast typist, Quicken can probably guess which category you're entering before you enter it. When you start typing **Ut**, for example, Quicken fills in the rest of the category name, "ilities," for you ("Ut" + "ilities" – "Utilities"). This feature is called *QuickFill,* and I talk about it in more detail in the section, "Working with a kooky (and clever) little thing named QuickFill," later in this chapter.

6. [Optional] Enter a class.

If, after reading about classes in Chapter 2, you decided to use classes, you can also enter a class into the Category field. To do this, type a / (slash) and then the class name after you type the category name. Just to make this a bit more clear, suppose that you're using classes to segregate expenses by house because you actually own two homes: your principle residence and a cabin in the mountains. If you've set up two classes — *principle* and *cabin* — you record utilities expenses for your principle residence by entering **utilities/principle** into the Category field. You record utilities expenses for your cabin by entering **utilities/cabin** into the Category field.

TIP

A neat little trick

You can expand and edit the list box of Num entries that Quicken displays. If you want to add some new Num entry to the Num drop-down list box, for example, do the following:

1. **Click the Edit List button, which appears at the bottom of the Num drop-down list.**

 Quicken displays the Edit Num List dialog box.

2. **Click the New button and then complete the dialog box that Quicken displays.**

 You can also remove any new Num entries you add by using the Edit Num List dialog box.

 I won't spend any more time describing how this works, so if you want to figure it all out, just experiment. You can't hurt anything.

7. **[Optional] Enter a memo description.**

 Move the cursor to the Memo field and describe the specific reason that you're paying the check. You may identify the cable payment as the June payment, for example. If you're using Quicken for a business, use this field to identify the paid invoice — usually by entering the invoice number you're paying. You don't have to enter anything into this field, by the way.

8. **Click the Enter button.**

 Click the Enter button that appears in the transaction's row of the register. This option tells Quicken that you want to record the transaction into your register. Quicken beeps in acknowledgment, calculates the new account balance, and moves the cursor to the next slot, or row, in the register.

Figure 4-3 shows the cable television check recorded into the register. You can't see it in the figure, but the amount in the Balance field after the $25.50 check shows up in red. This red number indicates that you've overdrawn your account. I don't need to tell you what that means: overdraft charges.

Changing a check you've entered

What if you need to change a check that you've already entered? Suppose that you make a terrible mistake, such as recording a $52.50 check as $25.20. Can you fix it? Sure. Just use the arrow keys or click the mouse to highlight the check transaction that you want to change. Use the Tab and Shift+Tab keys to move the cursor to the field you want to change. (You can also select the field by clicking it with the mouse.) Then make your fix. Click the Enter button when you finish or press Enter on the keyboard.

Figure 4-3:
The Quicken
register
after
recording
the check to
Movies
Galore.

Packing more checks into the register

Normally, Quicken displays two rows of information about each check that you enter. It also displays two rows of information about each of the other types of transactions you enter. If you want to pack more checks into a visible portion of the register, click the View button (which appears near the top-right corner of the Register tab) and then choose the One-Line Display command from the menu that Quicken displays. After you do, Quicken displays all the register information — except the Memo field — in a single-line format (as shown in Figure 4-4). To return to the double-line format, choose View⇨ One-Line Display again.

If you click the View button, you notice that it also displays a bunch of commands that begin with the word *Sort.* These commands all work the same basic way. They let you reorganize the transactions shown in the register in some new way: by date, amount, check number, and so on.

Don't worry. I'm not going to waste your precious time telling you things like the Sort By Date command sorts transactions by their dates or that the Sort By Amount (Largest First) command sorts transactions by descending size of the transaction amounts.

Memorized payees

Quicken provides another feature — memorized payees — which is almost irrelevant to day-to-day Quicken use now that the QuickFill feature exists. But because you may hear about this tool, I briefly describe how it works.

A *memorized payee* is one that you've stored or that Quicken has stored on a special list. (To store the transaction, you select it in the register and choose Edit⇨Transaction⇨Memorize Payee.)

To later use or abuse a memorized transaction, choose Tools⇨Memorized Payee List to display a list of previously memorized payees. When Quicken displays the list, select the payee you want to reuse and click Use.

A memorized payees list is a handy tool. But if you're feeling a little overwhelmed, don't spin your wheels trying to get up to speed on this feature. QuickFill almost always does the job for you because — get this — it automatically grabs memorized payees from the list.

If you point to the column heading for the Payee field, the Payment field, or the Cleared Status field (labeled with Clr), Quicken displays a pop-up command that you can use to re-sort the transactions in the register. These options are self-explanatory. The one that appears when you point to the Payee field is Sort Payees In Alphabetic Order. And the one that appears when you point to the Cleared Status field is Sort Transactions Into Groups of Reconciled, Cleared, and Uncleared Transactions. You get the picture.

Working with a kooky (and clever) little thing named QuickFill

Here's kind of a funny quirk about Quicken: If Quicken can guess what you're typing into a field, it fills in the rest of the field for you. Earlier in this chapter, I mention how this QuickFill feature works when you type category names. But it gets even better than that.

The second time you use a payee name, for example, Quicken knows that it's the second time. Quicken also figures that, "Hey, some stuff from the last Movies Galore transaction will probably be the same for this transaction." When you type the first few letters of the payee name, Quicken supplies a payee name for you. After you press the Tab key to accept the name, Quicken uses the last transaction's information to fill in all the current transaction's fields.

Figure 4-4:
How the register looks with the One-line Display format.

This feature is a real timesaver. Suppose that you did write a $25.50 check to Movies Galore for your June cable television bill. When you type **Movies Galore** to record July's cable television check, the amount will probably be the same. The complete payee name will certainly be the same, and the category will also be the same. So Quicken fills in all these fields, too.

QuickFill doesn't do everything for you, however. You still need to make sure that the date and check number are correct. If Quicken QuickFills a field with the wrong information, just replace the wrong information with the right information.

Recording Deposits

Recording a deposit works almost the same way as recording a check. The only difference is that you enter the deposit amount in the Deposit field rather than enter the check amount in the Payment field.

Entering a deposit into the register

Suppose that you receive $100 as a birthday gift from your elderly Aunt Enid and deposit it into your checking account. Here's how you record this deposit in the register:

1. **Enter the deposit date.**

 Move the cursor to the Date field of the next empty row of the register (if it isn't already there) and type the date. Use the *MM/DD* format. You enter June 8, 2007, for example, as **6/8**. As with check dates, you have to enter the year only if the current year number, which Quicken retrieves from the little clock inside your computer, is wrong.

 You can adjust the date in a Date field in Quicken by using the + and – keys. The + key adds one day to the current date; the – key subtracts one day from the current date.

2. **Type the code** DEP **(for deposit) into the Num field.**

 Are you the meticulous type? Then go ahead and move the cursor to the Num field. Open the Num drop-down list box and select Deposit.

3. **Type the name of the person from whom you received the deposit.**

 In this case, move the cursor to the Payee field and type **Aunt Enid**. (I don't mean to sound presumptuous, but, well, the next time Aunt Enid sends you birthday money, you'll be able to select her name from the Payee drop-down list box.)

4. **Enter the deposit amount.**

 Move the cursor to the Deposit field and type **100**. Don't type the dollar sign — or any other punctuation. (If Aunt Enid sweats money and sometimes passes out $1,000 gifts, for example, you record the deposit as **1000** — not 1,000 or $1,000.)

5. **Enter the category.**

 You know how this works by now. Move the cursor to the Category field. Open the Category drop-down list box, if necessary, and select the appropriate category. Alternatively, if you like living on the edge, try typing in the category name. You may describe Aunt Enid's check as **Gift Received**. (This income category is on the standard home category list.)

 To add a category, type a name in the Category field and move to another field. When Quicken doesn't recognize the category name, it asks you whether you want to add the category. Click Yes, and Quicken displays the Set Up Category dialog box. Refer to Chapter 2 if you have questions about how this works.

6. **[Optional] Enter a memo description.**

 Move the cursor to the Memo field and describe something, such as the reason for the deposit. Aunt Enid's money may be described as **birthday gift**. If you're a business depositing a customer's check, use this entry to identify the invoice the customer is paying.

7. **Click the Enter button.**

 This command tells Quicken that you want to record the transaction in your register. Quicken beeps in protest but then adds the transaction.

Figure 4-5 shows the Checking register after you enter Aunt Enid's thoughtful gift. Your account is no longer overdrawn — so you have that going for you. Maybe before you go any further, you should call Aunt Enid to thank her.

See the ending balance given at the bottom of the register window? The ending balance shows the account balance after every register transaction. If you enter future-dated transactions, the register window shows both a current balance — the balance as of the current date — and an ending balance, which is the balance after all the transactions.

Figure 4-5:
A Checking register after you record your first deposit.

Quicken also includes a Paycheck Wizard that you can use to describe the taxes withheld from your paycheck and categorize the deductions from your paycheck. That much said, you probably don't need to keep track of these amounts unless, for some reason, you want precise estimates of the income taxes you pay. Remember that your employer already does this accounting. Also remember that you must use the employer's data, which appears on your W-2 form — and not your Quicken data — when you prepare your U.S. taxes. If you do decide to use the Paycheck Wizard, just choose Tax⇨Tax Activities⇨Set Up My Paycheck. Quicken launches the Paycheck Wizard, which asks you a few general questions about your deductions and then provides a dialog box similar to a Split Transaction window where you can enter and categorize your deductions. For more information about splitting transactions, refer to the "Splitting Transactions" section, later in this chapter.

Changing a deposit you've already entered

Big surprise here — changing a deposit works just like changing a check. First, use the arrow keys or click with the mouse to select the deposit. Use the Tab and Shift+Tab keys to move the cursor to the field you want to change. Tab moves the cursor to the next field. Shift+Tab moves the cursor to the previous field. (You can also select the field by clicking it with the mouse.) Then make your fix and click the Enter button.

Recording Account Transfers

Account transfers occur when you move money from one account, such as your savings account, to another account, such as your checking account. But jeepers, why am I telling you this? If you have one of those combined savings and checking accounts, you probably do this sort of thing all the time.

Oh, now I remember why I brought this up — Quicken makes quick work of account transfers as long as you already have *both* accounts set up.

If you don't have the second account set up, you need to do that first. If you don't know how, flip back to Chapter 2.

Entering an account transfer

Buckle up. I speed through the steps for recording an account transfer. For the most part, you record an account transfer the same way you record a check or deposit.

Suppose that you want to record the transfer of $50 from your checking account to your savings account. Maybe you want to set aside a little money — *little,* presumably, being a key adjective — to purchase a gift for your generous Aunt Enid.

Say that you're working with your checking account and want to record a transfer to your savings account. Here's what you need to do:

1. **Enter the transfer date.**

 Move the cursor to the Date field. Then type the date that you move the money from one account to another.

2. **Flag the transaction as a transfer.**

 Move the cursor to the Num field. Open the drop-down list box and select the Transfer entry. Quicken abbreviates "transfer" as TXFR.

3. **Enter a description of the transaction.**

 Use the Description field to describe the transfer — for example, **Birthday**. You know how this works by now, don't you? You just move the cursor to the field. Then you pound away at the keyboard. Bang. Bang. Bang.

4. **Enter the transfer amount.**

 You enter amounts that you transfer out of an account in the Payment field, and you enter amounts that you transfer into an account in the Deposit field. So move the cursor to the right field (*right* as in *right and wrong,* not *right and left*) and then enter the transfer amount.

5. **Indicate the other account.**

 Move the cursor to the Category field, which has a modified name of Xfer Acct (standing for *Transfer Account*) and, when Quicken drops down a list box of accounts, select the other account. In Figure 4-6, I show the transfer as going to an account named "Savings." I set up this account secretly, while you weren't watching. But note that the steps for setting up a savings account parallel those for setting up a checking account. Refer to Chapter 2 for more information.

6. **[Optional] Enter a memo description.**

 Enter more information about the transaction (if you need to) in the Memo field. Perhaps a gift idea for Aunt Enid?

7. **Click the Enter button.**

 This command tells Quicken that you want to record the transfer transaction into your register.

Figure 4-6 shows the Checking register after you transfer money from your checking account to your savings account so that you'll have money to purchase something nice for Aunt Enid's next birthday — maybe that new Robert Plant CD.

Figure 4-6:
The
Checking
register
after you
enter the
transfer
transaction.

Take a look at the Category field. Notice that Quicken uses brackets — [] — to identify the Category field entry as an account and not as an income or expense category.

Working with the other half of the transfer

Here's the cool thing about transfer transactions: Quicken automatically records the other half of the transfer for you. Figure 4-6 shows the $50 reduction in the checking account because of the transfer. Quicken uses this information to record a $50 increase in the savings account. Automatically. Biddabam. Biddaboom.

To see the other half of a transfer transaction, select the transfer transaction by using the arrow keys or the mouse. Then choose Edit⇨Transaction⇨Go To Matching Transfer. Quicken displays the other account in a new register window, as shown in Figure 4-7.

Figure 4-7:
The other
half of the
transfer
transaction.

Changing a transfer you've already entered

Predictably, this activity works just like changing a check or a deposit:

1. **Select the transfer by using the arrow keys or by clicking the mouse.**

2. **Use the Tab and Shift+Tab keys to move the cursor to the field that you want to change.**

3. **Make your fix, click the Enter button, and then go to lunch.**

Splitting Transactions

Here's a sort of Quicken riddle for you: Suppose that you have a check that pays more than one kind of expense. You trot down to the grocery store, for example, and pick up $10 worth of junk food and junk beverages (which you should categorize as a Groceries expense) and $10 worth of 10W-40 motor oil (which you should categorize as an Auto expense). How do you categorize a transaction like this? Well, I'll tell you. You use a *split category*.

Here's how a split category works: When you're ready to categorize the check, you click the Split button and Quicken displays the Split Transaction window, shown in Figure 4-8.

Figure 4-8:
The Split
Transaction
window.

Steps for splitting a check

Being a clever sort, you probably already know how the Split Transaction window works. I go through the steps anyway. Suppose that you want to categorize a $20 check that includes $10 for groceries and $10 for motor oil.

To categorize a check in the Split Transaction window, do the following:

1. **Enter the first category name in the first Category field.**

 Move the cursor to the Category field (if it isn't already there). Activate the drop-down list box by pressing Alt+S or by clicking the down arrow and then selecting the category name.

 (Despite what a dietitian may say, you can call the soda and candy "Groceries.")

2. **Enter a memo description for the first categorized portion of the check.**

 Move the cursor to the first Memo field and then type whatever you want. (Maybe a description of the food you bought. Er, then again, maybe if you're buying real junk, you should just leave this blank.)

3. Enter the amount spent for the first category.

Move the cursor to the first Amount field and then type, well, the amount. If the first category is what you're calling Groceries and you spent $10 on this, you type **10**.

4. Repeat Steps 1, 2, and 3 for each spending category.

If you spent another $10 on motor oil, for example, move the cursor to the second Category field and enter the category and optionally the subcategory you use to summarize auto maintenance expenses. In Figure 4-9, for example, I use the category-subcategory combination Auto:Service. Optionally, move the cursor to the second Memo field and enter a memo description of the expenditure, such as **oil**. Move the cursor to the second Amount field and enter the amount of the expenditure, such as **10**.

Figure 4-9 shows a Split Transaction window that is complete. A split transaction can have up to 30 pieces. Use the scroll bar and PgUp and PgDn keys to scroll through the list of split amounts.

Figure 4-9:
The completed Split Transaction window.

5. Verify that the Split Transaction window shows no uncategorized spending.

If you find extra spending — this shows up as the Remainder amount — either add the category you need or delete the split transaction line that's uncategorized. To delete a split transaction line, move the cursor to one of the fields in the line and choose Edit⇨Delete. You can also click the Adjust button to get rid of the Remainder amount — but in this case, Quicken adjusts the amount originally entered into the register so that it agrees with the details you've supplied in the Split Transaction window.

If you want to insert a new line, move the selection cursor to the line above where you want to make your insertion and choose Edit⇨Insert. If you're fed up and want to start over from scratch, choose Edit⇨ Clear All (which causes Quicken to erase all the split transaction lines).

6. Click OK.

After you complete the Split Transaction window — that is, after you completely and correctly categorize all the little pieces of the transaction — click OK. Quicken closes the Split Transaction window. If you didn't enter an amount in the Payment column of the register before opening the Split Transaction window, Quicken displays a dialog box that asks whether the transaction is a payment or a deposit. You select an option button to make your choice known.

To let you know that the transaction is one that you've split, the Category field shows the word --Split-- when you select the split transaction. Take a peek at Figure 4-10 to see for yourself.

7. Click the Enter button.

This command tells Quicken that you want to record the transaction in your register.

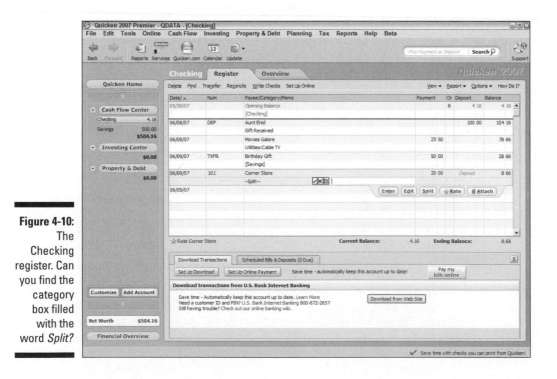

Figure 4-10:
The Checking register. Can you find the category box filled with the word *Split?*

Splitting hairs

Quicken assumes that any transaction amount you enter in the register should agree with the total of the individual split transaction amounts entered in the Split Transaction window.

If you're not sure what the split transaction amount's total is, your best bet is to NOT — I repeat, *NOT* — enter the amount on the Register tab. Instead, enter the individual split transaction amounts in the Split Transaction window. When you leave the Split Transaction window, Quicken totals your individual split amounts and then prompts you to see whether the total is a payment or a deposit. Then it plugs this total into either the Payment or the Deposit field.

If you've already entered either a payment amount or a deposit amount but you're not sure that the split transaction amounts agree with what you entered, you can tell Quicken to adjust the Payment or Deposit amount on the Register tab to whatever the individual split transaction amounts total. To do so, click the Split Transaction window Adjust button. Quicken then adds up the split transaction lines and plugs the total into the register. (This approach may best be called, "I don't care if it's a round hole; I want to pound this square peg into it.")

By the way, Quicken shows any difference between the amount shown on the Register tab and the individual split transaction amounts. It shows this difference as the last split transaction line, so you can tell whether the individual splits agree with the payment or deposit amount shown in the register.

Editing and deleting split categories

You can delete or change any individual line of a split category. To do so, first select the transaction (to display the Split Transaction window) and then click the check mark button, which appears in the register's Category field after you record the transaction. After Quicken dutifully displays the Split Transaction window, you can edit a field by selecting it and then typing over its contents. You can delete any line of the split category by choosing Edit⇨Delete. (If you want to delete all the lines of the split category so you can start over, choose Clear All instead.)

If you want to unsplit the transaction so that you can assign it to a single category, you need to use a little trick. Click the X button that appears in the register's Category field after you record the transaction.

Steps for splitting deposits and transfers

Wondering if you can split deposits and transfers? Well, you can. The steps for doing so work just like the steps for splitting categories for a check transaction. The basic trick — if you can call it a trick — is to use the Split Transaction window to list all the category names and amounts.

Sort of a voiding bug . . .

When you mark a transaction as void — you do this by selecting a transaction and choosing Edit⇨Transaction⇨Void Transaction(s) — Quicken does three things: It sticks the word VOID at the start of the Payee field, it marks the transaction as cleared, and it erases the amount in the Payment or Deposit field. So far, so good. But if you later fill in the Payment or Deposit field and don't pay attention to the warning from Quicken that you're editing a reconciled transaction, Quicken uses the payment or deposit amount that you enter to adjust the account balance — even though Quicken still shows the transaction as void. I keep thinking the folks at Intuit will fix this, but they haven't — at least not yet. The bottom line is that you need to make sure that you don't edit transactions after you void them. Otherwise, you can all too easily foul up your account balance — perhaps even overdraw your account. I won't tell you about how I happened to learn this. . . .

One other point I should make here is that you can mix and match categories and transfers in the Split Transaction window. Some of the splits, for example, can be categories, and some can be transfer accounts. This type of transaction is common in a business setting. (See Chapter 15 for more information.)

Deleting and Voiding Transactions

You can delete and void register transactions by using the Edit button's Delete and Void Transaction(s) commands. If you've looked at the Edit button — it appears just beneath the selected transaction when you're entering data — you've probably already guessed as much.

Using either command is a snap: Just highlight the transaction you want to delete or void by using the arrow keys or by clicking the mouse. Then click the Edit button and choose the command. And that's that.

Use the Void Transaction(s) command any time you void a check. Quicken leaves voided transactions in the register but marks them as void and erases the Payment or Deposit amount. So by using the Void Transaction(s) command, you keep a record of voided, or canceled, transactions.

Use the Delete command if you want to remove the transaction from your register.

The Big Register Phenomenon

If you start entering a bunch of checks, deposits, and transfers into your registers, you'll soon find yourself with registers that contain hundreds and even thousands of transactions. You can still work with one of these big registers by using the tools and techniques I talk about in the preceding paragraphs. Nevertheless, let me give you some more help for dealing with . . . (drumroll, please) . . . the big register phenomenon.

Moving through a big register

You can use the PgUp and PgDn keys to page up and down through your register a screenful of transactions at a time. Some people call this *scrolling*. You can call it whatever you want.

You can press Ctrl+Home to move to the first transaction in a register and Ctrl+End to move to the last transaction in a register.

You can also use the vertical scroll bar along the right edge of the Register tab. Click either above or below the square scroll bar marker to page back and forth through the register. Or, if you have no qualms about dragging the mouse around, you can drag the scroll bar marker up and down the scroll bar. If you drag the scroll bar marker to scroll through the register, Quicken displays a pop-up box that shows the transaction date you've scrolled to.

Finding that darn transaction

Want to find a specific check, deposit, or transfer? No problem. The Find command provides a handy way for doing just that. Here's what you do:

1. **Choose Edit⇨Find & Replace⇨Find, or click the Find button on the Register tab.**

 Quicken, with restrained but obvious enthusiasm, displays the Quicken Find dialog box (shown in Figure 4-11). You use this dialog box to describe the transaction you want to find in as much detail as possible. (Notice that you don't click the Edit command on the Register tab to get to this command; you click the menu bar's Edit menu.)

2. **Enter the piece of text or number that identifies the transaction you want to locate.**

 Move the cursor to the Find text box. Then type the text or number. By the way, the case of the text doesn't matter. If you type **aunt**, for example, Quicken finds *AUNT* or *Aunt*.

Figure 4-11:
The Quicken
Find dialog
box.

Quicken Find			
Search:	Memo ▼		Find
Match if:	Contains ▼		Find All
Find:	Aunit		Close
	✓ Search Backwards		Help

3. **Specify which pieces, or fields, of the register transaction you want Quicken to look at.**

 Click the arrow to the right of the Search box and then from the drop-down list, select the field Quicken should look at during the search: Amount, Cleared Status (the Clr field), Memo, Date, Category/Class (whatever is in the Category field), Check Number (what's in the Num field), or Payee. Or get truly crazy and pick the All Fields list entry so that Quicken looks both high and low.

4. **Tell Quicken whether you're using a shotgun or a rifle.**

 You need to specify how closely what you stuck in the Find text box needs to match whatever you selected in the Search drop-down list box. To do so, open the Match If drop-down list box. Then select the appropriate matching rule:

 • **Contains:** Select this rule if the field or fields you're searching just need to use a piece of text. If you enter **Aunt** into the Find text box and use this matching rule to search Payee fields, Quicken finds transactions that use the following payee names: *Aunt Enid, Aunt Enid and Uncle Joob, Uncle Harry and Aunt Edna,* and — well, you get the idea.

 • **Exact:** Select this rule if the field you're searching needs to exactly match your Find text box entry. If you enter the Find text box entry as **Aunt**, for example, and you're searching Payee fields, Quicken looks for transactions where the Payee field shows *Aunt* — and nothing more or nothing less.

 • **Starts With:** Select this rule if the field you're searching for just needs to start with what you entered in the Find text box. For example, if you enter **Aunt** in the Find text box and you're searching the Payee fields, Quicken looks for transactions where the Payee field starts with the word *Aunt* — such as *Aunt Enid* or *Aunt Enid and Uncle Joob.* (Uncle Joob and Aunt Enid wouldn't cut the mustard in this case, though.)

 • **Ends With:** Select this rule if the field you're searching for just needs to end with what you entered in the Find text box.

- **Greater:** Select this rule if the field you're searching for needs to hold a value that exceeds the number you entered in the Find text box. This makes sense, right? Like you're looking for checks you wrote for more than $100?

- **Greater or Equal:** Select this rule if the field you're searching for needs to hold a value that either exceeds or equals the number you entered in the Find text box.

- **Less:** Select this rule if the field you're searching for needs to hold a value that is less than the number you entered in the Find text box.

- **Less or Equal:** Select this rule if the field you're searching for needs to hold a value that is less than or equal to the number you entered in the Find text box.

5. **Tell Quicken whether you want it to search forward or backward from the selected transaction.**

 Select the Search Backwards check box if you want to look backward starting from the selected transaction.

6. **Let the search begin.**

 You click either the Find or Find All button to begin the search. If you click Find, Quicken looks through the register, and if it can find a transaction like you describe, it highlights the transaction.

 If you click Find All, Quicken looks through the register and builds a list of all the transactions that are like the one you describe. Then it displays the list in an expanded version of the Quicken Search Results window (as shown in Figure 4-12). To edit a found transaction, select the transaction and click the Edit Transaction(s) button.

Figure 4-12:
The Quicken Search Results window with a transaction that matches the search criteria.

Quicken supplies another command that is similar to Find. The Edit menu's Find/Replace command lets you both locate and modify transactions that look like the one you describe. (To use the Find/Replace command, choose Edit➪Find & Replace➪Find/Replace.) For example, you may want to locate transactions showing Aunt Enid as the payee so that you can replace *Aunt* with *Great Aunt*. The Find/Replace command works in a similar fashion to the Find command except that you need to describe what you want to modify in the found transactions. After you complete the initial dialog box that Quicken displays when you choose the command, Quicken displays a window listing the transactions it has found. (This window looks like the one shown in Figure 4-13.) You mark — by clicking — the transactions you want to modify, describe the replacement information, and then click the Replace button.

Figure 4-13:
The Find
And
Replace
dialog box.

You can't use the Find/Replace command to find and replace categories, but you can use another command: Recategorize. (To use the Recategorize command, choose Edit➪Find & Replace➪Recategorize.) For example, you may want to recategorize all your cable television payments as the Entertainment category (where earlier, you placed them in the Utilities category). When you choose the Recategorize command, Quicken displays the Recategorize window (shown in Figure 4-14). Enter the category you want to replace in the Find Category text box and the new replacement category in the Recategorize Selected Transaction(s) With text box. Next, click the Find All button to tell Quicken to display a list of transactions that use the category you want to replace. Click the transactions you want to recategorize (to mark them), supply the replacement category, and then click the Recategorize button.

Figure 4-14:
The Recate-
gorize
window.

Pop-Up Calendars and Calculators

Can I tell you just a couple more things? (If not, skip this section. If so, read on.) Quicken provides a pop-up calendar anytime you move the selection cursor to a Date field. To get to the calendar, click the button that appears at the right end of the Date field. Quicken displays a calendar for the current month (as shown in Figure 4-15). All you have to do is select the day you want as the date. (If you want to see a calendar for a different month, click the << and >> buttons.)

Quicken also provides a pop-up calculator anytime you move the selection cursor to an Amount field. To get to the calculator, click the button that appears at the right end of the Amount field.

Quicken displays a calculator like the one shown in Figure 4-16 when you choose the Tools⇨Calculator command. This baby works like a regular hand-held calculator. You just type the math you want to perform. Quicken displays the calculation result in the Amount field.

Do the calculator keys make sense? Table 4-1 shows how they work.

Table 4-1	A Handyman's Guide to the Quicken Calculator Keys
Key Name	*Operation*
/ (slash)	Division
X	Multiplication
– (minus)	Subtraction
+ (plus)	Addition
. (period)	Indicates the decimal point
%	Indicates that the number you just typed is a percentage and should be converted to a decimal value
= (equal sign)	Calculates the amount and removes the pop-up calculator
<-	Removes, or clears, the last digit you entered
CE	Clears the last number entered into the calculator
C	Clears the Amount field

Figure 4-15:
The pop-up calculator.

Figure 4-16:
The pop up
calculator.

If you type a number into the Amount field and then type any one of the math operand keys (+ – / *), Quicken pops open the calculator to continue the calculation. You don't have to click the calculator button first.

Attaching Flags, Notes, and Images

Inside the register window, just to the right of the Split button, Quicken provides an Attach button. If you wouldn't mind, take a minute and see if you can find the Attach button — it shows a picture of a paperclip.

Okay, here's why this button may interest you: When you click this button, Quicken displays a menu of commands that you can use to attach a follow-up flag, a little note, or even a PDF image of the check or other receipt. You choose the command that corresponds to the flag, note, or image you want to attach, or connect, to the register transaction. Quicken then displays a dialog box that you use to provide the flag or note or to identify the PDF file that holds the check or receipt image.

Chapter 5

Printing 101

- -

In This Chapter

▶ Printing a check

▶ Recovering from a mistake after you've printed the check

▶ Printing a register

- -

1 bet you can't guess what this chapter describes. Gee, you guessed it — how to print checks and reports.

Printing Checks

Printing checks in Quicken is, well, quick. All you basically need to do is enter the information you want to print on the check form and the number you want Quicken to use to identify the check. Sounds simple enough, doesn't it? It is, as you can read in the steps that follow.

To enter the information on a check form, follow these steps:

1. **Display the Write Checks window by choosing Cash Flow⇨Write Checks or by pressing Ctrl+W.**

 Figure 5-1 shows the Write Checks: Checking window.

2. **Select the account on which you want to write the check.**

 This step is very important! To select the account you want to use, open the Write Checks From drop-down list at the top of the window. (You can do this by clicking the arrow button that's just to the right of the box.) When Quicken displays the list of accounts, choose the one you want to use.

Figure 5-1:
The Write
Checks
window.

3. Enter the check date.

First, use the mouse or Tab key to move the cursor to the Date field. Then, type the date that you're going to print the check (probably today's date). Remember to type the date in a *MM/DD/YYYY* format — enter June 8, 2007, as **6/8/2007**. You don't need to enter the year if the year number that Quicken retrieves from your computer's internal system clock is correct. You can adjust the date by a day by using + and – from the numeric keypad. You can also click the button at the end of the Date field to display your friend, the pop-up calendar.

4. Enter the name of the person or business you're paying.

Move the cursor to the Pay To The Order Of field and type away. For example, to write a check to me, type **Steve Nelson**. (Feel free to do so, by the way. If you send me a check, I'll even cash it as a sort of public service.) If you've written a check to the payee before, when you start to type the name, Quicken recognizes it and fills in the rest for you.

5. Enter the amount of the check.

Move the cursor to the $ text box and type the amount. (If you're sending a check to me, be sure to make the amount nominal — for sure, not more than $10 or $20. . . .) When you press the Tab key, the cursor moves down to the next field, and Quicken writes the amount in words on the line under the payee name and before the word `Dollars`.

6. Enter the payee's address.

If you plan to mail the check in a window envelope, move the cursor to the Address field. (You can do this by clicking inside the field.) Then enter the name and address of the person or business you're paying.

Here's a little address-entry trick: You can copy the payee name from the Pay To The Order Of text box to the first line of the Address field. Click the mouse or select the first line of the address field. Then press the ' (apostrophe) key. Now fill in the rest of the address block, including the street number and name, city, state, and zip code. Once entered, Quicken memorizes these address details for the next time you use this payee.

7. [Optional] Enter a memo description of the check.

Move the cursor to the Memo field and enter a description (such as an account number or an invoice number) of why you're sending your money to this person or business. Or, if you're sending someone a check because you didn't have time to go out and buy a real gift, type **Happy Birthday** in the Memo field. It's the little things that make a difference.

8. Enter the category.

Move the cursor to the Category field and type the category name for the expense you're paying with the check. If you don't remember the category name, scroll down the category list to find the category. Figure 5-2 shows the completed window for a check payable to Movies Galore, the local cable TV company.

Figure 5-2:
A completed check.

You can assign a check to more than a single category by using the Split Transaction window. Using the Split Transaction window with the Write Checks window works the same way as using the Split Transaction window with the Register tab. (I describe using the Split Transaction window with the Register tab in Chapter 4.) Okay. So why do I bring this up? You use the Split Transaction window when a check pays more than one type of expense or is transferred to more than one account.

For example, if you're writing a check to pay your mortgage, with part of the check paying the actual mortgage and part of the check going into an escrow account for property taxes, you can use the Split Transaction window to describe the transaction's individual components. To split a check amount so that the amount is assigned to multiple spending categories, click the Split button or press Ctrl+S. Either way, Quicken displays the Split Transaction window for you to indicate the categories and categorized amounts that make up the check total. If you have questions about how split transactions work, refer to Chapter 4.

9. **Click the Record Check button.**

Quicken records the check. It displays the current account balance and the ending account balance, and it even adds a Checks To Print total at the bottom of the window. If you're working with a monitor that supports a high screen resolution, you'll also see a Checks To Print window that lists all the nitty-gritty about the checks you have to print, as shown earlier in Figure 5-2. Shoot, when you're finished with one check, Quicken even scrolls the completed check off the screen and replaces it with a new, blank check that you can use to pay your next bill. It doesn't get much better than this, does it?

What if you make a mistake entering a check?

Don't worry. If you haven't yet printed the check, fixing mistakes is easy. If you press the PgUp and PgDn keys with the Write Checks window displayed, Quicken pages you through the check transactions. That way, you can display any check that you wrote — but have not yet printed — in the Write Check window. Or, an even easier way if you've got a lot of checks is to double-click the check in the list that appears beneath the check form. (Quicken adds a check to this list when you click the Record Check button.)

With the check redisplayed, you can fix the mistake in two ways:

 ✔ If you incorrectly entered some bit of check information, move the cursor to the field with the incorrect data and just type over the data.

> ✔ If you're really mad or frustrated, you can delete the entire check by clicking the Delete button. (I should 'fess up here and suggest that you delete the check if you accidentally entered a check to me, for example.) Then you can re-enter the check — only this time, correctly.

Don't use this method to delete a check that you've already printed. To *void* a check that you've already printed, follow these steps:

1. **You must first go into the Register tab. To display the register, you can click the QuickTab for the account.**

 The QuickTab shows beneath the Cash Flow Center button.

2. **Find the check on the Register tab, select the check, and void it by clicking the Edit button and choosing the drop-down list's Void Transaction command.**

3. **You should also write something, such as VOID, in large letters across the face of the printed check.**

Printing a check you've entered

Printing checks is easy. Here's what you need to do.

1. **Load the checks into your printer.**

 You do so the same way you load any other paper into your printer. If you have questions about it, refer to your printer documentation. (Sorry I can't help more on this process, but with a million different printers on the market, I can't guess which one you have.)

2. **Click the Print button at the top of the Write Checks window or choose File⇨Print Checks or press Ctrl+P.**

 Quicken displays the Select Checks To Print: Checking dialog box, as shown in Figure 5-3. At the top of the dialog box, Quicken shows how many checks you have to print and the total dollar amount for those checks.

3. **Enter the first check number.**

 Move the cursor to the First Check Number text box and type the number printed on the first check form you'll print. Figure 5-3 shows 1001, for example, so the first check form is numbered 1001. To quickly increase or decrease the check numbers, use + or – on the numeric keypad.

Select Checks to Print: Checking

You have 1 check to print for $25.50.

First check number: 1001

Print
- All checks
- Checks dated through: 06/30/07
- Selected checks Choose...

OK
Cancel
Print First...
Help

Check style: Standard checks

Standard business checks are formatted three to a page for fast printing. Order standard checks...

Checks on First Page
- Three
- Two
- One

Options
- Print your logo
- Additional copies: 0

Figure 5-3:
The Select
Checks
To Print:
Checking
dialog box.

4. **Indicate which checks Quicken should print by selecting one of these options:**

 • **All Checks:** Select this option button if you want Quicken to print all the checks you've entered by using the Write Checks window, which is the usual case. (If you select this option, skip to Step 6.)

 • **Checks Dated Through:** Select this option button if you want to print all the checks through a certain date; then type that date in the text box. (If you select this option, skip to Step 6.)

 • **Selected Checks:** Select this option button if you want to pick and choose which checks to print.

5. **If you say that you want to select which checks to print, click the Choose button.**

 Quicken, with some annoyance, displays the Select Checks To Print window, shown in Figure 5-4. Initially, Quicken marks all the checks dated on or earlier than the current date by placing a check mark in the Print column. If you don't want to print a check, either leave the Print field for that check clear (unchecked) or click the field to remove the check mark. When only the checks you want to print are marked to be printed, click Done to continue with this crazy little thing called check printing. Quicken, happy with your progress, redisplays the Select Checks To Print: Checking dialog box (refer to Figure 5-3).

6. **Indicate which Quicken check form you're using.**

 Move the cursor to the Check Style drop-down list box, click the arrow so that the list drops down, and then select the check form you purchased: standard, voucher, or wallet checks.

Figure 5-4:
The Select
Checks
To Print
window.

7. **Tell Quicken if you're printing a partial page.**

 If you're printing a partial page, use the Checks On First Page option buttons to indicate the number of check forms on the partial page. Select the Three option button if you have three checks, the Two option button if you have two checks, or the One option button if you have one check.

8. **Indicate whether you want extra copies of the check form.**

 To do so, type the number of copies you want in the Additional Copies text box. (This text box appears only if you're set up for the voucher check style.)

 If you use Quicken for business to keep accounts payable files, make copies of checks to attach to the invoices that the checks pay. Then if a vendor calls later, starts hassling you, and asks which check paid an invoice, you can easily check your accounts payable files, quickly answer that question, and basically cover your derrière.

9. **Click OK and let the games begin.**

 If you're using a partial starting page of forms, your printer may prompt you to feed the first page of forms manually. When it finishes, Quicken asks whether it printed your checks correctly (as shown in Figure 5-5).

Figure 5-5:
The Did
Check(s)
Print OK?
dialog box.

10. **If the checks printed correctly, click OK. You're done. If the checks didn't print correctly, enter the number of the first check that printed incorrectly and click OK; then repeat Steps 3 through 9.**

11. **Sign the printed checks.**

Then — and I guess you probably don't need my help here — put the checks in the mail.

What if you discover a mistake after you print the check?

This problem isn't as big as you may think.

If you've already mailed the check, you can't do a whole lot. You can try to get the check back (if the person you paid hasn't cashed it) and replace it with the correct check. (Good luck on this one.)

If the person has cashed the check, you can't get the check back. If you overpaid the person by writing the check for too much, you need to get the person to pay you the overpayment amount. If you underpaid the person, you need to write another check for the amount of the underpayment.

If you printed the check but haven't mailed it, void the printed check. First, write the word **VOID** in large letters — in ink — across the face of the check form. (Use a ballpoint pen if you're using multipart forms so that the second and third parts also show as VOID.) Second, display the Register tab, highlight the check, and then click the Edit button and choose the Void Transaction command. (This option marks the check as one that has been voided in the system so that Quicken doesn't use the voided check in calculating your account balance.)

Oh, where, oh, where, do the unprinted checks go?

The register stores unprinted checks — those you've entered by using the Write Checks: Checking window but haven't yet printed. To identify them as unprinted checks, Quicken sets their check numbers as Print. After you tell Quicken to print the unprinted checks, Quicken prints the checks in your register that have Print in the check-number field and replaces the word Print with the actual check number.

This information is of little practical value in most instances, but it results in several interesting possibilities. For example, you can enter the checks you want to print directly into the register — all you need to do is enter the check number as **Print**. (Notice that you can't enter an address anywhere in the register, so this process isn't practical if you enter addresses that will be printed on your checks.) You also can cause a check you've printed once to print again by changing its check number from, say, 007 to Print. I can't think of many good reasons why you would want to change a check number. The only one I can think of is that you accidentally printed a check on plain paper and want to reprint it on a real check form.

A few words about check printing

Check printing is kind of complicated at first, isn't it?

For the record, I'm with you on this one. But you'll find that printing checks does get easier after the first few times.

Pretty soon, you'll be running instead of walking through the steps. Pretty soon, you'll just skate around things like check-form alignment problems. Pretty soon, you'll know all this stuff and never have to read "pretty soon" again.

Printing a Check Register

You can print a check register or a register for any other account. To print a register, follow these magic steps:

1. **First, display the register by clicking the QuickTab for the account, and then choose File⇨Print Register.**

 Quicken displays the Print Register dialog box, as shown in Figure 5-6.

Figure 5-6:
The Print
Register
dialog box.

2. **[Optional] Enter a register title.**

 If you're the sort who likes to add your own special titles to things, move the cursor to the Title text box. Then type the report title or description that you want Quicken to print at the top of every page of the register.

3. **[Optional] Limit the range of dates.**

 To print a register of something other than the current year-to-date transactions, use the Print Transactions From and To text boxes. This is pretty dang obvious, isn't it? You just move the cursor to the From and To text boxes and type the range of dates the register should include.

4. **[Optional] Tell Quicken to print split transaction information.**

 To print the split transaction information — categories, memos, and amounts — move the cursor to the Print Split Transactions check box. Then press the spacebar or select the check box.

5. **Click Print.**

 Quicken displays the Print dialog box (shown in Figure 5-7). You don't have to fool around with this dialog box. If you want to print a register pronto, just click OK. Then again, if you're the sort of person who likes to fool around with this kind of stuff, carry on with the rest of these steps.

Figure 5-7:
The Print
dialog box.

If you want to see the effect that the different register-printing text boxes and check boxes have, just experiment. You can't hurt anything or anybody.

The rest of these steps are optional. Do them if you feel like it.

6. **[Optional] Print the report to disk if you want.**

 To print the report to disk as a text file, select one of the following options from the Export To drop-down list:

 • **ASCII Disk File** if you want to create a text file, such as when you want to import the register into a word-processing program.

 • **Tab-delimited (Excel compatible) Disk File,** such as when you want to import the register into a database program. (Oooh . . . fancy. . . .)

 • **123 (.PRN) Disk File,** such as when you want to import the register into Lotus 1-2-3 or any spreadsheet program that will open 1-2-3 files (which, basically, means any spreadsheet program, including Microsoft Excel).

If you do indicate that you want a disk file, after you click the Print button to start the ol' printing process, Quicken displays the Create Disk File dialog box, as shown in Figure 5-8. This dialog box asks for the filename that Quicken should create as part of printing the file to disk and asks where you want to store the file. Just enter the filename you want into — you guessed it — the File Name text box. (Use a valid filename, of course.) Use the Save In text box to indicate where you want to store the file. Or don't do anything, and Quicken creates the file in the active Quicken directory — probably QUICKENW. And what do you do with the disk file? You're on your own here. . . .

Figure 5-8:
The Create
Disk File
dialog box.

7. [Optional] Tell Quicken which pages to print.

Use the Print Range option buttons and text boxes to limit the pages Quicken prints (refer to Figure 5-7). How? Select the Pages option button and then type the range of page numbers you want to print. That's simple enough, right?

8. [Optional] Color your world.

If you have a color printer and want to print your register in color, select the Print In Color check box on the Print dialog box (refer to Figure 5-7).

9. [Optional] Trade speed for quality.

Or you can select the Print In Draft Mode check box to tell Quicken it should print faster and spend less time worrying about the quality of the printing job (refer to Figure 5-7). In other words, you can use this check box to trade print quality for print speed. Life is full of trade-offs, isn't it?

10. [Optional] Tell Quicken to scrunch the information so that it fits across the page.

Use the Fit To One Page Wide check box to tell Quicken that you want its register information to fit across the width of the page (refer to Figure 5-7).

11. **Click OK.**

Quicken finally prints the register. I'm not going to show a printed copy of the register here. All it is, really, is just a printed copy of the same account detail information you see on the Register tab.

Should you save a printed copy of your register?

Here's a question for you: Should you save a printed copy of your register? I don't know. The case for printing a copy of your register and then having it handy in case, well, just in case, is this: If your computer goes haywire and you need to re-enter your transactions or you need a hard-copy record of your transactions and for some reason don't have access to Quicken, having a printed register will make things much easier for you. You know what, though? I think that most people, if they religiously back up their Quicken data files (something I describe in Chapter 9), don't really need to print copies of their registers.

Now, I should say that if you're someone who likes to keep meticulous records of your income and spending and you always double-check to make sure that you haven't left the iron on or even plugged in whenever you leave your house, you could print a copy of the register. And what I would suggest is that you print a copy of the register at the end of the year and then file this report away with your tax return.

By the way, I've been using Quicken since 1988 and have never needed a printed copy of my register. I've made frequent use of other reports. But never have I needed a hard, paper copy of my register. Anytime I have had a question, I've simply looked through the online version of my current register or archived files from previous years.

Chapter 6

Online and In Charge

*M*any banks now offer electronic banking services in a big, big way. This is a step toward providing a pretty impressive variety of online services to the general consumer. (You and me.) This chapter covers the Quicken electronic banking services: Online Account Access and Online Bill Payment.

What Are Online Account Access and Online Bill Payment?

I'm going to start with the basics — a definition of these two services.

Online services means that you can connect your computer to your bank's computer electronically through your Internet connection. You may think that doing so sounds scary, but Online Account Access and Online Bill Payment provide some very neat benefits:

- ✔ With Online Bill Payment, you can tell your bank or, in a pinch, Intuit's online financial services unit to make payments to specific individuals or businesses. In other words, rather than providing all this information in the usual way (on checks), you send the same information — the payees' names, their addresses, the amounts, and so on — and then the bank writes the checks. You can tell the bank to make automatic recurring payments for bills that you pay on a regular basis, such as a rent or mortgage payment. You can use Online Bill Payment at any bank.

- ✔ With Online Account Access, you can get transaction information — such as information about which checks and deposits cleared your account and what bank service fees you've been charged — from the bank's computer. You can also transfer money between accounts — such as from

your savings account to your checking account and from your checking account to your credit card account (to pay a credit card bill). To use Quicken for Online Account Access, your bank must support the Quicken Online Account Access service.

Wise Whys and Wherefores

Neither Online Account Access nor Online Bill Payment feature is difficult to use. And despite the nightmares that people with delusional paranoia may develop about electronic banking, the service is safe, secure, and very solid. Nevertheless, before you too, jump onto the Online Account Access and Online Bill Payment bandwagon, you should probably consider a few points:

- ✔ As I note in the preceding section, if you want to use the Online Account Access feature, your bank must be a part of the Quicken Online Account Access program. (See the next section for details on how to find out whether your bank qualifies.)

- ✔ To sign up for and use Online Account Access or Online Bill Payment services, you need an Internet connection.

- ✔ You should be fairly comfortable with Quicken, especially with account transactions and transferring money between accounts. (Therefore, if you're new to Quicken, you should at least record a handful of checks, make some deposits, and reconcile your account before venturing into Online Account Access. This ramping up of your Quicken skills should take, oh, I don't know, about two weeks.)

- ✔ Make sure that your records are completely up to date and reconciled with the last statements you've received from the bank.

This stuff usually ain't free. I can't tell you how much these two services will cost because your bank sets the charges. A good guess is $10 to $15 a month — and that adds up over the course of a year. But in choosing to use Online Account Access or Online Bill Payment, do consider all the hidden costs of the normal way of banking and paying bills. Gasoline, time, and postage can all add up, and these almost-hidden costs may make the costs of the online services appear more reasonable. (Besides, you won't have to deal with all that nasty glue on your tongue from licking envelopes.)

Banking with Online Account Access and Online Bill Payment

To begin using either the Online Account Access or the Online Bill Payment service, you have to sign up. If you want to use Online Account Access, you

sign up with your bank. Just visit your bank's Web site or call your local branch and ask someone whether the bank supports Online Account Access with Quicken. (If your bank doesn't support Online Account Access, you can still sign up with Intuit for Online Bill Payment — check the Quicken.com Web site for details.) Then do whatever the folks at the bank tell you to do to sign up. You'll probably have to fill out an application, agree to pay some extra fees, and then wait a few days for a customer identification number and a *PIN*, or personal identification number.

After the bank does its preparation and sends you its welcome letter, you can set up Quicken for Online Account Access. To set up Quicken to use Online Account Access or Online Bill Payment services, display the account for which you want to activate online services. You can do this, for example, by following these steps:

1. **Click the Cash Flow Center button and then click the account.**

2. **Tell Quicken you want to set up online banking or bill payment.**

 Click the Set Up Now button, which appears at the bottom of the register area (as shown in Figure 6-1).

Figure 6-1:
Click the Set Up Now button for online banking.

3. Identify yourself.

When Quicken displays the Quicken Account Setup dialog box (see Figure 6-2), supply a customer identification number and a personal identification number, or PIN.

Figure 6-2:
The Quicken
Account
Setup dialog
box.

Let me say a couple more quick things about setting up Online Account Access or Online Bill Payment. Your bank or the Quicken folks may, as part of the application process, send you a letter asking for more information, a canceled check, or a signature. (If they do, of course, be sure to respond.)

Using Online Account Access and Online Bill Payment is extremely easy. You pay bills in pretty much the usual manner. You make account transfers in the same manner. And then you reconcile transactions with a mouse click.

Finding an online bank — online

You can also find out which banks support Online Account Access by using your Internet connection. To do so, choose the Online⇨Participating Financial Institutions command. When you choose this command, Quicken starts your Web browser and then opens a page that lists the banks that allow you to bank online or provide other online services to Quicken. This list of financial institutions tells you which banks work well with Quicken. (The Quicken.com Web site may require you to register before it will supply a current list of banks that will take your money for providing online services.)

Paying bills

You have three ways to record online payments. If you're comfortable using the Write Checks window, you write a check in the usual way. You enter the payee name, an amount, probably a category, and so on. Just make sure that you select the Online Payment check box. The Online Payment check box appears in the lower-right corner of the on-screen check form.

If you have questions about how the Write Checks window works, Chapter 5 shows you — among other things — how to use the Write Checks window to describe checks you want to print. You use the same basic procedure to describe online payments that you want to make.

Honest Steve's evaluation of online services

I'm pretty much a cynic when it comes to new bells and whistles — or at least the kinds of bells and whistles that software companies like to add to the mature versions of their products. And I hate making financial record-keeping more complicated. I like things simple. But all that said, I think Online Bill Payment and, in particular, Online Account Access are slick.

If you're using Quicken to keep your financial records, you get to pay your bills and reconcile your bank accounts for basically no extra work. Well, okay, you have to click your mouse an extra time. And initially, you need to provide addresses and account numbers for your payees (which takes about five minutes). So you do have to do a little extra work at the beginning. But Online Account Access saves you time and hassle when it comes to bill paying and banking.

The only catch — and this is a big one for some Quicken users — is that to use Online Account Access, your bank needs to have its act together. (Note that if your bank doesn't support Online Account Access with Quicken, you can still use Online Bill Payment by signing up for online payment with Intuit, as detailed at the Quicken.com Web site.)

Now, all that said, I want to close with two caveats. Here's the first one: Online Account Access isn't worth it if it means you end up banking at some poorly run bank. I, er, well, yeah, you see, I've been there. And it isn't pretty. To make a long, sorry story short, a long time ago I had the experience of moving my banking from a well-run bank that didn't have Online Account Access to a poorly managed bank that did. Online Account Access is not — I repeat, is not — such a cool tool that you'll be happy banking at First National Idiots.

And now a second caveat: I have to tell you that online payments aren't, in my experience, as reliable as writing a regular check and then sending that check through the mail. I don't know why this is. But it's been my experience that online payments more frequently get lost, and they sometimes get delayed. I've been using online banking and bill payment for several years now, and a time or two a year, people or businesses call and say, "Dude, we never got your payment" or "Dude, we got your check late — you owe us a late fee." In comparison, my experience is that the U.S. Postal Service almost never loses my mailed payments.

If you're more comfortable using the register to record payments, you can make online payments with that, too. In the Num column, just specify the payment number as Send.

If you have questions about how the register works, you may want to refer to Chapter 4. Chapter 4 describes — in some detail, I might add — how the Quicken register works.

By the way, the first time you make an online payment to someone, Quicken asks for some information in the Set Up Online Payee dialog box: where the person lives or where the business is located, and what account number Quicken can use to identify the person or business. You can also describe online payees by choosing Online⇨Online Payee List, which displays a list of online payees. Then click the New button, which displays the Set Up Online Payee dialog box.

After you record a payment, you send it to the bank. To do so, choose the Online⇨One Step Update command.

Quicken connects to your Internet service provider and then, through the Internet, to your bank's computer. As part of making this connection, you need to provide a personal identification number, or PIN. When Quicken finishes sending your payment instructions to your bank, it displays a summary that basically says you've connected to the bank's computer and sent it some payment instructions. At this point, you're done.

Note: The first time that you use Online Account Access, Quicken asks you to change your personal identification number, or PIN.

Note: You can have Quicken regularly update your account information. To do this, choose the Online⇨Schedule Updates command and follow the on-screen instructions.

I need to make an important point here. You must send your payment instructions to the bank several days in advance of the time the bill needs to be paid. For obvious reasons, the bank needs a day or two to process the bill. And then the check probably has to go through the U.S. Postal Service. . . . (I say "probably" in the previous sentence because only a few payments get made electronically.)

Transferring money between accounts

As you may expect, you record Online Account Access transfers in the same way you record regular transfers — or at least in almost the same way. For online transfers, you can use the register in the normal way, but you need to specify that the transaction is an online transfer. You do this by activating the Num drop-down list box and selecting the Online Transfer entry.

Are you still with me?

Okay, I'm going to take a little breather here — just to make sure that you understand what's going on. When you boil everything down to its essence, online payments are really just payment instructions you send to your bank. And when you make an online transfer, you are effectively just calling the bank and saying, "Please transfer money from one account to that other account."

This makes sense, right? You're really just giving instructions to the bank. And then the bank (or

actually the bank's computer) goes off and does whatever you've told it to do. It's pretty simple.

Is Online Account Access anything to get all excited about? Is it really as slick as some people think? I think so. Sure, it's not always cheap. But after you get going, you get away from that business of finding your checkbook, signing checks, finding stamps, and then, on occasion, running down to the post office to drop off some overdue bill.

If you have a credit card with a bank that supports Online Account Access and if you also set up the credit card for Online Account Access, you can pay your credit card bill by transferring money from a bank account to your credit card account. You probably already thought of this if you have a credit card account. But I thought I'd mention it anyway. (For more information about credit card accounts, refer to Chapter 11.)

Updating your Quicken accounts

One major advantage of Online Account Access is that you can get the most up-to-date information regarding your accounts. Let me explain: When you use the Online menu's One Step Update or Schedule Updates command, your bank automatically sends current transactions to your computer. If Quicken can match the bank's records with your records, no problem. Everything is fine.

If Quicken can't match the bank records with your records, however, it lists the mystery transactions on the Downloaded Transactions tab of the account register window. You then examine them before they go into your records. You can add downloaded transactions from the bank's list to your register by clicking.

By regularly downloading transactions into your online accounts and matching transactions between your Quicken records and the bank's records, you don't need to reconcile your account. In effect, you reconcile your account just by downloading and matching. You can also get information about checks and debit card transactions that you've forgotten to record much earlier (because you don't have to wait until the end of the month).

Chapter 7

Reports, Charts, and Other Cool Tools

*Q*uicken enables you to summarize, slice, and dice register and account information in a variety of ways. This chapter describes how to use reports and produce graphs easily. This stuff is much easier to understand if you know how to print a register first (a trick I describe at the end of Chapter 5).

Creating and Printing Reports

After you know how to print checks and registers, all other printing in Quicken is easy, easy, easy.

Printing the facts, and nothing but the facts

The transactions you enter in the register window and the checks you enter in the Write Checks window determine the information in a report. To print a report, just choose the Reports menu and tell Quicken which report you want to print.

Quicken produces a bunch of different reports. To make sense of what may otherwise become mass confusion, Quicken arranges all its reports into groups: Banking, Spending, Comparison, Investing reports, Tax reports, and Net Worth & Balances reports. (These sort of sound like PBS documentaries, don't they? "Tonight, Joob Taylor explores the truth about tax evasion in the lemonade stand industry in the Tax Report.")

To see the reports in one of these groups, select the report group from the Reports menu. If you read the fast-paced and exciting Appendix A, you know that those little triangles to the right of menu command names tell you that another menu follows.

Figure 7-1 shows the Banking group of reports. Pretty exciting stuff so far, don't you think?

To create a Cash Flow report (or any other report, for that matter) on the fly, choose the report from the appropriate menu. For example, to create the Cash Flow report, choose Reports➪Banking➪Cash Flow. Quicken then creates the report, placing it inside a newly opened window. Figure 7-2, for example, shows Cash Flow report. After you create a report, you can change the report date or date range by using the boxes at the top of the report.

Figure 7-1: The Banking group of reports.

Figure 7-2:
The Cash
Flow in a
report
window.

To find out what type of information a report includes before you create the report, or to preview a report, choose Reports⊅Reports & Graphs Center. This displays the Reports & Graphs window, shown in Figure 7-3. Select a report group by clicking a topic on the left side and then select the report with the report group that you want to create. (In Figure 7-3, the Spending report group is selected and therefore shown. Within the Spending report group, the Spending By Category report is selected and therefore shown.)

You can change the report date or date range by using the box(es) provided. Click Show Report to create the report. If you don't enter a new range of dates, Quicken assumes that you want to include transactions from the start of the current calendar year through the present date.

Reports that show account balances — such as the Account Balances report, the Net Worth report, the Balance Sheet report, or the Portfolio Value report — don't need a range of dates because these reports show account balances as of a specific date. In these cases, if you don't enter a date, Quicken assumes that you want account balances for the current system date from your computer's internal clock.

You can't see the entire on-screen version of a report unless your report is very small (or your screen is monstrously large). Press the PgUp and PgDn keys to scroll up and down and use Tab and Shift+Tab to move right and left. Or if you're a mouse lover, you can click-and-drag various pieces of the scroll bars.

Figure 7-3:
The Reports
& Graphs
window.

To print your report, follow these steps:

1. **Click the Print Report button.**

 Quicken displays the Print dialog box (see Figure 7-4).

Figure 7-4:
The Print
dialog box.

2. **To accept the given specifications — which are almost always fine — just click Print.**

 You'll never guess what happens next: Quicken prints the report!

3. **(Optional) To modify the default printing suggestions, use the Print dialog box's buttons and boxes to mix it up a bit and then click Print:**

 Print To: The Print To option buttons let you tell Quicken where it should send the report it produces: to the printer or to a disk file. If you choose to print it to a file, Quicken displays another dialog box you use to specify where the print file should be located and what the print file should be named. (I describe how this print to file option works in Chapter 5, so I won't repeat the discussion here. If you want the scoop, refer to the section about printing a check register.)

 Print Range: Printing a long report? Consider using the Print Range buttons and box to specify that you want to print only a specified range of pages. As you might guess if you're a clever person, to do this, you mark the Pages button and then specify the individual pages (separating each page by a comma) or the range of pages (separating the start and end of a page range with a hyphen). The pages specification below, for example, says, "Hey Quicken, print pages 1, 4, and 5 and, oh shoot, I don't know, maybe the page range 34 through 41 as well."

 1, 4, 5, 34–41

 Copies: As you probably guessed, the Number Of Copies box tells Quicken to print multiple copies of a report.

 Page Scaling: For some reports — although not all — you can use the Page Scaling option buttons and boxes to tell Quicken that it should try to squish the report onto a smaller number of pages. Ever the thoughtful software program that it is, Quicken provides two squishing methods. You can mark the Page Scaling Adjust To button and then enter a squishing percentage. Or you can mark the Page Scaling Fit To button and then specify the report size as a certain number of pages wide by a certain number of pages tall.

 Print What: The Print What check boxes let you flip flop between printing a graph and printing a report of the Quicken data you've said you want to see a report on. The easiest way to see what this report option does is to click and unclick.

 Orientation: The Orientation buttons allow you to specify how Quicken prints a report on pages: vertically in what's called a Portrait Orientation or horizontally in what's called a Landscape Orientation. Again, if you're confused about this option, experiment by clicking the different buttons.

Note: When you click a Print dialog box button or enter some value into a Print dialog box field, Quicken redraws the Preview box to show you what the report looks like with your new specification.

Ink Color: If you use a color printer, Quicken provides Ink Color option buttons, which let you choose whether you want to print the report in expensive colored ink, in cheap black ink, or in shades of gray so you can go all film noire about your finances.

Change Font: The Change Font buttons let you customize the look of your report by changing the font settings (point size, font, style, and so on) of the text used for your report's header text and body text. I feel kind of like a broken record saying this, but, dude, seriously, the way to most easily learn what these options do is simply to experiment. You can't foul up or corrupt your Quicken data by fiddle-faddling with the Print dialog box's printing settings. And this is true even if you do something truly visually outrageous.

Adjust Margins: Click the Adjust Margins button to add margin-setting boxes to the Preview area of the Print dialog box. After Quicken adds these margin setting boxes, you can change the printed report's margins by changing the margin settings.

Reviewing standard reports

Tables 7-1 through 7-6 describe Quicken's reports by group. (Some of these babies won't make sense unless you understand how to collect the information that goes into the report, as I describe in Chapters 13 and 14.)

Table 7-1	Quicken Banking Reports
Report	*Description*
Banking Summary	Summarizes spending totals by category.
Cash Flow	Summarizes the money that flows into and out of an account by income and expense categories and by transfers. Cash is king, dude, so this report only includes transactions that you record in your bank, cash, and credit card accounts.
Missing Checks	Lists all the checks you've written and flags any gaps in the check number sequence. This report helps you identify missing checks.

Report	Description
Reconciliation	Summarizes an account reconciliation that you've performed. You don't need this report, really, unless you've got a clinical anxiety disorder and need to prove to yourself or your accountant that you really did reconcile your account.
Transaction	Lets you list transactions in multiple accounts chronologically.

Table 7-2	Quicken Spending Reports
Report	**Description**
Itemized Categories	Lists transactions by category.
Itemized Payees	Lists transactions by payee.
Spending By Category	Graphs spending and lists transactions by category.
Spending By Payee	Graphs spending and lists transactions by payee.
Current Spending Vs. Average Spending By Category	Summarizes spending by category and compares category totals to the average category total over the last six months.
Current Spending Vs. Average Spending By Payee	Summarizes spending by payee and compares payee totals to the average payee total over the last six months.
Income And Expense By Category	Summarizes income and spending by category.
Income And Expense By Payee	Summarizes income and spending by payee.
Budget	Summarizes income and expense categories and compares actual category totals for the year to budgeted category amounts. This report includes only transactions that you record in your bank, cash, and credit card accounts. (For this report to work, of course, you need to have a budget set up.)
Monthly Budget	Summarizes income and expense categories and compares actual category totals for a month to monthly budgeted category amounts. This report includes only transactions that you record in your bank, cash, and credit card accounts. (For this report to work, of course, you need to have a budget set up.)

Table 7-3	Quicken Comparison Reports
Report	*Description*
Current Spending Vs. Average Spending By Category	Summarizes spending by category and compares category totals to the average category total over the last six months.
Current Spending Vs. Average Spending By Payee	Summarizes spending by payee and compares payee totals to the average payee total over the last six months.
Cash Flow Comparison	Lets you compare category totals from two periods. You can use this report to compare January's activity with February's activity, for example. ***Remember:*** Because you are comparing two periods, you need to enter two transaction date ranges.
Income And Expense Comparison By Category	Summarizes spending totals by category for two time periods.
Income And Expense Comparison By Payee	Summarizes spending totals by payee for two time periods.

Table 7-4	Quicken Investing Reports
Report	*Description*
Capital Gains	Lists all the realized gains on individual investments you hold. (A *capital gain* occurs when an investment is worth more than you paid for it. When you sell the investment, you realize the gain.)
Investing Activity	Shows investment transactions grouped by activity.
Investment Asset Allocation	Shows investments by asset class.
Investment Income	Summarizes income and expense categories for the transactions you record in your investment accounts.
Investment Performance	A power-user report. This report calculates the internal rates of return delivered by each of the individual investments in your portfolio.

Report	Description
Investment Transactions	Lists recorded transactions for all your investment accounts.
Portfolio Value	Lists the current value of all securities in your investment accounts.
Portfolio Value & Cost Basis	Lists the current value and cost of all securities in your investment accounts.

Table 7-5	Quicken Tax Reports
Report	**Description**
Capital Gains	Lists all the realized gains on individual investments you hold. (A *capital gain* occurs when an investment is worth more than you paid for it. When you sell the investment, you realize the gain.)
Schedule A-Itemized Deductions	Lists and summarizes transactions that probably belong on your Schedule A tax form as itemized deductions: mortgage interest, property taxes, charitable contributions, and so on.
Schedule B-Interest And Dividends	Lists and summarizes interest and dividend income transactions that need to be reported on your Schedule B tax form.
Schedule D-Capital Gains And Losses	Lists and summarizes capital gain and loss transactions that need to be reported on your Schedule D tax form.
Tax Schedule	Lists all transactions you've entered as tax-related and subtotals them by line item.
Tax Summary	Lists all transactions you've described as falling into tax-related categories.

Table 7-6	Quicken Net Worth & Balances Reports
Report	**Description**
Net Worth	Lists all accounts, their balances, and the difference between the sum of the asset accounts and the sum of the liabilities accounts, which the report identifies as your *net worth*.
Account Balances	Lists all accounts and their balances.

Finding the report you want

Okay, if you've read or even skimmed the reports I describe in Tables 7-1 through 7-6, you're probably a little overwhelmed. Quicken produces a bunch of different reports. How do you know which one provides the answers you want? What are you supposed to do? Sift your way through a couple dozen of these babies?

Thankfully, the answer is no. Quicken also provides something called EasyAnswer reports. In effect, EasyAnswer reports let you identify the question that you want a report to answer. After you identify the question, Quicken produces the appropriate report. Here's how this all works:

1. **Choose Reports⇨EasyAnswer.**

 Quicken displays the EasyAnswer topic of the Reports & Graphs window.

2. **Indicate your question.**

 To tell Quicken what your question is, click one of the questions and then use the drop-down list boxes that accompany each question to further refine your question. For example, the "Where did I spend my money?" question lets you pick the period of time you're asking about: Last Year, Last Month, Current Year, Month to Date, and so on.

3. **Click Show Report.**

 Quicken produces a report that answers your questions. If you ask the question, "Where did I spend my money last year?" for example, Quicken produces a cash flow report that summarizes the previous year's income and expenses by category.

Going to the printing dog-and-pony show

You can do some neat things with the reports you create. I won't spend a bunch of time talking about these things, but I do want to give you a quick rundown of some of the most valuable tricks.

Got a question about a number? Just zoom it

If you don't understand where a number in a report came from, point to it with the mouse. As you point to numbers, Quicken changes the mouse pointer to a magnifying glass marked with a +. Double-click the mouse, and Quicken displays a list of all the transactions that make up that number.

This feature, called QuickZoom, is extremely handy for understanding the figures that appear on your reports. If you double-click the Utilities number in the report in Figure 7-2, for example, Quicken displays the QuickZoom report shown in Figure 7-5.

Ah, yes. Two cable TV bills. And you're not even buying the premium channels package. Yikes.

See a problem? Fix it

You can sometimes fix erroneous report data right in a report window. If you select a report transaction and Quicken enables the Edit button (shown in the upper-left corner of the report window), you can click the button to display an Edit menu. The menu lists editing commands you can use to delete the selected transaction or to change the category, payee, or memo information.

Got a question about register transactions? Use minireport

If you're looking at the Quicken register and you select either the Payee or Category field, Quicken adds a minireport button to the end of the field. (The actual minireport button looks like a small piece of paper.) If you click the minireport button, Quicken creates a small report that summarizes the transactions falling into the same category or transactions with the same payee, as shown in Figure 7-6.

If you click the Show Report button, which appears in the minireport window, Quicken creates a transaction report for the same information shown in the minireport.

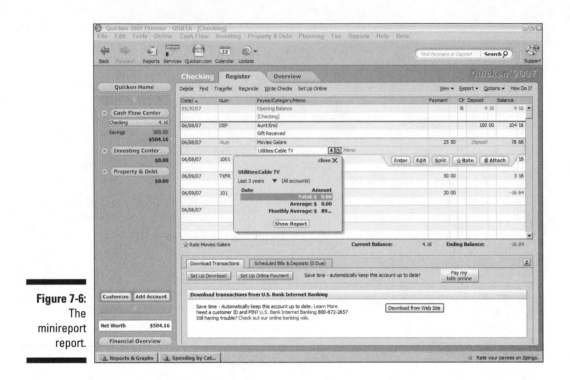

Figure 7-6:
The
minireport
report.

Sharing report data with spreadsheets

If you use Microsoft Excel, you can export the report to the spreadsheet program. Just click the Export Data button and choose Report to Excel Compatible Format. Quicken displays a dialog box you use to name and locate a tab delimited text file. (Any spreadsheet program worth its salt can open a tab delimited text file.) You may need to use this feature if you want to use a spreadsheet to analyze the report data.

You can also copy the stuff that shows in a report window to the Clipboard. Just click the Export Data button and choose the Copy Report To Clipboard command. Then, to use the copied report, start your spreadsheet (or other) program and choose Edit⇨Paste to paste the stuff from the Clipboard. This process really isn't very hard, so go ahead and try it.

Sharing report data in PDF files

You can create a PDF version of the report. To do this, click the Export Data button and choose the Export To PDF option. Quicken displays a dialog box that you use to name and locate the PDF file it will momentarily create. A PDF file of the report is an electronic version of the report.

Customizing your reports

If you want to extract some financial tidbit, you can usually get what you want from one of the reports listed on the Reports menu, especially if you use the EasyAnswer feature to find the right report!

I should tell you something: Quicken is remarkably sophisticated in its reporting. You can customize any report you see in the Reports menu.

To customize these reports, click the Customize button to get to the nuts and bolts of your selected report.

I'm not going to describe the customization process. I feel kind of bad about this omission because a few people are probably out there who, late one night, will decide that they want to know how to filter, sort, and customize. Of course, there are also people who will decide late some night that they want to know how to replace the transmission on a 1971 Triumph Spitfire. And I'm not describing that here, either.

If you really want to customize your reports, just noodle around. You can't hurt anything.

If you do play around with these items, you can save any custom report specifications that you create. To do so, click the Save Report button at the top of the report window. Quicken displays a dialog box that asks you to supply a name for your customized report. (You can also provide a default report date range.) After you name the customized report, Quicken lists it whenever you choose Reports⊅Saved Reports & Graphs Conter.

Editing and rearranging reports

You may notice that when Quicken displays the report window, it also displays a row of buttons, including (roughly left to right) Delete, Export Data, Sort, Save Report (refer to Figure 7-2), Preferences, and Customize. Also appearing are the Date Range and the Subtotal By drop-down list boxes. Earlier in the chapter, in "Printing the facts, and nothing but the facts," I talk about what the Date Range drop-down list box does. So in the interest of fair play, I briefly discuss what the other buttons do. (Not all these buttons are available in every report document window. And sometimes Quicken uses different names to refer to them. I don't know why, really. Maybe it's just to keep you guessing.)

You really don't need to worry about these other buttons. Read through the discussion that follows only if you're feeling comfortable, relaxed, and truly mellow. Okay?

Delete

The Delete button deletes the current report from the report list. You can use this button to, in effect, undo any changes you've made to a report and return to the default report specifications.

Export Data

I already talked about this option in "Sharing report data with spreadsheets" and "Sharing report data in PDF files" earlier in this chapter. Look there if you have questions.

Sorting

The Sort button displays a list of sorting options that you can use for arranging information on the report. Enough said.

Save Report

Say you get into this customization thing. If you do, you should know that you can save your customized reports by clicking the Save Report button. When you click Save Report, Quicken displays the Save Report dialog box, shown in Figure 7-7. Mostly, Quicken displays this dialog box so that you can give your creation a name. You also use this dialog box to indicate in which financial activity center Quicken should save your report.

Figure 7-7: The Save Report dialog box.

By the way, after you create a saved report, you can reproduce it by choosing Reports⇨Saved Reports & Graphs Center and then selecting the saved report name.

What's the Preferences button for?

When you click the Preferences button, Quicken displays a Preferences dialog box with a bunch of boxes and buttons that let you change the way the window looks or works.

If I were a really great writer — the Stephen King of computer books, for example — I might be able to whip up a riveting discussion of how the Preferences dialog box works. I'm going to do both you and my publisher a favor, however, by making a suggestion: Just play with these option settings if you're interested. You'll find it more fun and a better learning experience.

Date Range

I briefly mention the Date Range box earlier in the chapter, but here I provide a slightly more detailed description. The Date Range box displays a drop-down list that you can use to specify what time period you want listed on your report: the current month, last year, the current quarter to date, and so on.

Column subtotaling

The Column box displays a list that enables you to tell Quicken you want subtotal amounts by some criterion, as shown in Figure 7-8. Just select the criterion. Note that sometimes the Column box is replaced with a Subtotal By box.

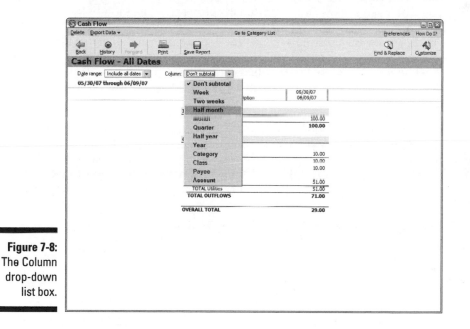

Figure 7-8:
The Column drop-down list box.

Customizing

The Customize button works pretty much the same no matter which report shows in the document window.

When you click this button, Quicken displays a dialog box that lets you enter the report title and specify the range of dates the report should cover by using text boxes. It also lets you choose from a variety of other options, too, such as which accounts to use, which transactions to use, and how the report's information should be arranged.

Charts Only Look Tricky

I love charts. I know that sounds goofy. But *data graphics* — as the snobs and academics call it — open up wonderful opportunities for communicating. And Quicken charts are really easy to use.

To produce a Quicken chart, just produce the report you want using the Reports & Graphs window, which you get to by choosing the EasyAnswer command from the Reports & Graphs window. Then, select the report you want and click the Show Graph button. That's it. Easy as rolling off a log.

Note: Not all reports provide data that can be plotted in a graph. Accordingly, you won't see a Show Graph button in every report window.

Figure 7-9 shows a picture of a bar graph of income and expense figures. But you'll have much more fun looking at your own data in a picture. By the way, you can use QuickZoom (described earlier in this chapter in "Got a question about a number? Just zoom it") on a chart to see a report that describes the data being plotted.

Note: The Quicken report window provides clickable links — Hide Graph and Hide Report — which you can use to remove a report and remove a graph from the window. If you hide a report or graph, Quicken replaces the Hide Graph and Hide Report links with Show Graph and Show Report links. Click the Show Graph and Show Report links to show previously hidden items.

Figure 7-9:
The Income/
Expense
graph.

You can memorize customized graphs the same way you memorize customized reports. Just click the Save Report button at the top of the graph window. Then, when Quicken prompts you, give the graph a name. To later reuse the graph, choose Reports⊅Saved Reports & Graphs Center, select the saved graph from the menu that Quicken displays, and click OK.

QuickReports: Last but Not Least

Before I forget, I need to tell you about one other variant of the Quicken reporting feature: QuickReports. Ah, yes, QuickReports. Here's the deal. Quicken supplies a quick-and-dirty report called, cleverly enough, a QuickReport. If you're working with the register, you can produce a quick report that summarizes things, such as the checks written to a particular payee or the transactions assigned to a specific income or expense category.

To produce a QuickReport, first move the cursor to the field that you want to summarize in the report. Then click the Report button at the top of the register window. Choose the report you want from the Report menu that drops down. The report shown in Figure 7-10, for example, is a QuickReport that shows the money you've received from your Aunt Enid. She is *such* a sweetheart.

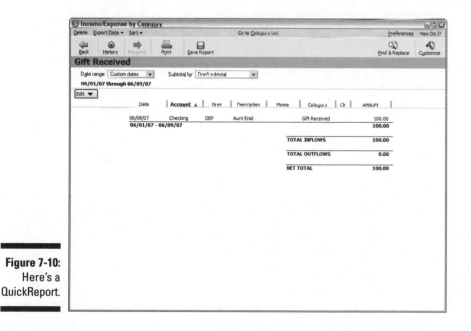

Figure 7-10:
Here's a
QuickReport.

Chapter 8

A Matter of Balance

- -

In This Chapter

▶ Choosing the account you want to balance

▶ Telling Quicken to balance an account

▶ Giving Quicken the bank statement balance

▶ Entering monthly service charges and Interest income

▶ Marking account transactions as cleared or uncleared

▶ Verifying that uncleared transactions explain the account difference

▶ Checking for errors: What you should do if your account doesn't balance

- -

I want to start this chapter with an important point: Balancing a bank account in Quicken is quick and easy.

I'm not just trying to get you pumped up about an otherwise painfully boring topic. I don't think balancing a bank account is any more exciting than you do. (At the Nelson house, we never answer the "What should we do tonight?" question by saying, "Hey, let's balance an account!")

My point is this: Because bank account balancing can be tedious and boring, use Quicken to speed up the drudgery.

Note: If you're using online banking for accounting and you regularly download account transactions, you don't need to reconcile your account. When you compare the downloaded transactions to your register, you, in effect, reconcile your account. See Chapter 6 for more information about online banking.

Selecting the Account You Want to Balance

This step is easy. And you probably already know how to do it, too.

1. **Click the Cash Flow Center button.**

 Quicken displays the Cash Flow Center window.

2. **Next, click the account that you want to balance.**

 Quicken displays the register window, which lists information about the account (shown in Figure 8-1).

Figure 8-1:
The Cash Flow Center window.

Balancing a Bank Account

As I said, balancing a bank account is remarkably easy. In fact, I'll go so far as to say that if you have any problems, they'll stem from . . . well, sloppy record keeping that preceded your use of Quicken.

Telling Quicken, "Hey, man, I want to balance this account"

To tell Quicken that you want to *balance,* or *reconcile,* your account records with the bank's records, click the Reconcile button. The Reconcile button appears at the top of the register window. Quicken displays the Statement Summary: Checking dialog box, shown in Figure 8-2.

Figure 8-2: The Statement Summary: Checking dialog box.

Statement Summary: Checking

The last statement ending date: N/A

1. Enter the following from your bank statement.

Opening Balance: 4.16

Ending Balance: 0.16

New Statement Ending Date: 06/06/07

2. Enter and categorize your interest and bank charges, if any.

Service Charge: 3.00 Date: 06/06/07

Category: Bank Charge

Interest Earned: Date: 06/06/07

Category: Interest Inc

OK Cancel Help

Giving Quicken the bank's information

As you probably know, in a reconciliation, you compare your records of a bank account with the bank's records of the same account. You should be able to explain any difference between the two accounts — usually by pointing to checks that you've written but that haven't cleared. (Sometimes deposits fall into the same category; you've recorded and mailed a deposit, but the bank hasn't yet credited your account.)

The first step, then, is to supply Quicken with the bank's account information. This information comes from your monthly statement. Supply Quicken with the figures it needs as follows:

1. **Verify the opening balance.**

 Quicken displays a figure in the Opening Balance text box. If this figure isn't correct, replace it with the correct figure. To do so, move the cursor to the text box and type over the given figure. (If you're reconciling your account for the first time, Quicken gets this opening balance figure from your starting account balance. If you've reconciled before, Quicken uses the Ending Balance that you specified the last time you reconciled as the Opening Balance.)

2. **Enter the ending balance.**

 Move the cursor to the Ending Balance text box and type the ending, or closing, balance shown on your bank statement.

3. **Provide the statement's ending balance date.**

 Move the cursor to the New Statement Ending Date text box and type the ending date for the statement you're using to reconcile.

4. **Enter the bank's service charge.**

 If your bank statement shows a service charge and you haven't already entered it, move the cursor to the Service Charge text box and type the amount.

5. **Type a transaction date for the service charge transaction.**

 Quicken supplies its best guess for the date. If you're reconciling for the first time, Quicken uses the current system date from your computer's clock. If you've reconciled the account before, Quicken picks a date one month later from the last time you reconciled the account. If the date Quicken picks isn't correct, type the correct date.

 You can adjust a date one day at a time by using either the + or – key.

6. **Assign the bank's service charge to a category.**

 Quicken helps you out by displaying the Bank Charge category in the first Category text box — the one beneath the Service Charge text box. If you want to use a different category, click the down arrow in the Category text box to open the Category drop-down list box; then select a category by scrolling down the list and pressing Enter.

7. **Enter the account's interest income.**

 If the account earned interest for the month and you haven't already entered this figure, type the amount in the Interest Earned text box.

8. **Enter a transaction date for the interest income transaction.**

 You already know how to enter dates. I won't bore you by explaining it again (but see Step 5 if you're having trouble).

9. **Assign the interest to a category.**

 Type an appropriate income category for any interest — perhaps something like, er, **Interest Income**.

10. **Tell Quicken that the bank statement is complete.**

 To do so, just click OK. Quicken displays the reconcile window, which I describe in the next section.

Explaining the difference between your records and the bank's records

Next, Quicken compares your register's account balance with the bank statement's ending account balance. Then it builds a list of checks and deposits that your register shows but that haven't yet *cleared* (haven't been recorded by the bank). Figure 8-3 shows the Statement Summary: Checking window that Quicken displays to provide you with this information.

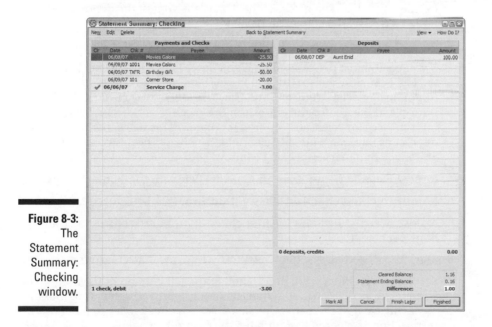

Figure 8-3:
The Statement Summary: Checking window.

As Figure 8-3 shows, the Statement Summary: Checking window is basically just two lists — one of account withdrawals and one of account deposits. The window also displays some extra information at the bottom of the screen: the Cleared Balance (which is your account balance including only those transactions that you or Quicken have marked as cleared), the Statement Ending Balance, and the Difference between these two figures.

 If you don't like the order in which withdrawals and deposits are arranged, you can change it. Click the View button and choose Sort By Date, and Quicken reorders the transactions by date. (You can also sort by check number, payee, or amount.)

Marking cleared checks and deposits

You need to tell Quicken which deposits and checks have cleared at the bank. (Refer to your bank statement for this information.)

1. **Identify the first deposit that has cleared.**

 You know how to do so, I'm sure. Just leaf through the bank statement and find the first deposit listed.

2. **Mark the first cleared deposit as cleared.**

 Scroll through the transactions listed in the right column of the Statement Summary: Checking window, find the deposit, and then mark it as cleared by clicking it. Quicken places a check mark in front of the deposit and updates the cleared statement balance.

3. **Record any cleared but missing deposits.**

 If you can't find a deposit, you haven't entered it into the Quicken register yet. I can only guess why you haven't entered it. Maybe you just forgot. In any event, return to the Quicken register by clicking the Edit button and then enter the deposit in the register in the usual way — but type a **c** (for "cleared") in the Clr column. This mark identifies the deposit as one that's already cleared at the bank. To return to the Statement Summary: Checking window, click the Reconcile button.

4. **Repeat Steps 1, 2, and 3 for all deposits listed on the bank statement.**

5. **Identify the first check or other withdrawal that has cleared.**

 No sweat, right? Just find the first check or withdrawal listed on the bank statement.

6. **Mark the first cleared check or other withdrawal as cleared.**

 Scroll through the transactions listed in the left column of the Statement Summary: Checking window, find the first check, and select it to mark it as having cleared the bank. Quicken inserts a check mark to label this transaction as cleared and updates the Cleared Balance.

7. Record any missing but cleared checks or withdrawals.

If you can't find a check or withdrawal — guess what? — you haven't entered it in the Quicken register yet. Display the Quicken register by clicking the Edit button. Then enter the check or withdrawal in the register. Be sure to type a **c** (for "cleared") in the Clr column to identify this check or withdrawal as one that's already cleared the bank. To return to the Statement Summary: Checking window, click the Reconcile button.

8. Repeat Steps 5, 6, and 7 for withdrawals listed on the bank statement.

By the way, these steps don't take very long. It takes me about two minutes to reconcile my account each month. And I'm not joking. By two minutes, I really mean two minutes.

Making sure that the difference equals zero

After you mark all the cleared checks and deposits, the difference between the cleared balance for the account and the bank statement's ending balance should equal zero. Notice that I said *should*, not *will*. Figure 8-4 shows a Statement Summary: Checking window in which everything is hunky-dory, and life is grand.

If the difference does equal zero, you're done. Just click the Finished button to tell Quicken that you're done. Quicken displays a congratulatory message telling you how proud it is of you, and then it asks whether you want to print a Reconciliation report.

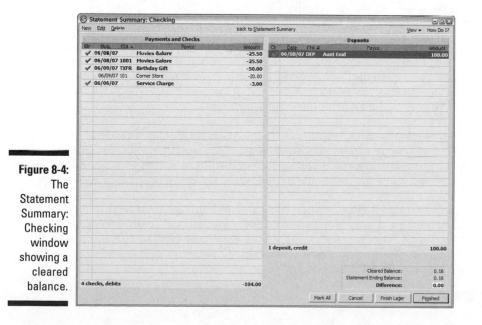

Figure 8-4:
The Statement Summary: Checking window showing a cleared balance.

As part of the finishing-up process, Quicken changes all the cs to Rs. There's no great magic in this transformation. Quicken makes the changes to identify the transactions that have already been reconciled.

Can't decide whether to print the Reconciliation report? Unless you're a business bookkeeper or an accountant reconciling a bank account for someone else — your employer or a client, for example — you don't need to print the Reconciliation report. All printing does is prove that you reconciled the account. (Basically, this proof is the reason you should print the report if you *are* a bookkeeper or an accountant — the person for whom you're reconciling the account will know that you did your job and will have a piece of paper to come back to later if he or she has questions.)

If the difference doesn't equal zero, you have a problem. If you click Finished, Quicken provides some cursory explanations as to why your account doesn't balance (via the Adjust Balance dialog box shown in Figure 8-5). This dialog box tells you, in effect, that you can force the two amounts to agree by clicking the Adjust button.

Figure 8-5:
The Adjust
Balance
dialog box.

Forcing the two amounts to agree isn't a very good idea. To do so, Quicken adds a cleared and reconciled transaction equal to the difference. (I talk about this transaction in the upcoming section, "Ten Things You Should Do If Your Account Doesn't Balance.")

If you want to reconcile later without saving your unfinished work, click Cancel in the Statement Summary: Checking window and then click Yes when Quicken asks you whether you really want to quit without saving your work. The next time you click the Reconcile button, you'll have to start over from scratch.

If you can't get your account to reconcile but want to save your work, click the Finish Later button. Quicken leaves your reconciliation work basically half done. The transactions that you marked as cleared still show a c in the Clr field. And you still have an unexplainable difference between the bank statement and your register.

Either way, postponing a reconciliation and not choosing to adjust the bank account balance is usually the best approach. It enables you to locate and correct problems. (I give you some ideas about how to do so in the next section.) Then you can restart the reconciliation and finish your work. (You restart a reconciliation in the same way that you originate one.)

Ten Things You Should Do If Your Account Doesn't Balance

I have some suggestions for reconciling an account that's causing you problems. If you're sitting in front of your computer wringing your hands, try the following tips.

Make sure that you're working with the right account

Sounds dumb, doesn't it? If you have a bunch of different bank accounts, however, ending up in the wrong account is pretty darn easy. So go ahead and confirm, for example, that you're trying to reconcile your checking account at Mammoth International Bank by using the Mammoth International checking account statement.

Look for transactions that the bank has recorded but you haven't

Go through your bank statement and make sure that you have recorded every transaction that your bank has recorded. Cash machine withdrawals, special fees or service charges (such as for checks or your safety deposit box), automatic withdrawals, direct deposits, and so on are easily overlooked.

If the difference is positive — that is, the bank thinks you have less money than you think you should — you may be missing a withdrawal transaction. If the difference is negative, you may be missing a deposit transaction.

Look for reversed transactions

Here's a tricky one. If you accidentally enter a transaction backwards — a deposit as a withdrawal or a withdrawal as a deposit — your account won't balance. And the error can be difficult to find. The Statement Summary: Checking window shows all the correct transactions, but a transaction amount appears positive when it should be negative or negative when it should be positive. The check you wrote to Mrs. Travis for your son's piano lessons appears as a positive number (a deposit) instead of a negative number (a check), for example.

Look for a transaction that's equal to half the difference

One handy way to find a transaction that you entered backwards — *if* you only have one — is to look for a transaction that's equal to half the irreconcilable difference. For example, if the difference is $200, you may have entered a $100 deposit as a withdrawal or a $100 withdrawal as a deposit.

I don't want to beat a dead horse, but the sign (that is, positive or negative) of the difference should help you find the problem. If the difference is positive — the bank thinks you have less money than your register indicates — you may have mistakenly entered a withdrawal as a deposit. If the difference is negative — the bank thinks you have more money than your register says — you may be missing a deposit transaction.

Look for a transaction that's equal to the difference

While I'm on the subject of explaining the difference by looking at individual transactions, let me make an obvious point. If the difference between the bank's records and yours equals one of the transactions listed in your register, you may have incorrectly marked the transaction as cleared or incorrectly left the transaction marked as uncleared.

I don't know. Maybe that was too obvious.

Check for transposed numbers

Transposed numbers occur when you flip-flop two digits in a number. For example, you enter $45.89 as $48.59.

These turkeys always cause accountants and bookkeepers headaches. If you look at the numbers, detecting an error is often difficult because the digits are the same. For example, when comparing a check amount of $45.89 in your register with a check for $48.59 shown on your bank statement, both check amounts show the same digits: 4, 5, 8, and 9. They just show them in different orders.

Transposed numbers are tough to find, but here's a trick you can try. Divide the difference shown on the Statement Summary: Checking window by nine. If the result is an even number of dollars or cents, you may have a transposed number somewhere.

Have someone else look over your work

This idea may seem pretty obvious, but I'm amazed at how often a second pair of eyes can find something that you've been overlooking.

If you're using Quicken at home, ask your spouse. If you're using Quicken at work, ask the owner or one of your coworkers (preferably that one person who always seems to have way too much free time).

Look out for multiple errors

By the way, if you find an error by using this laundry list and still can't balance your account, you should start checking at the top of the list again. You may, for example, discover — after you find a transposed number — that you entered another transaction backwards or incorrectly cleared or uncleared a transaction.

Try again next month (and maybe the month after that)

If the difference isn't huge in relation to the size of your bank account, you may want to wait until next month and attempt to reconcile your account again.

Before my carefree attitude puts you in a panic, consider the following example. You reconcile your account in January, and the difference is $24.02. Then you reconcile the account in February, and the difference is $24.02. Then you reconcile the account in March, and, surprise, surprise, the difference is still $24.02.

What's going on here? Well, your starting account balance was probably off by $24.02. (The more months you try to reconcile your account and find that you're always mysteriously $24.02 off, the more likely it is that this type of error is to blame.)

After the second or third month, I think it's pretty reasonable to tell Quicken that it should enter an adjusting transaction for $24.02 so that your account balances. (In my opinion, this is the only circumstance that merits your adjusting an account to match the bank's figure.)

By the way, if you've successfully reconciled your account with Quicken before, your work may not be at fault. The mistake could be (drum roll, please) the bank's! And in this case, you should do something else. . . .

Get in your car, drive to the bank, and beg for help

As an alternative to the preceding idea — which supposes that the bank's statement is correct and that your records are incorrect — I propose this idea: Ask the folks at the bank to help you reconcile the account. (Check to see whether they charge for this service first, of course.) Hint that you think that the mistake is probably theirs. Smile a great deal. And one other thing — be sure to ask about whatever product they're currently advertising in the lobby. (This behavior encourages them to think that you're interested in that 180-month certificate of deposit, and they'll be extra nice to you.)

In general, the bank's record keeping is usually pretty darn good. I've never had a problem as a business-banking client or as an individual. (I've also been lucky enough to deal with big, well-run banks.)

Nevertheless, your bank may have made a mistake, so ask the people there to help you. (*Note:* Be sure to have them explain any transactions that you discover only by seeing them on your bank statement.)

Chapter 9

Housekeeping for Quicken

● ●

In This Chapter

▶ Backing up your Quicken data

▶ Knowing when and how often to back up your data

▶ Knowing what to do if you lose your Quicken data

▶ Creating and working with more than one set of Quicken data

▶ Setting up a new file password

▶ Changing a file password

● ●

*O*kay, you don't have to worry about chasing dust bunnies in Quicken, but you do have to take care of little housekeeping tasks. This chapter describes these chores and how to do them right, with minimal hassle.

Backing Up Is Hard to Do

You should back up the files that Quicken uses to store your financial records. But you need to know how to back up before you can back up.

Backing up the quick-and-dirty way

You're busy. You don't have time to fool around. You just want to do a passable job backing up files. Sound like your situation? Then follow these steps:

1. **Insert a blank, formatted floppy disk, a writeable CD, or a blank Zip disk into the appropriate drive.**

 You can back up to any disk you can write to — this can be a floppy disk, writeable CD, or Zip disk. You should know which letters your computer uses to label its drives. If you don't, consult the documentation that came with your computer. (Usually, a floppy drive is named drive A.)

2. **Verify that the file you want to back up is active.**

 Display the Register tab and make sure that it displays one of the accounts in the file you want to back up. You can do so by clicking the register's QuickTab, which appears under the Cash Flow Center button. (If you don't remember setting up multiple files, don't worry. You probably have only one file — the usual case.)

3. **Start the backup operation by choosing File⇨Backup from the menu bar.**

 Quicken displays the Quicken Backup dialog box, shown in Figure 9-1.

Figure 9-1:
The Quicken Backup dialog box.

Figure 9-2:
The Browse For Folder dialog box.

4. **Identify the backup drive.**

 Select the On My Computer option button. Then verify that the disk letter shown in the text box is the one you want to use for backing up. If it isn't, click the Browse button. When Quicken displays the Browse For Folder dialog box, shown in Figure 9-2, select the correct disk.

Again, note that you don't have to use a floppy disk to back up. You can use any removable disk, including a Zip disk or a recordable CD. In real life, I use a Zip disk, just in case you're interested.

5. Click OK.

You see a message on-screen that says, "Aye, Cap'n, I'm working just as fast as I can" (or something to that effect). Then you see a message that says the backup is complete. Don't worry. You'll never see a message that says, "She's starting to break up, Cap'n. She can't take Warp-9 much longer." You will see a warning message if the file you want to back up is too large. In this case, you need to shrink the file, use a different disk, or use multiple disks.

As Figure 9-1 indicates, you can also back up Quicken online. When you select the Online option button and click OK, Quicken explains the service and gets you started. Just so you know, an online backup gets stored on Intuit's computers — Intuit makes Quicken — rather than on your computer's disks. Online backup works the same basic way as disk backup, except you need an Internet connection, and the online backup service costs money. The service costs from $6.95 to $19.95 a month at the time I'm writing this book, depending on the level of service you choose. But that seems too expensive to me for saving a couple of mouse clicks a week. Sorry, Intuit. . . .

Deciding when to back up

Sure, I can give you some tricky, technical examples of fancy backup strategies, but they have no point here. You want to know the basics, right? So here's what I do to back up my files. I back up every month after I reconcile. Then I stick the disk in my briefcase, so if something terrible happens at home, I don't lose both my computer and the backup disk with the data.

I admit that my strategy has a few problems, however. For example, because I'm backing up only once a month, I may have to re-enter as much as a month's worth of data if the computer crashes toward the end of the month. In my case, I wouldn't lose all that much work. However, if you have really heavy transaction volumes — if you write hundreds of checks a month, for example — you may want to back up more frequently than monthly, such as once a week. If you use the same disk or set of disks to back up your Quicken file, Quicken will warn you before it replaces the old file with the new one. You can go ahead and let Quicken do this, as long as you're sure that you won't want to access the old file anymore.

A second problem with my strategy is only remotely possible but is still worth mentioning. If something bad does happen to the Quicken files stored on my computer's hard drive *and* the files stored on the backup disk, I'm up the proverbial creek without a paddle. I should also note that a removable disk is far more likely to fail than a hard drive. If this worst-case scenario actually occurs, I'll need to start over from scratch from the beginning of the year. To prevent this scenario from happening, some people — those who are religiously careful — make more than one backup copy of their Quicken files.

By the way, Quicken periodically prompts you to back up when you try to exit. (You'll see a message that basically says, "Friend, backing up is a darn good idea.") You can, of course, choose to ignore this message. Or you can take Quicken's advice and do the backup thing as I describe earlier in this chapter, in the section, "Backing up the quick-and-dirty way."

You know what else? Here's a secret feature of Quicken: Quicken adds a subdirectory called Backup to the Quicken directory. And Quicken will stick a backup copy of your files in this directory every few days. (Sorry to be vague on this point, but it's hard to be specific and concrete when it comes to undocumented features.) You can find out more on this later in this chapter in the section, "Losing your Quicken data when you haven't backed up."

Losing your Quicken data after you've backed up

What happens if you lose all your Quicken data? First of all, I encourage you to feel smug. Get a cup of coffee. Lean back in your chair. Gloat for a couple of minutes. You, my friend, will have no problem.

After you've sufficiently gloated, carefully do the following to reinstate your Quicken data on the computer:

1. **Get your backup disk.**

 Find the backup disk you created and carefully insert it into one of your disk drives. (If you can't find the backup disk, forget what I said about feeling smug — stop gloating and skip to the next section.)

2. **Start Quicken.**

 You already know how to do this, right? By the way, if the disaster that caused you to lose your data also trashed other parts of your computer, you may need to reinstall Quicken. Shoot. I suppose it's possible that you may even need to reinstall Windows.

3. **Choose File⇨Restore Backup File from the menu.**

 Quicken probably displays a menu listing the backup copies of the Quicken data file that you've previously made. If that's the case, you simply select the backup copy you want to use. Alternatively, you can choose the Browse command from this little menu.

 Quicken looks at the selected folder or disk and displays a list of the files stored there, as shown in Figure 9-3. If your computer has another disk in it and this other disk has the backup copy of the file, use the Look In drop-down list box to select the other drive.

 Note: If you work with only a single Quicken file and Quicken knows where the backup copy is located, you may only need to choose the File⇨Restore Backup File command. In this special case, Quicken figures, heck, it doesn't need to ask you which file to restore or where the file is located because it already knows all this stuff.

Figure 9-3:
The Restore Quicken File dialog box.

4. **Select the file you want to restore and click OK.**

 Use the arrow keys or the mouse to select the file that you want to restore.

 If the file you select is the one Quicken used last, the program displays a message asking whether it's okay to *overwrite,* or replace, the file with the one stored on the disk.

 When you restore a file, you replace the current, in-memory version of the file with the backup version stored on the disk. Don't restore a file for fun. Don't restore a file for entertainment. Restore a file only if the current version is trashed, and you want to start over by using the version stored on the backup disk.

5. **Click OK.**

Quicken replaces the file it's currently using with the one from the backup disk. After it finishes, Quicken displays a message telling you that it has restored the file. You're almost done.

6. **Update the account registers as necessary.**

Using the register windows for each of the accounts in a file, re-enter each of the transactions you recorded since you created the backup. Be sure that you update your accounts because you've almost certainly entered transactions since the last time you backed up.

Just to be on the safe side, you should back up the file after you complete this process. Using a new disk is probably a good idea, too. I have heard that lightning never strikes the same place twice, but I'm not sure that the old saying is true. If you have hard drive problems or another recurring problem, whatever fouled up your file this time may rear its ugly head again — and soon.

Losing your Quicken data when you haven't backed up

What do you do if you haven't backed up your files in a while and you lose all the data in your Quicken files? Okay. Stay calm. All may not be lost.

First, you can try restoring the files from the Quicken backup directory. To do so, you follow the same file restoration steps I cover in the preceding section, with one minor exception. When you get to the Restore Quicken File dialog box (refer to Figure 9-3), you select your C drive. Then use the Look In box to indicate that you want to see the backup files in the backup folder.

At this point, you'll probably see a list of files with names similar to the file you lost. If the file you lost had the name QDATA, for example, you may see files named QDATA1 and QDATA2. If you named your Quicken data file STEVE in honor of me, you might see STEVE1, STEVE2, and so on. Select the newest file, which is the one with the "1" suffix, as in QDATA1 or STEVE1; then click OK. Quicken uses the file to restore the current file. As I alluded to earlier in this chapter, this may just work. And if it does, you should feel very lucky. Very lucky indeed.

Okay. So suppose that you've tried the approach described in the preceding paragraph, and it didn't work. What next?

You have to re-enter all the transactions for the entire year. Yeah. I know. It's a bummer. This method isn't quick, and it isn't pretty, but it works.

If you have copies of the registers, of course, you can use these as your information source to re-enter the information in your files. If you don't have copies of the registers, you need to use your bank statements and any other paper financial records you have.

If, for some unfortunate reason, the only copy you have of your Quicken data seems to have become corrupted, you can have Quicken try to rebuild the file. To do so, choose File⇨File Operations⇨Validate and enter the name of the file you want rebuilt in the File Name text box. You typically do this, however, only when instructed by Quicken or Intuit technical support people.

Working with Files, Files, and More Files

As part of setting up Quicken, you create what Quicken calls a *file:* a place where Quicken stores all your accounts (bank accounts, credit card accounts, investment accounts, and so on).

You can have more than one Quicken file at any time. Most people won't want to do this. But, for example, you can use different files to keep your personal financial records separate from business financial records.

Using multiple files does have a little drawback, however. You can't easily record, in one fell swoop, account transfer transactions between accounts in different files. You need to record the transaction twice — once in the *source account,* the file where the transaction originates, and again in the *destination account,* the file where you are transferring the transaction.

If the two accounts involved in a transfer are in the same file, just enter the account name in the Category text box. Quicken then records the transfer in the other account for you.

Setting up a new file

To set up a new file so that you can create accounts in it, follow these steps:

1. **Choose File⇨New from the menu bar.**

 Quicken displays the Creating New File: Dude, Are You Sure? dialog box, shown in Figure 9-4.

Figure 9-4:
The
Creating
New File:
Are You
Sure? dialog
box.

Figure 9-4:
The
Creating
New File:
Are You
Sure? dialog
box.

> **Creating new file: Are you sure?**
>
> Create
>
> ⦿ New Quicken File
> A Quicken file is a collection of accounts, categories, memorized items, and so on.
>
> ○ New Quicken Account
> A Quicken account is a list of transactions for a single bank account, credit card or other financial item.
>
> OK
> Cancel
> Help

2. Select the New Quicken File option button and then click OK or press Enter.

Quicken displays the Create Quicken File dialog box, shown in Figure 9-5.

Figure 9-5:
The Create
Quicken File
dialog box.

> **Create Quicken File**
>
> Save in: ☐ Quicken
>
> ☐ BACKUP
> ⬙ QDATA.QDF
>
> My Recent Documents
> Desktop
> My Documents
> My Computer
> My Network Places
>
> File name:
> Save as type: Quicken Files (*.QDF)
>
> OK
> Cancel
> Help

3. Enter a name for the Quicken file.

Position the cursor in the File Name text box and type some meaningful combination of letters and numbers. You don't need to enter a file extension because Quicken supplies the correct file extension, QDF, for you.

Note: You can use the symbol characters on your keyboard, but doing so gets a little tricky. If you must use symbol characters in the filename, refer to the Quicken user documentation.

4. Use the default file location.

Accept Quicken's suggestion to store the file in the QUICKEN directory — I can think of no good reason to put the file in another location.

5. Click OK.

Quicken displays the Quicken New User Setup dialog box, shown in Figure 9-6.

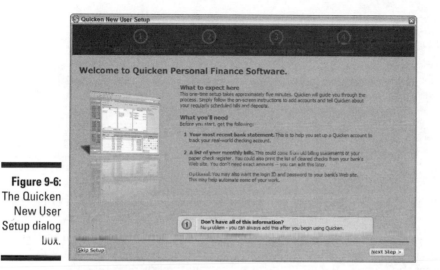

Figure 9-6:
The Quicken
New User
Setup dialog
box.

6. Run the New User Setup.

To set up the new Quicken file, run the New User Setup and answer its questions. If you have questions about the steps, refer to Chapter 1.

Flip-flopping between files

You can work with only one file at a time. So, after you create a second file, you need to know how to flip-flop between your files. If you're recording business stuff, for example, you want to be using the business file. However, what if a transaction comes in that clearly is meant for your personal file and you want to enter it there immediately? Flip-flopping allows you to get from one file to another in no time.

Flip-flopping is easy:

1. Just choose File⇨Open.

Quicken displays the Open Quicken File dialog box (see Figure 9-7).

Open Quicken File

Look in: ▢ Quicken

▢ BACKUP
▢ business.QDF
▢ QDATA.QDF
▢ steve.QDF

My Recent Documents

Desktop

My Documents

My Computer

Figure 9-7:
The Open
Quicken File
dialog box.

My Network Places

File name: OK

Files of type: Quicken Files (*.QDF;*.QDB;*.QDT) Cancel

Help

2. **Pick the file you want from the File Name text box and then click OK.**

 Zap! You are in the new file.

If you really want to switch to another file with lightning speed, you can select the name of the other file directly from the bottom of the File menu, where Quicken lists the last four files you used.

When files get too big for their own good

You can enter a large number of transactions in a Quicken file; in fact, you can record tens of thousands of transactions in a single account or file. Wowsers!

In spite of these huge numbers, I can think of some good reasons to work with smaller files if you can. For example, you can fit only about 5,000 transactions on a double-density 3½-inch floppy disk. So working with files of a manageable size means that you can more easily back them up on a floppy disk. Also, fewer transactions mean that Quicken runs faster because more memory is available for Windows. (Windows likes lots of memory — the same way that some people like lots of ice cream.)

Note: My technical editor, though, wants me to remind you that there are good reasons to work with large files when you can. Having several years of data at your fingertips, for example, is handy. With several years of data, you can easily get answers to all sorts of questions: how much money wealthy relatives have given you over the years, how much cable television has gone up in price, and so on.

For people who just have to be in the know....

What Quicken refers to as a *file* is really a set of data and index files with the same filename, such as HOME, but different file extensions, such as QDF, QPH, QEL, and QSD. So when Quicken refers to the HOME file, it really is referring to the set of files that includes HOME.QDF, HOME.QPH, HOME.QEL, and HOME.QSD.

In most cases, you never need to know the distinction between the files in the set, but the knowledge may come in handy someday. For example, if you happen to stumble onto the Quicken directory, knowing about the set of HOME files keeps you from panicking when you see all the multiple copies of the HOME file. Or, on a more serious note, if you use a third-party backup utility, you need to know that all of these files contain data that should be backed up.

If your files have gotten too big for their own good, you can knock them down to size by creating a new file that contains only the current year's transactions. You end up with a copy of the big file that you won't use anymore and a smaller, shrunken file with just the current year's transactions. Working with a smaller file probably means that Quicken will run faster. (The memory thing comes into play again.) And smaller files should make backing up easier because you can probably keep your files small enough to fit on a single, double-density floppy disk.

Call me a Nervous Nellie — or a Nervous Nelson — but because shrinking a file involves wholesale change, I'd really feel more comfortable helping you through this process if you first back up the file you're about to shrink. I don't think that you need to be anxious about anything, but just in case something does go wrong during the shrinking process, I know that you would like to have a backup copy of the file to fall back on.

To shrink a Quicken file, follow these steps:

1. **Choose File⇨File Operations⇨Year-End Copy from the menu bar.**

 Quicken displays a portrait of Barry Nelson, the first actor to portray James Bond. No, not really — I just wanted to see whether you were awake. Actually, Quicken displays the Year-End Copy dialog box, shown in Figure 9-8.

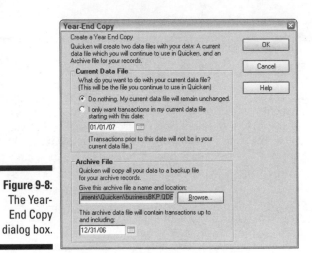

Figure 9-8:
The Year-
End Copy
dialog box.

2. **Describe what you want in the current data file.**

 Your next step in creating a year-end copy is to describe what informa-
 tion you want in the current data file, which is the Quicken file that
 you'll continue to work with. As the Year-End Copy dialog box suggests,
 you have two choices: The Do Nothing choice leaves the Quicken data
 file alone. The Do Something (please!) choice creates a copy of the
 Quicken data file using only balances and transactions after a specified
 date. To shrink the current Quicken file, you predictably use the Do
 Something (please!) option by selecting the appropriate option button
 and then specifying the cutoff date.

 When you archive, you make a copy of the Quicken data file, but (typi-
 cally) just through the end of the previous year. You continue to work
 with the big, everything-is-still-there data file. Why archive? So that you
 can have a copy of the Quicken data file as it existed at a point in time.
 You might archive the Quicken data file on a floppy or CD and store the
 archive file with your tax return, for example. By doing this, you'd be
 sure of always being able to later look at the Quicken data file that
 explained your tax deductions.

3. **Confirm the name in the Give This Archive File A Name text box.**

 You can actually ignore the filename and folder location information that
 Quicken enters into the Give This Archive File A Name box. However, if
 you really must have it your way, you do have the option of replacing

what Quicken suggests with another name. You can also click the Browse button and choose another folder location by using the dialog box Quicken displays.

4. **Specify a starting date.**

Using the Specify Starting Date text box, type a cutoff date. (Nowadays, the folks at Quicken are calling this the This Archive Data File Will Contain Transactions Up To And Including dialog box, but you guessed that, didn't you? Quicken deletes all cleared transactions with dates that fall before this cutoff date from the current Quicken file. (*Remember:* This file is the one you work with and want to shrink.) I chose 12/31/2006 as the cutoff date in Figure 9-8 so that I could create a new file for all 2007 transactions. (*Note:* Quicken doesn't delete uncleared transactions, and it doesn't delete investment transactions.)

5. **Click OK.**

Quicken creates an old-transactions "archive file" with the filename discussed in Step 3. If you told it to, Quicken also deletes all the old transactions from the current file so that your current file contains only the transactions that are dated after the cutoff date.

Quicken then displays the dialog box shown in Figure 9-9, which tells you the file was successfully copied. Select the Current File option button if you want to use the current file you've just shrunk. Select the Archive File option button if you want to use the old-transactions file. Click OK after you make your choice.

Figure 9-9:
The File
Archived
Successfully
dialog box.

If you want to see the old-transactions, or archive, file again, you can select it from the Open dialog box (accessed by choosing File⇨Open). You should *not* enter any new transactions in the old-transactions file, however, because these new transactions will change the old file's ending account balance without changing the current file's beginning account balance.

Using and Abusing Passwords

I have mixed feelings about Quicken passwords. Theoretically, they let you lock up your Quicken data so that your rebellious teenagers (if you're using Quicken at home) or the night janitors (if you're using Quicken in a business) can't come in and print checks, process automatic payments, and just generally mess things up.

Using passwords sounds pretty good, of course. But before you set up a password and then start relying on it to protect your information, let me remind you that a Quicken password only prevents someone from accessing your data with Quicken. Using a password doesn't prevent someone from fooling around with your computer itself. If the night janitors — or, heaven forbid, your teenagers — are the nefarious types, they can erase your files with Windows or scramble them with another program, such as a spreadsheet or word-processing program. And they may even be able to get in and manipulate the data with another checkbook or accounting program.

Passwords come with one other little annoying problem, too. Darn it, you have to remember them.

For these reasons, I think that passwords are best left to computer systems that use them on a global basis to control access to all programs and to computer systems that can track all users (you, your teenagers, the night janitors, and anyone else) by name. Your PC doesn't fall into this category.

Setting up a file password

You still want a password? Okay. With much trepidation, I give you the following steps for setting up a password for a Quicken file:

1. **Select the file you want to protect with a password.**

 If the file you want to password-protect is not the active file, choose File⇨Open from the menu and then either double-click the file you want or select it and click OK.

2. **Choose File⇨Passwords from the menu bar.**

 Quicken displays the — you guessed it — Passwords submenu, which lists two commands: File and Transaction.

3. **Choose the File command.**

 Quicken displays the Quicken File Password dialog box, shown in Figure 9-10.

Figure 9-10:
The Quicken
File
Password
dialog box.

4. **Enter the password into the New Password text box.**

 You can use up to 16 characters. Quicken differentiates between lower-case and uppercase characters, by the way, so Washington, wASHINGTON, and WASHINGTON are all different from its point of view. Quicken doesn't display the actual characters you type; It displays asterisks instead. If you type **Dog**, for example, it displays ***. (Passwords require strict secrecy, you see.)

5. **Enter the password you want to use again — only this time into the Confirm Password text box — and click OK.**

 Congratulations! You're done.

So what are transaction passwords?

After you choose File⇨Passwords from the menu bar, you can create a file password or a transaction password by choosing File or Transaction from the Passwords submenu. In general, you use a *file password* to protect the access into a Quicken file.

A *transaction password* works like a file password except that the user has to enter the transaction password if he or she tries to enter a transaction that is dated before a specified date. You specify the date, called the *cutoff date,* when you set up the transaction password.

You would use transaction passwords, my guess is, when you want to "lock" the previous year's records. In other words, if you don't want people to intentionally or accidentally change last year's transactions — because that would mean they're screwing around with things like your records of tax deductions you've claimed on a return — you use a transaction password.

Transaction passwords are okay, I guess. But I'm going to go out on a limb here and suggest something different: You can create and safely store backup copies of the Quicken file for last year or last month. Or you can keep the idiots from fooling around with your Quicken files. Jeepers, if somebody can't understand an instruction such as, "Use the current date," do you really want them mucking about in your books?

Assigning a password to a file doesn't prevent you from doing anything with the file that you would normally do. However, the next time you try to use this file — after you start Quicken or when you try to select the file by using the File⇨Open command — Quicken will ask you for the file's password. You need to supply the password to gain access to the file.

Changing a file password

After you set up a file password, you're not stuck with it forever. You can either change the password or remove it by choosing File⇨Passwords⇨File.

If you've already set up a password, however, Quicken doesn't display the Quicken File Password dialog box shown in Figure 9-10. Instead, Quicken displays a mutated Quicken File Password dialog box that asks for the password you're now using and the new password you want to use in the future (as shown in Figure 9-11). Type the current password in the Old Password text box and the new password in the New Password and Confirm Password text boxes. Then press Enter or click OK. From now on, you need to use the new password to gain access to the file. If you don't want to use a password anymore, just leave the New Password and Confirm Password text boxes blank.

Figure 9-11:
The
Quicken File
Password
dialog box.

Quicken File Password

Old Password: ********
New Password:
Confirm Password:

Secure passwords are typically longer than six characters, should include a combination of letters and number, and should not contain obvious words such as your name.

Note: To remove old password, leave new and Confirm fields blank. Also note that passwords are case sensitive.

Help Cancel OK

Chapter 10

Compound Interest Magic and Other Mysteries

*T*he folks at Intuit provide several nifty little calculators (most are dialog boxes) with Quicken. I strongly encourage you to use these tools. At the very least, the calculators should make your work easier. And if you invest a little time, you should gain some enormously valuable perspectives on your financial affairs.

What's more, the most recent versions of Quicken Deluxe and Quicken Premier include a handful of more powerful financial planning wizards that I want you to know about. I won't walk you through the steps to using these wizards. But I do want to preview them in the same way that a restaurant critic tells you what you should and shouldn't order at some nice restaurant. You know what I mean. "Darling, you absolutely must try the *foie gras,* but do stay away from the chocolate mousse. It's abominable. . . ."

Noodling Around with Your Investments

My favorite Quicken calculator is the Investment Savings Calculator. I guess I just like to forecast portfolio future values and other similar stuff.

Using the Investment Savings Calculator

Suppose that you want to know how much you'll accumulate if you save $3,000 a year for 35 years in a stock mutual fund that you anticipate will earn 10 percent annually. Use the Investment Savings Calculator to estimate how much you should ultimately accumulate. To use it, follow these steps:

1. **Choose Planning⇨Financial Calculators⇨Savings Calculator.**

 Quicken displays the Investment Savings Calculator dialog box (see Figure 10-1).

Figure 10-1:
The
Investment
Savings
Calculator
dialog box.

2. **Enter what you've already accumulated as your Opening Savings Balance.**

 Move the cursor to the Opening Savings Balance text box and then type the amount of your current investments. If this amount is zero, for example, type **0**.

3. **Enter the Annual Yield that you expect your investments to earn.**

 Move the cursor to the Annual Yield text box and type the percent. If you plan to invest in the stock market and expect your savings to match the market's usual return of about 10 percent, for example, type **10** (don't type **.10**).

4. **Indicate how long you plan to let your investments earn income.**

 Move the cursor to the Number Of drop-down list box and select the time period appropriate to your investment planning. (Usually, you'll select Years, as Figure 10-1 shows.) Then move the cursor to the Number Of text box and indicate how long (enter the number of time periods) you want to maintain these investments. For example, if you select Years in the drop-down list box and you plan to let your investments grow for 35 years, you type **35**.

5. **Enter the amount you plan to add to your investments every period.**

 Move the cursor to the Contribution Each text box and type the amount you plan to add. (Figure 10-1 shows how to calculate an IRA's future value assuming a $3,000 annual contribution.)

6. **Enter the anticipated inflation rate.**

 Move the cursor to the Predicted Inflation text box and type the inflation rate. By the way, over the twentieth century, the inflation rate averaged just over 3 percent.

7. **Indicate whether you plan to increase your annual contribution as a result of inflation.**

 Select the Inflate Contributions check box if you plan to annually increase — by the annual inflation rate — the amount you add to your investment portfolio. Don't select the check box if you don't want to inflate the payments.

8. **After you enter all the information, click Calculate.**

 The Ending Savings Balance field shows how much you'll accumulate in present-day, uninflated dollars: $206,045.30. Hmmm. Sweet.

If you want to know the amount you'll accumulate in future-day, inflated dollars, deselect the Ending Balance in Today's $ check box.

To get more information on the annual deposits, balances, and so on, click the Schedule button, which appears at the bottom of the Investment Savings Calculator dialog box. Quicken whips up a quick little report showing the annual deposits and ending balance for each year you plan to add into the savings. Try it. You may like it.

Trying to become a millionaire

So you want to be a millionaire some day.

To find out how to realize this childhood dream, use the Calculate For option buttons, which appear on the Investment Savings Calculator dialog box (refer to Figure 10-1). With these option buttons, you click the financial variable

(Opening Savings Balance, Regular Contribution, or Ending Savings Balance) you want to calculate. For example, to determine the annual amount you need to contribute to your investment so that your portfolio reaches $1,000,000, here's what you do:

1. **Select the Regular Contribution option button.**

2. **Select the Inflate Contributions check box.**

3. **Deselect the Ending Balance In Today's $ check box.**

4. **Enter all the other input variables.**

 Remember to set the Ending Savings Balance text box to 1000000 (the Ending Savings Balance field becomes a text box after you select the Regular Contribution option).

 The Investment Savings Calculator computes how much you need to save annually to hit your $1,000,000 target.

Starting from scratch, it'll take 35 years of roughly $2,500-a-year payments to reach $1,000,000.00, as shown in Figure 10-2. (All those zeros look rather nice, don't they?) Note that this calculation assumes a 10 percent annual yield.

Figure 10-2:
The secret to your success: $2,500 a year for 35 years.

"Jeepers, creepers," you say. "This seems too darn good to be true, Steve."

Well, unfortunately, the calculation is a little misleading. With 4 percent inflation, your million bucks will be worth *only* $253,415.55 in current-day dollars. (To confirm this present value calculation, select the Ending Savings Balance option button and then the Ending Balance In Today's $ check box.)

A timing assumption you should know

The Investment Savings Calculator assumes that you'll add to your portfolio at the end of the period — what financial planners call an *ordinary annuity*.

One of my pet ideas is that it really is possible for most people to become millionaires. There are just three tricks to doing so. First, make sure that you use tax-advantaged investments like 401(k) plans and IRAs. Second, invest this money into an index stock mutual fund like the Vanguard Total Stock Market Portfolio to make sure that, over time, your returns average out to the average. Third, use Quicken and your computer to make smarter financial decisions — by doing this, you can rather easily free up an extra $50, $100, or even $200 a month. I talk about this subject in Chapter 18.

The Often Unbearable Burden of Debt

To help you better manage your debts, Quicken provides a neat Loan Calculator that computes loan payments and balances.

Using the Loan Calculator to figure payments

Suppose that one afternoon, you're wondering what the mortgage payment is on one of those monstrous houses: tens of thousands of square feet, acres of grounds, cottages for the domestic help, and so on. You get the picture — something that's a really vulgar display of wealth.

To calculate what you would pay on a 30-year, $5,000,000 mortgage if the money costs 6 percent, use the Loan Calculator:

1. **Choose Planning⇨Financial Calculators⇨Loan Calculator.**

 Quicken displays the Loan Calculator dialog box. (See Figure 10-3 for a picture of this handy tool.)

Figure 10-3:
The Loan
Calculator
shows that
you can't
afford that
huge
mansion.

2. **Enter the loan amount.**

 Move the cursor to the Loan Amount text box and type the amount of
 the loan. (If you're checking the lifestyle of the ostentatious and vulgar,
 type **5,000,000**.)

3. **Enter the annual interest rate.**

 Move the cursor to the Annual Interest Rate text box and type the inter-
 est rate percent. If a loan charges 6 percent interest, for example, type **6**.

4. **Enter the number of years you want to take to repay the loan.**

 Move the cursor to the Number Of Years text box and type the number
 of years you plan to make payments.

5. **Indicate how many loan payments you plan to make a year.**

 Move the cursor to the Periods Per Year text box and type the number
 of loan payments you plan to make in a year. If you want to make
 monthly payments, for example, type **12**.

6. **Indicate how frequently the lender will calculate, or compound, interest.**

 Move the cursor to the Compounding Period box and select the interest
 compounding period. If a loan uses monthly compounding, for example,
 select monthly. (By the way, just so you know, most loans use compound-
 ing periods equal to the payment period. Some don't. But most do.)

If you click Calculate or move the selection cursor, Quicken calculates the
loan payment and displays the amount in the Payment Per Period field. Hey,
wait. $29,977.53. That doesn't seem so bad, does it? I mean, you could almost
make an annual — oh, never mind. That's a monthly payment, isn't it? Yikes!

I guess if you have to ask how much the mortgage payment is, you really can't afford it.

To get more information on the loan payments, interest and principal portions of payments, and outstanding loan balances, click the Schedule button, which appears on the face of the Loan Calculator dialog box. Quicken whips up a quick loan amortization schedule showing all this stuff.

Calculating loan balances

To calculate the loan principal amount, select the Loan Amount option button under Calculate For in the Loan Calculator dialog box. Then enter all the other variables.

For example, those $29,977.53-per-month payments for the monster mansion seem a little ridiculous. So calculate how much you can borrow if you make $1,500-per-month payments over 30 years and the annual interest rate is 6 percent:

1. **Select the Loan Amount option button.**

2. **Type** 6 **in the Annual Interest Rate text box.**

3. **Type** 30 **in the Number Of Years text box.**

4. **Type** 12 **in the Periods Per Year text box.**

5. **Type** 1500 **in the Payment Per Period text box.**

After you click the Calculator button or move the selection cursor, the Loan Calculator computes a loan amount of $250,187.42, as shown in Figure 10-4.

Figure 10-4:
The Loan
Calculator
dialog box.

The Refinance Calculator

You won't read about the Refinance Calculator here — but not because I'm lazy. Believe it or not, I enjoy writing about things that help you make better financial decisions. The Refinance Calculator merely calculates the difference in mortgage payments if you make lower payments; then it tells you how long it would take with these lower payments to pay back the refinancing costs you incur.

For example, if you save $50 a month because you refinance and it costs $500 to refinance, the Refinance Calculator tells you that it would take ten months of $50-per-month savings to recoup your $500.

You know what? Although you may want to know how long it would take to recoup the refinance costs, that information doesn't tell you whether refinancing is a good idea. Deciding whether to refinance is very, very complicated. You can't just look at your next few payments, like the Refinance Calculator does. You also need to look at the total interest you would pay with the old mortgage and the new mortgage.

I can't think of any good reason to use the Refinance Calculator; it just doesn't do what it purports to do.

So that I don't leave you hanging, however, let me give you two general rules to help you make smarter refinancing decisions:

✔ First, if you want to save interest costs, don't use refinancing as a way to stretch out your borrowing. That is, if you refinance, make sure that you make payments large enough to pay off the new mortgage by the same time you would have paid off the old mortgage. In other words, if you have 23 years left on your old mortgage, don't go out and get a 30-year mortgage. Find a lender who will let you pay off the new mortgage in 23 years.

✔ Here's a second trick, if you can find a willing lender. Ask the lender to calculate the *annual percentage rate* (APR) on the new mortgage, assuming that you'll pay off the mortgage by the same time you would have paid off the old mortgage. (An APR includes all the loan's costs — interest, points, miscellaneous fees, and so on — and calculates an implicit interest rate.) If the APR on the new loan is lower than the current loan's interest rate, refinancing would probably save you money.

Let me issue one caveat. When you base your refinancing decision on the comparison between the new loan's APR and the current loan's interest rate, you assume that you'll live in your current house until the mortgage is paid.

I hope this information helps. As I said, mortgage-refinancing decisions are tough if you truly want to save money.

The Retirement Calculator

I think that this section is the most important one in this book. No joke. Your financial future is much too consequential to go for easy laughs or cheap shots.

The dilemma in a nutshell

By the time the 30-something and 40-something crowd reaches retirement, Social Security coverage almost certainly will be scaled back.

But the problem isn't just Social Security. More and more often, employer-provided pension plans are *defined contribution plans,* which add specific amounts to your pension (such as 2 percent of your salary), rather than *defined benefit plans,* which promise specific pension amounts (such as $1,000 a month). As a result, although you know that someone will throw a few grand into your account every so often, you don't know how much you'll have when you retire.

So what does all this mean? In a nutshell, you need to think about your retirement now. Fortunately, the Quicken Retirement Calculator can help you.

The truth about Social Security

Every so often, the Social Security Administration sends you a Personal Earnings and Benefits Summary, sometimes known by the acronym PEBS. You want to pay close attention to both the statement and the accompanying letter. The statement shows you how much you can expect to receive in the way of retirement savings based on your past earnings, assuming you continue to earn similar amounts in the future. The statement also typically tells you that if Congress does nothing, there will only be money to cover "X" percent of your benefits at some point a few decades in the future. For example, the statement may say something along the lines of "Blah, blah, blah, and if Congress does nothing to fix the funding challenges faced by the nation's aging workers, in 2039 the trust fund will be depleted, and Social Security tax receipts will be only enough to pay

70 percent of the retirees and other recipients' benefits. . . ." Okay, that's a bummer. I know.

But think about the worst-case scenario. If Congress really does nothing, the Social Security Administration now tells you, implicitly through the PEBS statement, by what amount your benefits will be cut. The last PEBS that I saw, for example, suggested that the trust fund runs out of money in roughly 35 years, and, at that point, benefits will have to be cut back to 70 percent of their current level. For example, someone who would have gotten $800 a month will get only $560. Okay, that's not good. But as long as you're not depending solely on Social Security, it isn't quite a financial meltdown either. You can easily save just a bit more money yourself and more than make up the difference.

REMEMBER

More about timing

The Retirement Calculator assumes that you or your employer will add to your retirement savings at the end of the year — what financial planners call an *ordinary annuity.* If you or your employer adds to your retirement savings at the beginning of the year, you earn an extra year of interest. As a result, your after-tax income will be more than Quicken shows.

Retirement planning calculations

Imagine that you decide to jump into your employer's *401(k)* thing (a type of profit-sharing plan) and that it allows you to plop $6,000 into a retirement account that you think will earn about 9 percent annually.

Fortunately, you don't need to be a rocket scientist to figure this stuff out. You can just use the Retirement Calculator:

1. **Choose Planning⟹Financial Calculators⟹Retirement Calculator.**

 Quicken displays the Retirement Calculator dialog box, shown in Figure 10-5.

Figure 10-5:
The Retirement Calculator dialog box.

2. **Enter what you've already saved as your current savings.**

 Move the cursor to the Current Savings text box and type your current retirement savings (for example, if you have some Individual Retirement Account money or you've accumulated a balance in an employer-sponsored 401(k) account). Don't worry if you don't have anything saved — most people don't.

3. Enter the annual yield that you expect your retirement savings to earn.

Move the cursor to the Annual Yield text box and type the percent. In the little example shown in Figure 10-5, I say the annual yield is 9 percent. This is, I'll remind you, about the average return that the stock market produces over long periods of time.

4. Enter the annual amount added to your retirement savings.

Move the cursor to the Annual Contribution text box and type the amount that you or your employer will add to your retirement savings at the end of each year. In the example, I say that I plan to add $6,000 (refer to Figure 10-5).

5. Enter your current age.

Move the cursor to the Current Age text box and type a number. You're on your own here, but let me suggest that this is a time to be honest.

6. Enter your retirement age.

Move the cursor to the Retirement Age text box and type a number. Again, this is purely a personal matter. (Figure 10-5 shows this age as 65, but you should retire when you want.)

7. Enter the age to which you want to continue withdrawals.

Move the cursor to the Withdraw Until Age field and type a number. I don't want to beat around the bush here. This number is how old you think you'll be when you die. I don't like the idea any better than you do. Let me say, though, that ideally you want to run out of steam — there, that's a safe metaphor — before you run out of money. So go ahead and make this age something pretty old — like 95.

8. Enter any other income you'll receive — such as Social Security.

Move the cursor to the Other Income (SSI, Etc.) text box and type a value. (Figure 10-5 shows $15,000.) Note that this income is in current-day, or uninflated, dollars. By the way, you can request an estimate of your future Social Security benefits (this is the PEBS statement I talk about in the "The truth about Social Security" sidebar earlier in this chapter) by visiting the Social Security Administration's Web site at www.ssa.gov or by contacting your local Social Security Administration office. Also, note that if you haven't received a benefits estimate already, the Social Security Administration is actually supposed to be sending every worker an estimate of his or her future benefits.

9. Indicate whether you plan to save retirement money in a tax-sheltered investment.

Select the Tax Sheltered Investment option button if your retirement savings earns untaxed money. Select the Non-Sheltered Investment option button if the money is taxed. *Tax-sheltered investments* are such things as

Individual Retirement Accounts, annuities, and employer-sponsored 401(k)s and 403(b)s. (A *403(b)* is kind of a profit-sharing plan for a non-profit agency.)

As a practical matter, tax-sheltered investments are the only way to ride. By deferring income taxes on your earnings, you earn interest on the money you otherwise would have paid as income tax.

10. **Enter your current marginal tax rate, if needed.**

 If you're investing in taxable stuff, move the cursor to the Current Tax Rate text box. Then type the combined federal and state income tax rate that you pay on your last dollars of income.

11. **Enter your anticipated retirement tax rate.**

 Move the cursor to the Retirement Tax Rate text box, and then . . . hey, wait a minute. Who knows what the rates will be next year, let alone when you retire? I think that you should type **0**, but remember that the Annual Income After Taxes is really your pretax income (just as your current salary is really your pretax income).

12. **Enter the anticipated inflation rate.**

 Move the cursor to the Predicted Inflation text box and type the inflation rate. By the way, in recent history, the inflation rate has averaged just above 3 percent (refer to Figure 10-5).

13. **Indicate whether the annual additions will increase.**

 Select the Inflate Contributions check box if the additions will increase annually by the inflation rate. (Because your salary and 401(k) contributions will presumably inflate if there's inflation, Figure 10-5 shows the Inflate Contributions check box selected.)

14. **After you enter all the information, click Calculate and take a peek at the Annual Income After Taxes field.**

 Figure 10-5, for example, shows $28,838.76. Not bad really. If you want to see the after-tax income in future-day, inflated dollars, deselect the Annual Income In Today's $ check box but leave the Inflate Contributions check box checked.

To get more information on the annual deposits, balances, income, and so on, click the Schedule button, which appears on the face of the Retirement Calculator dialog box. Quicken whips up a quick little report showing the annual deposits, income, and ending retirement account balances for each year you plan to add to and withdraw from your retirement savings.

If you're now bummed out about retirement

First, don't feel depressed. At least you know *now* if your golden years seem a little tarnished. After all, you acquired Quicken to help you sort out your finances. Now you can use Quicken and your newly gained knowledge to help improve your financial lot.

Basically, retirement planning depends on just three things:

- ✔ The number of years that the retirement savings will accrue interest
- ✔ The *real yield* (that is, adjusted for inflation) you earn — in other words, the annual yield minus the predicted inflation
- ✔ The yearly payments

Anything you do to increase one of these variables increases your retirement income.

If you invest, for example, in something that delivers higher real yields, such as the stock market, you should see a big difference. (Of course, you usually bear more risk.) Or if you wait an extra year or two to retire, you wind up making more annual payments and earning more interest. Finally, if you boost the yearly payments (for example, by participating in an employer-sponsored 401(k) or 403(b) plan, where your employer matches a portion of your contribution), you'll see a huge change.

Noodle around with the variables. See what happens. You may be surprised.

Retirement roulette

Use the Calculate For option buttons in the Retirement Calculator (refer to Figure 10-5) to determine a retirement income variable. You can calculate current savings, annual contribution, or, as I describe earlier in the section, "Retirement planning calculations," the annual after-tax income.

To calculate the yearly payment required to produce a specific level of retirement income, for example, select the Annual Contribution option button. Then enter all the other variables — including the desired after-tax income and click Calculate. The Retirement Calculator figures how much you need to save to hit your target retirement income.

Cost of College

Ouch. I have a couple of daughters, so I know how you feel. Man, oh man, do I know how you feel.

The College Calculator

Suppose that you have a child who may attend college in 16 years, and you haven't started to save yet. If the local university costs $10,000 a year and you can earn 9 percent annually, how much should you save?

The College Calculator works like the Retirement Calculator:

1. **Choose Planning⇨Financial Calculators⇨College Calculator.**

 Quicken displays the College Calculator dialog box, shown in Figure 10-6.

Figure 10-6:
Use the College Calculator dialog box to determine whether you'll have to take out a second mortgage to pay for Junior's college education.

2. **Enter the annual college costs.**

 Move the cursor to the Annual College Costs text box. Then type the current annual costs at a school Junior may attend. Figure 10-6 shows this amount as $10,000.

3. **Enter the number of years until enrollment.**

 Move the cursor to the Years Until Enrollment text box and type a number. For example, if Junior will start college in 13 years, type **13**.

4. **Enter the number of years enrolled.**

 Move the cursor to the Number Of Years Enrolled text box and type a number. Assuming that Junior doesn't fool around, type **4** or **5**.

5. **Enter the amount of the current college savings.**

 Move the cursor to the Current College Savings field and type an amount. Figure 10-6 shows this amount as $0.00.

6. **Enter the annual yield that you expect the college savings to earn.**

 Move the cursor to the Annual Yield text box and type the percent. Figure 10-6 shows the yield as 9 percent.

7. **Enter the inflation rate anticipated in college tuition.**

 Move the cursor to the Predicted Inflation text box and type the inflation rate percent. Figure 10-6 shows this rate as 4 percent.

8. **Indicate whether you plan to increase your annual contribution as a result of inflation.**

 Select the Inflate Contributions check box if you plan to annually increase — by the annual inflation rate — the amount you save. Figure 10-6 shows this check box selected.

After you enter all the information, click Calculate or move the selection cursor. The Annual Contribution field shows how much you need to save each year until the child graduates from college.

Just to beat this thing to death, Figure 10-6 shows that the lucky student will attend five years at a college that currently costs $10,000 a year and that you expect to earn 9 percent annually and anticipate 4 percent annual inflation. Given these cold hard facts, you need to start saving $2,171.27 every year.

To get more information on the annual deposits, tuition, and balance, click the Schedule button, which appears on the face of the College Calculator dialog box. Quicken whips up a quick little report showing the annual deposits, tuition, and ending college savings account balances for each year you add to, and Junior withdraws from, the college savings money.

If you're now bummed out about college costs

Look at the positive side: You now understand the size of the problem and the solution.

College planning depends on four things:

- ✔ College costs
- ✔ The number of years that the savings earn interest
- ✔ The *real yield* (that is, adjusted for inflation) you earn — in other words, the annual yield minus the predicted inflation
- ✔ The yearly payments

I don't mean to sound like a simpleton, but you can successfully save for a college education in three basic ways:

- ✔ Reduce the costs (find a less expensive school)
- ✔ Invest in things that deliver higher yields
- ✔ Boost the yearly payments

Use the Calculate For option buttons (refer to Figure 10-6) to compute a specific financial variable. Select the variable you want to calculate and then input the other values. The College Calculator computes the flagged variable.

Finding a less expensive school isn't necessarily the same thing as looking for the cheapest tuition fees. Another huge factor these days is whether a program takes four years or five years to complete. A cheap-tuition school that requires five years may be more expensive than, say, a good private school that gets a student out — and working — in four years.

Planning for Taxes

Quicken also comes with a very powerful, very useful Tax Planner. The Tax Planner helps you make a precise estimate of the taxes that you'll owe. To use the Tax Planner, take the following steps:

1. **Choose Tax⇨Tax Planner.**

 Quicken displays the Tax Planner window. To move past the introductory information, click Let's Get Started and then click Next. Quicken shows the second page (see Figure 10-7).

 Note: Quicken may display a dialog box that asks whether you want to learn how TurboTax can help with year-round tax planning. Click No if you see this message. You've got my help.

Figure 10-7:
The second page of the Tax Planner window.

2. **Verify the tax year and filing status.**

In the upper-left corner of the Tax Planner window, notice that the tax year (labeled *Year*) and the filing status (labeled *Status*) appear. These are probably correct. Quicken can guess the year by looking at your computer's clock. It determines your filing status based on information that you supply when you set up Quicken. But if one of these bits of information is wrong, click the Year or Status hyperlink. The hyperlinks are those bits of text along the left edge of the Tax Planner window. Quicken displays the Tax Planner Options text boxes, which let you specify the Tax Year and the Filing Status and choose a Scenario.

Note: A *Scenario* is just a set of income tax inputs. You may have only one Scenario. Or you may have several Scenarios based on different guesses about your income and deductions.

3. **Enter the wages and salaries that you and your lovely or handsome spouse expect.**

Click the Wages hyperlink. Then, when Quicken displays the Wages text boxes, type your wages and, if you're married, those of your spouse. Quicken totals your wages and then makes a first rough calculation of the amount you'll owe in taxes. Of course, Quicken needs to collect some more data before this number is accurate, so don't freak out yet.

You can move to the next set of input text boxes by clicking the <u>Next</u> hyperlink and to the previous window of input text boxes by clicking the <u>Previous</u> hyperlink. The <u>Next</u> and <u>Previous</u> hyperlinks appear near the bottom of the Tax Planner window. (You may have to scroll down to see them on your computer.)

4. **Enter the other income you'll have from interest, dividends, capital gains, and so on.**

 To record the other income that you'll need to pay taxes on, click the <u>Interest/Dividend Inc</u>, <u>Business Income</u>, <u>Capital Gains</u>, and <u>Other Income</u> hyperlinks and provide the information that Quicken requests. Some of these numbers are pretty easy to guess. Some of them aren't. You can also look at last year's tax return or at the year-to-date information you've already collected by using Quicken.

5. **Identify any adjustments to your gross income.**

 Click the <u>Adjustments</u> hyperlink and then, using the Adjustments to Income text boxes, identify or estimate any adjustments to gross income that you'll have. Most people make only one adjustment — contributions to a deductible IRA. Self-employed individuals, however, also typically have several other adjustments, including half of their self-employment tax (which Quicken automatically calculates and enters), a portion of any health insurance paid, and Keogh and SEP pension contributions.

6. **Estimate your itemized deductions.**

 Click the <u>Deductions</u> hyperlink and then use the Standard and Itemized Deductions text boxes to estimate your deductions for expenses, such as state and local taxes, mortgage interest, and charitable contributions. Alternatively, if you'll probably or possibly use the standard deduction, carefully check any of the boxes that Quicken uses to determine which standard deduction you should use.

7. **Tell Quicken how many personal exemptions you'll claim.**

 Click the <u>Exemptions</u> hyperlink and then specify the number of dependents you'll claim on your return. The basic rule is that you get one exemption for every person in your family (you, your spouse if you're filing jointly, and your kids) as long as they live in your house. I should mention, however, that things become tricky if you have shirt-tail relatives (your Aunt Enid, for example) living at your house, if your kids live away from home or are married, or if some of the kids in the house have divorced parents. If you have questions because one of these situations sounds vaguely familiar, get the IRS preparation instructions and read the part about who is and is not a dependent.

8. **Indicate whether you owe any other taxes or have tax credits you can use to reduce your taxes.**

 Click the Other Tax, Credits hyperlink and then use the Other Taxes & Credits text boxes to describe any of the federal taxes you'll pay in addition to the usual federal income tax. The other taxes, by the way, typically include just two taxes: self-employment tax (which is the tax that self-employed people pay in place of Social Security and Medicare tax) and, in special cases, the alternative minimum tax. A bunch of different tax credits exist. You can very possibly look at your prior years' returns to see if they apply (typically) in your situation.

9. **Enter any estimated taxes you've paid or any federal income taxes your employer has withheld from your paycheck.**

 Click the Withholding hyperlink and use the Withholding text boxes to record how much money you've paid through withholding. Then click the Tax Payments hyperlink and use the Estimated Tax Payments text boxes to record how much you've paid in estimated tax payments and to guess how much you'll pay in the coming months.

10. **Return to the Tax Planner Summary and review the Quicken program's calculations.**

 After you complete the preceding steps, click the Tax Planner Summary hyperlink and review the calculations that Quicken makes. Quicken estimates the total tax you'll pay (which is useful and interesting in itself), the estimated refund or payment you'll have to make, and one other particularly useful bit of information — your marginal income tax rate (which Quicken labels *Marginal Rate*). If you want to print a copy of the Tax Planner's information and calculations, click Print (in the upper-right corner of the window).

Knowing your marginal income tax rate enables you to make more precise investment calculations. For example, the Retirement Calculator — described earlier in the chapter in the section cleverly titled, "The Retirement Calculator" — uses your marginal income tax rate to make more precise calculations. You can also use the marginal income tax rate to calculate the after-tax return that taxable investments deliver. Simply multiply the taxable return by the factor (1 − marginal tax rate).

The Other Planning Tools

In the preceding pages of this chapter, I talk about the personal financial planning tools that are most useful. Before I wrap up my discussion, let me quickly mention that Quicken provides some other interesting and, for some people, useful financial planning tools.

If you open the Planning menu, you'll notice commands named Retirement Planner, College Planner, Home Purchase Planner, Debt Reduction Planner, and Special Purchase Planner. These wizards walk you through the steps to planning for big important events. Like retirement. Or college. In my opinion, these are all special-interest tools. Most people won't be interested in taking the time to use the wizards. (The Retirement Planner, for example, takes about 30 minutes.) But if you're really serious or worried or compulsive about one of these topics, well, it just may be worth your time to explore a bit.

And now let me sneak in one other snidbit. If you choose Planning⇨Professional Planning Resources, Quicken displays a window that provides general information about personal financial planners. Go ahead and look at this stuff. But, well, can I be blunt? I think you need to be very careful about getting personal financial advice from a so-called personal financial advisor. Some advisors are very skilled. For example, I think anyone who's got the personal finance specialist (PFS) designation is a good bet. These persons are certified public accountants, which means that they're either college or graduate business school graduates who have passed a grueling three-day test and have spent time working with a publicly licensed CPA in a sort of apprenticeship. And these persons have also met a bunch of other knowledge and experience requirements.

I also think a tax attorney who specializes in estate tax planning usually provides pretty good advice. I don't think, however, that someone who's gone through a company-sponsored training program or a night school correspondence program — even one that leads to a professional designation — is automatically good. Okay, some are. I grant you that. But I would urge you to be very cautious about taking advice from someone who earns a commission by selling you financial products and services. Be careful. It's a jungle out there.

Part III
Home Finances

The 5th Wave By Rich Tennant

"I'm not sure – I like the mutual funds with rotating dollar signs, although the dancing stocks and bonds look good too."

In this part . . .

Are you going to be using Quicken for your personal financial stuff? If so, you should know that this program offers more than just the checkbook-on-a-computer business that I describe in Part II. Quicken can help you manage and monitor such things as credit cards, home mortgages, and investments. If this stuff sounds interesting, keep reading.

Chapter 11

Credit Cards, Petty Cash, and PayPal

. .

. .

*Y*ou can use Quicken to track your credit cards and even the cash in your pocket in much the same way that you use Quicken to keep a checkbook. Tracking these items uses a nearly identical process — with a few wrinkles.

First, however, I need to discuss whether you should even bother.

Tracking a Credit Card

Of course, if you do carry a credit card balance — and about 50 percent of people do — you can set up a Quicken credit card account and use it for tracking credit card purchases. If you just need to keep track of how much you charge during the month (even if you're going to pay the balance in full), you must also set up a credit card account and use it. I should make one other point: In order to track not just what you charge (by using spending categories) but also *where* you charge it (by using the Payee field), you must set up a credit card account and use it.

I don't use Quicken to track my credit card purchases because I pay my credit card balance in full every month. (Don't feel bad if you don't — it's like a natural law that CPAs like me must do this.) Therefore, I don't have an open credit card balance to track. What's more, when I pay the monthly credit card bill, I can easily use the Split Transaction window to describe my spending categories: $3.53 on food for lunch, $52.64 for car repair, and $217.54 for books (a dangerous, and ultimately destructive, personal weakness). If you're in the same boat — meaning you use a credit card but you don't carry a balance — you don't need anything special to track your credit card purchases, and, of course, you don't need to use Quicken to tell you your account balance because it's always zeroed out at the end of the month.

How to Set Up a Credit Card Account

If you want to track credit card spending and balances with Quicken, you must set up a special credit card account. (In comparison, you use bank accounts to track other things, such as the money that flows into and out of a checking account.)

Adding a credit card account

To set up a credit card account, you follow roughly the same steps as you do to set up a bank account. Here's what you do:

1. **Choose Tools➪Account List.**

 Quicken displays the Account List window, shown in Figure 11-1.

2. **Click the Add Account button.**

 Quicken displays the Quicken Account Setup dialog box, which you've seen about a thousand times before. As you may remember, what you need to do is enter the name of the credit card company into the text box that asks you for the name of your financial institution, at which point Quicken asks you to select the financial institution from its list — or just use the name you entered, as shown in Figure 11-2. You click Next to display the next Quicken Account Setup dialog box.

Figure 11-1:
The
Account List
window.

Figure 11-2:
The Quicken
Account
Setup dialog
box.

3. Tell Quicken you're setting up a credit card account.

Select the Credit Card option button when Quicken asks what type of account you want to set up (see Figure 11-3). Then, click Next to display the fourth Quicken Account Setup dialog box (not shown as a figure because it's really boring).

Figure 11-3:
The third Quicken Account Setup dialog box asks what type of account you want to set up.

4. Name the account, then click Next.

Why not? Move the cursor to the Name This Account text box and type a name. After you click Next, Quicken displays the fifth Quicken Account Setup dialog box, shown in Figure 11-4.

Figure 11-4:
The fifth Quicken Account Setup dialog box.

5. Enter the date on which you will start keeping records for the credit card account.

You should probably choose the date of your last statement, as Quicken suggests. Move the cursor to the Statement Date text box and type the date in *MM/DD/YY* format. June 6, 2007, for example, should be entered as **6/6/7**.

6. Enter the balance you owed at the end of the last credit card billing period after making your payment. Then click Next.

Move the cursor to the Ending Balance text box and type the balance value by using the number keys. After you click Next, Quicken displays the sixth Quicken Account setup dialog box, shown in Figure 11-5.

Figure 11-5:
The sixth
Quicken
Account
Setup dialog
box.

Quicken Account Setup

If you want, enter the credit limit for this account.

▶ Credit Limit, if Applicable:

| 5000 | 📅 (Optional) |

• If you enter your credit limit, Quicken displays your remaining credit in the account register.

(?) Cancel Back Done

7. [Optional] Type in the amount of your credit limit.

If you want, indicate the amount of your credit card limit by moving the cursor to the Credit Limit, If Applicable text box and then typing whatever number the credit card company has arbitrarily decided is a reasonable balance for you to shoulder.

8. Click Done.

Quicken may display a message that urges you to sign up for your credit card company's online banking services. For now, ignore this. (If you later want to sign up, just tell your bank, and it'll help you get all set up.) Just click Done again. Quicken finally gets the message and displays the new account's register.

Selecting a credit card account so that you can use it

To tell Quicken that you want to work with an account, you use the Account List window — the same window you saw in Figure 11-1. To get to the Account List window again, choose Tools⊅Account List and then select the new credit card account.

You can also get to the credit card account from the Cash Flow Center. Just click the Cash Flow Center button, and then click the credit card account's button.

After you select the account you want, Quicken displays the register for that account so that you can begin recording transactions (which I describe in the next section).

How to Enter Credit Card Transactions

After you select a credit card account, Quicken displays a special version of the register, as shown in Figure 11-6.

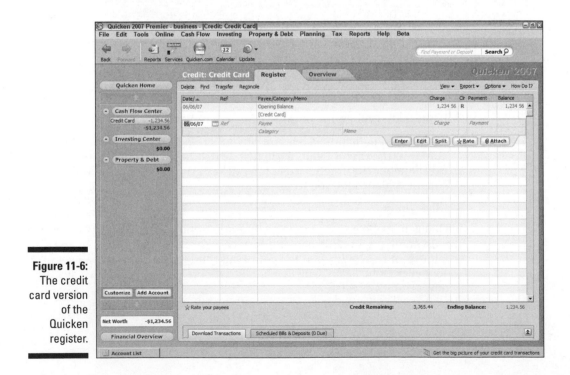

Figure 11-6:
The credit card version of the Quicken register.

Touring the credit card register

The credit card register works like the regular register that you use for a bank account. You enter transactions into the rows of the register. After you record a charge, Quicken updates the credit card balance and the remaining credit limit (if you entered the optional credit limit information when you set up the account).

You can use the same techniques and commands as you do for your regular ol' bank account register. I talk about these in earlier chapters, so I won't regurgitate those discussions here.

Recording a credit card charge

Recording a credit card charge is similar to recording a check or bank account withdrawal. For the sake of illustration, suppose that you charge $30.57 for dinner at your favorite Mexican restaurant. Here's how you record this charge:

1. **Enter the charge date.**

 Move the cursor to the Date field (if it isn't already there) and type the date using the *MM/DD* format. For example, enter June 6, 2007, as **6/6**. You usually don't have to type the year because Quicken retrieves the current year number from the little clock inside your computer. Or, if you want, get crazy — click the box that remotely resembles a calendar at the end of the field, and Quicken displays a pop-up calendar (see Chapter 4 for more information) from which you can select the appropriate month and day.

 Don't bother with the Ref field. Quicken supplies it so that you can record the credit card reference number — a bit of data that's usually about 20 characters long. You, my friend, have better things to do with your time, however. So just skip the field.

2. **Record the name of the business you paid with a credit card.**

 Move the cursor to the Payee field and type the name of the person or business you paid. If the restaurant is Florencia's Cantina, for example, type **Florencia's Cantina** into the Payee field.

3. **Enter the charge amount.**

 Move the cursor to the Charge field and type the total charge amount — **30.57** in this example. Don't type a dollar sign, but do type the period to indicate the decimal place and cents.

4. Enter the category.

Move the cursor to the Category field, open the drop-down list box, and select the appropriate category. You may categorize a restaurant charge as Dining, for example.

5. [Optional] Enter a memo description.

Move the cursor to the Memo field and type the specific reason you're charging the item, such as a special date with your spouse or an important business meeting.

6. Record the charge and click the Enter button.

Quicken beeps and then calculates both the new credit card balance and the remaining credit limit. Quicken then moves the cursor to the next slot in the register.

Figure 11-7 shows the charge at Florencia's. Good food and reasonable prices — you can't ask for much more than that.

Figure 11-7:
The charge at Florencia's Cantina.

Changing charges you've already entered

Use the arrow keys or click the mouse to highlight the charge that you want to change. Use Tab and Shift+Tab or the mouse to move the cursor to the field that contains the misinformation you want to fix. You can then fix the entry and record the transaction by clicking the Enter button. That's easy enough, isn't it?

Paying credit card bills

If you're tracking the credit card account balance with a credit card account like the one I'm describing here, Quicken provides two ways for you to pay a credit card bill.

Note: If you're not using a credit card account in Quicken, you record the check you send to pay a credit card bill in the same way you record any other check. And that means you don't have to read anything I'm about to say. Shoot, you shouldn't even be reading this chapter

A most bodacious way to pay a credit card bill

This method is pretty simple, so don't blink your eyes because you may miss the action.

Look at your credit card statement. Decide how much you want to pay. Select the bank account on which you'll write the check. Then write the check and record it in the bank account register — but as a transfer to the credit card account.

You're done. If you have questions, take a peek at the selected check transaction shown in Figure 11-8. It pays $30.57 of the credit card balance. The only trick — if you want to call it that — is that the credit card account is specified as the account to which the money is transferred. (You can see the other account by right-clicking the transaction and selecting Go To Transfer, or you can click the other account's QuickTab, of course.)

If you could look at the credit card account register now — of course, you can't because you're not sitting in front of my computer — you would see that this check reduces the credit card balance by $30.57.

Figure 11-8:
A check
transaction
that pays a
credit card
balance.

A less bodacious way to pay a credit card bill

You can also tell Quicken that you want to pay some portion of the credit card bill as part of reconciling the credit card's account balance. What will happen is that after you reconcile the credit card account, Quicken will (or may) ask whether you want to make a payment. If you say you do, Quicken prompts you to describe the payment.

I think that this method is slightly more difficult. But if you want to reconcile your credit card account, think about using this second method. If you're reconciling a credit card statement and paying some portion of the credit card balance at the same time, you may find this method more convenient. Who knows?

I describe how to reconcile a credit card account in the very next section.

Reconciling That Crazy Account

You know that trick in which you compare your checking account records with your bank's records of your checking account? The one in which you calculate the difference between what you think is your account balance and

what the bank thinks is your balance? And this difference is supposed to equal the total of the transactions floating around out there in the system? You can use this same trick on your credit card account.

To reconcile a credit card account, first get your credit card statement. Next, display the credit card account in a register window.

What the nasty credit card company says

To tell Quicken what that nasty credit card company says, follow these steps and put on some music if you can't seem to get the rhythm thing right:

1. **Click the Reconcile button on the register window.**

 Quicken displays the Statement Summary: Credit Card dialog box, shown in Figure 11-9.

Figure 11-9:
The
Statement
Summary:
Credit Card
dialog box.

(dialog box image)

Statement Summary: Credit Card

The last statement ending date: N/A

1. Enter the following from your statement.

Charges, Cash Advances: 30.57
(other than finance charges)

Payments, Credits: 30.57

Ending Balance: 1,294.55

New Statement Ending Date: 06/06/07

2. Enter and categorize your interest charges, if any.

Finance Charges: 50 Date: 06/06/07

Category: Interest Exp

OK Cancel Help

2. **Enter the charges and cash advances that your statement shows.**

 Move the cursor to the Charges, Cash Advances text box and then type the number.

3. **Enter the payment and credits that your statement shows.**

 You know the drill: Move the cursor to the Payments, Credits text box and type the number.

4. **Enter the new balance shown on the credit card statement.**

 Now I bet this is a surprise. Go ahead and type the figure in the Ending Balance text box — even if you just can't believe you charged that much.

5. **Enter the ending statement date.**

 I don't know why Quicken is now collecting this piece of information. For more than ten years, Quicken has been able to reconcile your credit card account (and any other account) without this snidbit of data.

6. **Enter the monthly interest charge by using the Finance Charges text box.**

 Pause for a moment of silence here if this topic makes you sad, sad, sad.

7. **Assign the monthly interest to the appropriate spending category, such as Interest Exp.**

 Move the cursor to the Category text box and type the category name. (Are you getting bored yet? I know: move and type . . . move and type . . . all I ever seem to say is "move and type.") Remember that you can click the little down arrow at the end of the text box to see a list of categories to select from.

8. **Click OK.**

 Quicken displays the Statement Summary: Credit Card window (see Figure 11-10). Use this window to tell Quicken which credit card charges and payments appear on your statement. (This step is akin to looking at a bank statement and noting which checks and deposits have cleared the bank.)

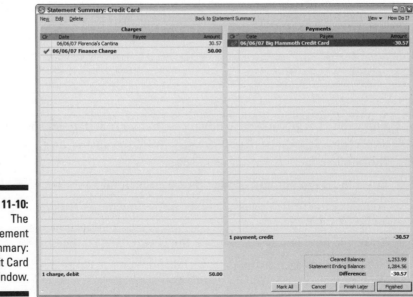

Figure 11-10:
The Statement Summary: Credit Card window.

Ouch! Did I really spend that much?

After you give Quicken an overview of your credit card situation, you can note which charges have cleared and which charges have not.

If you're comfortable whipping through a bank reconciliation, you can probably do this reconciliation with your eyes closed. If you need some help, leave your eyes open so that you can read these steps:

1. **Find the first charge listed on the credit card statement.**

2. **Mark the charge as cleared.**

 Charges are listed in the left list box. If you charged a bunch of stuff, scroll through the transactions listed in the Charges window until you find the charge. After you see a charge that appears on your credit card statement, click it. Or select the charge by using the arrow keys and then press the spacebar. Quicken adds the check mark symbol in front of the list entry in the Clr column to mark this charge as cleared and then updates the cleared statement balance.

3. **Enter any missing charges.**

 If you can't find a charge, you probably didn't enter it in the Quicken register yet. Open the credit card account register by clicking its tab and then enter the charge into the register in the usual way — except enter a c (the letter c) into the Clr column by clicking the Clr field. By doing so, you identify the charge as one that's already cleared. After you finish, click the Back To Statement Summary button to return to the Statement Summary: Credit Card window.

4. **Repeat Steps 1, 2, and 3 for charges listed on the credit card statement.**

 Or until you're blue in the face.

5. **Find the first payment or credit listed on the credit card statement.**

 Any payments and credits appear in the right list box.

6. **Mark the payment or credit as cleared.**

 Scroll through the transactions listed on the Payments window until you find the first payment or credit and then click it. Or select the credit and then press the spacebar. Quicken adds the check mark symbol in front of the list entry to mark the payment or credit as cleared and then updates the cleared statement balance.

7. **Enter any missing payments or credits.**

 If you can't find the payment or credit — you probably know what I'm going to say — it means you haven't entered it into the Quicken register

yet. Open the credit card account register by clicking its tab and then enter the payment or credit into the register in the usual way, but put a **c** in the Clr column. When you finish, click the Return To Reconcile button to return to the Statement Summary: Credit Card window.

8. **Repeat Steps 5, 6, and 7 for payments or credits listed on the credit card statement.**

If you record a transaction wrong, do this

As you're looking through the credit card statement, you may discover that you incorrectly recorded a transaction. If this happens, display the credit card register so that you can make the necessary fixes.

Oh, that explains the difference

After you mark all the cleared charges and payments, the difference between the cleared balance for the credit card and the statement's ending balance should be zero.

Figure 11-11 shows how this looks. By the way, reconciling with fictitious data is darned easy.

Figure 11-11:
When the difference between the cleared balance and the statement is zero, the reconciliation is complete.

If you're ready to finish

If the difference does equal zero, you're cool. You're golden. You're done. (Sort of makes you sound like fried chicken, doesn't it?)

All you need to do is click Finished to tell Quicken that you're done. Quicken asks you whether you want to make a credit card payment. Jump ahead to the "Paying the bill as part of the reconciliation" section for help doing just that.

If the difference doesn't equal zero, you have a problem. If you clicked Finished in spite of the problem, Quicken displays a message that has some cursory explanation as to why your account doesn't balance. This message also tells you that you can force the two amounts to agree by pressing Enter.

Forcing the two amounts to agree isn't a very good idea, though. To make the balances agree, Quicken adds a cleared transaction equal to the difference. (Quicken asks for a category if you choose the adjustment route.)

Despite the ease of making adjustments, you should still correct the error responsible for the difference.

Chapter 8 provides some ideas for trying to figure out why a bank account that should balance doesn't. You can apply the same list of tips to credit card reconciliations if you're in a bad way.

If you want to postpone the inevitable

You can postpone reconciling the account by clicking the Finish Later button. When you click this button, you abandon your reconciliation work. Transactions that you mark as cleared still show the c in the Clr text box. You still have an inexplicable difference between the credit card statement and your register. Even so, postponing a reconciliation is usually better than forcing the cleared balance to equal the credit card statement balance. By postponing a reconciliation, you can hopefully find the problem or problems and fix them. Then you can restart the reconciliation and finish your work. (You restart a credit card reconciliation in the same way that you originally start one.)

When you finish, Quicken redisplays the Register tab. You may notice that, as you mark credit card transactions as cleared, Quicken puts a c in the Clr column of the credit card register. When you finish reconciling the credit card account, Quicken changes all these cs to Rs. None of what Quicken does here is magical. Quicken just makes this change to identify the transactions that have already been through the reconciliation process. (The c shows that a transaction has been marked as cleared. The R shows that a transaction has been reconciled.)

Paying the bill as part of the reconciliation

After you finish reconciling the credit card account, Quicken does two things. First, if some of the stuff in the credit card register doesn't agree with the credit card statement, Quicken displays a message box to alert you to these, er, discrepancies and then suggests you let Quicken bring your records into agreement with the statement (see Figure 11-12). To synchronize your records with the credit card statement, verify that Quicken is using a reasonable expense category to "categorize" the discrepancy and then click Adjust.

Figure 11-12:
The Adjusting Register To Agree With Statement dialog box.

Quicken also does a second thing after you finish reconciling a credit card account. Quicken asks whether you want to pay the bill. Figure 11-13 shows the Make Credit Card Payment dialog box, which is the tool that Quicken uses to collect the necessary data. You simply identify the bank account on which you want to write the check and indicate whether you'll use a printed check or a handwritten check. Quicken then records a check that pays the credit card balance into the register. You can edit, print, and do whatever else you want to do with this check in the usual way.

Figure 11-13:
The Make Credit Card Payment dialog box.

The Online Banking Hoopla

As I briefly mention in Chapter 6, Quicken supports online banking. If you have your credit card with a credit card company — probably a bank — that is set up to handle Quicken online banking, you can grab your credit card statement directly from the credit card company. If you have a checking account at the bank that issued the credit card, you can also pay your credit card bill simply by transferring money from your checking account to your credit card. (This feature is actually pretty slick, I have to say.)

The big hoopla concerning this feature — at least as it relates to credit cards — is that you don't have to enter the credit card transactions into a register. Rather, you retrieve them by using an Internet connection.

Should you even bother?

Is the online-banking-with-a-credit-card-thing a feature that you should look into? Does it really save you time? Is it a good deal? Inquiring minds want to know, so I'll tell you what I think. (I should point out that what I'm about to say next is just my humble opinion.)

I think that online banking in general is well worth the fee you probably have to pay for the service when you consider the time savings. You'll probably pay only a few dollars a month. (What you pay depends on the bank issuing the credit card.)

Something bothers me about the whole deal, however: You really just receive an electronic version of your statement, which means — at least from my perspective — that you're more likely not to see erroneous transactions. And reconciling your bank statement against, well, your bank statement isn't going to make a whole heck of a lot of sense. (Golly, gee, Batman, the charge to Edna's Pet School appears on both statements, too!)

How to use Online Account Access with your credit card

Okay, so you've listened to my side of the story, but you still want to use the Quicken Online Account Access feature with your credit card — and your bank is one that provides this service. "What next?" you're wondering.

Here's the answer: You set up online credit card accounts the same way you set up online bank accounts. *Note:* For more information about the Quicken Online Account Access feature, see Chapter 6.

Petty Cash and Mad Money

You can track petty cash in your business as well as the petty cash in your wallet by using a special Quicken cash account. To track the cash, you must set up a cash account and then enter the increases and decreases into the cash account's register. Sure, this stuff isn't exactly rocket science, but shoot, I thought I'd just quickly go over it to show you how easy it really is. Okay?

Adding a cash account

To set up a cash account, you follow roughly the same steps as you do for setting up a bank account. Because you've probably already set up a bank account, you can move quickly through the following steps to set up a cash account:

1. **Display the Account List window.**

 Choose the Tools⇨Account List command. Quicken displays the Account List window (refer to Figure 11-1). You remember this puppy.

2. **Click the Add Account button to set up a new account.**

 Quicken, of course, is no fool, and so it displays the Quicken Account Setup dialog box.

3. **Set up a cash account.**

 You can guess how to do this, can't you? You simply step through Quicken's questions about the account you want to set up. You need to specify, for example, that this account isn't kept at some financial institution and that it's a cash account. You need to give the account a name, such as *pocket money*. And you need to provide a starting balance value using the faithful, the familiar Quicken Account Setup dialog box, shown in Figure 11-14.

Figure 11-14:
The final Quicken Account Setup dialog box used for cash accounts.

4. **Click Done.**

 When you finish describing the cash account, click Done. Quicken displays the new cash account in a register window.

Tracking cash inflows and outflows

After you set up a cash account, you can use it to track the cash you receive and spend in the same way that you track the deposits and checks for a bank account.

To record your cash inflows and outflows, use the QuickTab for the account, which should appear under the Cash Flow Center button. Figure 11-15 shows the cash account version of the register. Until you start entering transactions, only the first opening balance transaction shows.

Figure 11-15:
The cash account version of the register.

To record the amount of money you spend, fill in the Date, Payee, and Spend fields. To record the amount of money you receive, fill in the Date, Payee, and Receive fields. To track the reasons that you're receiving and spending the cash, use the Memo and Category fields.

Recording checks you cash instead of deposit

By the way, you don't necessarily need to set up a cash account if you like to spend cash (rather than, say, write checks or charge on a credit card). If you just cash a check and you do have a bank account set up, you can record the transaction in another way that may be simpler: Just use the Split Transaction window to show both the income category (Salary, for example, for an individual) and how you're going to use the money.

For example, if you cash a $1,000 check and you plan to use the $1,000 for spending money, you may show a positive $1,000 in the Salary category and a minus $1,000 in the Entertainment spending category. Figure 11-16 shows this trick.

Figure 11-16:
A zero-amount transaction is one handy trick.

Note that the transaction shown in Figure 11-16 produces a transaction that equals zero. This is correct. Cashing a check that you never deposited doesn't affect your checking account balance. But by filling out the Split Transaction window as shown in Figure 11-16, you do end up recording both the $1,000 of income and the $1,000 of expense.

Don't worry. I won't ask why you're carrying around $1,000 in cash.

Updating cash balances

You can update a register's cash balance to reflect what you actually have in petty cash, your wallet, under the mattress, in the cookie jar, or wherever else you keep your cash by taking the following steps:

1. **Display the cash account register.**

2. **Click the Update Balance button.**

 Quicken displays the Update Account Balance: Cash Account dialog box, shown in Figure 11-17.

Figure 11-17: The Update Account Balance: Cash Account dialog box.

3. **Enter the actual cash balance in the Update Balance To text box.**

4. **Enter a date in the Adjustment Date text box.**

5. **Choose the category that you want to update in the Category For Adjustment drop-down list box.**

 After you click the arrow to the right of the drop-down list box, you get a list of all the categories that you have set up.

6. **After you finish, click OK.**

 Quicken updates the cash account's balance.

And that, my friend, is that.

PayPal Can Be Quicken's Friend

One final point before we end this discussion.

If you use PayPal, you can and should use Quicken to track the money flowing into and out of your PayPal account. Fortunately, tracking a PayPal account with Quicken is pretty dang easy.

To track PayPal using Quicken, you just want to remember these three points:

- ✔ A PayPal account is really just another bank account — albeit a special sort of bank account. Accordingly, you want to set up a Quicken PayPal account in the same way that you set up any other Quicken bank account. (Refer to Chapter 2 for additional information about setting up a bank account.)

- ✔ If you use your credit card to pay money into the PayPal account, you're actually transferring money from your credit card account to your PayPal account. To record this transfer, you record a credit card charge into your credit card register (similar to the charge made to Florencia's Cantina shown in Figure 11-7). However, rather than use a Quicken category, you specify the PayPal account.

- ✔ You should reconcile your PayPal account just like any other bank account or credit card account. During this reconciliation, be sure to record any PayPal charges.

And one final snidbit for people who really want to push the envelope: PayPal will allow you to download your transaction history into a .QIF file, which can then be imported into Quicken. You may want to refer to Quicken's and PayPal's online help for more information.

Chapter 12

Other People's Money

∙ ∙

In This Chapter

▶ Tracking loans, mortgages, and other debts

▶ Setting up liability accounts

▶ Calculating the principal and interest portions of a payment

▶ Recording loan payments

▶ Handling mortgage escrow accounts

▶ Adjusting principal and interest breakdowns

▶ Scheduling automatic loan payments

∙ ∙

A popular, financial self-help writer thinks that one of the secrets to financial success is using other people's money: the bank's, the mortgage company's, the credit people's, your brother-in-law's. . . . You get the idea.

Me? I'm not so sure that using other people's money is the key to financial success. Borrowing other people's money can turn into a nightmare.

Quicken can help you here. No, the folks at Intuit won't make your loan payments for you. But in a way, they do something even better: They provide you with a tool to monitor the money you owe other people and the costs of your debts.

Should You Bother to Track Your Debts?

I think that tracking your debts — car loans, mortgages, student loans, and so on — is a good idea when lenders fail to tell you the amount that you're paying in annual interest or the amount you owe after each and every payment.

If your lenders are doing a good job at keeping you informed, I don't think that using Quicken for this purpose makes much sense. Heck, it's their money. They can do the work, right?

Let me make one more observation. If lenders have half a clue, they send you a United States 1098 tax form at the end of every year. The number shown on that form equals your tax deduction if the interest stems from a mortgage, business, or investment loan. Note that personal interest expenses aren't deductible anymore, so you shouldn't track them unless you really want to be mean to yourself.

How Do You Get Started?

To track other people's money with Quicken, you must set up a *liability account.* Setting up one of these babies is easy. Just remember that you must set up a liability account for every loan or debt you want to track: one account for your mortgage, another for your car loan, still another for your student loan, and so on.

Setting up a liability account for an amortized loan

An *amortized loan* is one on which you make regular, equal-sized payments. Over time, the principal portion of each payment pays off, or *amortizes,* the loan principal. If you borrowed money to purchase a house, a car, a Winnebago, or anything else that's really expensive and that you pay off over several years, chances are that your loan is of the amortizing variety.

Setting up a loan account requires a couple of dozen steps. But none of the steps is difficult. And none takes that much time to complete. As long as you have your loan information handy — the loan amount, interest rate, balance, and so on — setting up this type of account is a snap.

Here's the recipe for setting up a liability account:

1. **Click the Property & Debt button.**

 Quicken displays the Property & Debt Center window.

2. **Click the Add Loan button in the Property & Debt Center window.**

 Quicken displays the Loan Setup dialog box. Click the Summary tab to see the dialog box exactly as it's shown here (see Figure 12-1).

Figure 12-1:
The Loan
Setup dialog
box.

3. **Provide some basic background information. Then click Next.**

Use the Loan Type option buttons to specify whether you're borrowing money or lending money. Use the New Account box to name the new loan account something clever like *mortgage* or *car loan*. And use the Have Any Payments Been Made? option buttons to indicate, well, whether you've started making payments yet. After you click Next, Quicken displays another set of boxes and buttons, as shown in Figure 12-2.

Figure 12-2:
Another
Loan Setup
dialog box.

4. **Enter the date that you borrowed the money in the Opening Date text box, or if your loan has a grace period (like a student loan), enter the date when your loan enters the repayment period.**

Quicken needs to know this date so that it can calculate the interest the loan started to accrue when you borrowed the money. The program suggests the current system date as the Opening Date, but this is probably wrong.

5. **Enter the original loan balance.**

 Enter the original loan amount into the Original Balance text box. You can get this amount, if you're unsure, from the original loan documents.

6. **Enter the loan term in years in the Original Length text box.**

 If you set up a 30-year mortgage, for example, type **30**. You may have to perform one tiny trick when entering this figure: If you set up a loan that includes a balloon payment, enter the number of years over which the loan will be fully paid — not the number of years used for calculating the loan payment. For example, loan payments may be calculated based on a 30-year term, but the loan may require a balloon payment at the end of seven years. In this case, type **7** in the Original Length text box.

7. **Indicate how often the bank calculates loan interest.**

 Use the Compounding Period box to specify how often the bank calculates interest on the loan. The interest-compounding period usually equals the payment period.

8. **Describe how often you make a loan payment by using the Payment Period options.**

 If you make regular monthly payments, for example, select the Standard Period option button and then open the Standard Period drop-down list box and select Monthly. If you can't find an entry in the Standard Period drop-down list box that describes how often you make payments, select the Other Period option button and then type the number of payments you make each year in the Payments Per Year text box.

9. **Click Next.**

 Quicken displays another set of boxes and buttons in the Summary tab (as shown in Figure 12-3).

10. **Describe the balloon payment — if you have one.**

 The balloon payment option buttons and boxes let you alert Quicken to any balloon payment you must make in addition to the last regular loan payment. If the loan doesn't have a balloon payment, ignore this stuff and make sure that the No Balloon Payment option is selected.

 If the loan does have a balloon, select the Amortized Length option button; then use the Amortized Length text box and drop-down list box to specify the number of years or months (or whatever) the loan is amortized over. If you know that you have a loan payment (and know the loan payment amount) but don't know what the amount is or when it occurs, select the Balloon Information's Calculate option button.

Figure 12-3:
Some more
buttons and
boxes you
can use to
describe the
amortized
loan.

11. Enter the Current Balance if you've made any payments.

If you indicated that you have already made payments on the loan, specify how much you still owe on the loan after making the last payment by using the Current Balance text box. If you don't know the current balance, call the lender and ask for it. If you haven't made any payments yet, skip to Step 12. You know the drill by now. Just move the cursor to the text box and pound a few number keys.

12. Enter the date as of which the current balance is, well, current.

Use the As Of field to indicate the date for which you've entered the current balance. All the standard date entry and date-editing tricks apply to this text box. You can press the + and – keys, for example, to move the date ahead and back by one day. And you can click that icon at the right end of the As Of text box to display a pop-up calendar.

13. Specify the interest rate.

Enter the loan's interest rate into the Interest Rate text box in the Payment section of this window. The loan interest rate, by the way, isn't the same thing as the *APR,* or annual percentage rate. You want to enter the actual interest rate used to calculate your payments. Enter the interest rate as a decimal amount. For example, don't type 7⅝, type **7.625**. You should be able to get this rate from the lender or the prospective lender.

14. Describe the payment in more detail — if necessary.

If you've entered all the loan information that Quicken has requested in the preceding steps, you can just select the Payment's Calculate option button. Quicken then calculates the loan payment by using the loan balance, term, balloon payment information, and interest rate you've already entered. If you haven't entered all this information — say you left out the balloon payment information because you don't know what

it is — select the Payment Amount (P+I) option button and then enter the loan principal and interest amount into the Payment Amount (P+I) text box. If necessary, edit the next payment date in the Due On drop-down list box.

15. Click Done.

If you asked Quicken to calculate anything for you, a dialog box pops up telling you that Quicken did so. Click OK. Make sure that the Quicken calculations make sense and then click Done again. Quicken displays the Set Up Loan Payment dialog box (shown in Figure 12-4).

Figure 12-4:
The Set Up Loan Payment dialog box.

16. Verify the principal and interest payment calculated by the program.

If it's wrong, you can keep going, but let me point out a minor yet annoying problem. You probably entered one of the loan calculation inputs incorrectly, such as the loan balance, the loan term, or the interest rate. Fortunately, these errors are only a minor bummer. Later in this chapter (in the "Fixing loan stuff" section), I describe how to restart.

17. [Optional] Indicate any amounts you pay besides principal and interest.

Click the Edit button. Quicken displays the Split Transaction dialog box (see Figure 12-5), which you can use to describe any additional amounts the lender requires you to pay. In the case of a mortgage, for example, you may be required to pay property taxes or private mortgage insurance. After you enter the information and click OK, Quicken calculates the full payment and redisplays the Set Up Loan Payment dialog box (refer to Figure 12-4).

18. **Indicate how you make payments in the Type drop-down list box.**

Select one of the payment transaction types listed in the Type drop-down list box. *Payment* means that you hand-write checks; *Print Check* means that you print checks by using Quicken; and *Online Pmt* means that you use Quicken Online Banking to make electronic payments.

If you print checks by using Quicken and want to put the payee's address on the check, click the Address button in the Set Up Loan Payment dialog box. Quicken displays a dialog box that you can use to input the payee's address, as shown in Figure 12-6. When you finish providing name and address information, click OK and go get another cup of coffee. When you come back, Quicken will have redisplayed the Set Up Loan Payment dialog box.

19. Type the lender's name in the Payee text box.

The payee is just the name of the person or business that loaned you the money.

20. [Optional] Type a memo description.

Does the lender always get mixed up when you send the check? Stick the loan account number in the check's Memo text box. I refrain from using this text box to comment on the fairness of the bank's interest rate, to mock the intelligence of the loan payment processors, or to perform other emotionally gratifying, but generally unproductive, acts.

21. Type the date of your next loan payment in the Next Payment Date text box.

22. Enter the interest category.

Open the Category For Interest drop-down list and select the appropriate category.

Quicken lets you *schedule* (have Quicken automatically enter) or *memorize* (just have Quicken remind you to enter) loan payments and electronic payments. I assume that you don't want to be doing this kind of stuff — at least not yet. If I'm assuming incorrectly, click the Payment Method button. Then fill out the dialog box that appears. It's not all that difficult. If you're still confused, I explain how you can use the Calendar to schedule loan payments later in this chapter.

23. With the Set Up Loan Payment dialog box displayed, click OK.

Quicken removes the Set Up Loan Payment dialog box and asks whether any asset is associated with the loan. If you want to associate an asset with your loan, Quicken walks you through the steps for setting up an asset account. But you know what? Don't worry about setting up an asset account. It actually isn't worth it. Just click No. Quicken displays the Property & Debt Center. You probably want to see the new liability you've set up in its own register, so click the new account. Quicken displays the register, as shown in Figure 12-7.

By the way, I want to apologize to you for describing a 23-step process. I couldn't do anything about it, but I feel bad anyway.

Fixing loan stuff

Nobody's perfect, right? You may have made a tiny little mistake in setting up either the loan or the loan payment. This mistake doesn't need to be a major financial or personal crisis, however. Just use the View Loans window to identify the incorrectly described loan and then make your corrections, as shown in Figure 12-8. To display the View Loans window, just choose Property & Debt⇨Loans.

Figure 12-7:
The Liability:
Mortgage
register.

Figure 12-8:
The View
Loans
window.

If you have multiple loans set up, click the Choose Loan (x) button and select
the loan you want to change from the drop-down list that appears. Quicken
gives you all the dirt on the selected loan in the View Loans window.

Hey, can I mention one other thing about the View Loans window? See those two tabs labeled Payment Schedule and Payment Graph? You can probably guess what they do, but if you click the Payment Schedule tab, an amortization schedule shows the interest and principal portions of each loan payment. If you click the Payment Graph tab, Quicken displays a line chart that shows how you pay off the loan balance over time. You may want to take a minute and experiment with these two tabs. They're pretty neat.

Changing loan or loan payment information

If you want to change something about the loan, click the Edit Loan button. Quicken displays the Edit Loan dialog box. It works like the Loan Setup dialog boxes in Figures 12-1 and 12-2. Make the changes and click OK.

To change something about the payment, click the Edit Payment button. Quicken displays the Edit Loan Payment dialog box. Make your changes and click OK.

Working with adjustable rate loans

Before I wrap up this discussion, let me mention a couple other things. If you have a variable rate loan, you can click the Rate Changes button to display the Loan Rate Changes dialog box (shown in Figure 12-9). This dialog box has a very simple purpose: It lists the interest rates you entered for a loan and the dates these interest rates were used in loan calculations.

Figure 12-9:
The Loan
Rate
Changes
dialog box.

Loan Rate Changes			
New Edit Delete		Print Close How Do I?	
Date	**Rate**	**Principal and Interest**	
07/06...	7.0%		599.55

If you want to record new interest rates — because you have a variable rate loan and the interest rate changes, for example — follow these steps in the Loan Rate Changes dialog box:

1. **Indicate that you want to record a new interest rate.**

 Click the New button in the Loan Rate Changes dialog box or right-click in the dialog box and choose New from the shortcut menu that appears. Quicken displays the Insert An Interest Rate Change dialog box, shown in Figure 12-10.

Figure 12-10:
Changing a
loan's
interest
rate.

Insert an Interest Rate Change

Effective Date:	06/06/07	OK
Interest Rate:	6%	Cancel
Regular Payment:	599.55	Help

2. **Provide the effective date of the interest rate change.**

 Use the Effective Date text box to indicate when the new interest rate becomes effective. You can either type in a date or open the drop-down list box and select a date from the calendar.

3. **Give the new interest rate.**

 Type the new interest rate in the Interest Rate text box. When you move the selection cursor to a new box, Quicken refigures the loan payment and sticks the new loan payment figure in the Regular Payment text box.

4. **Click OK.**

Removing and adding loans

You can delete (remove) and add loans by using the Loan Summary tab of the View Loans window (refer to Figure 12-8).

Delete a loan that you no longer need or shouldn't have added in the first place by clicking the Choose Loan (x) button and selecting the loan account. Then click the Delete button. Quicken then warns you that you're about to delete your loan and asks you whether you'd like to save the account for your records. Saving the account keeps the account available in your Accounts window but eliminates it from your View Loans window. You can hide the saved account later if you'd like it to disappear from your Accounts window. (To do so, choose Tools⇨Account List, click the Manage Accounts tab when Quicken displays the Account List window, and then check the Hide In Quicken check box for the account.)

You can add loans from the View Loans window, too (refer to Figure 12-8). To do so, click the View Loans window's New button. Quicken displays the Loan

Setup dialog box and walks you through the sequence of steps that I describe earlier in the "Setting up a liability account for an amortized loan" section to set up the loan. For example, you fill out both the Loan Setup dialog box (refer to Figures 12-1 and 12-2) and the Set Up Loan Payment dialog box (refer to Figure 12-4).

Delivering a Pound of Flesh (Also Known as Making a Payment)

After you set up a liability account, you're ready to hand over a pound of your flesh — that is, make a payment. Before you say that this phrase is just some sort of populist bull-dweeble, I want to remind you that this metaphor comes from Shakespeare's *The Merchant of Venice,* in which a loan is guaranteed with a pound of human flesh. Ouch.

Recording the payment

After you set up the loan and the loan payment, you're ready to record the payment in (drumroll, please) the register.

I'm trying to make the old Quicken register more exciting for you because you're probably becoming pretty darn familiar with it. And familiarity, as they say, breeds contempt.

Anyway, complete the following steps to record a payment:

1. **Display the View Loans window by choosing Property & Debt⇨Loans.**

2. **Display the loan you want to pay.**

 To do so, click the Choose Loan (x) button at the top of the dialog box and select the loan from the drop-down list.

3. **Click the Make Payment button.**

 Quicken displays a message box that asks whether the payment you're making is a regular payment (one the lender expects) or an extra payment (perhaps to amortize the loan more quickly). After you select the payment type, Quicken displays either the Make Regular Payment or the Make Extra Payment dialog box. Figure 12-11 shows the Make Regular Payment dialog box; the Make Extra Payment dialog box looks almost exactly the same.

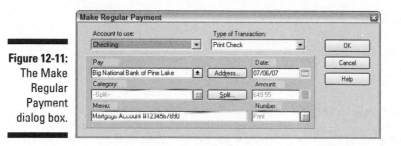

4. **Describe the loan payment.**

 I'm not going to give you the blow-by-blow account here. If you've gotten this far, you don't need my help. (Mostly, as you know, you just type stuff in boxes.)

5. **Click OK.**

 Quicken enters the loan payment in the liability register and bank account register. You're done.

Handling mortgage escrow accounts

I should talk about one minor mortgage record keeping annoyance — mortgage escrow accounts.

If you have a mortgage, you know the basic procedure. Although your mortgage payment may be $599.55 a month, your friendly mortgage company (while insisting that it trusts you completely) makes you pay an extra $50 a month for property taxes and other such things. In other words, even though you're paying only $599.55 a month in principal and interest, your monthly payment to the mortgage company is, according to this example, $649.55 ($599.55 + $50).

The mortgage company, as you probably know, saves this money for you in an escrow account or a set of escrow accounts. A couple of times a year, the mortgage company pays your property taxes, and a time or two a year, it pays your homeowner's insurance. If you have private mortgage insurance, it may pay this fee every month as well. And so it goes.

The question, then, is how do you treat this stuff? As with most things, you can take the easy way, which is rough, dirty, and unshaven, or the hard way, which is precise, sophisticated, and cumbersome.

You can choose whichever method you want. It's your life.

The rough, dirty, and unshaven method

Suppose that you do pay an extra $50 a month. You can treat this extra $50 as another expense category, such as Tax Property or Other Housing or Property Expenses. (I'm just making up these categories. If you can think of better ones, use your own.)

Nice. Easy. No fuss. These words and phrases pop into my head when I think about the rough, dirty, and unshaven method of mortgage escrow record keeping. Figure 12-12 shows a sample Split Transaction window filled out this way. If the Split Transaction window seems like too much fuss, mosey on over to Chapter 4 where I give you the rundown on using it.

Figure 12-12: A mortgage payment with an escrow account treated as an expense.

I use the rough, dirty, and unshaven method. Let me make a confession, though. This approach doesn't tell you how much moolah you have stashed away in your escrow accounts. It also doesn't tell you how much you really spend in the way of homeowner's insurance, what you're entitled to claim as a property tax deduction, or how much they're bleeding you for private mortgage insurance.

To get these figures, you have to peruse the monthly and annual mortgage account statements — that is, if you get them. Or you have to call the mortgage lender and rattle a cage or two.

Still, with all its shortcomings, I like the easy-to-use, rough, dirty, unshaven method.

The precise, sophisticated, and cumbersome approach

You say you can't live with the uncertainty, the stress, the not knowing? Then I have another approach just for you.

You can set up an *asset account* for each escrow account for which the mortgage company collects money.

You set up asset accounts as you set up a checking account. And, in fact, you should think of escrow accounts as, essentially, special checking accounts into which your lender deposits money collected from you so that it can pay your property taxes and insurance.

Because I explain this "setting up a checking account" process in Chapter 1, I'll just cover it quickly. You set up an asset account with its starting balance equal to the current escrow account balance. To do so, follow these steps:

1. **Choose Tools⇨Account List to display the Account List window.**

2. **Click the Add Account button to indicate that you want to create a new account.**

3. **As you step through the seemingly interminable account setup process, identify the account as an asset account and give it a name.**

4. **Tell Quicken how much money is in the account as of a specific date.**

 If you've set up an account or two in your time, this process should take you about 40 seconds.

After you set up your asset account and record its current balance, you're ready to cruise. Record payments in the escrow as account transfers whenever you record the actual loan payment.

You need to do one other thing. When you set up an escrow account, you must record the payments that the bank makes from your escrow account to the county assessor (for property taxes) and to the insurance company (for things such as homeowner's and private mortgage insurance). You don't know when these payments are really made, so watch your monthly mortgage account statements.

When the mortgage company disburses money from the escrow account to pay your first property tax assessment, for example, you need to record a decrease equal to the payment for property taxes and then categorize the transaction as a property tax expense. This process isn't tricky in terms of mechanics. The account increases after every loan payment and decreases after a disbursement.

Basically, the Asset Account register mirrors the Checking Account register. The only difference is that the Payment and Deposit fields in the latter are labeled Decrease and Increase in the former. To get to this account's register, click its QuickTab underneath the Property & Debt button.

This second approach doesn't seem like all that much work, does it? And if you use this approach, you can track escrow balances and escrow spending precisely. You can, for example, pull your property tax deduction right from Quicken. Jeepers, maybe I should try the sophisticated approach next year.

Your Principal-Interest Breakdown Won't Be Right

Not to bum you out, but your principal-interest breakdown will often be wrong. You may calculate interest expense as $544.55 when your bank calculates it as $544.56. A few pennies here, a few pennies there, and pretty soon your account balance and interest expense tallies are a few pennies off.

So you can't change the world

You can try calling the bank, telling whomever you talk to what a bozo he (or she) is, and then demanding that someone there correct your balance. (If this approach works for you, let me know.)

Or (and this method is really more practical) you can adjust your records to agree with the bank's records. Here's how:

1. **Display the register for the liability.**

 To get to this account's register, you just click its QuickTab underneath the Property & Debt button.

2. **Click the Update Balance button.**

 (Go ahead. Tap your keys very hard if you're angry that the bank won't adjust its records.) Quicken displays the Update Account Balance dialog box, as shown in Figure 12-13.

3. **Enter the correct account balance (that is, the one that the bank says is correct).**

 Type the correct figure in the Update Balance To text box. (The amount probably comes from the year-end or month-end loan statement.)

Figure 12-13:
The Update
Account
Balance:
Mortgage
dialog box.

> **Update Account Balance: Mortgage**
>
> This Account Last Updated: N/A
>
> 1. Enter the current balance for this account.
>
> Update Balance to: `99,900.50`
>
> Adjustment Date: `06/06/07`
>
> 2. Choose a category for the balance adjustment.
>
> Category for Adjustment: `Interest Exp`
>
> [OK] [Cancel] [Help]

4. **Enter the last day of the month or year for which you're making the adjustment.**

 Enter a transaction date in the Adjustment Date text box. (You must use a transaction date that sticks the adjustment transaction — which fixes the principal-interest split — into the right month or year.)

5. **Enter your interest expense category.**

 Type the correct category name in the Category For Adjustment text box. (To see a list of categories, open the drop-down list box.)

6. **Record the adjustment.**

7. **When the Update Account Balance dialog box correctly describes the needed adjustment, click OK.**

Think this adjustment business is kooky?

Does the whole adjustment transaction business make sense to you? At times, it can seem kind of backwards, so let me throw out a quick observation.

As you record loan payments, you split the loan payment between the interest expense category and a principal account transfer that reduces the liability. Here's what's tricky: When the liability gets reduced either too much or not enough, you must fix the liability balance *and* the principal-interest split.

Let me give you an example. Suppose that over the course of a year, you record $0.17 too little interest expense and, therefore, record $0.17 too much principal reduction, despite your best efforts to be accurate. You need to increase the liability account balance by $0.17 in this case, but you also need to increase the interest expense figure by $0.17. By entering the interest expense category in the Category For Adjustment field, Quicken does these adjustments for you. Pretty cool, huh?

Automatic Payments

Quicken has a couple of nifty features called Scheduled Transactions and the Calendar that can help you with automatic loan payments.

The Calendar and Scheduled Transactions features may be useful in other instances as well. For example, a business may use the Scheduled Transactions and Calendar features to schedule and plan employee payroll checks, tax returns, and deposits. But I think that they're both most useful in the case of a loan. So I talk about both of them here.

Scheduling a payment

If a payment occurs regularly—the payment might be for a loan or some other regular bill like your cable TV service–you can set it up as a scheduled payment. When you do so, Quicken automatically records the payment for you based on a schedule.

Follow these steps to set up such a scheduled transaction:

1. **Choose Cash Flow➪Calendar or press Ctrl+K.**

 Quicken displays the Calendar window, as shown in Figure 12-14. The figure shows a calendar for the current month and, optionally, a list of memorized payees.

 Note: If you can't see the list of transactions along the right edge of the Calendar window, choose Options➪Memorized Payees List.

2. **Display the first month for which you want to schedule the transaction.**

 Using the Prev Month and Next Month buttons, select the starting month for the scheduled transaction. You can also click the Go To Date button. If you do so, Quicken displays a dialog box that you can use to specify the precise date you want to schedule a payment for.

3. **Identify the scheduled transaction and date.**

 Select the transaction for which you want to create a schedule. In Figure 12-14, for example, you may want to schedule the payment to Movies Galore to fall on the 15th. To do so, select Movies Galore from the payee list by clicking it.

 Then drag Movies Galore to the 15th. When you release the mouse button, Quicken displays the Add Transaction dialog box (see Figure 12-15).

Figure 12-14:
The
Calendar
window.

4. **Identify the account from which the payment should be made.**

 Open the Account To Use drop-down list box and then select the appropriate account.

5. **Verify that the transaction type is Payment.**

 Open the Method drop-down list box and select Payment. (Of course, if you were setting up some other type of payment, you might choose something else, such as Printed Check.)

6. **Check the payment scheduling stuff.**

 Verify that the Start On box shows the correct date for the first payment. If this is a recurring payment, use the How Often box to specify how frequently Quicken should remind you about this payment. Finally, if you want to get really crazy, use the Scheduling Options buttons and boxes to more precisely specify when you want to make payments or be reminded about payments.

Figure 12-15:
The Add
Transaction
dialog box.

7. **Verify that the Pay To, Category, Start On date, and Memo fields are correct.**

They probably are. But I have kind of a compulsive personality. Because I've been telling you to check all this other stuff, I thought I'd also suggest that you check these fields.

8. **Click OK.**

Quicken adds the payee's transaction to the calendar.

Note: When you schedule payments, you may implicitly break your budget. If you've set up a budget and scheduling a payment does "break" the budget, Quicken alerts you. Quicken also asks (in the nicest way possible) if you want to update your budget. For more information about budgeting, refer to Chapter 3.

Working with scheduled transactions

By dragging payees to the calendar, you add transactions to the register one at a time. However, Quicken also allows you to automatically schedule the adding of transactions.

To create these scheduled transactions, you choose the Tools⇨Scheduled Transaction List command. Quicken displays the Bills & Deposits window (see Figure 12-16).

To create a scheduled transaction, click the Create New button and select Scheduled Transaction to display a dialog box that you use to describe automatically scheduled transactions (see Figure 12-17). Note that you can automatically schedule any kind of transaction — loan payments, insurance premiums, child support, or whatever. (I'm describing the automatically scheduled transactions feature here in this chapter, though, because loan payments are one of the most common ways to use this Quicken feature.)

Figure 12-16: The Bills & Deposits window.

Figure 12-17: The Add Scheduled Transaction dialog box.

To schedule a transaction, describe the account to use, the transaction method, the payee, category, amount, and so on. You shouldn't have any trouble figuring out what goes into these boxes. They're the same boxes you use to record a check into the register.

After you describe the transaction, use the Scheduling options to describe the payment schedule. The Start On box, for example, lets you describe when the first payment occurs. The Remind Me options let you tell Quicken when you want to be reminded about the payment. The Frequency options let you describe the payment pattern: every month on the 13th, the second Friday of every month, and so on (see Figure 12-17). You can also use the Ending On boxes to identify when the payments stop.

Checking out the Calendar

The bar along the top of the Calendar (refer to Figure 12-14) provides some other tools that you may want to use. I'm not going to spend much time on them; you'll have more fun trying them out yourself than you would reading about them. Nevertheless, let me give you a bird's-eye view:

- ✔ The Add Note button lets you post a note on a calendar day. You use this feature to create reminder notes that will also appear in the Alerts area of the Cash Flow Center. For example, you may want to post a note saying "Remember Wedding Anniversary" on the big day. After you click this button, Quicken displays a dialog box in which you type the message. Then you click Save My Butt. The program also marks the calendar day with a little yellow square — a miniature stick-on note. Click the square to read the message.

- ✔ The Options button displays a menu of commands that let you specify which transactions should appear in the Calendar, add an account balances graph to the Calendar window, and fiddle with the memorized transactions list. The transactions shown in that list box along the right edge of the Calendar window, by the way, are memorized transactions. (Chapter 4 briefly discusses memorized transactions.)

Chapter 13

Mutual Funds

. .

In This Chapter

▶ Knowing when to use Quicken investment record keeping

▶ Setting up a mutual fund investment account

▶ Recording your initial mutual fund investment

▶ Buying mutual fund shares

▶ Recording mutual fund profits

▶ Selling mutual fund shares

▶ Adjusting your mutual fund shares and price information

. .

Mutual fund record keeping is something that more of us need to think about. More of us are investing as the population ages and we prepare for retirement. And with the prevalence of battered 401(k) and brokerage accounts, many of us need to more closely monitor our mutual funds.

Fortunately, Quicken provides great tools for managing your mutual fund investments. And this chapter talks about those tools. But first, I should talk about whether you even need to do this.

Deciding to Use Investment Features

The Quicken investment record keeping feature lets you do three important things:

↳ Track your interest and dividend income

↳ Track real and potential capital gains and losses

↳ Measure an investment's performance by calculating the annual return from an investment

If you're a serious investor, these things probably sound worthwhile. But before you invest any time learning how Quicken investment record keeping works, be sure that you need all this power.

Are your investments tax-deferred?

If your investments are tax-deferred — if, for example, you're using individual retirement accounts (IRAs), 401(k)s, or Keoghs — you don't really need to track investment income and capital gains and losses. Tax-deferred investments have no effect on your personal income taxes in the United States. You get a tax deduction for the money you stick into IRAs, for example, and anything you take out is taxable. (Or in the case of a Roth IRA, you don't get a deduction for amounts you stick into the account, but then you also don't get taxed on amounts taken out of the account — which means that you don't need to closely account for Roth IRA investments, at least for tax accounting reasons.)

With tax-deferred investments — like deductible IRAs, 401(k)s, and Keoghs — you record all that you should need to know via your checking account. Checks earmarked for investment are categorized as *IRA Deductions,* for example, while investment account withdrawals deposited into your checking account are categorized as *IRA Distributions.* In other words, you don't need to set up special accounts for tracking your investments. Your bank accounts track everything you need to keep track of.

Are you a mutual fund fanatic?

If you're a fan of mutual funds, you don't need Quicken to measure the funds' annual returns. Fund managers provide these figures for you in quarterly and annual reports. In fact, part of what you're paying the mutual fund manager for is record keeping and performance management.

Some investors don't need Quicken

Let me give you an example of someone who doesn't need to use the Quicken program's investments feature — me. Once upon a time, I bought and sold common stocks, fooled around with half a dozen mutual funds, and learned firsthand why junk bonds are called junk bonds. (Apparently, junk bonds are more risky. And so fluctuate wildly in value.) Over the last few years, though, I've simplified my financial affairs considerably.

I don't invest directly in stocks, bonds, or mutual funds these days; instead, I stick money into an IRA. My investments don't produce taxable dividends or interest income, nor do they produce taxable or tax-saving capital gains or losses. Money I put into the IRA is tax-deductible. And money I ultimately take out of the IRA will be taxable.

I'm also sticking with a handful of mutual funds, but I don't need to calculate the annual return — that's what mutual fund managers do. So I don't need to figure, for example, what my shares of Vanguard Total Stock Market Portfolio (my favorite mutual fund) delivered as an annual return when I include both the 3 percent dividend and the 10 percent price drop.

Because I don't need to track investment income, or track capital gains and losses, or calculate the progress of my investment portfolio, I don't need Quicken investment record keeping for my personal use.

Many investors do need Quicken

Of course, many people — including mutual fund investors — do benefit from Quicken investment record keeping. If you routinely buy stocks and bonds, you probably want to calculate your annual returns. What's more, if you try to monitor your capital gains and losses intelligently — and you should — you want to know both what you originally paid for your securities and what they're worth currently.

The size of your investment portfolio isn't an issue. For example, I have two daughters who are saving money for college. (Actually, in a cruel twist of fate, *I* am saving; they're simply accumulating.) Although Beth and Britt haven't saved much money, and although they use mutual funds to keep things simple, they do three things that cause nightmarishly complex record keeping for their poor, overworked, and grossly underpaid accountant — Dad. They reinvest their quarterly dividend income, pay annual maintenance fees, and coerce their parents into adding more and more money to their investment portfolios.

What's the big deal? All three things adjust the *basis* in the fund. And when Beth and Britt sell their mutual fund shares, their gain (or loss) will be determined by subtracting the *basis* (the purchase price and all out-of-pocket costs) from the sales proceeds.

The bottom line: Though Beth and Britt don't have much money, the Bob Cratchit of this little story needs to use Quicken to track their investments.

How to pick a mutual fund

Would you mind terribly if I took a minute and provided a handful of tips about how to pick a mutual fund? I guess I'm thinking that maybe, just maybe, my observations might be useful to you. I am not, after all, trying to earn a commission by selling you some financial product or service. So maybe I can be a bit more objective. I'm also rather over-educated (with a couple of masters' degrees, one in finance and one in taxation). And I've been a CPA for, jeepers, 25 years and so have seen countless real-life examples of people's investing successes and mistakes. . . .

Here, then, are my tips:

1. Carefully, carefully, watch your investment expenses, including both commissions and the mutual fund management fees. Why? Despite what you may have been told, in my experience, you absolutely don't get extra investment returns by paying extra for investment advice or financial planning. And note that every bit of financial research — the kind that finance professors do — supports this statement. Usually, you want to pick the cheapest mutual fund alternative. Almost always, that's an index fund.

2. Use tax-deferred investment accounts like 401(k)s, 403(b)s, and IRAs for your investments. Income taxes can be a huge drag on your investment returns. And over the decades that you'll be investing, minimizing your income taxes will add at least tens of thousands of dollars and potentially hundreds of thousands of dollars to your wealth.

3. To diversify, use an inexpensive index fund, one per investment category. For example,

you can diversify by investing in one index fund that invests in the U.S. stock market, another index fund that invests in corporate bonds, another that invests in real estate investment trusts, and so on. Diversification reduces your investment risk.

4. Consider one of the new target retirement funds such as those offered by Vanguard or Fidelity. With one of these babies, you don't worry about trying to diversify. You don't worry about asset allocation or rebalancing. You don't worry about adjusting your investment mix as you get older. You just pick a single fund that's tied to your retirement year. For example, if you will retire in 2025, you would buy the target retirement that assumes you'll retire in 2025. That's it. That's the last investment decision you need to make.

5. For goodness sakes, don't trade, attempting to buy low and sell high. Trading rarely works. And it's always expensive. Be a long-term investor who buys inexpensive mutual funds and holds them for the long term.

6. Invest some time and money in beefing up your investment knowledge. You can do this by reading pretty much anything that Burton Malkiel or John Bogle has written. I particularly like and recommend Burton Malkiel's *A Random Walk Guide to Investing* (published by W. W. Norton & Company). I also think the *Wall Street Journal's* Jonathan Clements is about the most common-sensed journalist writing on personal finance. (He writes a weekly column.)

Tracking a Mutual Fund

If you need to track a mutual fund investment, you need to know how to set up a mutual fund account and then record your investment activities.

Even if you don't invest in mutual funds, you shouldn't skip this section. Understanding how mutual fund record keeping works makes tracking other, more complicated investments — like stocks, bonds, Krugerrands, and commodity options — much, much easier for you.

Setting up a mutual fund investment account

Setting up an investment account to track a mutual fund works the same way as setting up any other account:

1. **Click the Investing Center button**

 The Investing Center button, as a careful examination reveals, appears in that row of buttons along the left edge of the window. Quicken, ever the faithful companion, displays the Investing Center window. You may need to click the Today's Data tab if it isn't shown by default.

2. **Click the Add Account button on the Investing Center window.**

 Quicken dutifully displays the first Quicken Account Setup dialog box that you use to add a new Quicken account. You've seen this dialog box a million times by now. It just asks you to name the financial institution holding your investment account.

3. **Identify the financial institution and then click Next.**

 Name the financial institution (bank, brokerage firm, or mutual fund management company) holding your mutual fund investment account. As you type the name, Quicken displays a list of companies that match what you type. When you see the right name, click it and then click Next. And, oh, if you don't see the right name, indicate that you just want to use the name you've typed and not a name from the list.

 Note: If you select a financial institution that supports online setup, Quicken displays a dialog box that asks whether you want to set the account up manually or use a new, special online method. I'm assuming here that you'll set up the account manually.

 After you complete Step 3, Quicken displays the second Quicken Account Setup dialog box, as shown in Figure 13-1.

Figure 13-1:
The second
Quicken
Account
Setup dialog
box.

4. **Identify the account type.**

 Use the dialog box shown in Figure 13-1 to indicate that you want to create a mutual fund account.

 Note: Quicken lets you set up a 401(k)-type or 403(b) account. Although I recommend that you not bother tracking tax-deferred investments — especially when someone else already does the record keeping for you — you can set up an account for a 401(k) or 403(b) account. And then you can use that account to monitor the account's performance. The steps I describe here for working with a mutual fund investment are the same basic steps you use for working with a 401(k) or 403(b) account.

5. **Click Next and then name the investment, then click Next again.**

 Quicken displays the third Quicken Account Setup dialog box (shown in Figure 13-2). Move the cursor to the Name This Account text box and type a name for the mutual fund. If you're investing in the Vanguard Index 500 Trust mutual fund, you might type **Vanguard Index**. There's also a little box that asks if the account is tax deferred. If the account is tax deferred, you can check that box. Of course, if the account is tax deferred, as discussed earlier in the chapter, I wonder why you're even doing this. But hey, that's not really my business.

 After you click Next, Quicken displays the fourth Quicken Account Setup dialog box.

6. **Provide the last statement date and then click Next.**

 The fourth Quicken Account Setup dialog box asks for the date of the statement you're using to enter your mutual fund shares, cost, and value information. This date is the starting date, in essence, for your mutual fund record keeping with Quicken. Enter the date and then click Next.

Figure 13-2:
The third
Quicken
Account
Setup dialog
box.

7. **Provide the ticker symbol and then click Next.**

All this fifth dialog box does is collect the mutual fund's ticker symbol so that you can download share prices several times during the day and drive yourself half mad with anxiety (see Figure 13-3). If you don't know the ticker symbol, click the Ticker Symbol Lookup button to display a Quicken.com Web page that lets you find the ticker symbol.

Figure 13-3:
The fifth
Quicken
Account
Setup dialog
box.

After you click Next, Quicken displays the sixth Quicken Account Setup dialog box, shown in Figure 13-4.

Figure 13-4:
The sixth
Quicken
Account
Setup dialog
box.

8. **Provide a total shares count.**

 Enter the number of shares you hold in the mutual fund.

9. **Click Next.**

 Quicken displays a dialog box summarizing the mutual fund investment that you've just entered. If something seems amiss, click the Back button to find the Quicken Account Setup dialog box where you entered some incorrect bit of information. If everything seems okay, click Done. Quicken displays the Investing Center window. (You can also display this window any other time simply by clicking the Investing Center button.) You want to see the details concerning the account you've just added. To do this, click the account's name on the Investing Center window. Quicken displays the Summary window for the new mutual fund investment, as shown in Figure 13-5.

Recording your initial investment

After you set up a mutual fund investment account and describe the security, you can record an initial purchase of fund shares.

Of course, you need to know the original price of those first shares. So dig through that kitchen drawer where you stuff bank statements, financial records, and those kooky birthday cards from Aunt Enid.

Figure 13-5:
The
Summary
investment
window.

When you find the proper paperwork that shows the number of shares you purchased and the price per share, here's what you do:

1. **Open the investment account, if it isn't already open.**

 Display the Investing Center window; then open the investment account by clicking the account name.

2. **Tell Quicken you want to enter cost basis data.**

 Click the Enter hyperlink in the Cost Basis column. Quicken displays the Enter Missing Transactions dialog box, shown in Figure 13-6.

3. **Click the Enter Missing Transaction button.**

 Quicken displays the Buy - Shares Bought dialog box, as shown in Figure 13-7. If you don't see the Add - Add Shares dialog box — sometimes Quicken seems to get confused — select Add - Shares Added from the Enter Transaction drop-down list box.

Figure 13-6:
The Enter
Missing
Transactions
dialog box.

Figure 13-7:
The Buy -
Shares
Bought
dialog box.

Note: For you history buffs, let me mention that an investment record-keeping tool available in old versions of Quicken, the investment register, is no longer available in the newest versions of Quicken. This makes me a bit nostalgic. Was it really such a bad feature that they had to kill it? That seems a little harsh to me. But no sense crying over spilt coffee. After you and I are used to the new, register-less way of doing things, I think we'll both be happier and more productive.

4. **Enter the date you first purchased the fund shares into the Transaction Date text box.**

Move the cursor to the Transaction Date text box and enter the date by using the *MM/DD/YY* format. Enter January 1, 2001, for example, as **1/1/1**. You may also select the date from the pop-up calendar.

5. [Optional] Enter a memo description.

If you want to tie the purchase to a confirmation order number, for example, enter the data into the Memo text box. I suppose that you could use this text box to record anything: *Kilroy was here. Save the Whales. Don't tread on me.*

6. Indicate the size of your purchase.

To enter the total number of shares, move the cursor to the Number Of Shares text box. (Fractional shares are okay.)

7. Indicate what you paid per share.

With the cursor on the Price Paid text box, enter the amount you paid for the lot. After you supply Quicken with the adjusted cost basis, it calculates the total cost.

8. Record the initial purchase of mutual fund shares by clicking the Enter/Done button.

Quicken redisplays the Enter Missing Transactions dialog box (refer to Figure 13-6).

9. Repeat Steps 2 through 8 if necessary.

You need to repeat Steps 2 through 8 to record any other lots you purchased. For example, if you own 1,000 shares of Vanguard Total Stock Market Index but you accumulated these shares by buying 200 shares five different times, you need to record five separate lots of 200 shares a piece. The first time through Steps 2 through 8, you record the first lot of 200 shares. The second time through the steps, you record the second lot of 200 shares. The third and subsequent times through the steps, if you're setting up a mutual fund investment account that you didn't really need to set up, you ask yourself why you didn't listen to me when I said you don't need and therefore don't want to do this for tax-deferred investments.

After you describe each lot that makes up your holdings of the mutual fund investment, the Enter Missing Transactions dialog box shows that there aren't any placeholders for missing transactions because the shares placeholder and the cost placeholder should both equal zero (see Figure 13-8). You can click Done.

Figure 13-8:
The Enter
Missing
Transactions
dialog box
after one
enters all
the missing
transac-
tions.

Enter Missing Transactions		☒

Enter Missing Transactions for Vanguard Total Stock Market Index

This security is missing all or part of its transaction history. When you downloaded or manually entered transactions, the total number of shares in those transactions did not equal the total number of shares you own. Quicken has added a Placeholder Entry to account for missing transactions.

To get complete performance reporting and tax calculations, enter the missing transactions now.

Vanguard Total Stock Market Index Transactions as of 01/01/07

Date	Transaction	Description		
01/01/01	Bought	200 shares @ 15	Edit	Delete
01/01/02	Bought	200 shares @ 20	Edit	Delete
01/01/03	Bought	200 shares @ 25	Edit	Delete
01/01/04	Bought	200 shares @ 30	Edit	Delete
01/01/05	Bought	200 shares @ 35	Edit	Delete

Holdings as of 01/01/07	Shares	Cost
Total shares you own:	1,000	25,000.00
Shares from transactions (above)	1,000	25,000.00
Shares in Placeholder Entry	**0**	**0.00**

Enter Missing Transaction... | Estimate Average Cost

Help | Done

If you make a mistake in entering a transaction, you can click the Edit or
Delete button to the right of the transaction to change or remove the erro-
neous data.

Buying investments

As you purchase shares — by sending a check to the mutual fund manage-
ment company or by reinvesting dividends and capital gain distributions —
record the transactions for the investment account.

By writing a check

If you buy shares by writing a check, display the investment window (such as
by clicking the Investment Center button and then the investment account),
and then record the purchase by following these steps:

1. **Click the Enter Transactions button.**

 Quicken displays the dialog box used to enter investment transactions.

2. **Select Buy - Shares Bought from the Enter Transaction drop-down list
 box.**

 Quicken displays the Buy - Shares Bought version of the investment
 transaction entry dialog box, as shown in Figure 13-9.

3. **Enter the purchase date into the Transaction Date text box.**

4. **[Optional] Enter a description in the Memo text box.**

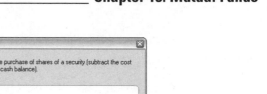

Figure 13-9:
The Buy -
Shares
Bought
dialog box.

5. **Enter the bank account on which you'll write the check that pays for the shares.**

 Select the account name from the From drop-down list box.

6. **Indicate the size of your purchase by using the Number Of Shares and the Price Paid text boxes.**

 Tell Quicken the size of your investment by giving the number of shares purchased and the price paid per share.

7. **Enter the commission or fee that you paid.**

 Move the cursor to the Commission text box and enter the commission or fee you paid to purchase the shares. (The amount shown in the Total Cost text box includes this figure.)

8. **Record the purchase.**

 Click the Enter/New button if you want to record the transaction and enter another new transaction. Or click the Enter/Done button if you want to record just the single transaction. Quicken records your purchase of new shares. You are now a capitalist. Congratulations.

By reinvesting dividends, interest, or capital gains

When you reinvest your dividends, interest, or capital gains, you also must record your reinvestment transactions. Essentially, you're buying new shares using the dividend or capital gain proceeds you could have received. To record the reinvestment of mutual fund distributions, display the investment window (by clicking the Investment Center button and then clicking the investment account), and then follow these steps:

1. **Click the Enter Transactions button.**

 Quicken displays the dialog box used to enter investments transactions.

2. **Select Reinvest - Income Reinvested from the Enter Transaction drop-down list box.**

 Quicken displays the Reinvest - Income Reinvested version of the investment transaction entry dialog box, as shown in Figure 13-10.

Figure 13-10: The Reinvest - Income Reinvested dialog box.

3. **Enter the purchase date (in this case, the reinvestment date) into the Transaction Date text box.**

4. **[Optional] Type a brief explanation of the transaction into the Memo text box.**

5. **Use the Amount and Shares columns to describe the reinvestment.**

 Take another look at Figure 13-10. No, really, go ahead. I'll wait. See those rows labeled Dividend, Interest, Short-Term Cap Gain Dist, Mid-Term Cap Gain Dist, and Long-Term Cap Gain Dist? And see the columns labeled Amount and Shares? Use these rows and columns to record the amounts of dividends, interest, and capital gains distributed to you by the mutual fund and to record the numbers of shares you purchase by reinvesting these amounts. For example, if you receive $100 of dividends and use this amount to purchase 2 shares, you enter **100** into the Dividend Amount box and **2** into the Dividend Shares box.

6. **Record the reinvestment transaction.**

Click the Enter/New button if you want to record the transaction and enter another new transaction. Or click the Enter/Done button if you want to record just the single transaction.

Figure 13-10 shows $100 of dividends being reinvested in the mutual fund by buying 2 more shares, $25 of interest being reinvested by buying 0.5 (or half of a) share, and $200 of short-term capital gains being reinvested by buying 4 shares.

Recording your profits

Every so often, you may receive distributions directly from the mutual fund company. Retirees, for example, often receive mutual fund dividend checks and capital gains directly rather than reinvesting the amounts.

To record these kinds of distributions, you follow a process very similar to those I describe in the preceding set of steps. For example, to record an income transaction directly into the investment account, follow these steps:

1. **Click the Enter Transactions button.**

 Display the investment window — such as by clicking the Investing Center button and then clicking the Enter Transactions button. Quicken displays the dialog box used to enter investment transactions.

2. **Select Inc - Income (Div, Int, Etc.) from the Enter Transaction drop-down list box.**

 Quicken displays the Inc - Income (Div, Int, Etc.) version of the investment transaction entry dialog box, as shown in Figure 13-11.

Figure 13-11: The Inc - Income (Div, Int, Etc.) dialog box.

3. **Enter the distribution date into the Transaction Date text box.**

4. **Use the Transfer Account drop-down list to identify the account into which you'll deposit the check the mutual fund company sends you.**

5. **[Optional] Type a brief description of the distribution in the Memo text box.**

 Be creative — type your wedding anniversary, the name of your dog, or even a piece of data related to the dividend or distribution.

6. **Indicate the dividend or capital gains distribution amount.**

 Enter the amount in the appropriate amount text box. A dividend, I hope you can guess, goes into the Dividend box. A short-term capital gain goes into the Short-Term Cap Gain Dist box, and so on.

7. **Record the dividend or distribution transaction.**

 When you click either the Enter/New or Enter/Done button, you record the dividend. If you click the Enter/New button, Quicken leaves the dialog box open so that you can enter some other transactions.

Figure 13-11 shows a $50 deposit of dividends into your checking account.

Selling investments

Selling mutual fund shares works basically the same way as buying them — only in reverse. To record the sale of shares held in an investment account, perform the following actions:

1. **Click the Enter Transactions button.**

 Display the investment window by clicking the Investing Center button and then clicking the Enter Transactions button. Quicken displays the dialog box used to enter investment transactions.

2. **Select Sell - Shares Sold from the Enter Transaction drop-down list box.**

 Quicken displays the Sell - Shares Sold version of the investment transaction entry dialog box, as shown in Figure 13-12.

3. **Enter the sale's date into the Transaction Date text box.**

4. **[Optional] Type a brief description of the sale in the Memo text box.**

5. **If you're selling all your shares, mark the Sell All Shares In This Account check box.**

6. **Give Quicken the number of shares you're selling.**

 Use the Number Of Shares box to specify the number of shares you're selling (if you didn't click the Sell All Shares check box in Step 5).

7. **Indicate the price per share that you received by using the Price Received text box.**

 With a little luck, your selling price is more than you paid.

8. **Enter the commission or fee you paid to sell the shares in the Commission text box.**

 No wonder Bernie, your broker, does so well, huh? He makes money even if you don't.

 Quicken calculates whatever you don't enter. For example, if you tell Quicken how many dollars you sell (by using the Price Received text box), it calculates the number of shares you sell by dividing the total sales amount by the price per share. If you tell Quicken how many shares you sell (using the Number Of Shares text box), it calculates the total sales amount by multiplying the number of shares by the price per share. I guess this feature is handy.

9. **Enter the bank account into which you're going to deposit the sale's proceeds.**

 Open the To drop-down list box and select the appropriate account.

10. **[Optional] Indicate whether you want to use specific identification.**

If you have purchased share lots at different prices or at different times, you can click the Specify Lots button to open the Specify Lots For Investment dialog box. Here, you can pick and choose which lots to sell so that you can minimize the capital gains taxes you'll owe. (Good idea, huh?) A *lot* is simply a batch, or set, of shares that you purchase at one time. If you sell the most expensive lots, you reduce your capital gains and the taxes on those gains.

- To pick an entire lot, double-click it. (You need to double-click the date field, by the way.)

- To pick a portion of a lot, select it and then type the number of shares from the lot you want to sell in the Selected text box.

- To clear your selections and start over, click the Reset button.

The Specify Lots For Investment dialog box also provides nifty command buttons for automating the process of selecting lots. If you click the Maximum Gain or Minimum Gain button, Quicken picks lots for you in a way that produces the largest possible or smallest possible capital gain. Alternatively, you can click the First Shares In or Last Shares In buttons to sell either the oldest shares or newest shares first. This business about picking the lots you sell is rather arbitrary, of course. By letting Quicken pick lots, you can manipulate the capital gain you'll have and the capital gains taxes you'll pay. But it's all legal (as long as you specifically tell the mutual fund management company which lots you're selling). And honorable. And it can save you money because you can time your capital gains so that they occur when they'll cost you the least.

If you're someone who has large capital loss carryforwards — as many investors do after the brutal last few years — your capital loss carryforwards may totally wipe out any gains you have to recognize over the next few years (or decades, gulp). In this case, you may not get much benefit from fooling around with this specific identification business. Consult your tax advisor for details.

11. Click one of the Enter buttons.

Quicken records your sale.

Correcting a mistake

If you make a mistake, don't worry — it's not a problem. You can edit an investment transaction. To edit a particular transaction, you first need to display the investment transactions list. Start by clicking the Investing Center button, clicking the investment account you want to work with, and then clicking the Transactions tab in the investment account's window (see Figure 13-13).

Figure 13-13:
The Transactions tab of the investment account window.

To edit one of the transactions you see listed for the investment account, click the transaction and then click the Edit button. Quicken opens the dialog box you originally used to record the transaction (such as the one shown in Figure 13-14), and you use it to make your changes.

Figure 13-14:
The Edit Inc-Income (Div, Int, Etc.) dialog box appears when you indicate you want to edit a reinvestment transaction.

For example, you can click the fields with the incorrect entries, fix them, and then record the new, corrected transaction.

Working with slightly tricky mutual fund transactions

I haven't described every possible mutual fund transaction — although I have described every one I've encountered in the last 10 or 12 years. You should know, however, that Quicken does let you record three additional transactions by specifying several almost-magical actions: shares out, stock split, and reminder transactions.

How do I remove shares from an account?

You can tell Quicken to remove shares from an account — without moving the money represented by the shares — to some other account. Why would you want to remove shares from an account using a *shares-removed* transaction? I can think of two situations:

- ✔ You erroneously added shares to the account with the shares added transaction action and now you need to remove them.
- ✔ You're using an investment account to record old investment activity, such as activity from last year.

The first instance is self-explanatory because you're simply correcting an error that you made. In the second case, however, you don't want to transfer the proceeds of a mutual fund sale to a checking account because the money from the sale was already recorded as a deposit at some point in the past.

You can record a shares-removed transaction directly into Quicken by clicking the Enter Transaction button and selecting Remove - Shares Removed from the Enter Transaction drop-down list box. Then fill in the rest of the fields in the dialog box the same way that you would for a regular ol' sell transaction. The only difference is that you won't give a transfer account for the sale proceeds — because there aren't any proceeds.

What? The stock split and then doubled?

Stock splits don't occur very often with mutual funds; however, when they do occur, the mutual fund manager, in effect, gives you a certain number of new shares (such as two) for each old share you own.

To record a stock split, you click the Enter Transactions button and select Stock Split from the Enter Transaction drop-down list box. When Quicken displays the Stock Split version of the dialog box used to enter investment transactions (see Figure 13-15), you indicate the ratio of new shares to old shares. For a two-for-one split, for example, you indicate that you get two new split shares for each old unsplit share. The whole process is pretty easy.

Quicken, will you remind me of something?

A *reminder* transaction is the electronic equivalent of a yellow stick-on note. If you put a reminder transaction in an investment account, Quicken gives you a reminder message on the reminder date. You can't goof up anything by trying out reminders, so if you're curious, enter a reminder transaction for tomorrow and see what happens.

You can post a reminder note by clicking the Enter Transactions button, selecting Reminder Transaction from the Enter Transaction drop-down list box, and filling out the dialog box that Quicken displays (see Figure 13-16).

Figure 13-15: The Stock Split version of the investment transaction entry dialog box.

Reminder Transaction

Enter transaction: Reminder Transaction ▾ Create a reminder for yourself (will appear with your investment alerts in Quicken and on Quicken.com).

Reminder Transaction:

Transaction date: 12/31/07

Account: Vanguard Index ▾

Memo: Description:
 Phone home

Cancel Clear Help Enter/New Enter/Done

Figure 13-16:
The Reminder Transaction version of the investment transaction entry dialog box.

Reconciling an account

You reconcile a mutual fund investment account the same basic way that you reconcile a bank account. The only real difference — and it doesn't affect reconciliation mechanics — is that you focus on mutual fund shares and not on account balance dollars. To begin reconciling a mutual fund investment account, choose Investing⇨Investing Activities⇨Reconcile An Account. If you have questions about what to do next, refer to Chapter 8. It describes how you reconcile a bank account, but the same procedures apply to a mutual fund account.

Trying reports

I just want to say one thing about Quicken reports as they relate to your investments: *Remember that the reports are available.* (For more information, see Chapter 7.)

Using menu commands and other stuff

For the most part, the commands and menus available for an investment account are the same as those available for all the other accounts Quicken supplies. I write about the commands that I think are most helpful to new

users in the preceding chapters of this book. If you have a question about how the Void Transaction command works, for example, refer to the index, which directs you to a specific discussion of that command.

Updating Securities Prices

You can collect current market prices and store this information with your accounts. Just display the investment account that has the mutual fund shares. Then click the Portfolio button or choose Investing⇨Portfolio. Either way, Quicken displays the Portfolio tab (see Figure 13-17).

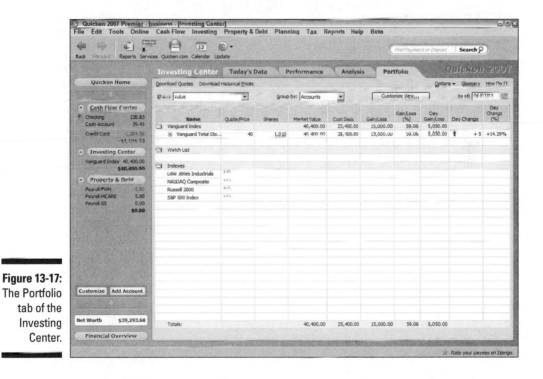

Figure 13-17:
The Portfolio
tab of the
Investing
Center.

To record the current market price for a security, use the arrow keys or click the mouse to select the security. Then move the cursor to the Quote/Price text box and enter the current price.

Quicken updates the Market Value field in the Portfolio tab as well as the Market Value figure at the bottom of the register window. After you update the market price, you can return to the investment account window register by clicking the investment account name on the Portfolio tab.

If you invest exclusively in mutual funds, the information in this chapter should be all you need. If you also invest directly in such things as stocks and bonds, you may want to turn to the next chapter. It describes how you use a Quicken investment account to track a brokerage account.

The Portfolio tab

You can do more with the Portfolio tab (refer to Figure 13-17) than just update share prices.

The Portfolio As Of field lets you specify the date on which you want to see and set market prices and values. The Show drop-down list box lets you customize how Quicken reports on your investment holdings. The Investing Center window has two other useful tabs of investment data — Today's Data and Analysis — that show you the details of your investing in other ways.

I'm not going to go into more detail here about what all these extra bells and whistles do. If you're a serious investor, however, take the time to explore these commands. You may gain some interesting insights into your financial investments.

Chapter 14

Stocks and Bonds

. .

In This Chapter

▶ Setting up a brokerage account

▶ Describing the securities in a brokerage account

▶ Transferring cash to and from a brokerage account

▶ Buying stocks and bonds from a brokerage account

▶ Recording income from securities held in a brokerage account

▶ Recording margin interest, miscellaneous income and expenses, and return of capital

▶ Updating securities prices

▶ Adjusting your brokerage cash balance

▶ Adjusting your brokerage account shares

. .

*A*fter you understand how Quicken handles mutual fund investments, working with a brokerage account (or *cash investment account* as Quicken calls it) is a snap.

 If you haven't yet used Quicken for mutual fund record keeping or read Chapter 13, I recommend you at least skim Chapter 13. That chapter provides some useful information about the fundamentals of investment record keeping with Quicken.

Setting Up a Brokerage Account

Setting up a brokerage account is similar to setting up a regular mutual fund account, except for a couple of minor — but predictable — differences. If you're still fairly new to this process, you can use the following steps as a guide:

1. **Click the Investing Center button.**

 Quicken displays the Investing Center window. You may also need to click the Today's Data tab if it isn't displayed by default.

2. **Click the Add Account button in the Investment & Retirement Accounts area.**

 When Quicken displays that first Quicken Account Setup dialog box, identify the financial institution holding the account by entering its name into the This Account Is Held At The Following Institution text box. When you do this, Quicken displays a list of financial institution names that (sort of) match what you enter. Select the one that really does match and click Next.

 Quicken displays the second Quicken Account Setup dialog box.

3. **Set up the manual way.**

 When Quicken asks whether you want to use the manual or online setup method, indicate that you'll use the manual method by clicking the Manual button. Then click Next to display the third Quicken Account Setup dialog box (shown in Figure 14-1).

Figure 14-1:
The third
Quicken
Account
Setup dialog
box.

4. **Select the Standard Brokerage option button and then click Next.**

 Indicate that you're setting up a standard brokerage account by selecting the, duh, Standard Brokerage option button.

5. **Name the investment and then click Next.**

 When Quicken displays the fourth Quicken Account Setup dialog box, use the Name This Account text box to provide a name for the new investment account.

 After you click Next, Quicken displays the fifth Quicken Account Setup dialog box (shown in Figure 14-2).

Figure 14-2:
The fifth
Quicken
Account
Setup dialog
box.

6. **Describe the cash balance associated with the brokerage account and then click Next.**

As you probably already know if you're investing through a broker, your brokerage account will have a cash account associated with the brokerage account. The cash in this account, of course, provides the money you use for additional investments. And when you receive cash from selling some investment or from some dividend, the money goes into this account.

To describe this cash account, use the Statement Date, Cash, and Money Market Fund boxes to give the date as of which you'll use Quicken and the opening balances. You can probably guess this, but at the risk of being redundant, the information that you provide to set up a cash account or money market fund mirrors the information you provide to set up a regular ol' checking account.

After you click Next, Quicken displays the sixth Quicken Account Setup dialog box, as shown in Figure 14-3.

Figure 14-3:
The sixth
Quicken
Account
Setup dialog
box.

7. **Provide the ticker symbols for the securities held in your investment account and then click Next.**

 All this sixth dialog box does is collect the ticker symbols for the stocks, bonds, and mutual funds you hold in the investment account. If you don't know the ticker symbols, don't freak on me. You can click the Ticker Symbol Lookup hyperlink to display a Quicken.com Web page that lets you look up the ticker symbols.

 After you click Next, Quicken displays the seventh Quicken Account Setup dialog box.

8. **Provide a total shares count.**

 Enter the number of shares you hold in the investment account.

9. **Click Next, pause briefly, and click Done.**

 Quicken displays the eighth and essentially final Quicken Account Setup dialog box. I don't show this dialog box here. All it does is summarize the information that you entered in the previous two Quicken Account Setup dialog boxes. You can review this information to make sure that you've done your part correctly and then click Done.

Recording your initial share balances

Did you happen to read or skim Chapter 13, which talks about using Quicken to track mutual funds? If you did, you may remember that there's a section titled, "Recording your initial investment." That little section explains how to tell Quicken what you paid for the mutual fund shares held in your mutual fund investment account.

Okay. So here's the deal. Just as you need to describe your starting share balances when you set up a new mutual fund investment account, you need to describe your starting share balances when you set up a new brokerage investment account. In other words, if you own three stocks in your brokerage account — IBM, GE, and Boeing — you need to describe how much you paid and when you purchased your IBM, GE, and Boeing shares.

Rather than copy that earlier discussion (I'd literally be copying and pasting material from Chapter 13), let me refer you to the "Recording your initial investment" section in Chapter 13. Go through the nine-step process described there for each stock you hold.

Working with brokerage accounts

Brokerage accounts work like mutual fund accounts, which I describe in Chapter 13, except for a handful of minor differences. Therefore, if you haven't already used Quicken for mutual fund record keeping or haven't already read Chapter 13, I need to ask you now to do that. If you already read the first part of Chapter 13, as directed in the preceding paragraph, you can just focus on the Chapter 13 sections titled "Buying investments," "Recording your profits," and "Selling investments."

After you understand the way that mutual fund investment accounts work, brokerage accounts make a lot of sense. Essentially, only three general differences exist between mutual fund investment accounts and brokerage investment accounts:

- ✔ Brokerage accounts use security lists (whereas mutual fund investment accounts don't).

- ✔ Brokerage accounts have cash accounts (whereas mutual fund investments don't).

- ✔ Brokerage accounts let you record a handful of goofy transactions that mutual fund investment accounts don't (because they don't make sense in the context of mutual fund investments).

I spend the next few paragraphs of this chapter describing these unique-to-brokerage-accounts features.

Setting up security lists

Typically, a brokerage account probably contains more than one type of *security.* You may have shares of Boeing, General Motors, or Chase Manhattan. You name it, and someone owns it.

Therefore, a brokerage account uses a list of securities — and you, as the investor, need to create and maintain the list of securities (stocks, bonds, and so on) that your account holds.

To do so, set up the brokerage account (as described in the first part of this chapter) and then complete the following steps:

1. **Choose Investing⇨Security List.**

 Quicken displays the Security List window, shown in Figure 14-4. Note that any mutual funds you've already set up appear in the list as securities.

Figure 14-4:
The Security
List window.

2. **Click the New button in the Security List window.**

 Quicken displays the first Add Security To Quicken dialog box, shown in Figure 14-5.

Figure 14-5:
The first
Add
Security To
Quicken
dialog box.

3. **Enter the stock symbol for the security in the Ticker Symbol text box.**

 If you don't know the symbol, make sure that you have the name of the security correct and then click the Look Up button to search for the ticker symbol at Quicken.com.

4. **Click Next to continue.**

 Quicken retrieves information about the stock whose ticker symbol you entered and displays it in another Add Security To Quicken dialog box.

5. **Click Done.**

 Quicken adds the security to the security list and redisplays the Security List window. If you have additional securities, you can add them by repeating Steps 2 through 4. Also, you can add securities on the fly as you're recording the purchase of a security for the first time. When you do this, Quicken starts this little "Oh, let's add another security to the list" process for you at Step 3.

 Before I quit this discussion of the security list, let me just make a couple of observations for your benefit. See those buttons at the top of the Security List window? (Go ahead and flip back to Figure 14-4.) You can use them to do useful stuff. For example, click Edit to change security information. Click Delete, predictably, to remove a security from the list. Use Hide to hide the selected security, Print to print the list, and Options to view or "un-view" (is that a real word?) previously hidden securities. Just thought you'd want to know.

Working with cash

One of the big differences between a brokerage account and a mutual fund account is that a cash management, or *money market,* account is attached to the brokerage account.

When you initially set up a brokerage account, your money goes into this account. (The broker bought you a doughnut and coffee in this meeting, remember?)

You purchase your first shares with the cash from this account. And when you sell shares, all cash proceeds go into this account.

Transferring cash to and from an account

Because you work with cash in a brokerage account, you need to know how to record the cash that flows into and out of the account.

To transfer cash to an account, follow these steps:

1. **Display the investment account's window.**

 You can do this in more than one way, as luck would have it, but one easy way to display an investment account's window is to click the Investing Center button and then click the investment account. The investment account window should look something like the one shown in Figure 14-6. If you're lucky.

Figure 14-6:
An
investment
account
window.

2. Indicate that you're transferring money.

Click the Enter Transactions button. Quicken displays the dialog box shown in Figure 14-7. Choose Cash Transferred Into Account from the Enter Transaction drop-down list box.

Figure 14-7:
The dialog
box used to
record
transfers
into an
account.

3. **Record the transaction date, amount, and account.**

 To record the amount of a cash transfer, confirm the transaction date (shown in the Transaction Date text box), enter the dollar amount in the Amount To Transfer text box, and then specify the checking account supplying the cash in the Transfer Account drop-down list box. Then click the Enter/New or the Enter/Done button. (If you click Enter/New, Quicken records the transaction but leaves the dialog box open so that you can record some more transactions.)

To transfer cash from an account, follow these steps:

1. **Display the investment account window.**

2. **Indicate that you're transferring money from an account.**

 Click the Enter Transactions button. Quicken displays the dialog box shown in Figure 14-8. Choose the Cash Transferred Out Of Account option from the Enter Transaction drop-down list box.

Figure 14-8:
The dialog box used to transfer cash out of a brokerage investment account.

3. **Record the transaction date, amount, and account.**

 To record the amount of a cash transfer, again confirm the transaction date (using the Transaction Date text box), enter the dollar amount in the Amount To Transfer text box, and specify the checking account receiving the cash in the Transfer Account drop-down list box. Then click either the Enter/New or the Enter/Done button.

Mutual (fund) acquaintance

Treat mutual fund shares that you hold in a brokerage account the same way that you treat other stocks and bonds that you hold in the account. If you're confused, think of it this way: Although brokers sell many mutual funds to their clients, the mutual fund manager sells some mutual funds directly to the public.

I don't want to get into the subject of load mutual funds versus no-load mutual funds — you pay a commission to buy load funds, and you don't pay a commission to buy no-load funds — but if you're interested in how these two types of funds work, flip open the *Wall Street Journal* and look for advertisements from no-load fund managers such as Vanguard, Scudder, and T. Rowe Price. Give them a call, and they'll tell you why they think that you should bypass the middleman — your broker. Next, talk to a broker, who will tell you why you *shouldn't* bypass the middleman. Then you make the decision.

What? You want *my* opinion? With much trepidation, I'll tell you: I always use no-load mutual funds because I'm a big fan of the do-it-yourself approach. You save substantial amounts both in commissions and, typically, in annual maintenance fees. Quite honestly, if you can figure out how to use Quicken and are reading a chapter like this, you've got enough smarts to choose your own mutual funds (especially if you're willing to do a bit of research through reading). Try Andrew Tobias's classic, *The Only Investment Guide You'll Ever Need* (Harvest Books) or Burton Malkiel's *A Random Walk Guide to Investing* (W.W. Norton & Company). However, I also think that a good broker — *good* is the operative word here — is well worth the commission fee if he or she helps you avoid expensive mistakes. It is not, however, necessarily easy to find a good broker or financial planner.

Buying near and selling dear

Buying and selling securities in a brokerage account is very similar to buying and selling shares of a mutual fund. You fill out almost the exact same fields.

1. **Display the investment account window.**

2. **Click the Enter Transactions button. When Quicken displays the dialog box, choose Buy - Shares Bought from the Enter Transaction drop-down list box.**

 Quicken, ever responsive to your needs, displays the Buy - Shares Bought dialog box (shown in Figure 14-9). When Quicken displays this dialog box, provide the transaction date. Select the security from the Security Name drop-down list box. Use the Number Of Shares, Price Paid, and Commission text boxes to describe your purchase. (You can get this information from your order confirmation slip.)

Buy - Shares Bought

Enter transaction: [Buy - Shares Bought ▼] Enter the purchase of shares of a security (subtract the cost from my cash balance).

Buy - Shares Bought:

Transaction date: [06/30/07] Security name: [IBM ▼]

Account: [Brokerage ▼] Number of shares: [100]

Memo: Price paid: [75] per share

[] Commission: [0.00]

 Total cost: [7,500.00]

— Use cash for this transaction —
(•) From this account's cash balance
() From [▼]

[Cancel] [Clear] [Help] [Enter/New] [Enter/Done]

Figure 14-9:
The Buy -
Shares
Bought
dialog box.

3. Indicate whether Quicken should adjust a cash account.

Use the From This Account's Cash Balance or From option button to specify which cash account Quicken should adjust for the transaction. You can say the usual cash account (by selecting the From This Account's Cash Balance option button) or specify some different account (by marking the From option button and then choosing the account from the From drop-down list box).

4. Click the Enter/New or the Enter/Done button when you're finished.

Pretty simple, right?

Selling a security works in the same basic way as buying a security:

1. Display the investment account window and then click the Enter Transactions button.

2. When Quicken displays the dialog box, choose Sell - Shares Sold from the Enter Transaction drop-down list box.

Quicken displays the Sell - Shares Sold dialog box (shown in Figure 14-10). Use the Transaction Date box to provide the sales date. Use the Security Name drop-down list box to identify the stock, bond, or mutual fund you're selling. You use the Number Of Shares, Price Received, and Commission text boxes to describe your sale, and you use the To This Account's Cash Balance or To option button to specify whether Quicken should adjust some bank account balance for this transaction.

Figure 14-10:
The Sell -
Shares Sold
dialog box.

[Sell - Shares Sold dialog box]

Enter transaction: Sell - Shares Sold Enter the sale of shares of a security (add the proceeds to my cash balance).

Sell - Shares Sold:

Transaction date: 06/30/07 Security name: IBM

Account: Brokerage ☐ Sell all shares in this account

Memo: Number of shares: 100

 Price received: 80 per share

 Commission: 10.00

Record proceeds? Specify Lots

⦿ To this account's cash balance Total sale: 7,990.00

◯ To:

Cancel Clear Help Enter/New Enter/Done

3. **Click the Specify Lots button.**

 If you want to control which lots are sold — a *lot* is just a chunk of secu-rities you purchase together — you can click the Specify Lots button in the Shares Sold dialog box. Clicking this button tells Quicken to display a dialog box where you can specify which lots you're selling. (I describe how to use this dialog box in Chapter 13 if you need more information.)

4. **Click the Enter/New or the Enter/Done button.**

Recording dividends, capital gains, and other goodies

Taking care of this stuff is easy. Any time you receive investment income, click the Enter Transactions button and choose Inc – Income (Div, Int, Etc.) from the Enter Transaction drop-down list box. When Quicken displays the dialog box used to record income, use the Security Name drop-down list box to confirm the stock, bond, or mutual fund producing income and then use the Dividend, Interest, Short-Term Cap Gain Dist, Mid-Term Cap Gain Dist, Long-Term Cap Gain Dist, and Miscellaneous text boxes to record the amount and type of income, as shown in Figure 14-11.

Note: You use the Transfer Account drop-down list box to identify the account into which income amounts are deposited when you don't use the investment account's regular cash account.

To record dividends, capital gains, and other income when you reinvest the money you receive, click the Enter Transactions button and choose Income Reinvested from the Enter Transaction drop-down list box. When Quicken dis-plays the dialog box, describe the amounts received and how you've reinvested.

Figure 14-11:
The dialog box used to record income.

Recording other not-so-tricky transactions

Quicken lets you record all sorts of transactions in a brokerage account. Not only can you do reminder and stock split actions (which I describe for mutual fund accounts in Chapter 13), but you can also do a bunch of other things.

I briefly describe these other transactions and explain how to record them.

Bonds . . . James Bonds . . .

If you invest in bonds, you know that a bond's price is actually quoted as a percentage of its face value. A bond that sells for $950 with a face value of $1,000, for example, is quoted as 95 because the $950 price is 95 percent of the $1,000 face value. Quicken, however, doesn't let you describe a bond's price as a percent. You must enter the bond price as its price in dollars and cents.

Going for the gold

You can use Quicken to record precious-metal investments. Suppose, for example, that you're hoarding *Krugerrands* (1-ounce gold coins minted in South Africa). For this investment, the price is the price per Krugerrand, and the shares figure is actually the number of ounces (equal to the number of Krugerrands). Because Quicken doesn't supply price-per-ounce or number-of-ounces fields, you insert the information into the Price and Shares fields on the Investment register.

Recording margin interest expenses

To record margin interest expense, click the Enter Transactions button and select Margin Interest Expense from the Enter Transaction drop-down list box. When you do, Quicken displays the margin interest expense version of the investment transaction entry dialog box, which you use to describe the cost of your financial adventure. Only the most sophisticated investors should be using margin interest expense anyway. If you're one of these financial cowboys or cowgirls, then I assume that you're smart enough to figure out this stuff on your own.

Paying a miscellaneous expense

Sometimes you need to pay an expense. One rarely sees these occur for stock or bond investments. Expenses sometimes do arise with real estate partnership interests (which can be treated like common stock shares) or precious-metal investments (which can also be treated like common stock shares).

If you need to pay a fee for account handling or for storing your stash of South African Krugerrands, for example, you can record such an expense by clicking the Enter Transactions button and then choosing Miscellaneous Expense from the Enter Transactions drop-down list box. When Quicken displays the dialog box, fill out the boxes on the miscellaneous expense version of the investment transaction entry dialog box.

Recording a return of capital

The old *return of capital* trick. Sometimes, the money you receive because you own a security isn't really income. Rather, it's a refund of part of the purchase price.

Consider this example: You buy a mortgage-backed security — such as a Ginnie Mae bond — for which the *mortgagee* (the person who borrowed the mortgage money) pays not only periodic interest but also a portion of the mortgage principal.

Obviously, you shouldn't record the principal portion of the payment you receive as income. You must record this payment as a mortgage principal reduction or — in the parlance of investment record keeping — as a *return of capital*.

As another example, suppose that you invest in a limited partnership or real estate investment trust that begins liquidating. Some of the money that the investors receive in this case is really a return of their original investment, or a return of capital.

To record a return of capital action, click the Enter Transactions button. When Quicken displays the return of capital version of the investment transaction entry dialog box, choose Return Of Capital from the Enter Transaction drop-down list box and describe the security that's returning capital.

Special investment transactions

Quicken also supplies some other investment transaction types. Quicken provides special investment transactions to record the receipt of stock options, exercise of stock options, and repricing of stock options. Quicken also supplies investment transaction types for short selling and investment transactions for dealing with corporate mergers, spinoffs, and reorganizations. To use these other special investment transactions, you follow the same general approach described in the preceding sections.

More Quick Stuff about Brokerage Accounts

Let me tell you a couple other quick things. You'll almost certainly find these tidbits helpful.

Monitoring and updating securities' values

Regardless of whether you're working with a mutual fund account or with securities in a brokerage account, you can collect current market prices and store them with the Quicken account information.

To do so, use the Portfolio window (which you can open by choosing Investing⇨Portfolio) to display the investment account with the mutual fund shares or the securities that you want to update.

To record the current market price for a security, use the up-arrow and down-arrow keys to select the security (or click the security with the mouse). Then move the cursor to the Quote/Price field and enter the current price.

Researching investments

If you choose Investing⇨Online Research Tools, Quicken displays a short menu of commands for accessing online research resources available through the Quicken.com Web site. I think that the Mutual Fund Finder is particularly valuable. And the other tools can also be pretty darn useful. By the way, if you do use the Mutual Fund Finder to look for good mutual funds, you should know that investment management fees are highly, highly negatively correlated with long-term investment performance. In other words, the higher the investment management fees, the lower the returns over long periods of time.

Adjusting errors

You can adjust the cash balance in a brokerage account and the shares balance in brokerage accounts if for some reason the figures are incorrect.

Oops, my brokerage cash balance is wrong

How you adjust the cash balance in a brokerage account depends on how you set up the account.

To adjust an investment account's cash balance when the cash balance information isn't tracked in a separate linked cash account, you open the investment account's register (such as by clicking its QuickTab), and then you choose Investing⇨Investing Activities⇨Update Cash Balance. When Quicken displays the Update Cash Balance dialog box, shown in Figure 14-12, specify the correct cash balance and the date as of when the figure you enter is correct.

Figure 14-12:
The Update
Cash
Balance
dialog box.

To adjust an investment account's cash balance (or "cash management account" as some brokerage houses call them), you reconcile the account in the usual way. For information about how to reconcile a linked cash account, refer to Chapter 8. Chapter 8 describes how to reconcile a bank account, but reconciling a linked cash account works the same way.

Oops, my brokerage account shares balance is wrong

To adjust the shares balance for a security in a brokerage account, open the brokerage account's register and choose Investing⇨Investing Activities⇨Update Share Balance.

Quicken next displays the Adjust Share Balance dialog box, shown in Figure 14-13, where you specify the security, the correct number of shares balance, and the date for which you're entering the balance. Fill in the text boxes and click OK. Quicken adjusts the shares balance for the security you specified.

Figure 14-13:
The Adjust
Share
Balance
dialog box.

A few words on the investment account window

If you've read this whole chapter, you know that I mostly describe how you get information into the investment account window. But before I stop talking about the investment account window, I want to give you a little more information on how you can use the window to monitor your investments.

The first thing to notice is that the investment account window provides several tabs, each of which provides its own information: Today's Data, Performance, Analysis, and Portfolio:

- ✔ **The Today's Data tab** (see Figure 14-14) shows the current value of your investments, daily gain or loss, and overall gain or loss. (I'm not sure that the focus on short-term investment performance is good, but lots of people are interested in watching their investments this closely.)

- ✔ **The Performance tab** graphs your investment account values and lets you compare these values to some external benchmark, such as the S&P 500.

- ✔ **The Analysis tab** provides charts and tables of information that let you see how your overall investments are allocated (see Figure 14-15). For what it's worth (and I have an MBA in finance, a master's of science in taxation, and two-plus decades of professional experience), I think this asset allocation information is useful and can lead you to better diversify your portfolio and more prudently bear financial risks. (Malkiel's book, *A Random Walk Guide to Investing,* which I reference earlier in this chapter, is a great little guide to picking investments and appropriate allocations.)

Figure 14-14:
The Today's
Data tab of
the
investment
account
window.

Figure 14-15:
The
Analysis tab
of the
investment
account
window.

> ✔ **The Portfolio tab** provides overall summary information about all your investment accounts (see Figure 14-16).

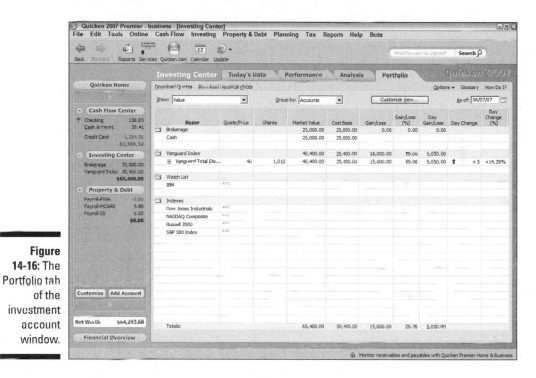

Figure 14-16: The Portfolio tab of the investment account window.

Online Investing with Quicken

Before I wrap up this chapter, let me mention one other quick thing: If you have Quicken and you have an online investment account with someone who supports the Quicken program's online investing, you can download your investment transactions from your online broker's Web site right into the appropriate Quicken investment account.

If you want to do this, first check with the online broker to see whether his or her firm supports this feature. If the firm does support this feature, choose Investing➪Online Investing Setup. Then follow the on-screen instructions. After you do this, you can easily download investment transactions from your online investment broker. Online investing works the same way that online banking does.

Part IV
Serious Business

The 5th Wave
By Rich Tennant

"You know kids – you can't buy them just <u>any</u> accounting software."

In this part . . .

If you use Quicken in a business, you'll need some information about how to use the program for payroll, customer receivables, and vendor payables. Sure, you can learn these things by sitting down with your certified public accountant, having a cup of coffee, and paying about $185 an hour.

Or you can read on, pretend that we're chitchatting over coffee, and save the $185.

Chapter 15

Payroll

In This Chapter

▶ Creating categories and accounts necessary to prepare payroll

▶ Getting an employer ID number

▶ Getting Social Security, Medicare, and federal income tax withholding information

▶ Calculating an employee's gross wages, payroll deductions, and net wages

▶ Recording a payroll check in Quicken

▶ Making federal tax deposits

▶ Filing quarterly and annual payroll tax returns

▶ Producing annual wage statements, such as W-2s

▶ Handling state payroll taxes

A lot of people with small businesses or a household employee (a nanny, for example) need to deal with payroll. Unfortunately, while all the payroll tax forms and tedious calculations might make you want to have someone else — such as a bookkeeper or payroll service — do the work, that's often not an economical solution. Payroll service bureaus (including Intuit's) often charge at least $1,000 a year — even if you've only got a single employee. For this reason, I want to provide you with some quick-and-dirty instructions about how to handle simple payroll situations with Quicken. Oh, sure. It won't be pretty. But I promise you it'll be cheap.

If you're planning to use Quicken for doing a lot of payroll, do yourself a favor and either buy QuickBooks (another Intuit product) or upgrade to Quicken Premier Home & Business (which is actually available on your CD and can be activated online for about $20). Quicken Premier Home & Business includes QuickPayroll, which lets you more easily calculate withholding amounts and prepare paychecks.

However, if you've got only a simple payroll need (such as for a nanny who's paid the same amount each month), this chapter explains how you do so.

For more information about Quicken Premier Home & Business, choose Help➪Add Business Tools. For more information about QuickBooks, see the Web site www.quickbooks.com. Would it be terrible if I told you that I'm also the author of *QuickBooks For Dummies?* And that there's lots of information about small business accounting in it? I hope not.

Getting Ready for Payroll

To prepare payroll checks and summarize the payroll information that you need to prepare quarterly and annual returns, you need to set up some special accounts and categories. You also need to do some paperwork stuff. I describe how to do both things in this section.

Getting Quicken ready

To do payroll in Quicken, you need to set up several liability accounts, a payroll expense category, and several payroll expense subcategories. Fortunately, doing so is not particularly difficult.

I'm going to describe how you do this task for purposes of U.S. federal income and payroll taxes. If you employ people in one of the states that has a state income tax — California, say — you may also have to deal with state payroll taxes. But you can track and process these the same way you process the federal taxes. (Some counties and cities even have income taxes, but these should also work the same way.)

I should say that you might also have other taxes to pay if you employ people outside the United States. But, hey, with a couple hundred countries in the world, your best bet is to get specific advice from someone of authority or expertise in the country of employment.

Setting up liability accounts

You need to set up three liability accounts to deal with federal payroll and income taxes:

- **Payroll-SS:** to track Social Security

- **Payroll-MCARE:** to track Medicare

- **Payroll-FWH (for *Federal Withholding*):** to track federal income taxes owed

(I should confess that these aren't my names. They're the names that Quicken expects you to use.)

To set up a llability account for any of these payroll tax liabilities, follow these steps:

1. **Click the Property & Debt button.**

 Quicken displays the Property & Debt Center window. You've probably seen this window about a hundred times before. If you want to see the window right now, though, choose the command and look at your screen.

2. **Click the Add Account button in the Property & Debt Center window.**

 Quicken displays the Quicken Account Setup dialog box, shown in Figure 15-1.

Figure 15-1: Choosing the account type.

3. **Select the Liability option button and then click Next.**

 Doing so tells Quicken that you're going to set up a Liability account. Quicken displays the next Quicken Account Setup dialog box, shown in Figure 15-2.

4. **Type the appropriate account name:** Payroll-SS, Payroll-MCARE, or Payroll-FWH.

 Move the cursor to the Name This Account text box and type the correct name.

5. **Click Next.**

 Quicken displays the next Quicken Account Setup dialog box, shown in Figure 15-3, which provides text boxes for specifying how much you already owe.

Figure 15-2:
Naming the account.

Figure 15-3:
Entering the ending date and balance.

6. **Enter the starting date in the As Of Date text box.**

 Move the cursor to the As Of Date text box. Type the date — probably the current date — on which you owe the balance that you enter in the Value text box.

7. **Enter the current amount you owe for the payroll tax liability.**

 Move the cursor to the Value text box and enter whatever you already owe. Or, if you're just starting and owe nothing, type **0**. (If you do owe something but don't have a clue in the world as to how much, you should figure out what you owe now before going any further. Sorry.)

8. **Click Done.**

 Quicken displays a message box that asks whether you want to set up an amortized loan for this liability.

9. **Click No.**

 This choice tells Quicken that you don't want to set up an amortized loan for the liability account. Quicken, only slightly bent out of shape, displays the Account Register window, which shows your new account.

10. **Close the Account Register window by clicking its Close box.**

11. **Repeat Steps 2 through 10 for all the other payroll tax liability accounts you want to add.**

 Remember that you need at least three payroll tax liability accounts — Payroll-SS, Payroll-MCARE, and Payroll-FWH — for the people you employ in the United States. And if you live in a state with income taxes, you either need to move or set up a fourth account: Payroll-SWH.

 The only trick to naming other payroll tax liability accounts is that you need to start each liability account name with the word *Payroll*. No, I didn't just make up this rule arbitrarily. I have a reason for this policy. You can easily create a report that prints information on all the accounts and categories that start with the word *Payroll*.

Setting up a payroll expense category

You also need to set up a payroll expense category. Here's all you do:

1. **Choose Tools⇨Category List.**

 Quicken, with no hesitation, displays the Category List window. Figure 15-4 shows this puppy.

Figure 15-4:
The
Category
List window.

2. **Click New.**

 Quicken displays the Set Up Category dialog box (see Figure 15-5).

Figure 15-5:
The Set Up
Category
dialog box.

3. **Enter Payroll as the category name.**

 Move the cursor to the Name text box and type **Payroll**.

4. **[Optional] Enter a description of the category.**

 If you want, you can type a description in the Description text box.

5. **In the Type section, select the Expense option button.**

 This choice tells Quicken that you're setting up an expense category.

6. **Describe the tax characteristics of this category.**

 If you're preparing payroll for a business, select the Tax-Related check box.

 If you're prepaying payroll for a household employee — like a nanny, say — don't select the Tax-Related check box. This little check box merely tells Quicken to include this category on the Tax Summary report. Household employee payroll expenses aren't tax-deductible — as you probably know.

 Optionally, if you want, you can select the tax form from the Tax Line Item drop-down list box on which this category should be reported for U.S. federal tax purposes.

7. **Click OK.**

 Quicken adds the category to the category list and redisplays the Category List window.

Setting up the payroll subcategories

You need to do one more thing to get Quicken ready for payroll: You need to set up subcategory expenses for employee gross wages, the company's share of the Social Security taxes, and the company's share of the Medicare taxes. Quicken expects you to use *Gross, Comp SS,* and *Comp MCARE* as subcategory names. So that's what I use in the following steps:

1. **Display the Category List window if it isn't showing already.**

 Choose Tools➪Category List. If you can't remember what this window looks like, refer to Figure 15-4.

2. **Click the New button.**

 Quicken displays the Set Up Category dialog box (refer to Figure 15-5).

3. **Type the appropriate payroll expense subcategory name:** Gross, Comp SS, or Comp MCARE.

 For example, move the cursor to the Name field and type **Gross** or **Comp SS** or **Comp MCARE**.

4. **Enter a description of the subcategory in the Description text box.**

 Because the subcategory names are a little more cryptic, you may want to use the Description text box to document things such as what *Comp SS* means. (I recommend entering **Company Social Security**.)

5. **In the Type section, select the Subcategory Of option button.**

 This option tells Quicken that you're setting up a subcategory.

6. **Indicate that the subcategory falls into the Payroll expense category by moving the cursor to the Subcategory Of text box and typing** P **for Payroll.**

 Or, because this is a drop-down list box, you can open the list box and select the payroll expense category from it.

7. **Click OK.**

 Quicken adds the subcategory to the category list and redisplays the Category List window. It also automatically adds the tax information you specified for the Payroll category.

8. **Repeat Steps 2 through 7 for all the remaining payroll expense subcategories you need.**

For employees working in the United States, you need at least three subcategories: Gross (for tracking gross wages), Comp SS (for tracking company Social Security taxes), and Comp MCARE (for tracking employer Medicare taxes).

Congratulations, Mr. Bond. You saved the world again. You created the liability accounts and categories that you need to track the amounts you pay employees and the payroll taxes you withhold and owe.

By the way, if you have state or local income taxes, these taxes should be handled the same way as federal income taxes. Just set up equivalent accounts for state and local taxes withheld. If you have state or local payroll taxes that you (the employer) pay, you need to set up accounts and categories like those for tracking the employer's portion of Social Security and Medicare. If you have state or local payroll taxes that your employee pays, you need to set up accounts and categories like those for tracking the employee's portion of Social Security and Medicare.

Getting the taxes stuff right

You also need to do a couple other things if you want to do payroll the right way in the U.S. of A.

Requesting (or demanding) an employer ID number

First, you need to file the SS-4, or Request for Employer Identification Number form, with the Internal Revenue Service (IRS) so that you can get an Employer Identification Number. You can get this form by calling the IRS and asking for one or by visiting the IRS Web site (www.irs.gov).

In one of its cooler moves, the IRS changed its ways. You can apply for and receive an Employer Identification Number over the telephone. You still need to fill out the SS-4 form, however, so that you can answer questions the IRS asks during the short, telephone-application process. (You also need to mail or fax the form to the service after your telephone conversation.)

Or, even cooler, you can apply right online. Here's the URL:

```
https://sa1.www4.irs.gov/sa_vign/newFormSS4.do
```

So what about Social Security, Medicare, and withholding taxes?

You need to do two things before you can figure out how to handle all those taxes. First, you need your employees to fill out W-4 forms to let you know what filing status they'll use and how many personal exemptions they'll claim. Guess where you get blank W-4 forms? That's right . . . from your friendly IRS agent.

You also need to get a *Circular E Employer's Tax Guide* publication. The *Circular E* publication is the pamphlet that tells you how much you should withhold in federal income taxes, Social Security, and Medicare from a person's salary. You can get this form, as well as the additional federal forms that you must fill out to satisfy the government requirements for hiring employees, by calling those friendly people at the Internal Revenue Service or by visiting the IRS's Web site, www.irs.gov. To get state tax forms, contact the equivalent tax agency in your state.

Paying someone for a job well done

After you tell Quicken to get ready to do payroll and you collect the necessary tax information, you're ready to pay someone.

Figuring out the gross wages figure

Determining how much to pay your employees should be pretty easy. Does Raoul make $15 an hour? Did he work 40 hours? Then you owe him $600 because $15 times 40 equals $600. Is Betty's salary $400 a week? Then you owe her $400 for the week.

Calculating that deductions stuff

Your next step — after you know how much you're supposed to pay Raoul and Betty — is to figure out what Uncle Sam says you must withhold.

To determine this amount, you need both Raoul's and Betty's W-4s to find out their filing statuses and personal exemptions. Then just flip to the page in the *Circular E* that describes withholding for persons claiming those filing statuses and weekly pay.

If Raoul is single and claims just one personal exemption, for example, you need to flip to the page like the one shown in Figure 15-6. Remember that Raoul is paid each week based on the number of hours he worked. I circled the number in the table in Figure 15-6 that shows what Raoul is supposed to pay in federal income taxes.

And Betty? Remember that Betty's pay is $400 a week. If Betty's filing status is married filing jointly and she has three personal exemptions, you need to flip to the page that resembles Figure 15-7. Again, I circled the number in the table in Figure 15-7 that shows what Betty is supposed to pay.

SINGLE Persons—WEEKLY Payroll Period

If the wages are —		And the number of withholding allowances claimed is —										
At least	But less than	0	1	2	3	4	5	6	7	8	9	10
		The amount of income tax to be withheld is—										
$600	$610	94	79	67	59	51	43	36	28	20	12	4
610	620	96	81	69	61	53	45	37	29	21	13	5
620	630	99	84	70	62	54	46	39	31	23	15	7
630	640	102	87	72	64	56	48	40	32	24	16	8
640	650	105	90	75	65	57	49	42	34	26	18	10
650	660	108	93	78	67	59	51	43	35	27	19	11
660	670	110	95	81	68	60	52	45	37	29	21	13
670	680	113	98	83	70	62	54	46	38	30	22	14
680	690	116	101	86	71	63	55	48	40	32	24	16
690	700	119	104	89	74	65	57	49	41	33	25	17
700	710	122	107	92	77	66	58	51	43	35	27	19
710	720	124	109	95	80	68	60	52	44	36	28	20
720	730	127	112	97	83	69	61	54	46	38	30	22
730	740	130	115	100	85	71	63	55	47	39	31	23
740	750	133	118	103	88	73	64	57	49	41	33	25
750	760	136	121	106	91	76	66	58	50	42	34	26
760	770	138	123	109	94	79	67	60	52	44	36	28
770	780	141	126	111	97	82	69	61	53	45	37	29
780	790	144	129	114	99	85	70	63	55	47	39	31
790	800	147	132	117	102	87	73	64	56	48	40	32
800	810	150	135	120	105	90	75	66	58	50	42	34
810	820	152	137	123	108	93	78	67	59	51	43	35
820	830	155	140	125	111	96	81	69	61	53	45	37
830	840	158	143	128	113	99	84	70	62	54	46	38
840	850	161	146	131	116	101	87	72	64	56	48	40
850	860	164	149	134	119	104	89	75	65	57	49	41
860	870	166	151	137	122	107	92	77	67	59	51	43
870	880	169	154	139	125	110	95	80	68	60	52	44
880	890	172	157	142	127	113	98	83	70	62	54	46
890	900	175	160	145	130	115	101	86	71	63	55	47
900	910	178	163	148	133	118	103	89	74	65	57	49
910	920	180	165	151	136	121	106	91	77	66	58	50
920	930	183	168	153	139	124	109	94	79	68	60	52
930	940	186	171	156	141	127	112	97	82	69	61	53
940	950	189	174	159	144	129	115	100	85	71	63	55
950	960	192	177	162	147	132	117	103	88	73	64	56
960	970	194	179	165	150	135	120	105	91	76	66	58
970	980	197	182	167	153	138	123	108	93	79	67	59
980	990	200	185	170	155	141	126	111	96	81	69	61
990	1,000	203	188	173	158	143	129	114	99	84	70	62
1,000	1,010	206	191	176	161	146	131	117	102	87	72	64
1,010	1,020	208	193	179	164	149	134	119	105	90	75	65
1,020	1,030	211	196	181	167	152	137	122	107	93	78	67
1,030	1,040	214	199	184	169	155	140	125	110	95	81	68
1,040	1,050	217	202	187	172	157	143	128	113	98	83	70
1,050	1,060	220	205	190	175	160	145	131	116	101	86	71
1,060	1,070	222	207	193	178	163	148	133	119	104	89	74
1,070	1,080	225	210	195	181	166	151	136	121	107	92	77
1,080	1,090	228	213	198	183	169	154	139	124	109	95	80
1,090	1,100	231	216	201	186	171	157	142	127	112	97	83
1,100	1,110	234	219	204	189	174	159	145	130	115	100	85
1,110	1,120	236	221	207	192	177	162	147	133	118	103	88
1,120	1,130	239	224	209	195	180	165	150	135	121	106	91
1,130	1,140	242	227	212	197	183	168	153	138	123	109	94
1,140	1,150	245	230	215	200	185	171	156	141	126	111	97
1,150	1,160	248	233	218	203	188	173	159	144	129	114	99
1,160	1,170	252	235	221	206	191	176	161	147	132	117	102
1,170	1,180	255	238	223	209	194	179	164	149	135	120	105
1,180	1,190	258	241	226	211	197	182	167	152	137	123	108
1,190	1,200	261	244	229	214	199	185	170	155	140	125	111
1,200	1,210	264	248	232	217	202	187	173	158	143	128	113
1,210	1,220	267	251	235	220	205	190	175	161	146	131	116
1,220	1,230	270	254	237	223	208	193	178	163	149	134	119
1,230	1,240	273	257	240	225	211	196	181	166	151	137	122
1,240	1,250	276	260	244	228	213	199	184	169	154	139	125

$1,250 and over Use Table 1(a) for a **SINGLE person** on page 34. Also see the instructions on page 32.

Figure 15-6: Raoul's tax deduction stuff.

MARRIED Persons—**WEEKLY** Payroll Period

If the wages are—		And the number of withholding allowances claimed is —										
At least	But less than	0	1	2	3	4	5	6	7	8	9	10
		The amount of income tax to be withheld is—										
$0	$125	0	0	0	0	0	0	0	0	0	0	0
125	130	1	0	0	0	0	0	0	0	0	0	0
130	135	1	0	0	0	0	0	0	0	0	0	0
135	140	2	0	0	0	0	0	0	0	0	0	0
140	145	3	0	0	0	0	0	0	0	0	0	0
145	150	4	0	0	0	0	0	0	0	0	0	0
150	155	4	0	0	0	0	0	0	0	0	0	0
155	160	5	0	0	0	0	0	0	0	0	0	0
160	165	6	0	0	0	0	0	0	0	0	0	0
165	170	7	0	0	0	0	0	0	0	0	0	0
170	175	7	0	0	0	0	0	0	0	0	0	0
175	180	8	0	0	0	0	0	0	0	0	0	0
180	185	9	1	0	0	0	0	0	0	0	0	0
185	190	10	2	0	0	0	0	0	0	0	0	0
190	195	10	2	0	0	0	0	0	0	0	0	0
195	200	11	3	0	0	0	0	0	0	0	0	0
200	210	12	4	0	0	0	0	0	0	0	0	0
210	220	14	6	0	0	0	0	0	0	0	0	0
220	230	15	7	0	0	0	0	0	0	0	0	0
230	240	17	9	1	0	0	0	0	0	0	0	0
240	250	18	10	2	0	0	0	0	0	0	0	0
250	260	20	12	4	0	0	0	0	0	0	0	0
260	270	21	13	5	0	0	0	0	0	0	0	0
270	280	23	15	7	0	0	0	0	0	0	0	0
280	290	24	16	8	0	0	0	0	0	0	0	0
290	300	26	18	10	2	0	0	0	0	0	0	0
300	310	27	19	11	3	0	0	0	0	0	0	0
310	320	29	21	13	5	0	0	0	0	0	0	0
320	330	30	22	14	6	0	0	0	0	0	0	0
330	340	32	24	16	8	0	0	0	0	0	0	0
340	350	33	25	17	9	1	0	0	0	0	0	0
350	360	35	27	19	11	3	0	0	0	0	0	0
360	370	36	28	20	12	4	0	0	0	0	0	0
370	380	38	30	22	14	6	0	0	0	0	0	0
380	390	39	31	23	15	7	0	0	0	0	0	0
390	400	41	33	25	17	9	1	0	0	0	0	0
400	410	42	34	26	18	10	2	0	0	0	0	0
410	420	44	36	28	20	12	4	0	0	0	0	0
420	430	45	37	29	21	13	5	0	0	0	0	0
430	440	47	39	31	23	15	7	0	0	0	0	0
440	450	48	40	32	24	16	8	1	0	0	0	0
450	460	50	42	34	26	18	10	2	0	0	0	0
460	470	51	43	35	27	19	11	4	0	0	0	0
470	480	53	45	37	29	21	13	5	0	0	0	0
480	490	54	46	38	30	22	14	7	0	0	0	0
490	500	56	48	40	32	24	16	8	0	0	0	0
500	510	57	49	41	33	25	17	10	2	0	0	0
510	520	59	51	43	35	27	19	11	3	0	0	0
520	530	60	52	44	36	28	20	13	5	0	0	0
530	540	62	54	46	38	30	22	14	6	0	0	0
540	550	63	55	47	39	31	23	16	8	0	0	0
550	560	65	57	49	41	33	25	17	9	1	0	0
560	570	66	58	50	42	34	26	19	11	3	0	0
570	580	68	60	52	44	36	28	20	12	4	0	0
580	590	69	61	53	45	37	29	22	14	6	0	0
590	600	71	63	55	47	39	31	23	15	7	0	0
600	610	72	64	56	48	40	32	25	17	9	1	0
610	620	74	66	58	50	42	34	26	18	10	2	0
620	630	75	67	59	51	43	35	28	20	12	4	0
630	640	77	69	61	53	45	37	29	21	13	5	0
640	650	78	70	62	54	46	38	31	23	15	7	0
650	660	80	72	64	56	48	40	32	24	16	8	0
660	670	81	73	65	57	49	41	34	26	18	10	2
670	680	83	75	67	59	51	43	35	27	19	11	3
680	690	84	76	68	60	52	44	37	29	21	13	5
690	700	86	78	70	62	54	46	38	30	22	14	6
700	710	87	79	71	63	55	47	40	32	24	16	8
710	720	89	81	73	65	57	49	41	33	25	17	9
720	730	90	82	74	66	58	50	43	35	27	19	11
730	740	92	84	76	68	60	52	44	36	28	20	12

Figure 15-7: Betty's tax deduction stuff.

Always use up-to-date information. The numbers you use for federal income tax withholding change annually. Therefore, *don't* use the tables shown in Figures 15-6 and 15-7. They'll be long out-of-date by the time you read this.

You determine Social Security and Medicare amounts by multiplying the gross wage figure by a set percentage. Social Security is 6.2 percent of the gross wages up to roughly $100,000. The Medicare tax is 1.45 percent of the gross wages with no wage limit. Be sure to check your faithful *Circular E* if you think limits come into play for a particular employee. Note, too, that as I'm writing this, Congress is tinkering with the tax laws again. But, of course, Congress is *always* tinkering with the tax laws.

Figuring out someone's net wages

Table 15-1 summarizes the payroll calculations shown in Figures 15-6 and 15-7, earlier in this chapter.

Table 15-1	Payroll for Raoul and Betty		
Item	*Raoul*	*Betty*	*Explanation*
Gross Wages	$600	$400	Their pay
Withholding	$79	$18	From *Circular E*
Social Security	$37.20	$24.80	6.2% of gross wages
Medicare	$8.70	$5.80	1.45% of gross wages
Net Wages	$475.10	$351.40	What's left over

Does Table 15-1 make sense? If it doesn't, take another look at the marked information in Figures 15-6 and 15-7 and read my earlier discussion of how to figure out deductions stuff. All I've really done in the table is reorganize some information, calculate the Social Security and Medicare taxes, and show how Raoul's and Betty's gross pay gets nickeled and dimed by the various taxes they owe.

Working with other taxes and deductions

If you have other taxes and deductions to make and you know how the federal income taxes, Social Security taxes, and Medicare taxes work, you won't have any problem working with other taxes — whatever they are.

State income tax withholding, for example, works like the federal income tax withholding. (Of course, you need to get the state's equivalent to the *Circular F* guide.)

In general, you treat other taxes and the amounts the employee pays similarly.

In fact, the only thing that you need to be careful about is what affects your employees' gross pay for income taxes but not their Social Security taxes — things such as 401(k) deductions and certain fringe benefits. If you have these kinds of things to deal with and you need help, just ask your accountant. (Providing general answers that will work for everyone who reads this paragraph is just too difficult — and actually kind of dangerous, too. Sorry.)

Recording a payroll check

After you make the tax deduction and net wages calculation, you're ready to record the check. Doing so is a little bit tricky, but stick with me; I'll get you through it in no time.

If Betty is milling around your computer, whining, and saying things like, "Gee, Boss, how much longer? I want to get to the bank before it closes," tell her to cool her heels for about three minutes.

Suppose that you're going to record the check by using the Register window for your checking account. (As you know, recording the check into the Write Checks window works the same basic way. The difference is that by using the Write Checks window, you can more easily print the payroll check.)

After you display the Checking Account Register window and highlight the first empty row of the register, follow these steps:

1. **Enter the date of the payroll check in the Date field.**

2. **Enter the payroll check number in the Num field.**

3. **Enter the employee name in the Payee field.**

4. **Enter the net wages amount in the Payment field.**

5. **Open the Split Transaction window (see Figure 15-8).**

 You can do so by clicking the Split button.

6. **In the first row of the Split Transaction window, enter the category and gross wages amount in the correct fields.**

 Enter the category **Payroll:Gross**. The amount, of course, should be the gross wages figure (**400.00** in the example).

Figure 15-8:
The Split
Transaction
window
recording
Betty's $400
wages and
her $351.40
paycheck.

7. **Enter the employee's federal withholding tax and account in the second row of the Split Transaction window.**

 Instead of a category in the Category field, enter a liability account **[Payroll-FWH]** or select it from the drop-down list box (in this case, it would be Transfer To/From [Payroll-FWH]). This tax-withheld amount comes from the *Circular E* form (**18.00** in this example).

8. **Enter the employee's Social Security tax withheld and account in the third row of the Split Transaction window.**

 In the Category field, enter the liability account **[Payroll-SS]** or select Transfer To/From [Payroll-SS] from the drop-down list box. The amount of the Social Security tax withheld should be 6.2 percent of the employee's gross wages (**24.80** in this example). Type this number in the Amount field.

9. **Enter the employee's Medicare tax withheld and account in the fourth row of the Split Transaction window.**

 In the Category field, enter the liability account **[Payroll-MCARE]** or select the account from the drop-down list box. The amount of the Medicare tax withheld should be 1.45 percent of the employee's gross wages (**5.80** in this example).

 Figure 15-8 shows the Split Transaction window filled out to record Betty's $400 of wages, the taxes poor Betty has to pay on these earnings, and the net wages figure of $351.40. If you have questions about any of these figures, take a peek again at Table 15-1.

10. **If you have other employee-paid payroll taxes, record them in the next empty rows, following the same set of procedures.**

11. **If you plan to print this paycheck on a payroll check that has a remittance advice or payroll stub, move down to line 17; otherwise just move to the next empty line.**

 (An *advice* is accounting jargon for the little slip of paper that's attached to the actual check form.)

 Only the first 16 lines of the Split Transaction window's information print on a payroll stub. So by using lines 17 and higher for the employer portions of the payroll tax, you won't confuse the employee about employee versus employer payroll taxes. If you aren't printing payroll stubs, you can just move to the next empty row.

12. **On the next two empty lines of the Split Transaction window, enter your (the employer's) matching share of the Social Security tax.**

 If the employee pays $24.80 of Social Security tax, for example, type **Payroll: Comp SS** in the Category field and **24.80** in the Amount field in the first empty line.

 Then type **[Payroll-SS]** in the Category field and **–24.80** in the Amount field in the next line to record the Social Security tax liability.

 Figure 15-9 shows the Social Security and Medicare payroll tax information.

Figure 15-9:
The employer's matching share of Social Security and Medicare taxes.

13. **On the next two empty lines of the Split Transaction window, enter your (the employer's) matching share of the Medicare tax.**

 If the employer pays $5.80 of Medicare, for example, use the first empty line to type **Payroll: Comp MCARE** in the Category field or choose the account from the drop-down list box; then type **5.80** in the Amount field.

Then type **[Payroll-MCARE]** in the Category section or choose the account from the drop-down list box; then enter **–5.80** in the Amount section in the next line to record the Medicare tax liability.

The accounts you use to show the payroll taxes withheld and owed are liability accounts. By looking at the balances of these accounts, you can easily see how much you owe the government.

14. **If you have other employer-paid payroll taxes, record these following the employer's matching share of the Social Security and Medicare taxes.**

 You can use this same basic approach to record federal and state unemployment taxes.

15. **After you finish entering the employer-paid payroll taxes, click OK to close the Split Transaction window.**

16. **To record the payroll check and related employer-paid payroll tax information in the register, click Enter.**

You did it! You recorded a payroll check and the related payroll taxes. Maybe it wasn't all that much fun, but at least it wasn't very difficult. (Chapter 5 describes how to print checks, just in case you're interested.)

Depositing Taxes

Make no mistake. Uncle Sam wants the money you withhold from an employee's payroll check for federal income taxes, Social Security, and Medicare. Uncle Sam also wants the payroll taxes you owe — such as matching Social Security and Medicare taxes and federal unemployment taxes.

Every so often, then, you need to pay Uncle Sam the amounts you owe.

Making this payment is simple. Just write a check payable for the account balances shown in the payroll tax liability accounts. If you've written only the one check to Betty (as shown in Figures 15-8 and 15-9), for example, your payroll liability accounts would show the following balances:

Liability Account	*Amount*
Payroll-SS	$49.60
Payroll-MCARE	$11.60
Payroll-FWH	$18.00
Total	$79.20

Notice that the Payroll-SS account balance and the Payroll-MCARE account balance include both the employee's and the employer's Social Security and Medicare taxes.

Then you write a check for the $79.20 you owe (see Figure 15-10). The only tricky thing about this transaction is that you transfer the check amount to the payroll liability accounts rather than assign the check amount to a payroll tax category. In effect, you transfer money from your checking account to the government to pay off the payroll taxes you owe.

Figure 15-10:
The Split Transaction window for paying Betty's payroll taxes.

The first time you see this sort of transfer, it can be a little confusing. So take a minute to think about it. If you write the check to the government, your checking account doesn't have the money in it anymore, and you don't owe the government the money anymore. Therefore, you need to decrease both the checking account balance and the liability account balance. In Quicken, you do so with an account transfer. (If you're a little shaky on doing the account transfer thing, you may want to take a quick peek at Chapter 4.)

When do you make payroll tax deposits? Good question. Fortunately, it's not one you have to answer. The Internal Revenue Service tells you when you're supposed to deposit your money. In my business, for example, I have to deposit payroll taxes within a couple of days of doing payroll. Some businesses have to deposit more frequently or more quickly. And some businesses get to deposit less quickly or less frequently.

While I am on federal payroll tax deposits, I should cover another general rule related to when you need to make the deposit: If your accumulated payroll taxes are less than $1,000, you can pay the taxes the next time you're supposed to remit payroll taxes: the next payroll date, the next month, or whatever. (This

is called the *De Minimis* rule — named after the Congresswoman Dee Minimis, I think.) Don't rely on this *rule,* however, without first checking with the Internal Revenue Service or your tax advisor.

To make a payroll tax deposit, just run your check with a federal tax deposit coupon to a financial institution qualified as a depository for federal taxes (probably your local bank) or to the Federal Reserve bank serving your geographical area. The IRS should have already sent you a book of coupons as a result of your requesting an employer ID number. And one other thing: Make your check payable to the depository or to the Federal Reserve.

Some businesses are either now, or will shortly be, required to electronically remit payroll tax deposits directly to the U.S. Treasury. The IRS should tell you when that's the case. Talk to your bank if you need to do this.

You might also want to sign up to pay tax deposits online at www.eftps.gov. By doing so, you can avoid a trip to the bank on tax deposit day.

Filing Quarterly Payroll Tax Returns

At the end of every quarter, you need to file a quarterly payroll tax return. (By *quarters* here, I'm referring to calendar quarters. You don't do this four times on a Sunday afternoon while you watch football.)

If you're a business, for example, you must file a Form 941 — which is a form you fill out to say how much you paid in gross wages, how much you withheld in federal taxes, and how much you owe for employer payroll taxes.

If you're not a business but have household employees — such as a nanny — you file a Form 942. You fill out this form to say how much you paid in gross wages, withheld in federal taxes, and owe in payroll taxes.

To get the gross wages totals and the balances in each of the payroll tax liability accounts, print a Cash Flow report for the quarter you need to report. You can do this by choosing Reports➪Banking➪Cash Flow. Quicken displays the Cash Flow report, but the dates will probably be wrong, so click the Customize button. Quicken displays the Customize Cash Flow dialog box, shown in Figure 15-11.

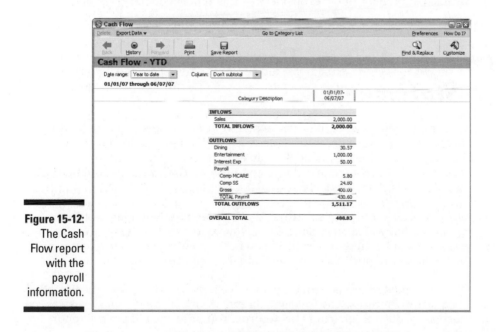

Figure 15-11:
The Customize Cash Flow dialog box.

Specify the range of dates as the start and end of the quarter for which you're preparing a quarterly report. Then click OK. Quicken produces a Cash Flow report, which you can easily use to fill out the quarterly payroll tax return. Figure 15-12 shows the on-screen version of the Cash Flow report. If you want to print a version of this report, click the Print button.

Figure 15-12:
The Cash Flow report with the payroll information.

The Gross amount in the Payroll Expenses section — $400 in the example — is the gross wages upon which employer payroll taxes are calculated.

The company's Social Security contributions and Medicare contributions are the amounts you recorded to date for the employer Social Security and Medicare taxes — so you need to double these figures to determine the actual Social Security and Medicare taxes you owe.

The transfers lines at the bottom of the report — these are all labeled as TO Payroll-FWH, TO Payroll-MCARE, TO Payroll-SS — represent the federal tax deposits you paid. If you're working off the on-screen report, you may need to scroll down to see this transfer information.

Note: If your accountant fills out the 941 or 942 for you, you don't even need to read this stuff. Your accountant won't have any problem completing the quarterly payroll tax return by using the Quicken report and, in fact — I kid you not — will probably even enjoy it.

Unlike earlier versions of Quicken, Quicken 2007 doesn't include a payroll report that provides just the payroll expense and transfer information. If you display the Reports And Graphs window (discussed in Chapter 7), you'll see a Payroll report. However, you need to upgrade to Quicken Premier Home & Business to produce this report. There are plenty of good reasons to upgrade to Quicken Premier Home & Business — this report isn't one of them.

Computing Annual Returns and Wage Statements

At year end, you need to file some annual returns — like the 940 federal unemployment tax return — and the W-2 and W-3 wage statements. (You'll need to prepare these by hand. Perhaps to protest all the work that small businesses have to go to in order to comply with tax laws, you could prepare these forms by hand using a cheap ballpoint pen. Just an idea.)

As a practical matter, the only thing that's different about filling out these reports is that you need to use a Cash Flow report that covers the entire year — not just a single quarter. So you need to enter the range of dates in the Cash Flow Report dialog box as January 1 and December 31.

The 940 annual return is darn easy if you've been wrestling with the 941 or 942 quarterly returns. The 940 annual return works the same basic way as those more difficult quarterly tax returns. You print the old payroll report, enter a few numbers, and then write a check for the amount you owe.

Note that you need to prepare state unemployment annual summaries before preparing the 940. The 940 requires information from the state returns.

For the W-2 statements and the summary W-3 (which summarizes your W-2s), you just print the old Cash Flow report and then, carefully following directions, enter the gross wages, the Social Security and Medicare taxes withheld, and the federal income taxes withheld into the appropriate blanks.

If you have a little trouble, call the IRS. If you have a lot of trouble, splurge on someone to do it. Any experienced bookkeeper can do the job for you.

Doing the State Payroll Taxes Thing

Yeah. I haven't talked about state payroll taxes — at least not in any great detail. I wish I could provide this sort of detailed, state-specific help to you. Unfortunately, doing so would make this chapter about 150 pages long. It would also cause me to go stark raving mad.

However, you still need to deal with the state payroll taxes. State payroll taxes follow the same basic mechanics you apply to the federal payroll taxes. For example, a state income tax works the same way the federal income tax works, employer-paid state unemployment taxes work the same way the employer-paid federal taxes work, and employee-paid state taxes work the same way the employee-paid Social Security and Medicare taxes work.

If you're tuned in to how federal payroll taxes work in Quicken, you really shouldn't have a problem with the mechanics of the state payroll taxes.

Chapter 16

Profits, Losses, Receivables, and Payables

. .

. .

*T*he most popular flavors of Quicken — Quicken Basic, Quicken Deluxe, and Quicken Premier — aren't really built for tracking the profits and losses of a small business nor the amounts that clients and customers owe you or that you owe your vendors. But you can do all this stuff as long as you don't try to get too fancy and as long as you don't have a long list of receivables or payables. This chapter describes how you can handle both situations *when you're not using Quicken Premier Home & Business.*

Note: If you *are* using Quicken Premier Home & Business, you track profits, losses, accounts receivable, and accounts payable using the tools built right into the Home & Business version of Quicken. I would recommend you consider stepping up to the Home & Business product if you're running a small business that does more than $10,000 in annual profits. If you're willing to learn a bit of accounting, I would also recommend you consider taking a slightly larger step — a step up to one of the flavors of QuickBooks that Intuit sells.

Tracking Profits and Losses

To track the profits and losses of a business, just set up a Quicken account for your business checking account. (How you do this, I describe in Chapter 2.)

Then when you deposit money into the account, categorize the deposit as income using a business income category named something like "Sales" or "Revenue." When you pay business expenses out of the account, categorize those payments as expenses using a business expense category. (In Chapter 2, I also describe how to add business income and expense categories.)

When you want to see how your business is doing — whether it's making money or losing money — just print out a cash flow or itemized categories report. That's it.

The accounting really can be this simple. But let me offer up one more tip: If you need some help, find a local CPA and get his or her help with any questions or problems you have with this accounting stuff. A good enrolled agent or bookkeeper may also be able to help you.

Tracking Customer Receivables

To track customer receivables, you must set up an asset account just for tracking customer receivables. If you know how to set up an asset account, just do it. If you don't, follow these steps:

1. **Click the Property & Debt button.**

 Quicken displays the Property & Debt Center window.

2. **Click the Add Account button.**

 Quicken asks you to choose the type of account you want to create: House (with or without Mortgage), Vehicle (with or without Loan), Asset, or Liability.

3. **Select the Asset option button.**

 Doing so tells Quicken that you're setting up a catchall asset account to track something besides a bank account, cash, or your investments.

4. **Click Next.**

 Quicken displays the Quicken Account Setup dialog box, as shown in Figure 16-1.

Figure 16-1:
The first
Quicken
Account
Setup dialog
box.

5. Name the account.

Move the cursor to the Name This Account text box and type a name, such as **Acct Rec**, to identify the account as the one that holds your accounts receivable. But one of the fun things about being in your own business is that *you* get to make the decisions about what you name your accounts — so go for it, dude, and be creative.

6. Click Next.

Quicken displays another Quicken Account Setup dialog box, shown in Figure 16-2, that lets you describe the asset's current balance.

Figure 16-2:
The second
Quicken
Account
Setup dialog
box.

7. **Leave the starting balance as zero.**

8. **Accept the default date.**

 You don't need to enter a date because you aren't entering a starting balance.

9. **Click Done.**

 Quicken displays the accounts receivable account you just created.

Tracking Customer Invoices and Payments

Because the popular versions of Quicken (Quicken Basic, Quicken Deluxe, and Quicken Premier) aren't designed to keep track of lots of receivables and don't generate their own invoices (see Chapter 2 for a refresher on what these versions of Quicken do and don't do), I think that you should just use Quicken to keep a list of your unpaid customer invoices. You can use a Quicken Other Asset account to bill customers and track their invoices, but this approach requires Rube Goldberg-esque complexity. What's more, if you do want to do all this complex stuff, you're really better off with either Quicken Premier Home & Business (which rather elegantly handles this stuff) or a real small business accounting system, such as QuickBooks by Intuit (which gives you full-powered invoicing and receivables accounting).

Now, back to the chase. . . .

For more information or to purchase Quicken Premier Home & Business, visit Intuit's Quicken Web site at www.quicken.com or choose the Help⇨Add Business Tools command.

Recording customer invoices

When you bill a customer — presumably you're going to do this by creating a nice-looking invoice in something like Microsoft Word or Excel — you just enter a transaction for the invoice amount in your Accounts Receivable register. You can follow these steps for recording a customer invoice in the next empty slot in the Accounts Receivable register:

1. **Open the register for the Accounts Receivable account (if necessary).**

 Click the Property & Debt button and double-click the accounts receivable account. Quicken displays the register window for the account.

2. **Enter the *invoice date* — the date you bill your customer or client — in the Date field.**

3. **Enter the invoice number in the Ref field.**

 The invoice number you enter is the number of the invoice you create yourself.

4. **Enter the customer or client name in the Payee field.**

 After the transaction has been recorded, the name appears in the Payee drop-down list box, and you can select the name from the list box any time you activate the list.

 Make sure that you use the same spelling of the customer's name every time you enter it because Quicken summarizes accounts receivable information by payee name: Quicken interprets *John Doe* and *Jonh Doe* as two different customers. In addition, you must take care with names because Quicken QuickFill works quickly in assuming that you mean a particular account name. If you first enter a customer name as *Mowgli's Lawn Service,* for example, and then later you type **Mowg** as an account name, Quicken assumes that you're entering another transaction for *Mowgli's Lawn Service* and fills the Payee field with the complete name. You can avoid trouble in both these instances by activating the Payee drop-down list and selecting the payee name from the list.

5. **Enter the invoice amount in the Increase field.**

6. **Click Enter to record the transaction.**

 If Quicken reminds you to enter a category, click No. You don't want to use a category in this step because you later categorize the invoice by using an income category when you record the customer deposit.

Figure 16-3 shows a register entry for a $750 invoice to Mowgli's Lawn Service. After you click Enter, the ending balance, shown in the lower-right corner, shows the sum of all the transactions in the register.

Figure 16-3:
An invoice entry in the Accounts Receivable register.

Recording customer payments

When you work with customer payments in Quicken, you need to do two things. First, you record the customer's check as a deposit in your bank account and categorize it as falling into one of your income categories. Because you can probably record this information with your eyes closed and one hand tied behind your back, I won't describe the process again here. (If you jumped straight to this exciting section, you may want to check out Chapter 4, where I talk all about deposits.)

Second, you must update your accounts receivable list for the customer's payment. To update the list, display the Accounts Receivable account's Register tab and mark the existing invoice the customer has paid by typing a **c** in the Clr (or cleared) field. (You can do so simply by clicking the Clr field.) Figure 16-4 shows that the first $750 invoice to Mowgli's Lawn Service has been paid.

Notice that I've gotten pretty crazy and entered some other invoices, too. It's my job.

Tracking Your Receivables

When you look at the Accounts Receivable register at this point, you can't tell the total of what your customers owe you. In Figure 16-4, for example, even though I've marked invoice #101 as paid, the account balance still shows $1,825 (the balance of all four invoices shown).

Discovering a dirty little secret about A/R reporting in Quicken

If you read the last section, you're aware of an unfortunate quirk in the way the popular versions of Quicken handle accounts receivable: The account balance for an asset account includes all the transactions entered in the register — even those you mark as being cleared. This quirk causes some problems. For example, you can't print an accurate balance sheet report because Quicken uses the account balance from an asset account on the balance sheet report, and this balance is not accurate.

Oh m'gosh — does this mean that you can't track receivables this way? Naw. It does mean, however, that you can't use the accounts receivable account balance for anything because the balance is really a meaningless number. What's more, the accounts receivable, total assets, and net worth figures on the Balance Sheet report are also meaningless numbers because the report uses the goofy accounts receivable account balances, too.

Producing an accurate balance sheet

Suppose that you do want to produce an accurate balance sheet. What do you do? You simply strip out the cleared transactions in a receivables register by deleting them one by one. Before you begin your deletions, however, print a copy of the Accounts Receivables register. You may want to keep track of the customer invoices that you billed.

What's that? You don't like the idea of stripping out the transactions? Okay. If you're willing to do slightly more work, you can fix the accounts receivable balance in another way. Using the Split Transaction window (see Chapter 15), go through and add split transaction information showing a reduction in the invoice total that results when the customer makes a payment.

For a $750 invoice on which the customer pays $400, for example, the Split Transaction window includes one line that records a positive number for the initial $750 invoice and another line that records a negative number for the $400 customer payment. So what you're left with is a transaction that equals $350 — the open balance on the invoice — because that's what the split transaction amounts add up to. Figure 16-5 shows an example of this.

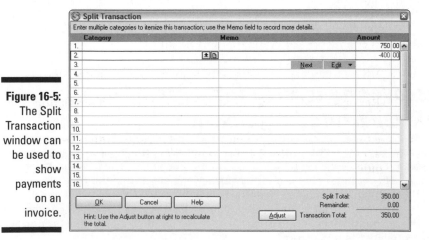

Figure 16-5:
The Split Transaction window can be used to show payments on an invoice.

If you use the Split Transaction window to show invoices being paid, don't mark partially paid invoices as cleared. If you do, they won't show up on the list of unpaid invoices. I talk a bit more about this report in the next section.

Getting a list of what customers owe you

You can also mitigate the problem of the inaccurate balance sheet by printing a list of unpaid invoices to summarize which people owe you and how much they owe. (Doing so won't suddenly make an inaccurate balance sheet accurate, of course, but it will let you know exactly who owes you what.)

Now let me point out a goofy change in recent versions of Quicken (specifically since Quicken 2005). In the past, Quicken let you easily print A/R By Customer reports — which were just lists of uncleared transactions, sorted by payees, from other asset accounts. In other words, in the past, Quicken let you easily print lists of unpaid invoices. Unfortunately, Intuit now makes it harder to do this. In fact, if you use the Reports And Graphs window (described in Chapter 7) to display a list of business reports, Quicken 2007 tells you that you can't produce an A/R By Customer report unless you unlock the report by upgrading to Quicken Premier Home & Business. As I say elsewhere in this book, Quicken Premier Home & Business is a great product. But you don't need to and shouldn't pay an upgrade fee merely for these reports.

You can, with just a bit of fiddling, produce an A/R By Customer report, which summarizes all uncleared transactions.

To Quicken, the first transaction in the typical accounts receivable register, Opening Balance, looks like a customer — even though it's not a real account. So that this phantom customer doesn't appear on your report, you may want to either delete it or mark it as cleared. The Edit menu's Transaction submenu supplies commands for doing this sort of stuff.

To print the A/R By Customer business report, follow these simple steps:

1. **Choose Reports➪Banking➪Transaction to display the Transaction report.**

2. **Click the Customize button if you've already created other asset accounts. In the Customize Transaction dialog box that appears, click the Accounts tab.**

 Your dialog box should look like the one shown in Figure 16-6.

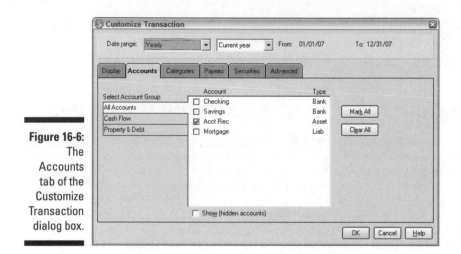

Figure 16-6:
The
Accounts
tab of the
Customize
Transaction
dialog box.

3. **Select which accounts with uncleared transactions you want on the Accounts Receivable report. Then to select an account, click the mouse or press the spacebar.**

 To do this, click the All Accounts item in the Select Account Group list, click the Clear All button, and then check your accounts receivable account's box. I've done this in Figure 16-6, by the way.

4. **Tell Quicken that only uncleared transactions should appear on the report.**

 To do this, click the Advanced tab and then deselect the Newly Cleared and Reconciled check boxes.

5. **Click OK.**

 Quicken redisplays the Transaction report. This time it lists all the uncleared transactions in your accounts receivable account, which represent your unpaid customer invoices. Figure 16-7 shows this Transaction report.

 You can save your customizations by clicking the Save Report button. When Quicken displays the Save Report dialog box, name the report something like *Accounts Receivable Listing* or *Unpaid Customer Invoices* and click OK.

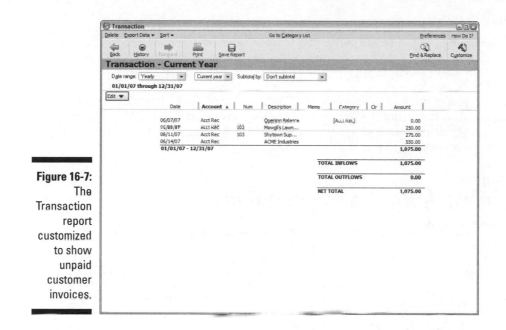

Figure 16-7:
The
Transaction
report
customized
to show
unpaid
customer
invoices.

Preparing to Track Vendor Payables

You really don't have to do anything special to begin tracking the amounts you know that you'll pay; however, you do need to have a bank account already set up. (I'm assuming that you do already have a bank account set up. If you don't — which is almost impossible to believe — refer to Chapters 1 and 2.)

Describing your vendor payables

You describe your vendor payables by filling in the checks you use to pay a vendor's bills in the Write Checks window. Don't print the checks, though. Quicken tracks these unprinted checks because they represent your unpaid vendor invoices. When you finally print the checks to actually pay the bills, then Quicken stops tracking them as unpaid bills. That's it.

I'm super-tempted to describe how you fill out the blanks of the Write Checks window — the result of the first tenet in the computer writer's boring old code of honor, "When in doubt, describe in detail." But really — as you probably know — filling out the Write Checks window is darn easy.

If you're not sure about how to fill out the Write Checks window, don't feel bad or think that the process requires an advanced degree. After all, you're still getting your feet wet. If you feel unsteady, peruse Chapter 5 and then go ahead and wail away at your keyboard.

Tracking vendor payables

Whenever you want to know how much money you owe someone, just print a report that summarizes the unprinted checks by payee name. Pretty easy, huh? All you have to do is print a Transaction report that lists only unprinted checks. Here's a blow-by-blow account of the steps you need to follow:

1. **Choose Reports⇨Banking⇨Transaction.**

2. **Click the Customize button.**

 Quicken, with little protest, displays the Customize Transaction dialog box. I showed you a copy of this dialog box earlier in Figure 16-6, so I'm not going to show you another one.

3. **Click the Advanced tab.**

 Quicken displays the Advanced tab, of course.

4. **Tell Quicken you want to see only unprinted checks on the report.**

 To do this, select Unprinted Checks from the Transaction Types drop-down list box.

5. **Produce your Accounts Payable report.**

 When you click OK to close the Customize Transaction report, Quicken summarizes the unprinted checks in your bank, cash, and credit card accounts.

6. **[Optional] Save your Accounts Payable report.**

 Click the Save Report button. When Quicken displays the Save Report dialog box, name the report something like *Accounts Payable Listing* or *Unpaid Vendor Invoices* and then click OK.

In the past, Quicken let you easily print Accounts Payable reports like the one I describe in the preceding paragraphs. In Quicken 2007, unfortunately, Intuit has made it harder to do this. In fact, if you use the Reports And Graphs window (described in Chapter 7) to display a list of business reports, Quicken 2007 tells you that you can't produce an Accounts Payable report unless you unlock the report by upgrading to Quicken Premier Home & Business. As I say elsewhere in this book, Quicken Premier Home & Business is a great product. But you don't need to and shouldn't pay an upgrade fee merely for these reports. You can, with just a bit of fiddling as shown here, produce an Accounts Payable report that summarizes all unprinted checks.

Explaining how Quicken handles payables

Before I conclude this wonderfully interesting, terribly exciting discussion about how you track unpaid bills in Quicken, let me make one final, quick point: An unprinted check is counted as an expense only after you print it. Does this news sound like much ado about nothing? It probably is.

But let me take a minute to explain the accounting system that Quicken uses. For example, if you record a $1,000 check to your landlord on December 31, but you don't print the check until January, Quicken doesn't count the $1,000 as an expense in December. It instead counts the $1,000 as an expense in January of the next year.

By the way, the Quicken register shows two balances: the current balance, which shows, well, the current balance (the balance that's in your account even as you read this sentence), and the ending balance, which shows the balance after adjusting for all the future, or post-dated, transactions you've entered.

If you know a little about cash-basis accounting versus accrual-basis accounting, you've probably already said to yourself, "Hey, man, Quicken uses cash-basis accounting." And you're right, of course.

This little subtlety between the two accounting systems can cause confusion, especially if you've already been working with a regular, full-featured accounting system that uses an accounts payable module with accrual-basis accounting. In one of these systems, the $1,000 check to your landlord probably gets counted as an expense as soon as you enter it in the system.

How Quicken identifies an unprinted check

Here's a little tidbit of information that you may (or may not) find useful: When you describe a check you want to print by using the Write Checks window, Quicken records the check in the register but uses the word *Print* in place of the check number. The word *Print* identifies the check as the one that you want to print and signals Quicken to look at the check and say to itself, "Aha! — an unprinted check!" *Print* is, to say the least, an important word.

If you're someone who has decided to get truly wild and crazy and use the Quicken electronic bill-paying feature, untransmitted payments

show up in the register, too. This time, Quicken uses the word *XMIT* to look at and say, "Aha! — an untransmitted electronic payment!" Untransmitted payments, however, don't appear on the Accounts Payable report. Go figure.

Electronic payments can be wild and crazy? What a concept! Yes, the entire Quicken program can be just that, if wild and crazy means being fun and adventurous. You know, wild and crazy — as in ordering Thai food and saying, "How spicy? Make it Dragon, please." Or wild and crazy — as in not wearing any underwear. You understand.

Part V
The Part of Tens

The 5th Wave By Rich Tennant

"I think if you subtract the figure in the 'Days
I Go Home Early' column from the figure in the
'Snippy Attitude' column you'll reach a zero
sum figure."

In this part . . .

As a writing tool, laundry lists aren't something that high school English teachers encourage. But you know what? The old laundry list format is pretty handy for certain sorts of information.

With this idea in mind (and, of course, with deepest apologies to my high school English teacher, Mrs. O'Rourke), this part simply provides you with lists of information about Quicken. It includes answers to ten commonly asked questions about Quicken, ten things you should definitely not do unless you want to turn your financial life into a mess, and (nearly) ten troubleshooting tips you can try if you get into a messy situation.

Chapter 17

(Slightly More Than) Ten Questions I'm Frequently Asked about Quicken

. .

In This Chapter

▶ What are Quicken's best features?

▶ Does Quicken work for a corporation?

▶ What happens to stockholders' equity in Quicken?

▶ Does Quicken work for a partnership?

▶ Can I use Quicken to track more than one business?

▶ What kinds of businesses shouldn't use Quicken?

▶ Can I use Quicken for my real estate investments?

▶ Can I use Quicken retroactively?

▶ Can I do payroll with Quicken?

▶ Can I prepare invoices with Quicken?

▶ Can I import data from my old accounting system?

▶ What do you think of Quicken?

. .

*W*hen people find out that I've written a book about Quicken, they always ask a question or two. In this chapter, I list the most common questions and their answers.

What Are Quicken's Best Features?

Quicken has become more and more complicated over the years, so I think it may be fair to include a few sentences that review its most valuable and least valuable features. As far as what's best or most valuable, I would say that its checkbook feature is still clearly the most valuable. If you should use one feature in Quicken, it's the checkbook stuff. (To do so, set up a bank account for your checking account and then use Quicken to keep track of your balances, income, and expenditures as described in Chapter 4.)

I also have to say that I think that Intuit, the maker of Quicken, provides pretty neat stuff at its Quicken Web site, so I'd give that feature my vote as the second best. I don't talk about the Quicken.com Web site a whole lot in this book. But that's because you can have more fun and more success with Quicken.com by exploring the site on your own.

Just because I'm super-compulsive not only about my personal finances but also about yours, let me say that I think that the Quicken program's financial calculators (I describe them in Chapter 10) are also really valuable. If you're willing and able to do just a bit of planning right now, you'll be truly amazed by the positive impact that planning has on your financial affairs a few years down the road.

So this leads rather nicely to another question: What are Quicken's least valuable features? I think the answer really depends on the person. I used to pooh-pooh the online banking because my bank caused me headaches, and my at-home, dialup Internet connection was unreliable. (With a fast cable modem connection now, however, I really do like online banking.) The credit card stuff and cash account stuff don't do much for me. But you know what? Those tools may do wonderful things for you. It depends on the way you've organized your finances.

I guess the bottom line, to me, is that the least useful features depend on what you don't need to do. But what you don't need to do will probably differ from what I don't need to do. I'm sorry that I don't have more helpful criticism.

Does Quicken Work for a Corporation?

Sure. But let me talk for a minute about what's unique — at least from an accountant's perspective — about a corporation.

In addition to recording assets (such as bank accounts and receivables) and liabilities (such as mortgages and trade payables), a corporation needs to *track,* or keep records for, the stockholders' equity.

Stockholders' equity includes the amount people originally paid for their stock, any earnings the corporation has retained, cumulative income for the current year, and sometimes other stuff, too.

"Ugh," you're probably saying to yourself. "Ugh" is right. Accounting for stockholders' equity of a corporation is mighty complicated at times. It's so complicated, in fact, that Quicken can't track a corporation's stockholders' equity.

I'm not saying that you can't use Quicken if you're a corporation, and I'm not saying that you shouldn't. (I do business as a corporation, and I used to use Quicken just for laughs.) Just remember that someone — probably your poor accountant — periodically needs to calculate your stockholders' equity.

Fortunately, the financial information you collect with Quicken provides, in rough form, much of the information that your poor accountant needs in order to do things manually.

What Happens to Stockholders' Equity in Quicken?

Quicken doesn't exactly ignore a corporation's stockholders' equity. In an Account Balances report, the difference between the total assets and the total liabilities actually represents the total stockholders' equity. (Quicken labels this total Net Worth.) So, to the extent that your total assets and total liabilities figures are correct, you know your total stockholders' equity.

Does Quicken Work for a Partnership?

Yep, it does. But a partnership that uses Quicken faces the same basic problem as a corporation that uses Quicken. In a partnership, the partners want to track their partnership capital accounts (or at least they should). A partnership capital account simply shows what a partner has put into and taken out of a business.

As noted in the preceding section, Quicken calculates a net worth figure for you by subtracting total liabilities from total assets. So, to the extent that your total assets and total liabilities are accurately accounted for in Quicken, you know roughly the total partnership capital.

To solve this problem, you (or someone else) need to track what each partner puts into the business, earns as a partner in the business, and then takes out of the business. You can also (and I've helped clients do this) just use the Quicken loan accounts for partnership equity accounts. You just need to not get freaked out when your net worth shows as zero, and you need to remember that the partnership equity accounts aren't really loans — they're capital.

Can I Use Quicken for More Than One Business?

Yeah, but be very careful. *Very* careful. You must be especially diligent in keeping the two businesses' financial records separate.

Quicken provides a handy tool for keeping them straight: You can work with more than one file. Each file, in effect, is like a separate set of financial records. You can't record automatic transfers between accounts in different files; instead, you must record each side of the transaction separately. You can, however, keep truly separate business records.

To create a separate file, choose File⇨New.

If you've been using Quicken for a while, you can probably figure out for yourself how the File⇨New command works. If you need help, refer to my discussion of this command in Chapter 9.

Keeping separate bank accounts is a must. If you keep separate records for two distinct businesses in Quicken, you need to set up separate bank accounts for them. In fact, my attorney tells me that in the case of a corporation, you must set up a separate corporate bank account for the corporation to be truly considered as an independent legal entity. Talk to your attorney if you have questions; attorneys can tell you the specifics that apply to a particular state and situation.

What Kinds of Businesses Shouldn't Use Quicken?

You're probably saying to yourself, "Quicken works for corporations (sort of), and it works for partnerships (sort of). Does that mean that it works for just about any kind of business?"

The answer is no. Quicken is a darn good product. In fact, for many small businesses, it's a great product. But it doesn't work in every situation.

The following is a three-part test that you can use to determine whether your business should use Quicken. If you answer yes to two or three of the questions, you should seriously consider moving up to a full-featured, small-business accounting system (like QuickBooks).

✔ **Do you regularly need to produce business forms other than checks?**

- If you answer no to this question, you're in good shape with Quicken, which produces checks easily. And if all you need is an occasional invoice, you can create it easily enough on your computer. To produce a handful of invoices a month, for example, you can use your word processor. If you want to, you can also use a super-sized version of Quicken called Quicken Premier Home & Business, which not only does invoices but also does monthly customer statements.

- If you do produce a lot of forms besides checks and invoices — for example, purchase orders — you should probably consider moving to a small-business accounting system that produces the forms you want. If you've been using Quicken, for example, take a look at QuickBooks for Windows, another Intuit product. Another more powerful but wonderfully designed product you might try is Peachtree Accounting for Windows from Peachtree Software. You can probably buy either program at the local software or office supplies store. You can certainly buy either program by visiting www.quickbooks.com or www.peachtree.com.

✔ **Do you need to track assets other than cash, accounts receivable, or investments?**

For example, do you buy and resell inventory? Do you have a bunch of fixed assets (furniture, equipment, and stuff like that) that you need to track? An accounting system is usually helpful in tracking these items. Quicken doesn't do a very good job of tracking these other assets, so you may want to look at one of the other small-business accounting products — QuickBooks, for example.

✔ **Are you having problems measuring your profits with cash-basis accounting?**

I'm not going to get into a big, tangled discussion of cash-basis versus accrual-basis accounting. It wouldn't be any fun for you. It wouldn't be any fun for me, either. Nevertheless, you should know that if you can't accurately measure your business profits by using cash-basis accounting (which is what Quicken uses), you may be able to more accurately measure your business profits by using accrual-basis accounting. To do so, use an accounting system that supports accrual-basis accounting. I should be totally honest with you and tell you that to measure your profits the right way, you (or your accountant) need to use — horror of horrors — double-entry bookkeeping.

If you are a Quicken user but realize that you're outgrowing the checkbook-on-a-computer scene, check out QuickBooks. (No, I don't get a kickback from Intuit.) Here's the deal: QuickBooks looks and feels a lot like Quicken. Plus, it uses the data that you've already collected with Quicken, so you'll find that moving from Quicken to QuickBooks is only slightly more complicated than rolling off a log.

Can I Use Quicken for Real Estate Investing?

Yeah. Absolutely.

In a nutshell, all you need to do is set up an income category to track your rental income and then some expense categories to track your rental expenses. (In Chapter 2, in the section about changing a category list, I describe how to set up income and expense categories.)

To see which rental-expense categories you need, either look at the Schedule E tax form that went with last year's tax return (if you've already been investing in real estate), or grab a Schedule E tax form from www.irs.gov (if you're new to real estate investing).

Now before you stop reading and rush off to do the bookkeeping for your growing real estate empire, let me tell you one other critical thing: The Schedule E tax form on which you report your real estate income and deductions requires you to segregate your income and deductions by property. For example, if you have two rental properties — a duplex on Winston Street and a single-family cottage on Roosevelt Avenue — you'll need to break down your income and expenses by property.

To break down income and expense by property, you use a Quicken feature called *classes.* Oh, yes, it all sounds complicated. But all you need to do is include a / (slash) character and a name for the property after the category information in the Category field. For example, rather than entering **rent** in the Category field when recording a rent payment from your tenants living in the Winston Street duplex, you enter **rent/Winston**.

By appending the class information **/Winston** to the income category, you can later easily produce a cash flow that shows income and expenses for the Winston duplex.

Just to make sure that you understand this, let me give you another example. Rather than recording a check to pay the utilities expenses for the house on Roosevelt as **utilities**, enter **utilities/Roosevelt** in the Category field.

By appending the class information **/Roosevelt** to the expense category, you can easily produce a cash flow later that shows income and expenses for the Roosevelt cottage.

A couple of other notes about this: The first time you enter a slash followed by a name you select to identify a rental property into the Category field, Quicken asks whether you want to set up a class. When you click "heck yeah," Quicken prompts you for a bit of information about the class. After that, though, you just enter the class without fanfare or embarrassment.

To produce a report that summarizes income and deductions information by class, produce the report in the usual way. (You may choose to produce a cash-flow report, for example, by choosing Reports⇨Banking⇨Cash Flow.) However, when you see the report window, select Class from the Columns drop-down list box.

Can I Use Quicken Retroactively?

Yeah. And the idea is better than it may seem at first.

Entering a year's worth of transactions doesn't take long in Quicken (as long as you have decent records to work with). If you're a millionaire, the task may take you a couple of days. (Of course, in this case, you can hire someone to do it for you.) If you're a regular, ordinary person, I bet you can get it done on a rainy Saturday afternoon.

After you enter all the information into a Quicken register, you can easily monitor your spending in various categories, track your income and outgo, and reconcile your bank accounts. I know one professional who uses Quicken records to do these things every year. Hey, it's not the most efficient way to do things. And it's not a very good way to manage business or personal financial affairs. But it works. Sort of.

Can I Do Payroll with Quicken?

Yes. See Chapter 15 for more details.

By the way, if you have only one or two salaried employees who always earn the same amount — a nanny, for example — you can rather easily use Quicken for payroll. But if you have a bunch of employees or even a single hourly employee, you'll probably want to either purchase a full-featured, real-live, small business accounting program like QuickBooks or use a payroll service like Paychex or ADP to take care of the whole thing for you.

Intuit makes and sells QuickBooks, as you may guess by its name. You can get QuickBooks from the local software store, from one of the mail-order places, or by calling Intuit.

You can look up either payroll service — Paychex or ADP — in the telephone book. You can also look up either payroll service — Paychex or ADP — at www.paychex.com or www.adp.com.

Can I Prepare Invoices?

Not with Quicken Premier or Quicken Deluxe, but you can, very nicely thank you, with Quicken Premier Home & Business. If you want invoices, at least step up to Quicken Premier Home & Business. This requirement may also be a symptom indicating that you should consider moving up to a full-featured, small business accounting system, such as QuickBooks.

Can I Import Data from an Old Accounting System?

Someone had to ask this question, I guess. (Imagine me taking a deep breath here.) Yes, you can import data from your old accounting system. To do so, export the old system's data into a file that matches the Quicken Interchange Format, or .QIF, specification. (The QIF file just neatly organizes financial information in a well-documented structure so that other programs — and even people — can read and understand the data.) Then import this file into an empty Quicken file. Keep in mind, however, that this process isn't for the timid or faint-hearted. I would also say that it isn't for people who have better things to do with their time.

My advice to you? Go to a movie. Mow your lawn. Read a trashy novel. Forget all about this importing business.

What Do You Think about Quicken?

I think it's great. But I bet your question isn't really whether Quicken is good or not. Heck, the package has something like 10 million happy users, so we both know that the package is pretty good, right? My guess is that what you really want is my opinion about using Quicken in particular business or personal situations.

It's tough to answer this question in a one-way conversation. Even so, let me give you some of the best reasons for using Quicken:

- You always know your bank account balances, so you won't ever have to wonder whether you have enough money to pay a bill or charge a purchase.

- Reconciling your account takes about two minutes. (I'm not joking. It really does take only a couple of minutes.)

- You get a firm handle on what you're really making and spending.

- You can budget your spending and then track your spending against your budget.

- If you're a business, you can measure your profits as often as you want by using cash-basis accounting.

- If you're an investor, you can monitor your investments and measure their actual returns.

I hope these answers help. My guess is that if you think that a program such as Quicken will help you better manage your financial affairs, it probably will.

Chapter 18

(Almost) Ten Tips on How Not to Become a Millionaire

- -

In This Chapter

▶ Ignore the fact that one can build surprising wealth by investing in ownership investments and earning just average returns

▶ Ignore that one can get much, and maybe most, of the money from tax savings and employer matching

▶ Don't tap your computer's and the Quicken program's power to develop powerful, wealth-building insights

▶ Give up because it's too late to start anyway

▶ Get entangled in at least one "get-rich-quick" scheme

▶ Fake it with false affluence

▶ Give in to the first big temptation of wealth building

▶ Give in to the second big temptation of wealth building

- -

You read the chapter title right. But let me explain a couple of things. First, a few years ago I wrote a book about how to save a million dollars for one's retirement. That sounds a little money-grubbing, I'll agree, but my argument then (and now) is that most people need to accumulate a nice-sized nest egg for retirement because most of us can't or shouldn't really count on things like pensions and Social Security for all of our retirement needs.

If Congress does nothing — absolutely nothing — to save Social Security in the United States, the best studies show that, about 30–40 years from now, the government will need to reduce benefits to around 70 percent of the amount it pays today. For example, someone who may receive $1,000 per month today may instead receive $700 in the future. Likewise, someone who receives $400 today may instead receive $280 in the future. Although that dif-

ference isn't quite the financial meltdown some people think, it does mean that you and I really must prepare to augment our retirement income by having our own savings.

So, anyway, as part of promoting this book, I spent several weeks on the road doing radio call-in shows, bookstore appearances, and television talk shows. I learned several things from that experience. First, I learned that after one appears on some television show, it is, apparently, customary to remove the strange makeup that's applied for the cameras. This step is especially important if you plan to appear later in public.

I also learned something else in my travels and talking with people. Although everyone is interested in becoming a millionaire or in preparing financially for retirement, it turns out that most people are really more interested in how *not* to become a millionaire. In other words, they wanted me to explain in financial terms why people *don't* accumulate wealth.

At first, I thought that this was a little strange. But then finally somebody explained, "We all know you need to save and invest to build wealth. . . . What we *don't* know are those things that prevent or sabotage our attempts to do this." People in the audience didn't want to make the same mistakes.

And so that is what I want to cover here. I want to share with you my observations and research results about why people who know they should save at least some money for retirement don't end up building wealth. I've observed that eight really common problems or traps foul up most people.

Before I begin, note that one of the things that happens when you start talking about compound interest and future values is that inflation makes comparing apples to apples difficult. In other words, I can say something like, " . . . and then you'll have $3,000,000." But you then have to wonder what that amount will be worth factoring in inflation. To deal with this annoying complexity, I adjust for inflation all the numbers I use in the following paragraphs. I subtract the inflation amount and give you only the "adjusted-for-inflation" numbers in current-day dollars. Note that the Quicken financial planners also let you adjust for inflation by checking the Adjust For Inflation check box, which appears on most of the calculator dialog boxes.

Ignore the Fact That You Can Build Wealth by Investing in Ownership Investments and Earning Average Returns

You can build surprising wealth just by investing in ownership investments that produce average returns. By *ownership investments,* I mean basically stocks and maybe real estate. Here are three examples:

- Just by earning the stock market's average inflated adjusted return of around 6 percent, a 25-year-old saving $150 per month can build as much as $300,000 by age 65.

- Just by earning the stock market's average inflated adjusted return of around 6 percent, a 35-year-old saving $300 per month can build as much as $300,000 by age 65.

- Just by earning the stock market's average inflated adjusted return of around 6 percent, a 50-year-old saving $850 per month can build as much as $300,000 by age 65.

I want to stop here. An important truth here is that, sadly, most people miss this information. Consider what this means: You don't have to get fancy. You don't have to spend a bunch of time worrying. You don't need to spend a bunch of money on advisors, newsletters, or commissions — or even on books about using Quicken.

Compound interest is a powerful engine, and it creates wealth. And that means that you can build surprising wealth by investing in ownership investments and earning just average returns.

Note, too, that you can lock in average returns by choosing a low-cost index fund such as The Vanguard Group's Index 500 or Total Stock Market Portfolio mutual fund.

If you choose an actively managed mutual fund or a mutual fund that charges average fees for managing your money, you basically don't have a snowball's chance in you-know-where of actually earning an average return over time. Over the long investment horizon required to prepare for retirement, if you go this route, chances are you'll actually earn a return that's equal to the market's return *less the expense ratio that the mutual fund manager charges.* Expense ratios for actively managed funds run about 2 percent annually. So, rather than a 6- or 7-percent annual adjusted-for-inflation return, you'll actually earn a 4 or 5 percent annual adjusted-for-inflation return on actively managed mutual funds.

One final point: People see way more risk in this investing than really exists — particularly after the last few years. But over decades, which is how long you'll invest, the risk drops. If you had begun investing in the stock market in the mid-1920s and then continued systematically investing for 25 years through the crash of 1929, the global depression of the '30s, World War II, and the start of the Cold War, you would have earned about an 8 percent return on your money. Given that the inflation rate was just 2 percent over this same period of time, you still could have built wealth by investing in ownership investments producing average returns. I honestly expect similar real returns over the remaining decades (I hope) of my life.

Ignore the Fact That You Can Get Much, and Maybe Most, of the Money from Tax Savings and Employer Matching

Okay. I'm moving on to another really important point. It's fine to say that you need to invest just $300 a month, and that produces the wealth you need. The big question is this: *Where do you get that money?*

You've got bills to pay and a rent or mortgage check to write. You want to enjoy at least a few of the material pleasures — like food and drink — that life offers up. Where in the world does someone come up with this kind of money?

Well, the answer is mostly from the tax man and your employer. No kidding. Because of the way that employer-matching provisions work in things like 401(k) and Simple-IRA plans and because of the way our progressive income tax system works, you can get a lot of money from your employer and from the government in the form of tax-deduction savings. You may even be able to get most of the money you need for your retirement savings from these sources.

Table 18-1 shows how someone who wants to save $300 a month might come up with the money. And, in fact, the first line of Table 18-1 shows how much you want to save: $300.

The second line of the table shows how much you might get from your employer in a 401(k) or Simple-IRA plan. Note that an IRA obviously doesn't include employer matching. (This line shows up, therefore, as zero in Table 18-1.) But 401(k) plans commonly provide a 50 percent match on at least the first portion of your contribution. (This shows up as $100 in the table.) And basically by law, Simple-IRAs provide a 100 percent match on the first portion of your contribution (which shows up as $150 in the table).

Table 18-1	Ways to Come Up with $300 a Month		
	IRA	*401(k)*	*Simple-IRA*
What you want to save	$300	$300	$300
What you can get from employer	$0	$100	$150
What you can get from tax man	$90	$60	$45
What you come up with yourself	$210	$140	$105

The third line of the table shows how much you might get in the way of tax savings. For example, if you're contributing $300 a month to an IRA, you might actually enjoy $100 a month in federal and state income tax savings if the tax rate you pay on your last dollars of income equals 30 percent. (This rate would be the case for many readers.)

The fourth line of the table shows what you need to come up with yourself. The IRA is the worst case shown in the table. With an IRA and $300 a month of savings, you would need to come up with $210 yourself. The 401(k) plan looks better; with it, you need to come up with $140 yourself. The Simple-IRA is the best case in the table. With it, you need to come up with only $105.

I don't want to overload you with data. But please note that this is an incredibly powerful insight. Much, and maybe most, of the money you need to build wealth can come from other people — specifically the tax man and your employer, if you work someplace that offers a 401(k) or Simple-IRA plan.

Don't Tap Your Computer's Power to Develop Wealth-Building Insights

This is hard to describe in general terms because by definition, what the computer lets you do is get very specific. Consider this: Personal financial planning is essentially applied mathematics. What that means is that to make a decision, you often need to tally up the costs and benefits of Option A versus Option B, and then you need to make time/value of money calculations. (Practically speaking, this just means that you also need to figure in things like interest expense and investment income.) These sorts of tasks are the perfect applications for the personal computer.

When you use your computer to make better personal financial decisions, you develop powerful, wealth-building insights that often supply the rest of the money you need for your investing. More specifically, if you need to save $300 a month and you can get $150 of this from your employer and through tax savings, you still need to come up with that last $150 a month. But what I'm saying is that your computer can, and should, help you find this money.

Here's one example: Have you heard about early mortgage repayment? It sounds like a good idea, at least on the surface. If you add an extra $25 a month to the regular mortgage payment on a typical mortgage, you often save about $25,000 in interest. (Maybe more. How much you save depends on the interest rate, the mortgage balance, and the remaining number of payments.)

Based on that bit of financial data, early mortgage repayment sounds like a pretty good idea. Lots of people — encouraged by financial writers — have started doing this. But is it a good idea? It depends.

To determine whether this is truly a good idea, however, you need to weigh your options. If you can instead put an extra $25 a month into a 401(k), you end up with about $100,000.

So there you have it: Option A, which is early mortgage repayment, sounds pretty good because $25,000 of interest savings is a lot of money. But Option B, the 401(k) option, is clearly better because, for no extra pain or hassle, you end up with $100,000.

But other important financial decisions and personal financial planning issues often provide you with similar opportunities for free money or extra wealth because you use your computer:

✔ **ARMs:** Sometimes, these adjustable rate mortgages (ARMs) actually make you bear less risk and work better.

✔ **Buying a home:** Sometimes it isn't a good investment — even when it seems like it is.

✔ **Car leases:** They can be great deals or terrible deals. It all depends on the implicit interest rate that the lease charges.

In Chapter 10, I talk about how you use Quicken's financial planners to make better financial decisions. The Internet also provides a ton of tools, many helpful, for doing personal financial planning. I don't want to sound like your mother or some cranky uncle, but I urge you to use these sorts of computer-based financial tools to make wiser decisions. A little extra money here, a little there, and pretty soon you've found that last bit of money you need to save for a comfortable retirement. No kidding.

Give Up Because It's Too Late to Start Anyway

Another common trap that prevents people from saving money for retirement is they give up, thinking that it's too late to start. I have to tell you that, mathematically speaking, that's just dead wrong.

You may think that wealth-building schemes that rely on compound interest work only for young people. It's true that wealth building can be very easy for someone who's young. Often, young people need to make only a single, clever decision in order to build wealth. For example, if a 25-year-old, pack-a-day smoker quits smoking and puts the money he saves into savings, he can rather easily build $1,000,000 by retirement. All he needs to do is save his money in an IRA and select a small-company stock mutual index fund. (Remember, I adjust for inflation; so really, this person will probably have between $3,000,000 and $4,000,000 of inflated dollars.)

You can't do that if you're 50 years old. I mean, you can't make one decision and expect that single good decision to grow to $1,000,000.

But there's another angle in all of this: You aren't limited to making a single good decision. Oh, sure. That's easiest. But I really believe that if you make five or six or seven — maybe even ten — good decisions, you can still build substantial wealth by the time you stop working.

I don't think that surprises you if you're a mature investor. And I don't think it should discourage you. You possess more life experience and, I daresay, more wisdom, than someone who's 25. You can use your experience and wisdom to make a greater number of good decisions, and that can produce the wealth you need.

Get Entangled in at Least One "Get-Rich-Quick" Scheme

Get-rich-quick schemes don't work except for the person selling the scheme. And, in fact, they drain off energy and money you really should be using to build your investments. You know all this, of course. We all do. But I think that all of us have a tendency to assume that this one particular great investment or business we're presented with is different. Oh, sure, we know that other dummies get suckered, but "fill in the blank" is different.

I actually don't think trying the occasional flier is a bad idea. If you have some small percentage of your investment money chasing speculative returns, that's okay, but only as long as this iffy investing doesn't foul up your other, more important, boring-but-predictable wealth building for retirement. That's fair, right? If you or I want to try chasing down the hottest new mutual fund or try online day trading or invest in some friend's start-up business, that seems okay. But you can't allow these get-rich-quick schemes to foul up your meat-and-potatoes investing.

Unfortunately, I see that most of the people who get involved in get-rich-quick schemes try to use this speculation as a replacement for true, disciplined investing. And I have never seen a get-rich-quick scheme that consistently works.

I offer one other comment: Many, and perhaps even most, of the best-selling books about money and investment techniques amount to just new get-rich-quick schemes. I'm not going to name names here. Neither my attorney nor the publisher will let me. But any book that promises you some way to magically and consistently double or triple the returns that other investors earn is a get-rich-quick scheme.

However, some wonderful books out there show you how to better manage your money. For example, Eric Tyson's book, *Personal Finance For Dummies*, 4th edition, is a really good book about the basics. And I'm not just saying this to schmooze the publisher. (Both Eric's book and this book are published by Wiley.) I also love basically everything that Andrew Tobias writes

plus John Bogle's two books about mutual fund investing — *Bogle on Mutual Funds* (Irwin) and *Common Sense on Mutual Funds* (Wiley) — and Burton Malkiel's *A Random Walk Guide to Investing* (Norton). All of these books provide good, fact-based advice that leads you in the right direction.

Fake It with False Affluence

I talk about this a bit in Chapter 2, but it's an important point and worth repeating. When people spend all their money trying to look rich, they don't have any money left over to save and invest. That means that most people have to decide — either explicitly or implicitly — whether they want to be rich or look rich. Weird, right?

Yet, most millionaires live average lives. They live in average houses located in middle-class neighborhoods. They drive average cars.

Ironically, most of the people who live in big houses or drive expensive cars aren't rich. They may have high incomes, but they aren't rich. And yet that makes sense. You can't become rich if you're spending all your money trying to look rich.

Faking affluence is a trap that goofs up more people than you'd guess.

Give In to the First Big Temptation of Wealth Building

I think that when you boil everything down to its very essence, the big problem is that most people lack the commitment. We all must be culturally programmed this way or something. But most of us — I'm the same way — stumble over a couple of big temptations. So I mention these temptations here and in the next section.

Temptation #1: I can tell you, and so can any good financial planner, how to come up with an extra $100 or even $500 a month. Also, if you really do use Quicken in a disciplined way to manage your financial affairs, you'll find yourself freeing up money. You'll save a little bit of money here, waste a little less over there, and pretty soon you'll find yourself with a bit of extra cash. But you must have the commitment to save and invest that money. You and I have to decide to dedicate the next $100 or $500 to investments. If we do, we don't have to worry about financial security in retirement. And if we don't, we should

worry. But anyway, that's the first temptation. When you find some extra money, you need to have the discipline to save and invest those funds. And if you do start to do this, you'll rather quickly amass thousands of dollars.

Give In to the Second Big Temptation of Wealth Building

Ironically, resisting Temptation #1 leads rather quickly to

Temptation #2: After you collect an extra $5,000 or $25,000 or $50,000 in your portfolio, you need to have the commitment necessary to let that money grow. That seems obvious, of course. But I've also noticed that a lot of people don't do this. A lot of people, after they amass a nice little pot of money, decide it's time to abandon a strategy that has worked wonderfully. They decide to buy a bigger house or a boat. Or they change investment strategies, maybe by investing in some friend's or family member's new business. Or they turn their money into a hobby — perhaps deciding that they're going to use their retirement money to try out this online investing thing or leveraged real estate investing.

It's your money, of course. You get to do with it whatever you want. But I am going to be honest with you and say that if you really want to build up a nice nest egg for retirement, you need to be committed enough to resist these two big temptations.

Chapter 19

(Almost) Ten Troubleshooting Tips

After writing about Quicken for more than ten years, I've had a revelation of sorts. People not only want specific, step-by-step information about how to use the program, but also want troubleshooting advice. They want techniques and tactics that they can use to solve the inevitable problems they encounter while using Quicken in real-life settings. What follows is my list of the best troubleshooting techniques that I can offer you.

Tactics #1 and #2: Use Quicken's Help File and This Book

I know what you may be thinking. You may be thinking that you've got some problem that you can't solve by using Help, and it's either a bug or some glaring error in the Quicken documentation. And, of course, you've looked through this book, and it says nothing, absolutely nothing, about your question. In fact, upon further reflection, you may be thinking that you've encountered some problem that you can't possibly solve by consulting the Quicken Help file or this book.

Maybe you're right.

But in my experience (when I talk with people who have problems), about half the time, the problem is that people don't know enough about Quicken to know what to do. People simply experience a mechanical problem, and they can't make the program work because they haven't used Quicken enough to figure out how it works. Therefore, the right way to solve this sort of problem is to find out more about Quicken and try again. For example, if you're having problems printing a report, just finding out more about printing and reports often solves your problem.

In most cases, though not all, you should be able to find the information in this book by using either the Index or the Table of Contents.

Usually, you should be able to find the information (perhaps in a slightly less friendly form) in the Quicken Help file. To find information in the Quicken Help file, choose Help⇨Contents to display the Help window, click the Index tab, and then enter the word or phrase that you want to look up.

Tactic #3: Visit Quicken's Product Support Web Site

Another really good resource for troubleshooting is the Intuit product support Web site for Quicken. This Web site, available at `www.intuit.com/support/quicken`, supplies a rich database of troubleshooting information.

To use the Web site, you select the version of Quicken you're using from the Select Your Product drop-down list box. After you click your version, you see a Web page that lists common categories of problems or questions. You select a category, and you're on your way. The product support Web site then displays a list of troubleshooting articles that may help you solve your problem.

Tactics #4 and #5: Check Microsoft's or the Hardware Vendor's Product Support Web Site

Keep in mind the possibility that your problem may not be a problem with Quicken at all, but rather a problem with your computer and its hardware or with Microsoft Windows. If your problem stems from the hardware or the

operating system, you can consult the hardware or software maker's product support Web site for troubleshooting information. The Microsoft product support Web site, which is phenomenally rich in information, is available at support.microsoft.com. You can usually find the hardware maker's product support Web site easily by using a good Internet search engine. For example, to locate Dell Computer's product support Web site, type something like **Dell Computer product support** into a search engine such as www.google.com to search on the phrase *Dell Computer product support.*

You can find troubleshooting information about Intuit products at the Microsoft product support Web site. If the solutions that the site offers aren't very reassuring, at least you can find out whether others have experienced the same problem. Microsoft may suggest that you contact the vendor (which is Intuit) or that you upgrade to a newer version of the Quicken software. But knowing that the problem you've encountered is a real problem that Microsoft has logged in to its product support knowledge base (that's what Microsoft calls it) and described in some technical detail is often useful.

Tactic #6: Contact Intuit Directly

In addition to the option of using the Intuit product support Web site, you can also contact Intuit directly. As I write this, the price for this personalized service is $24.95 per telephone call, and the telephone number is 1-800-811-8766, but the price and even the telephone number may be different when you call. You can get an up-to-date list of support numbers as well as current pricing information at this Web address by searching on "phone support."

```
www.intuit.com/support/quicken
```

Tactic #7: Try a Quicken Newsgroup

If your problem with Quicken isn't really a program bug or can't be easily solved by getting more information, you can sometimes find an answer by consulting other Quicken users. One of the easiest ways to do this is by browsing the Quicken newsgroup at alt.comp.software.financial.quicken.

To browse the Quicken newsgroup, you need to use an Internet service provider that supports newsgroups and a newsgroup reader (such as Outlook Express). Assuming that you have these things, you can subscribe to the Quicken newsgroup and talk with other Quicken users about the problems you're encountering.

You may not need this background information, but I'm going to point out a few important things about newsgroups. A specific organization doesn't typically support or police newsgroups. For example, Intuit doesn't maintain or support the Quicken newsgroup. Newsgroups, including the Quicken newsgroup, really amount to freeform — and, sometimes, unruly — discussions among users. You can't expect to have your question answered. And good newsgroup etiquette suggests that, if you're going to ask questions, you should also try to answer questions.

Tactic #8: Install and Use Antivirus Software

Okay, this shouldn't really be tactic #8. This tactic deserves a higher ranking than that. But that's beside the point. The point is this: If you can't solve a problem and you've got Internet access and you've been downloading files or accepting e-mail messages with attachments from strangers, your computer may have a virus. And it may be that your Quicken problems (particularly Quicken problems that you can't solve in other ways) stem from the virus.

In this case, I'd buy, install, and use antivirus software such as Norton AntiVirus or McAfee VirusScan. Consider one of these software programs just another part of the price of Internet connectivity. To locate online stores where you can download antivirus software, use www.google.com to search for *Norton AntiVirus* or *McAfee VirusScan*.

Tactic #9: When All Else Fails . . .

If you use a CPA to prepare your federal and state income taxes, you can probably get a quick (and perhaps free) answer from him or her. CPAs, as you may guess, have spent years learning about and working with accounting systems. Commonly, the problems people have with Quicken aren't technical software problems but accounting or bookkeeping conundrums. So what you think is a Quicken bug may, er, really be an operator error.

Let me also mention that even if you don't have a CPA prepare your tax return, you may want to find one who you can ask for help and then pay him or her. Even if you're using Quicken for a small business or real estate investing — something a wee bit complicated — an hour or so of personalized training is often all you need to get all your questions answered.

Part VI

Appendixes

The 5th Wave By Rich Tennant

"Great! It comes with Quicken. Now maybe
we can figure out where all the money
around here is going."

In this part . . .

*I*f you're new to Windows, this part contains a lot of useful information, such as how to get the system up and running, how to find things you need, and how to get your computer to respond when you want it to do something.

I also include a glossary of the business, financial, and computer terms you see throughout the book. Throw around some of these terms in casual conversation and everybody will think you're an expert.

Appendix A

Quick-and-Dirty Windows

• •

*I*f you're new to Microsoft Windows — and by Windows, I mean Windows 95, 98, 98 Second Edition, NT, 2000, Me, XP, or for the truly brave, Vista — you need to know a few things about the Windows user interface. Although this appendix doesn't reveal anything earthshaking, it does provide a quick-and-dirty overview of what you need to know to get around.

If you've used other Windows applications, you probably don't need to read this appendix because you already know the material it covers.

I won't bore you with technical details. The information here, though, will enable you not only to operate Quicken but also to converse easily about the newest versions of Windows at cocktail parties, over lunch, or with the guy at the computer store.

If you want more information, you may want to read a book such as *Windows XP For Dummies,* 2nd Edition, by Andy Rathbone (published by Wiley).

What Is Windows?

Windows — and when I use the term *Windows* here, again, I mean any version of Microsoft Windows sold in the last few years — is an operating environment that manages your *system resources* (things like memory, your monitor, your printer, and so on).

Applications (programs such as Quicken) run on top of Windows. In other words, you first start Windows (by turning on your personal computer), and then, after Windows is running, you can start applications such as Quicken.

Windows provides a standard graphical interface. In English, Windows provides a common approach for using *visual elements* — icons, buttons, check boxes, and so on. (This appendix describes how the major pieces of this graphical interface work.)

Windows enables you to run more than one application at a time. You may, for example, run Quicken, a tax preparation package, and even a Windows accessory program, such as the Calculator.

Starting Windows

Starting Windows is easy. You just turn on your personal computer. If you can find the on-off switch, you're set.

If for some reason you can't find the on-off switch or it doesn't seem to work, don't feel silly. Ask someone who has used that computer. Sometimes the on-off switch is on the front of the computer and is labeled "on-off" (which makes good sense, of course). Sometimes, I'm afraid, manufacturers stick the on-off switch on the back of the computer or label the switch something really stupid, such as 0 and 1. Sometimes, too, people plug a computer and all its peripherals (such as printers, modems, and all that junk) into a power strip that needs to be turned on to turn on the computer. So just ask someone. (If you bought the computer, of course, you can just telephone the place you bought it from.)

Just so you don't feel like a complete imbecile, I have to tell you something. I once had to call someone to learn how to click the stupid mouse that I got with my laptop computer.

Figure A-1 shows a typical Windows XP desktop. The *desktop* is what you see after Windows XP has started. The other Windows desktops look similar.

Figure A-1:
The
Windows
desktop.

Starting Programs

To start a program like Quicken, you click the Start button so that Windows displays the Start menu. Then you click the All Programs menu option so Windows lists all the programs that you, Windows, or someone else has installed. And then you click one of the listed programs to start that program.

Some programs — such as Quicken — don't appear as options on the All Programs menu. They appear on Programs submenus. If you click Start and then choose the All Programs menu, you'll see a Quicken item, for example. (Pointing to some object like the Start button and then pressing the mouse's left button is called *clicking* the object.) Choosing the Quicken item from the All Programs menu displays the Quicken submenu, which lists a bunch of different options (which depend on the version of Quicken you've installed). To start Quicken, you choose All Programs⇨Quicken 2007⇨Quicken 2007 Premier.

To practice this starting business, try starting the WordPad application that comes with Windows by following these steps:

1. **Click the Start button.**

2. **Choose All Programs⇨Accessories⇨WordPad.**

When you follow these steps, Windows opens the WordPad program. Figure A-2 shows the WordPad application window. (An *application window* is just the window that a program like WordPad or Quicken displays.)

A tidbit about the taskbar

At the bottom of your screen, Windows displays a *taskbar.* It provides the Start button, which I talk about earlier in this chapter, so that you can start another program. (With Windows, you can run several programs at the same time.) The taskbar also provides buttons that you can click to move among the programs you're running. If you look closely at it while you're running WordPad, for example, you see a taskbar button for the WordPad program. You also see a taskbar button for any other program you're running at the same time. You probably will be glad to know that *multitasking,* which is what running multiple programs is called, is this easy to do — just click the buttons on the taskbar to switch from one running program to another. By the way, in this book, I hide the taskbar so it doesn't obscure any of the Quicken program window.

Figure A-2:
The
WordPad
window.

Choosing Commands from Menus

To set something in motion in Windows, you usually need to choose *commands* from menus.

I don't know why they're called commands. Perhaps because you often (but not always) use them to command Windows and Windows applications to do things. "Windows, I command thee to start this application," or "Quicken, I command thee to print this report."

Most application windows have a *menu bar* — a row of menus across the top of the window. Predictably, not every menu bar contains the same menus. But they're often darn similar. Some of the commands on the Quicken menus, for example, mirror commands on the WordPad menus.

This menu similarity isn't some nefarious conspiracy. The common command sets make things easier for users.

If you choose to read the next section, don't worry about what particular commands or menus do. Just focus on the mechanics of choosing commands.

Choosing commands with the furry little rodent

I think that the easiest way to choose a command is to use the mouse.

To select one of the menus by using a mouse, move the *mouse pointer* — the small arrow that moves across your screen as you physically roll the mouse across your desk — so that it points to the name of the menu that you want to select. Then click the mouse's left button: Windows or the Windows application displays the menu. Now click the command that you want to choose.

If you inadvertently display a menu, you can deselect it (that is, make it go away) by clicking anywhere outside the menu box.

Choosing commands by using the Alt+key combinations

Another way to choose a command is to use an *Alt* key (cleverly labeled Alt, these keys are usually at either end of the spacebar):

1. **Press the Alt key.**

 Doing so tells Windows or the Windows application that you want to choose a command.

2. **Press the underlined letter of the menu that you want to choose.**

 Doing so tells Windows or the Windows application which menu contains the command you want.

3. **Press the underlined letter of the command you want to choose.**

 Each command on a menu is usually underlined, too, so that you can tell the program which command you want to choose by pressing the underlined letter of that command. For example, if you've chosen the File menu, you can choose the last option, Exit, by pressing the letter *X*. (You can try choosing Exit if you want, but then restart WordPad so that you can continue to follow along, okay?)

Some Windows programs, Quicken included, don't show you the underlined letter that chooses menus and menu commands until you press the Alt key. Weird, huh?

Windows and Windows applications offer yet another way to choose menu commands. After you press the Alt key, use the left- and right-arrow keys to

highlight the menu that you want. Then press Enter. Windows or the Windows application displays the menu. Use the up- and down-arrow keys to highlight the command that you want to choose. Then press Enter.

For example, press Alt to activate the menu bar. Press the right-arrow key to highlight the Edit menu. Press Enter to display the Edit menu of commands (as shown in Figure A-3). Press the down-arrow key seven times to highlight the Find command. Then press Enter.

Figure A-3:
The
WordPad
Edit menu.

If you want to deselect a menu but still leave the menu bar activated, press the Esc key once. To deselect the displayed menu and, at the same time, deactivate the menu bar, press the Esc key twice.

Using shortcut-key combinations

For many menu commands, Windows and Windows applications offer shortcut-key combinations. When you press a shortcut-key combination, Windows or the Windows application simultaneously activates the menu bar, chooses a menu, and chooses a command.

Windows (and Windows applications, such as WordPad and Quicken) displays the shortcut-key combination that you can use for a command on the menu beside the command.

Using one of the menu selection techniques that I describe earlier, activate the Edit menu (refer to Figure A-3). Do you see the rather cryptic codes, or whatever, that follow the command name? Following the Undo command, for example, you can just barely make out the code Ctrl+Z. And following the Paste command, you can see the code Ctrl+V. These are the shortcut-key combinations. If you simultaneously press the two or three keys listed — the Ctrl key and the Z key, for example — you choose the command. (Shortcut-key combinations often use funny keys — such as Ctrl, Alt, and Shift — in combination with letters or numbers. If you're not familiar with some of these keys' locations, check your keyboard.)

Disabled commands

Oh, jeepers. I almost forgot to tell you something. Not every menu command makes sense in every situation. So Windows and Windows applications disable commands that would be just plain kooky to choose. To show you when a command has been disabled, the program displays disabled commands in gray letters. In comparison, commands you can choose show up in black letters. Take another look at Figure A-3. Several of the commands on that menu are disabled. That's why you can barely read some of their names.

Working with Dialog Boxes

Windows (and Windows applications like Quicken) uses a special type of window, called a *dialog box,* to communicate with you. In fact, after you choose a command, Windows and Windows applications often display a dialog box to get the information they need to carry out the command.

Dialog boxes have five unique design elements: text boxes, radio buttons (also called option buttons), check boxes, list boxes, and command buttons.

Text boxes

Text boxes provide a space into which you can enter text. To see what a text box looks like, start WordPad (if you haven't already), type **Semper fidelis**, and choose Edit⇨Find. WordPad, responding nicely to your deft touch, displays the Find dialog box (shown in Figure A-4). The text box is the box to the right of the words Find What.

Figure A-4:
The Find
dialog box.

If the *selection cursor* — the flashing line or outline that selects the active element of a dialog box — isn't already in the text box, you need to move it there. Then type in the text. If this "active element" mumbo jumbo seems too technical, just press Tab a bunch of times and watch the dialog box. See that thing that moves around from box to button to box? It selects the active element.

You can move the selection cursor several ways:

- ✔ Click the text box.
- ✔ Press Tab or Shift+Tab until the selection cursor is in the text box. (Pressing Tab moves the selection cursor to the next element; pressing Shift+Tab moves the selection cursor to the preceding element.)
- ✔ Press the Alt+key combination (for example, press Alt+N to move the selection cursor to the Find What text box).

If you make a typing mistake in the text box, use the Backspace key to erase incorrect characters. Other editing tricks are available, but I don't describe them here. (This chapter is just a quick-and-dirty overview of Windows.)

You also can move the *insertion bar* — the vertical line that shows where what you type gets placed — by using the left- and right-arrow keys. The left-arrow key moves the insertion bar one character to the left without deleting any characters. The right-arrow key moves the insertion bar one character to the right without deleting any characters.

Which commands display dialog boxes

Seeing which menu commands display dialog boxes is easy: Command names that prompt dialog boxes are followed by ellipses, as shown in the Edit menu in Figure A-3, after Paste Special, Find, and Replace. Choosing these commands always opens a dialog box.

Check boxes

Check boxes work like on-off switches. A check box is "on" if the box is selected with a check mark. A check box is "off" if the box is empty. Figure A-4 shows the Match Case check box turned off, whereas Figure A-5 shows the Options dialog box's Automatic Word Selection check box turned on. (WordPad displays the Options dialog box when you choose its View⇨Options command.)

Figure A-5:
A dialog box with some option buttons and a check box.

To turn a check box on or off with the mouse, click the check box. If the check box is on, your click turns the check box off. If the check box is off, your click turns the switch on.

You also can use the spacebar to select and deselect a check box. After you move the selection cursor to the check box, press the spacebar to alternatively select and deselect the check box. Toggle, toggle, toggle.

Tabs

You frequently see *tabs* on dialog boxes. Take another look at Figure A-5. See how the Options dialog box actually supplies several tabs of information, including the Options tab shown. To see another tab, you click it. For the Options dialog box shown in Figure A-5, for example, you can move to the Text tab by clicking the word *Text,* which marks the Text tab.

Option buttons

Option buttons (or *radio buttons*) are sets of buttons representing mutually exclusive choices. The Options dialog box, which appears when you choose WordPad View⇨Options, uses one set of option buttons, the Measurement Units options buttons: Inches, Points, Centimeters, and Picas (refer to Figure A-5).

You can select only one option button in a set. Windows or the Windows application identifies the selected button by putting a *bullet,* or darkened circle, inside the button. In Figure A-5, for example, the Inches option button is selected. The easiest way to select an option button is to click the option button you want.

Command buttons

Every dialog box has command buttons. *Command buttons* tell Windows or a Windows application what you want to do after you finish with a dialog box.

Figure A-5, for example, shows command buttons labeled OK and Cancel. If you use the Options dialog box to make some changes, you click OK after completing the rest of the dialog box. If you don't want to use the Options dialog box after all, you click Cancel.

To choose a command button, either click it or move the selection cursor to a command button and press Enter.

List boxes

List boxes list a series of possible choices. To see an example of a list box in WordPad, for example, choose the File⇨Open command. WordPad displays the Open dialog box (shown in Figure A-6).

Figure A-6:
The Open
dialog box.

Windows and Windows applications use two types of list boxes: a regular list box, which is always displayed, and a *drop-down* list box, which Windows won't display until you tell it to.

Regular list boxes show you a bunch of choices, and you make your choice by clicking one of the items listed. The big open area shown in Figure A-7, for example, is a regular list box. You can select any of those things listed (files in this case) by clicking.

Drop-down list boxes look like text boxes with a down-arrow button at the right end of the box. To open a drop-down list box — such as the Files Of Type list box shown in Figure A-6 — click the down-arrow button.

After it's opened, a drop-down list box works the same as a regular list box. After you select an item from the list box (by using the mouse or the arrow keys), press Enter.

Unfortunately, a list is sometimes too long for the list box to completely display. When this minor tragedy occurs, you can use the PgUp and PgDn keys to page through the list.

You also can use the *scroll bar* — the vertical bar with arrows at either end. Just drag the square scroll bar selector up or down. You also can click the arrows at either end of the scroll bar, or you can click the scroll bar itself. (This last trick moves the scroll bar selector toward the place where you clicked.)

Stopping Quicken for Windows

To stop a Windows application like Quicken for Windows, either click the application's Close box — the button with the X in it that appears in the top-right corner of the application window — or choose File➪Exit.

A Yelp for Help

Help, a separate application within Windows, has powerful tools to help you learn about Windows and Windows applications such as WordPad and Quicken. To access Help, select the Help menu or click the ? icon.

The Quicken Premier 2007 Help menu (see Figure A-7) lists 13 commands: Quicken Help, Current Window, Add Business Tools, Unlock Again, Product And Customer Support, Submit Feedback On Quicken, What's New In Quicken, Learn About Next Steps After Set Up, Learn About Downloading Transactions, User Manuals, Ask a Quicken User, About Quicken, and Privacy Statement. Different versions of Quicken have different Help menus and supply different commands. But, for the most part, they all work pretty much in the same way. So in the following paragraphs, I briefly describe how each command shown in Figure A-7 works.

If you exit Quicken the wrong way

If you exit Quicken by turning off (or resetting) your computer, the index file that Quicken uses to organize your financial records gets, well, wasted. Quicken rebuilds the index when you restart, but this process takes a few seconds.

Don't exit Quicken or Windows by turning off your computer. Doing so may not cause serious problems (let me say, though, that Windows isn't as forgiving as Quicken), but it is bad form — akin to eating the last potato chip or leaving the gas tank empty in your spouse's car.

Figure A-7.
The Quicken
Help menu.

The Quicken Help command

If you choose Help➪Quicken Help, the Help program displays a window (as shown in Figure A-8) that has three tabs: Contents, Index, and Search.

The Contents tab lists some of the major Help topic categories. To display the topics within a particular category, double-click the Help topic category. Help expands the list shown so that it shows the topics within each category. Double-click the topic to display the Help information on that topic.

The Index tab (shown in Figure A-9) lists all the Quicken Help topics in alphabetical order. To use the index, type the first few characters of the topic you're interested in or curious about into the text box. If you want to learn more about creating new accounts in Quicken, for example, you may type the word **new**. Then review the list of Help topics shown on the Index tab's list box. If you see one that matches the topic you have questions about, double-click it. Help then displays a dialog box that lists the specific Help topics related to the index entry. You *double-click,* or quickly click twice, the one you want. And that's that. Sort of like rolling off a log.

Figure A-8:
The
Contents
tab lists
major Help
topics.

Figure A-9:
Click the
Help menu's
Index tab to
display the
index of
Help topics.

Note: If you have the time, you can also use the Index tab by scrolling through its (lengthy!) alphabetical list of all Quicken Help topics until you find the one you want.

You can click the Search tab (shown in Figure A-10) to search through the Help topics. To use the Search tab, enter your search, or key, words into the first text box, and then select the Help topic from the last list box.

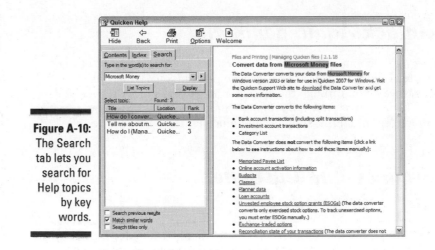

Figure A-10:
The Search tab lets you search for Help topics by key words.

The Current Window command

You can also get Help information specifically related to the active window (the window that appears on top of any others). To do so, either press F1 or choose the Help⇔Current Window command to start the Help program. I really don't need to say any more about this command. If you have questions about it, just try it.

The Add Business Tools command

The Add Business Tools command displays a Web page from the Quicken.com Web site, which describes the Home & Business version of Quicken. The Web page also provides a link so you can order the Home & Business version of Quicken. When you "order" the Home & Business version of Quicken, you don't actually get another copy of Quicken. Rather, you get a key that you can use to unlock all of the Home & Business features.

Just a quick editorial comment about the Home & Business version of Quicken: I love it. Quicken Home & Business is a wonderful accounting solution for small and home-based businesses that don't handle payroll in-house and that don't buy and resell inventory.

The Unlock Again command

The Unlock Again command (which is also called in some versions of
Quicken Enter Unlock Code) isn't really a Help command. What this com-
mand does is walk you through the steps for accessing a more powerful ver-
sion of Quicken, such as Quicken Premier Home & Business. (Essentially, you
pay an unlock fee, and Intuit supplies an unlock code.)

The Product And Customer
Support command

The Product And Customer Support command displays a dialog box that
describes the various ways that you can get help from Intuit, including the
Quicken troubleshooting feature, Intuit's Worldwide Web support, and fax
support. Basically, I guess, the folks at Intuit are looking for some way to give
you help — without actually having to talk to you in person. (This practice
sounds terrible, but if you end up having to talk with someone, Intuit will
probably spend more money paying people to talk to you than it will make
from your purchase.)

The Submit Feedback On
Quicken command

The Submit Feedback On Quicken command opens a Web page that you can
use to submit suggestions, share comments, or report bugs. If you've got
something you need to say, this is the way you do it.

The What's New In Quicken command

If you choose the What's New In Quicken command, Quicken displays a Web
page that you can read to learn about the features new to Quicken 2007. Note
that there's more than a single page of information about what's new, so you
click hyperlinks to get from the main page to other detailed pages.

The Learn About Next Steps After Set Up and the Learn About Downloading Transactions commands

The Learn About Next Steps After Set Up and Learn About Downloading Transactions commands display windows that list Quicken help topics related to (for the first command) getting the Quicken program set up and (for the second command) online banking and bill payment. The windows also provide clickable hyperlinks you can use to find out about setting up Quicken and setting up online banking.

The User Manuals command

The User Manuals command, in some misguided attempt at help, tells you that you should have received a user manual. The command also alerts you to the fact that an electronic copy of the user manual is stored on your hard drive (along with the other Quicken files) but that you'll need Adobe Acrobat Reader to print or read the thing.

The Ask A Quicken User command

This command connects you to the Quicken Support Forums Web site (www.quickenforums.com) so that you can discuss Quicken problems and solutions with other Quicken users.

The About Quicken command

The About Quicken command displays a dialog box that gives the application's complete name, Quicken 2007 Premier. To remove this dialog box from the screen, click OK.

The Privacy Statement command

This command displays information about the ways Intuit attempts to keep your financial data secure and about the business practices that Intuit employs.

Quitting Windows

To quit Windows, click the Start button and choose the Shut Down or Turn Off Computer command or something like that. Then wait until Windows says that turning off your computer is okay. When you get the go-ahead, flip the power switch — if that's even necessary.

Recent computers and versions of Windows may be able to turn off your computer without your intervention.

Appendix B

Glossary of Business, Financial, and Computer Terms

. .

940 Payroll Tax Form: The annual federal unemployment tax return. A 940EZ version is supposed to be EZ-er to fill out.

941 Payroll Tax Form: The quarterly federal payroll tax form that tells the IRS what federal employee payroll taxes (Social Security, Medicare, and Federal Withholding Tax) you've collected and remitted.

942 Payroll Tax Form: The quarterly payroll tax form that tells the IRS what domestic employee payroll taxes an employer has collected and remitted.

account: In Quicken, a list of the increases and decreases in an asset's value or in a liability's balance.

account balance: The value of an asset or the outstanding principal owed for a liability. For example, the value of a checking account is the cash value of the account. The balance of a mortgage liability is the principal you still owe.

account transfer: An amount you move from one account (such as a checking account) to another (such as a savings account).

account type: Quicken provides different versions, or types, of accounts. There are both accounts for keeping records of the things you own (checking, saving, money market, cash, brokerage, IRA or Keogh, 401(k), dividend reinvestment plan, other investments, house, and vehicle), and for keeping records of the amounts you owe (credit card and liability).

accounts payable: In a business, the amounts you owe your trade creditors — your landlord, the office supplies store, the distributor from whom you purchase your inventory, and so on. People who prefer monosyllabic speech often refer to accounts payable as *A/P.*

accounts receivable: In a business, the amounts your customers or clients owe you. People who prefer monosyllabic speech often refer to accounts receivable as *A/R.*

amortization: The itsy-bitsy principal payments you make over the course of repaying a loan. Eventually, these principal reductions pay off the loan.

ASCII: An acronym standing for the American Standard Code for Information Interchange. People usually use the term to refer to files — in other words, ASCII files — that contain just regular old text: letters, numbers, symbols from the keyboard, and so on.

backing up: Making a copy. If something terrible happens — fire, hard drive failure, thermonuclear exchange — you still have a copy on removable media, such as a CD or Zip disk, and safely stored away from your computer, preferably offsite.

balancing an account: The steps you take to explain the difference between what your records show as a balance and what the bank's records (statements) show as a balance. Also referred to as *reconciling an account.*

bookkeeper: Someone who keeps the "books," or financial records.

brokerage account: A Quicken account specifically set up to track a brokerage account that you use to invest in securities. Unlike a mutual fund account, a brokerage account includes a cash element. See also *account type*.

budget: A plan that says how you will make and spend money.

capital account: The money a sole proprietor leaves in or contributes to the sole proprietorship. Also, the money a partner leaves in or contributes to a partnership.

capital gain: What you earn by selling an investment for more than you paid. Capital gains (and losses) receive special treatment on your income tax return.

capital loss: What you lose by selling an investment for less than you paid.

category: In Quicken, how you summarize income and outgo. For example, you may use a category, such as Wages, to summarize your payroll check deposits. And you may use categories (such as Housing, Food, and Fun) to summarize your checks.

category list: The list of categories you can use. While setting up the first account in a file, Quicken suggests category lists for home users and for business users.

certified public accountant: Someone who's taken a bunch of undergraduate or graduate accounting courses, passed a rather challenging test, and worked for at least a few years under a CPA doing things like auditing, tax planning and preparation, and consulting. Real exciting stuff, in other words.

chart: A picture that shows numbers. In Quicken, you can produce pie charts, bar charts, line charts, and so on.

check date: The date you write your payment instructions, or check. Technically, the check date is the date on which your payment instructions to the bank become valid.

check form: The preprinted form that you use to provide payment instructions to your bank: "Okay, Mammoth National, pay Joe Shmoe $32 from my account, 00704-844." Theoretically, you could use just about anything as a check form — a scrap of paper, a block of wood, and so on. In fact, rumor has it that someone once used a cowhide. It's easier for your poor bank, though, if you use check forms that follow the usual style and provide OCR characters (OCR stands for optical character recognition) along the form's bottom edge.

Circular E: Instructions from the IRS to employers. This publication tells stuff like how much federal income tax to withhold. Call the IRS and request a copy if you need one. Or visit the IRS Web site (www.irs.gov).

class: Another way to summarize Quicken data when categories just aren't enough. This book doesn't really talk about classes much. Sorry. (In Chapter 17, just for the record, I do explain how to use classes for real estate investing.)

cleared: When a check or deposit has been received by the bank. An *uncleared* transaction hasn't been received by the bank.

commands: What you use to tell Quicken what it should do. For example, "Quicken, I command thee to print a report." Note that while you can use menu commands to navigate within Quicken, you can also use the buttons, QuickTabs, and the hyperlinks that appear within the Quicken windows. Just thought I'd mention this.

controller: A business's chief accountant — and usually the brunt of most accountant jokes. Also known as a *comptroller.*

corporation: A legal business entity created by state law, owned by shareholders, and managed by directors and officers. As a business entity, a corporation has unique advantages and some disadvantages. Ask your attorney for more information. But know that for small businesses, a limited liability company, or LLC, is usually better.

credit card account: A Quicken account specifically set up to track credit card charges, payments, and balances. See also **account type**.

deleted transaction: A transaction that Quicken has removed from the register. See also **voided transaction**.

disk: The thingamajig in your computer on which Windows stores your programs (such as Quicken) and your data files (such as the Quicken file for your financial records). A hard drive (or *hard disk*) inside your computer can store a great deal of information; removable disks (such as floppy disks and Zip disks) typically store a lot less data than a hard drive.

exit: To shut down, terminate, or stop a program. By the way, you want to always do this the right way, which means by using the File menu's Exit command or by clicking the program window's Close button. Don't just turn off your computer.

file: Where data is stored. Your Quicken financial records, for example, are stored in a set of files.

filename: The name of a file in which Quicken stores data. Actually, what Quicken calls a filename is actually the name used for several files. You don't need to worry about this unless you create multiple files.

financial wizards: People who believe that they know so much about the world of finance that it is actually their God-given duty to share their expertise with you. See also *wizard*.

Find: A tremendous bargain, as in: "At $22,000, the five-bedroom house was a real find." In Quicken, also an Edit menu command that you can use to locate transactions. See also *search criteria*.

fiscal year: A fiscal year is just the accounting year. Most of the time, a fiscal year is the same as the calendar year, starting on January 1 and ending on December 31. But some businesses and foreign taxpayers use a different fiscal year. (Why they do that is way, way beyond the scope of this book.)

folder: What Windows uses to organize your hard drive. Some people call folders *directories*.

formatting: Hey, this word is too complicated for a book like this, isn't it? Let me just say that formatting means doing some things to a disk so that you can write files to that disk. It can also mean setting up some nice typesetting "looks" in your printed documents.

Help: A program's online documentation — which can almost always be accessed by pressing F1. Also, a verbalized cry for assistance.

hyperlink: A bit of clickable text (and sometimes a clickable picture) that you can use (by clicking, of course) to move to some other Quicken feature or some other Web page. Quicken 2007, as you may have noticed, scatters hyperlinks everywhere. And I mean everywhere.

index fund: What almost everybody should use for their retirement investments but almost nobody does. . . . Alas.

internal rate of return: An investment's profit expressed as a percentage of the investment. If you go down to the bank and buy a certificate of deposit earning 7 percent interest, for example, 7 percent is the CD's internal rate of return. I don't want to give you the heebie jeebies, but internal rates of return can get really complicated really fast.

LLC: An acronym for *limited liability company.* LLCs are popular with tax accountants and tax attorneys because they, sort of, give you the best of both the corporation and partnership world. For small businesses, LLCs are nice because (compared to corporations) they offer both simplicity and less paperwork.

limited liability company: See *LLC.*

liability account: A Quicken account specifically set up for tracking loans, payments, the principal and interest portions of these payments, and the outstanding balance. See also *account type.*

memo: A brief description of a transaction. Because you also give the payee and category for a transaction, it usually makes sense to use the Memo field to record some other bit of information about a check or deposit.

menu: In Quicken, a list of commands. In a restaurant, a list of things you can order from the kitchen.

menu bar: Although it sounds like a place where menus go for a drink after work, a menu bar is a horizontally arranged row, or bar, of menus.

missing check: A gap in the check numbers. For example, if your register shows a check 101 and a check 103, check 102 is a missing check.

mutual fund account: A Quicken account specifically set up to track a mutual fund investment.

online banking: An extra service you can buy from your bank. With online banking, you record a payment in your Quicken register and then transmit the payment information to your bank so that it can make the actual payment. Online banking also lets you electronically transfer money between your accounts and grab your statement electronically.

Online Bill Payment: An extra service you can buy from Intuit, the folks who bring you Quicken. With Online Bill Payment, you record a payment in your Quicken register and then transmit the payment information to Intuit's computer or your bank. Intuit or your bank then uses this information to make the actual payment.

online investing: Quicken lets you automatically download transactions from many (and maybe even most) of the online brokerage services right into your investment accounts. If you're buying and selling securities, downloading these transactions (rather than entering them by hand) saves you time. This is a particularly valuable feature for people who want to see how quickly they can lose everything they own through day trading.

partnership: A business entity that combines two or more soon-to-be former friends. In general, each partner is liable for the entire debts of the partnership.

password: A word you have to give Quicken before Quicken gives you access to a file. The first password, "Open sesame," was used by Ali Baba.

payee: The person to whom a check is made payable. (If you write a check to me, Steve Nelson, for example, I'm the payee.) In Quicken, however, you can fill in a Payee field for deposits and for account transfers.

power user: Someone who's spent far more time than is healthy fooling around with a computer. Power users are good people to have as friends because they can often solve your worst technical nightmares. However, note that most people who describe themselves as power users aren't.

QIF: An acronym standing for *Quicken Interchange Format.* Basically, QIF is a set of rules that prescribes how an ASCII file must look if you want Quicken to read it. If you're a clever sort, you can import category lists and even transactions from ASCII files that follow the QIF rules.

Quicken: The name of the checkbook-on-a-computer program that this book is about. You didn't really need to look this up, did you?

Quicken.com: The Intuit Corporation Web site especially for Quicken users. Visit this Web site, my friend. It's really good.

Quicken Premier: A supercharged and multimedia version of Quicken that includes a bunch of extra whistles and bells, including multimedia help information, a really neat program for locating great mutual funds (called, cleverly enough, Mutual Fund Finder), and a Home Inventory System program. This book is about Quicken Premier, but Quicken Basic, Quicken Deluxe, and Quicken Premier Home & Business users can apply this book to their products. (All the products are similar in their core functionality.)

Quicken Quotes: Quicken Quotes is an online service that you can use to grab up-to-date price information on stocks and bonds. This book doesn't talk much about Quicken Quotes.

QuickFill: A clever little feature. If Quicken can guess what you're going to type next in a field, it types, or *QuickFills,* the field for you. QuickFill types in transactions, payee names, and category names.

QuickTabs: QuickTabs are the clickable hyperlinks that appear along the left edge of the Quicken application window underneath the financial center buttons. You can typically click a QuickTab to display an account's register.

QuickZoom: A clever, big feature. If you have a question about a figure in an on-screen report, double-click the figure. Quicken then lists all the individual transactions that go together to make the figure.

register: The list of increases and decreases in an account balance. Quicken displays a register in a window that looks remarkably similar to a crummy old paper register — your checkbook. To print a copy of the register that you see on your screen, press Ctrl+P and then press the Enter key.

report: An on-screen or printed summary of financial information from one or more registers.

restore: Replace the current version of a file with the backup version. You may need to do this after a fire, hard drive failure, or thermonuclear exchange. See also *backing up*.

savings goal accounts: Quicken includes a pseudo-account called a *savings goal account*. In effect, a savings goal account is a compartment in a banking account where you can "hide" or set aside money that you're saving for a special purpose. A new car. A boat. A trip to Montana. Whatever.

scroll bars: The vertical bars along the window's right edge and the horizontal bars along the window's bottom edge. Use them to scroll, or page, through your view of something that's too big to fit on one page.

search criteria: A description of the transaction that you want to locate. See also *Find*.

sole proprietorship: A business that's owned by just one person and that doesn't have a separate legal identity. In general, businesses are sole proprietorships, partnerships, corporations or limited liability companies.

split transactions: A transaction assigned to more than one category or transferred to more than one account. A split-check transaction, for example, might show a $50 check to the convenience store paying for both groceries and automobile expenses.

stockholders' equity: The money that shareholders have contributed to a corporation or allowed to be retained in the corporation. You can't track stockholders' equity with Quicken.

subcategory: A category within a category. For example, the suggested Quicken home categories list breaks down utilities spending into Cable TV, Gas and Electric, Telephone, and Water subcategories.

supercategory: A group of categories that you monitor as a group. You create supercategories so that you can monitor them.

tax deduction: For an individual, an amount that can be deducted from total income (such as alimony or IRA contributions) or used as an itemized deduction and deducted from adjusted gross income (such as home mortgage interest or charitable contributions). For a business, any amount that represents an ordinary and necessary business expense. Be sure to consult with your tax advisor if you have any questions about what is or isn't a valid tax deduction.

tax-deferred account: Some accounts aren't taxable — Individual Retirement Accounts, for one example, and 401(k) plans for another. To deal with this real-life complexity, Quicken lets you tag any account as being tax-deferred. As a practical matter, however, it'll probably be only investment accounts and the occasional bank account that are tax-deferred.

technogeek: Someone who believes that fooling around with a computer is more fun than anything else in the world.

transposition: Flip-flopped numbers — for example, 23.45 entered as 24.35 (the 3 and 4 are flip-flopped as 4 and 3). These common little mistakes have caused many bookkeepers and accountants to go insane.

voided transaction: A transaction that Quicken has marked as void (using the Payee field), marked as cleared, and set to zero. Voided transactions appear in a register, but because they are set to zero, they don't affect the account balance. See also *deleted transaction*.

W-2 and W-3: A W-2 is the annual wages statement that employers use to tell employees what they made and to tell the IRS what employees made. When employers send a stack of W-2s to the IRS, they also fill out a W-3 form that summarizes all the individual W-2s. W-2s and W-3s aren't much fun, but they're not hard to fill out.

Windows: The Microsoft Windows operating system. Quicken 2007 for Windows relies on Windows to do a bunch of system stuff, such as print. Refer to Appendix A for more information.

wizard: A little program that walks you through the steps to completing some tasks that some programmer thinks you're too dense to figure out on your own. While a wizard sounds bad, it actually isn't. Quicken supplies a bunch of cool wizards, including wizards for setting up accounts and setting up how you want to record a paycheck, planning for retirement, planning for your kid's college expenses, reducing your debts, and so on.

Index

• D •

BUSINESS, CAREERS & PERSONAL FINANCE

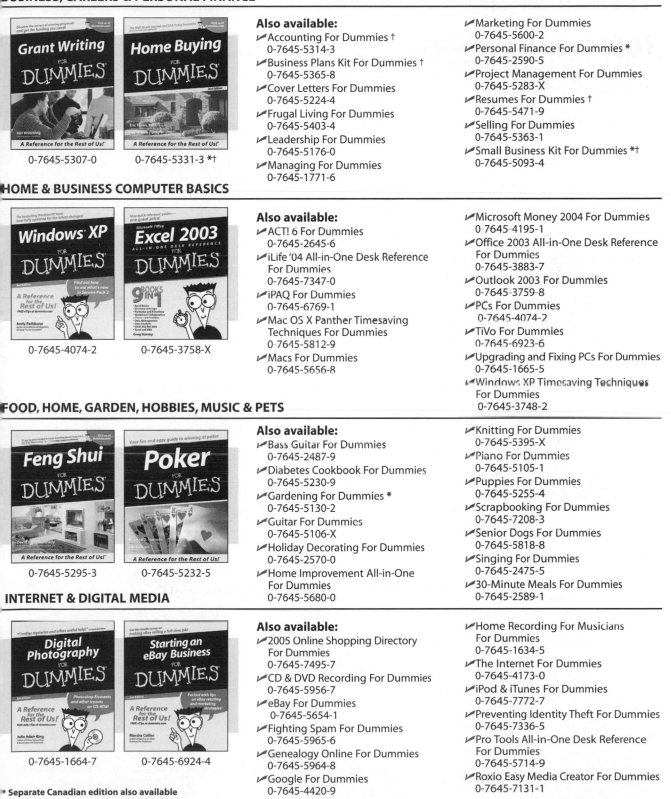

Grant Writing For Dummies
0-7645-5307-0

Home Buying For Dummies
0-7645-5331-3 *†

Also available:
- Accounting For Dummies †
 0-7645-5314-3
- Business Plans Kit For Dummies †
 0-7645-5365-8
- Cover Letters For Dummies
 0-7645-5224-4
- Frugal Living For Dummies
 0-7645-5403-4
- Leadership For Dummies
 0-7645-5176-0
- Managing For Dummies
 0-7645-1771-6

- Marketing For Dummies
 0-7645-5600-2
- Personal Finance For Dummies *
 0-7645-2590-5
- Project Management For Dummies
 0-7645-5283-X
- Resumes For Dummies †
 0-7645-5471-9
- Selling For Dummies
 0-7645-5363-1
- Small Business Kit For Dummies *†
 0-7645-5093-4

HOME & BUSINESS COMPUTER BASICS

Windows XP For Dummies
0-7645-4074-2

Excel 2003 All-in-One Desk Reference For Dummies
0-7645-3758-X

Also available:
- ACT! 6 For Dummies
 0-7645-2645-6
- iLife '04 All-in-One Desk Reference
 For Dummies
 0-7645-7347-0
- iPAQ For Dummies
 0-7645-6769-1
- Mac OS X Panther Timesaving
 Techniques For Dummies
 0-7645-5812-9
- Macs For Dummies
 0-7645-5656-8

- Microsoft Money 2004 For Dummies
 0-7645-4195-1
- Office 2003 All-in-One Desk Reference
 For Dummies
 0-7645-3883-7
- Outlook 2003 For Dummies
 0-7645-3759-8
- PCs For Dummies
 0-7645-4074-2
- TiVo For Dummies
 0-7645-6923-6
- Upgrading and Fixing PCs For Dummies
 0-7645-1665-5
- Windows XP Timesaving Techniques
 For Dummies
 0-7645-3748-2

FOOD, HOME, GARDEN, HOBBIES, MUSIC & PETS

Feng Shui For Dummies
0-7645-5295-3

Poker For Dummies
0-7645-5232-5

Also available:
- Bass Guitar For Dummies
 0-7645-2487-9
- Diabetes Cookbook For Dummies
 0-7645-5230-9
- Gardening For Dummies *
 0-7645-5130-2
- Guitar For Dummies
 0-7645-5106-X
- Holiday Decorating For Dummies
 0-7645-2570-0
- Home Improvement All-in-One
 For Dummies
 0-7645-5680-0

- Knitting For Dummies
 0-7645-5395-X
- Piano For Dummies
 0-7645-5105-1
- Puppies For Dummies
 0-7645-5255-4
- Scrapbooking For Dummies
 0-7645-7208-3
- Senior Dogs For Dummies
 0-7645-5818-8
- Singing For Dummies
 0-7645-2475-5
- 30-Minute Meals For Dummies
 0-7645-2589-1

INTERNET & DIGITAL MEDIA

Digital Photography For Dummies
0-7645-1664-7

Starting an eBay Business For Dummies
0-7645-6924-4

Also available:
- 2005 Online Shopping Directory
 For Dummies
 0-7645-7495-7
- CD & DVD Recording For Dummies
 0-7645-5956-7
- eBay For Dummies
 0-7645-5654-1
- Fighting Spam For Dummies
 0-7645-5965-6
- Genealogy Online For Dummies
 0-7645-5964-8
- Google For Dummies
 0-7645-4420-9

- Home Recording For Musicians
 For Dummies
 0-7645-1634-5
- The Internet For Dummies
 0-7645-4173-0
- iPod & iTunes For Dummies
 0-7645-7772-7
- Preventing Identity Theft For Dummies
 0-7645-7336-5
- Pro Tools All-in-One Desk Reference
 For Dummies
 0-7645-5714-9
- Roxio Easy Media Creator For Dummies
 0-7645-7131-1

* Separate Canadian edition also available
† Separate U.K. edition also available

Available wherever books are sold. For more information or to order direct: U.S. customers visit www.dummies.com or call 1-877-762-2974.
U.K. customers visit www.wileyeurope.com or call 0800 243407. Canadian customers visit www.wiley.ca or call 1-800-567-4797.

WILEY

SPORTS, FITNESS, PARENTING, RELIGION & SPIRITUALITY

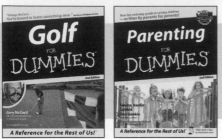

0-7645-5146-9

0-7645-5418-2

Also available:
- Adoption For Dummies
 0-7645-5488-3
- Basketball For Dummies
 0-7645-5248-1
- The Bible For Dummies
 0-7645-5296-1
- Buddhism For Dummies
 0-7645-5359-3
- Catholicism For Dummies
 0-7645-5391-7
- Hockey For Dummies
 0-7645-5228-7

- Judaism For Dummies
 0-7645-5299-6
- Martial Arts For Dummies
 0-7645-5358-5
- Pilates For Dummies
 0-7645-5397-6
- Religion For Dummies
 0-7645-5264-3
- Teaching Kids to Read For Dummies
 0-7645-4043-2
- Weight Training For Dummies
 0-7645-5168-X
- Yoga For Dummies
 0-7645-5117-5

TRAVEL

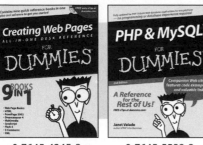

0-7645-5438-7

0-7645-5453-0

Also available:
- Alaska For Dummies
 0-7645-1761-9
- Arizona For Dummies
 0-7645-6938-4
- Cancún and the Yucatán For Dummies
 0-7645-2437-2
- Cruise Vacations For Dummies
 0-7645-6941-4
- Europe For Dummies
 0-7645-5456-5
- Ireland For Dummies
 0-7645-5455-7

- Las Vegas For Dummies
 0-7645-5448-4
- London For Dummies
 0-7645-4277-X
- New York City For Dummies
 0-7645-6945-7
- Paris For Dummies
 0-7645-5494-8
- RV Vacations For Dummies
 0-7645-5443-3
- Walt Disney World & Orlando For Dummies
 0-7645-6943-0

GRAPHICS, DESIGN & WEB DEVELOPMENT

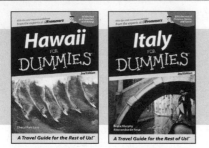

0-7645-4345-8

0-7645-5589-8

Also available:
- Adobe Acrobat 6 PDF For Dummies
 0-7645-3760-1
- Building a Web Site For Dummies
 0-7645-7144-3
- Dreamweaver MX 2004 For Dummies
 0-7645-4342-3
- FrontPage 2003 For Dummies
 0-7645-3882-9
- HTML 4 For Dummies
 0-7645-1995-6
- Illustrator CS For Dummies
 0-7645-4084-X

- Macromedia Flash MX 2004 For Dummies
 0-7645-4358-X
- Photoshop 7 All-in-One Desk Reference For Dummies
 0-7645-1667-1
- Photoshop CS Timesaving Techniques For Dummies
 0-7645-6782-9
- PHP 5 For Dummies
 0-7645-4166-8
- PowerPoint 2003 For Dummies
 0-7645-3908-6
- QuarkXPress 6 For Dummies
 0-7645-2593-X

NETWORKING, SECURITY, PROGRAMMING & DATABASES

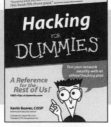

0-7645-6852-3

0-7645-5784-X

Also available:
- A+ Certification For Dummies
 0-7645-4187-0
- Access 2003 All-in-One Desk Reference For Dummies
 0-7645-3988-4
- Beginning Programming For Dummies
 0-7645-4997-9
- C For Dummies
 0-7645-7068-4
- Firewalls For Dummies
 0-7645-4048-3
- Home Networking For Dummies
 0-7645-42796

- Network Security For Dummies
 0-7645-1679-5
- Networking For Dummies
 0-7645-1677-9
- TCP/IP For Dummies
 0-7645-1760-0
- VBA For Dummies
 0-7645-3989-2
- Wireless All In-One Desk Reference For Dummies
 0-7645-7496-5
- Wireless Home Networking For Dummies
 0-7645-3910-8

THE
BATHING
SUIT
WORKOUT

JOYCE L. VEDRAL, PH.D.

THE
BATHING
SUIT
WORKOUT

WARNER BOOKS

A Time Warner Company

Warner Books, Inc., 1271 Avenue of the Americas, New York, NY 10020
Visit our Web site at www.warnerbooks.com

A Time Warner Company

Printed in the United States of America
First Printing: May 1999
10 9 8 7 6 5 4 3 2 1

Library of Congress Cataloging-in-Publication Data
Vedral, Joyce L.
 The bathing suit workout / Joyce L. Vedral.
 p. cm.
 Includes index.
 ISBN 0-446-67108-8
 1. Exercise for women. 2. Reducing exercises. 3. Low-fat diet.
 I. Title.
 GV482.V417 1999
 613.7'045—dc21 98-5297
 CIP

Cover design by Elaine Groh
Cover photo by Don Banks
Book design by Stanley Drate/ Folio Graphics Co., Inc.
Bodywear provided by Dance France, 1-800-421-1543
Photography by Don Banks
Gym shoes by Reebok International

To all of us,
the women who want
a bathing suit body—
whether or not
it's bathing suit season.

ACKNOWLEDGMENTS

To Jessica Papin, for your continual support and enthusiasm and for your kind willingness to go the extra mile.

To Mel Berger, my agent, for your cheerful wisdom.

To Diane Luger and Jacki Merri Meyer for your dedication to the cover art.

To Larry Kirshbaum, Mel Parker, and Emi Battaglia for being every author's dream when it comes to backing me up.

To Don Banks for your artistic photography.

Darriane, for your talent in hair design and makeup.

To Dance France for providing all of the workout clothing.

To Las Vegas Athletic Clubs in Las Vegas, Nevada, for providing a complete fitness facility (baby-sitting included) and to Chad and Karen Smith for your sensitivity and intelligence in management and personal attention.

To Joe and Betty Weider, who started it all!

To Rosa and Mike Tulane, true friends and enthusiastic supporters.

To you, the women who have written to me requesting such a book.

To Michelle, Kelley, Anita, Chris, and Ivonne for going the extra mile in your workouts.

CONTENTS

RECLAIM YOUR WAIST, HIPS, THIGHS, AND BUTT

Perhaps warmer weather is approaching, or maybe your planned vacation is coming up soon, but despite the promise of sunshine, you're filled with dread. It's bathing suit time! You picture yourself desperately searching through the stores to find a suit that will hide a multitude of sins. Well, there's good news.

You won't have to hide anything if you don't want to, and whether you choose to wear a conservative one-piece bathing suit or a daring bikini, you'll be proud of yourself and you'll never again have to dread donning a bathing suit. What's more, you'll be happy when you catch a glance of yourself when passing a mirror—in your underwear or even in the nude.

How long will this take? Here's the best part: *You can achieve a bathing suit body in thirty workout hours—and you can opt to put those hours in as fast as possible.* You can go on the 911 plan, where you zap your problem areas every day, or you can take the more relaxed road and work out every other day. You can do the regular plan, where you put in ten minutes a day, or the emergency plan, where you put in fifteen minutes a day. You can do it in record time because you'll be concentrating *only* on the problem areas, the spots that snug spandex does nothing to hide.

Busting the Bulge in Record Time

Most women have it—at least the women I've met, the women in the real world. It's that area in the middle of the body—you can even draw a circle around it. It begins at your waistline, goes down the front of your thighs to your knees, zooms around to your hips, butt, and

back thighs. It's the area that inspires us to cover in the safety of a voluminous T-shirt, the area we are determined to hide, to cover up!

I have good news for you. Finally, once and for all, you can flatten your stomach and reclaim your waistline, firm and shape your thighs—both front and back—rid them of cellulite in the process, bomb away the bulges from your hips, and reduce the size of your butt, while at the same time shaping and lifting it. You can do it whether you're a "fat-fat" (significantly overweight—in which case you'll also follow the eating plan in Chapter 7) or a "skinny-fat" (not really overweight, but flabby or badly out of shape).

How do you do this? Follow this new exercise plan that will *zap* that "bathing suit area" in a rapid-fire sequence of exercises designed to get you fit and firm—fast!

The Secret of This Workout: The Zap-the-Fat "Tri-Set"

In this book you will find a workout method not found in any of my other books: the tri-set. Simply explained, a tri-set takes three complementary muscle groups and exercises them in sequence, without stopping. You will work your three most troublesome body parts one after another: hips/buttocks, thighs (both front and back), and your stomach (upper and lower—that "pooch"—and your waistline). You'll be zooming around the circle of fat without resting.

Only after you have done one full revolution will you rest for fifteen seconds. (Later, when you get used to the workout, you can even opt to eliminate that rest, burning more fat and reducing your exercise time in the process.) You will continue to use the fat-zapping tri-set until you've transformed your body into a firm, defined, shapely vision of feminine muscularity.

The Magic Seven—The Emergency Ten

There are seven mandatory revolutions in all, with three additional cycles for those of you who are in an emergency and want to get into bathing suit shape as fast as possible.

Never Be Bored! It's Over Before You Know It

The secret of the tri-set is, that it presents a relatively painless way of exercising. You never get bored, and you never get a chance to feel fatigued, because you are doing three completely different exercises in se-

quence, rather than the same old thing over and over again. In this workout, you will do one exercise for hips/buttocks, one exercise for thighs, and one exercise for the stomach without stopping. But even though you keep moving, certain body parts are resting and recuperating.

Here's how it works. While your hips/buttocks muscles are working, your thighs and stomach are resting, and while your thighs are working, your hips/buttocks and stomach are resting, and while your stomach is working, your hips/buttocks and thighs are resting. *But you don't rest.* You keep going, and going, just like a certain bunny we know, burning maximum fat and tightening, toning, and defining your bathing suit area.

Thirty Workout Hours to the Bathing Suit Body of Your Dreams

How long will it take you to get rid of your circle of fat and to replace it with lean, firm muscle? It all depends upon how quickly you put in those thirty workout hours. If you do the maximum plan, you'll get there faster than you will if you do the minimum plan, but in either case you'll get there. If you are overweight, you'll follow the bathing suit eating plan—and you'll watch your fat melt away and uncover a tight, toned, feminine body. You will either achieve your goal in thirty workout hours or show so much improvement that you won't give up the workout until you do! (Details on what to expect are found in Chapter 3, "Before and After")

But They Say You Can't Get Rid of Cellulite

Sound of buzzer. Yes you can! You may have heard people say, "Cellulite is genetic." It is true that some people are more inclined toward "cottage cheese thighs" when they are overweight and/or out of shape, but the only reason for this is "thin skin." That's right. Most of us have bunched-up fat beneath the surface of the skin, but the thinner your skin, the more it shows. If you are among the thin-skinned, don't worry. By following this workout and following the bulge-busting diet, you will replace your cellulite with sleek muscle.

What exactly is cellulite anyway? Cellulite isn't a medical term. It's a term that was coined in the midseventies to describe bunched-up fat, fat that gives the appearance of an orange peel. This fat is made up of enlarged fat cells that conglomerate just beneath the surface of the skin, clinging to fibrous tissue for support.

As you follow my low-fat, balanced eating plan *and* you do the exercises in this workout, you build solid muscle under the skin, and

eventually, the cellulite-ridden area smooths out. No more orange-peel. No more craters. Just curving contours of firm skin.

At first you may find one or two lingering dimples. But if you continue to do this workout, and to follow the eating plan, over time even those few remaining dimples will probably disappear.

No Equipment Necessary

What? Am I kidding? No equipment? That's right. Except for optional dumbbells (handheld weights) for the thigh exercises, you need absolutely nothing to do this workout—nothing except yourself. This means you can do this workout at home, in the office, on vacation—anywhere, anytime, anyplace.

If you want to invest in the optional dumbbells, all the better. You'll get a more intense thigh workout. And in time, as your thighs grow stronger, you have the option of trading in your five-pound dumbbells for tens, and eventually fifteens or even twenties. You may want to do this if you have the sagging thigh problem—you know, where the skin from your lower thigh drops over your knee—the result of Father Time! (A discussion on when to do this is found on p. 52.)

Ten Minutes a Day!

Once you get used to the routine, you will be able to breeze through it in just over ten minutes. How is this possible? It only takes ten to fifteen seconds to perform a set of exercises. You will be doing three sets of each of seven tri-sets, consisting of three exercises each, or twenty-one sets in total for the regular workout. Twenty-one sets of fifteen seconds each takes five minutes and fifteen seconds. But you are resting fifteen seconds between each tri-set. That means you will take six rests. So add a minute and a half for the rests. Now you have seven minutes and forty-five seconds. And six of the exercises are done on one side of the body at a time, so add fifteen seconds times six—another minute and a half—making the grand total ten minutes and fifteen seconds.

Bear in mind that you work more quickly once you get used to the workout. In addition, you can eventually eliminate all the rests. In time, you can finish the regular workout in seven minutes or less.

In the beginning, while you're learning to do the moves correctly and safely and while your body is getting used to the new challenge, the workout will take you longer—maybe as long as twenty to thirty minutes. But that won't last. You'll see. And anyway, unless you are a seasoned exerciser, you won't be doing the entire workout in the begin-

ning. You'll be using a break-in-gently plan where you do no more than one third of the full workout. By the time you get to the full workout you'll be confident and up to speed!

Eleven to Fifteen Minutes for Quicker Results

For those of you who choose to add in one, two, or three exercises and do the Iron Woman, Steel Woman, or Titanium Woman workouts, add a minute or so each. The Iron Woman workout takes eleven minutes, the Steel Woman workout takes twelve minutes and forty-five seconds, and the Titanium Woman workout takes fourteen and a half minutes.

So there you have it. By investing only ten to fifteen minutes a day, and not even every day (you can work out three to six days a week—workout plans are discussed on pp. 43–44), you will have the bathing suit body of your dreams.

Why Isn't Dieting Enough to Get Your Hips/Buttocks, Thighs, and Stomach in Shape?

If you are overweight, dieting is absolutely necessary to get your middle body in shape. In fact, it is exactly this area of the body that provides the main storehouse for excess body fat. *But dieting alone cannot do the job.* No matter how strict your diet, once the fat is gone, unless you work out the right way, your body will feel soft and mushy and, even worse, your skin will sag. You may end up looking like a "skinny-fat."

The truth is, all you can hope to achieve from dieting alone is to fit into a smaller size. Dieting can't make your bathing suit area firm and shapely, nor can it give you definition. Only working out the right way can sculpt your body. You must do a series of specially designed exercises in a specific sequence in order to tighten, tone, and define your hips/buttocks, thighs, and abdominal muscles.

How We Get Tight and Toned

How does exercising the right way do the job? As you repeat a certain number of movements in a specific sequence, inevitably the muscle responds to the "work" being demanded of it. By moving the designated body part at carefully designed angles and planes, your working muscle eventually becomes not only stronger and harder (the muscle cells and fibers strengthen, become more concentrated, and increase, but it

also begins to take on a new shape. In other words, your out-of-shape body part will become reshaped by the work being required of it; you will go from flabby to tight, toned, and defined. Your toned muscle is firm to the touch and pleasing to the eye. In addition, the body part becomes stronger—able to do more without becoming tired.

Don't worry that you will look like a bodybuilder if you do this workout. Bodybuilders use heavy weights and work out for hours every day to achieve an exaggerated muscularity. The only weights you will be using for this workout are optional light handheld weights for your thighs. If you wish to put on more muscle, you can go heavier—up to twenty pounds. Bear in mind, however, that female bodybuilders use heavy weights for thigh work—two hundred pounds, not twenty.

What about the rest of the body? This book concentrates on areas most critical to women, the bathing suit area. Later, if you want to shape up the rest of your body, you can get one of my total-body workouts or videos. I discuss this in detail in Chapter 10.

What about Aerobics?

Aerobic exercises are great for getting your heart and lungs into shape and for burning overall excess body fat. Also, being in "aerobic shape" makes all physical activity easier, including the workout in this book. If you are in aerobic shape, you won't get out of breath as quickly as you did before—and you may even be able to eliminate all the rests in this workout. But aerobics, with all their health benefits, won't transform your body. They won't make you look fabulous in a bathing suit. Only targeting specific muscle groups with certain exercises can do that.

Why do people think they can get their thighs in shape, for example, by using a stair-stepping machine? They believe that the repeated movement of the body part will reshape that body part. This movement does help to strengthen the thighs and hips/buttocks, but it cannot sculpt and define the thighs and lift the skin that sags over the thigh to the knee, or lift and shape the butt. Why? You're doing too many repetitions of one exercise without a rest, and you are not hitting the muscle from a variety of angles.

Bodybuilders whose entire careers depend upon body shaping realized this long ago. If aerobics could reshape the body, bodybuilders the world over would be hopping up and down, grapevining or jogging their way to definition. But the truth is that many bodybuilders don't even do aerobics, and those who do rely upon them only for heart and lung conditioning and extra fat burning. Body reshaping is a science. You have to do it a certain way, in a certain sequence, and from certain angles.

Should you forget about aerobics? Of course not. In fact, I advise you to do three to six twenty-to-forty-minute aerobic sessions a week. See Chapter 8 for more about this.

What Kind of a Diet Will Be Required?

Don't worry. I'm not going to ask you to starve to death. In fact, you'll eat plenty of food, and there will be a selection of foods that you can eat anytime, night or day, as much as you want. But you will have to reduce your fat intake and limit most foods. What's more, you will have to eat more often!

Anyone Can Do It—Create Your Own Workout!

There are thirty exercises in this workout, each targeting a specific area of your bathing suit area: waist and stomach, hips, butt, and front and back thighs. No matter how fat you are and regardless of your medical problems (you can work with your doctor), you can create a program tailor-made for you. In other words, you have a selection of so many exercises that even if you cannot (or will not) do certain exercises the Bathing Suit Workout contains enough options for you to create a plan that will work for you. More about this in Chapter 5.

What You Can Expect from This Workout

- A tight, toned stomach: upper stomach, lower "pooch," a trim waistline

- Higher, rounder, tighter buttocks and no saddlebags

- Firm, shapely front and back thighs

- Removal of cellulite

- Increased energy and self-confidence

- The lifetime fitness maintenance plan

- If overweight, reduced dress sizes—up to a size every three weeks

- If overweight, a delicious eat-till-you-drop (if you wish) fat-loss plan

What I would look like if I didn't work out!

2

THE SKINNY
ON FAT!

You may have heard the expression "The rich get richer and the poor get poorer." For my purposes, I'd like to rephrase that. The rich get richer and the fat get fatter, and Americans, both rich and poor, are fat. Yes, despite the increased efforts of our health and fitness professionals and even the government itself, recent studies show that more Americans are overweight and out of shape than ever before. In fact, whereas only one fourth of adults were found to be overweight between 1960 and 1981, more than one third of adults are now considered overweight.

Why do people, in spite of all the emphasis on health and fitness, continue to grow fatter? Aside from the fact that we live in an increasingly sedentary society, in my opinion the answer is quite clear. People want to enjoy their lives, and they believe that eating what they want when they want is a big part of that enjoyment. Furthermore, they believe (wrongly) that in order to lose weight they would have to sacrifice eating pleasure forever.

If you are one of those people, I have some good news for you. You don't have to give up your eating pleasure completely, not even when you are losing your excess fat. Once you arrive at your fitness goal, you will be able to eat whatever you want once a week—and stay in shape for life. Because it contains the right combination of eating and exercise, the Bathing Suit Workout will show you a weight-loss plan you can stick to. In this chapter I'll talk about the food element that is the key to your weight-loss success—fat—and I'll explain why it tends to conglomerate on your stomach, hips, butt, and thighs. In Chapter 7, you'll get a full fat-loss diet!

To understand is to control. After reading this chapter, you will know the facts about fat—and this will help you to use your mind as a tool to control what you eat. Instead of resenting the fact that you must limit your fat intake as well as your overall daily calorie consumption, you will realize that it's the only logical thing to do, not only for your physical beauty, but for your health—indeed, for a longer, more energetic life.

What Is Contained in Food?

There are basic life-sustaining nutrients in all foods. These nutrients are broken down into three categories: water, micronutrients, and macronutrients. Water is the basic component of all foods. Without water we would die in a matter of days. Vitamins and minerals are the micronutrients found in all foods. They are needed in small quantities by the body. Without them we would suffer malnutrition and all kinds of unpleasant diseases. Carbohydrates, protein, and fats are macronutrients found in specific foods. They are required in greater quantities than any other food nutrients. However, for good health and a lean body, a careful macronutrient balance must be maintained. We should consume only about 12 to 15 percent of our total caloric intake in fat! (Most of the rest will be consumed in carbohydrates, and some in protein. I'll talk about this in Chapter 7.)

The Skinny on Fat

Fat is not all bad. In fact, it is absolutely necessary for the sustenance of your body, and indeed for your life. The problem with fat is not that we consume it, but that we consume too much of it. In fact, most Americans consume about 40 to 50 percent of their daily food intake in fat. The FDA says that for good health 30 percent of fat would be fine. Many medical doctors disagree. They feel that 20 percent would be a closer ideal percentage for good health, and even lower for fat loss. In fact, the Pritikin Longevity Center recommends that fat intake be as low as 10 percent, but never lower. Like most doctors, they agree that you will probably always feel hungry if your diet contains less than 10 percent fat. My fat-loss plan allows you to consume between 12 and 15 percent of fat—plenty to prevent hunger, and low enough to lose weight as fast as possible within the parameters of good health. You won't have to figure out percentages. I've done it for you by inventing a system where you only have to count fat grams. More about this later.

Why Do We Need Fat to Live?

It is fat that supplies the body with what are called "essential fatty acids." These are fatty acids that cannot be produced by the body itself, but must be supplied by fat intake from foods. These fatty acids are used by the body to produce hormonelike compounds that help to control blood clotting, blood pressure, and a host of other bodily operations. It is fat that comprises most of the cell membrane and sex hormones and helps to maintain healthy skin and hair. It also helps to transport fat-soluble vitamins D, A, E, and K through your bloodstream and helps to regulate your blood cholesterol level. You also need a certain amount of fat to cushion your internal organs. In addition, as mentioned above, if you keep your fat grams too low you will always feel hungry and you'll keep "picking" or "grazing." I used to do that until I wrote *Eat to Trim* (see Bibliography on p. 200) and upped my fat and lost twelve pounds—and I've kept those pounds off for over two years now. My new knowledge of fat and eating a balanced diet, in addition to the workout, is responsible for this success.

Why a Too-Low-Fat Diet Can Cause Overeating

If you don't have a certain amount of fat in your diet, no matter how much of other foods you eat, you'll still feel hungry because fat slows down the emptying of food from your stomach. You may find yourself constantly going back to the refrigerator. What you are really looking for is fat, but since you have forbidden yourself to eat it, you "pick," filling up on calorie-laden fat-free foods until you *gain* weight, even on a low-fat diet.

So don't become a fanatic and decide to eliminate all fat. If you consume 15 percent (about 15 to 25 grams of fat per day) of your total calorie intake in fat, you'll give yourself the benefit of the feeling full and at the same time you'll keep your fat intake low enough to lose as much weight as possible.

I'm not really worried that you will eliminate *all* fat from your diet. It would be very difficult to do so. There is at least a modest amount of fat in most foods. Even the humble apple has a gram of fat, and the lowest of low-fat protein fish and chicken sources have about one to two grams of fat per ounce. In Chapter 7 I'll give you a list of appropriate low-fat foods for your daily intake.

How We Get Fat

Simply put, we get fat when we eat more calories than we burn. As you may know, it takes 3,500 excess calories to cause one pound of fat to be stored on your body. But what are calories? A calories is a unit of chemical energy released to your body when you digest the food you have consumed. All foods contain calories, and you burn them all the time—when you're sleeping, and even breathing, burns about sixty calories an hour.

You Are What You Eat! Fat Calories Are Fatter than Other Calories

If you eat a high percentage of fat, you'll be fat! Why? There are more than double the number of calories in fat than in any other food. Fat has nine calories per gram while protein and carbohydrate have only four calories per gram. Obviously, it is much more diet efficient to eliminate as much fat from your food as you can than it is to go after protein and carbohydrate. (Later, I'll explain why carbohydrates are really the best food bargain of all.)

Fat gets even fatter! In fact, it is so fat and lazy that it does not go through the normal digestion process. When protein and carbohydrate are digested, they consume 20 to 25 percent of their own calories. But when fat is digested it uses up only 2 to 3 percent of its calories. It skips the whole cycle and goes straight to the place where it will be stored on your body—probably your hips, buttocks, thighs, and stomach.

Let's take a closer look at how this works. If you consume 100 calories of pure fat, say, for example, you eat a huge lump of full-fat cream cheese (standing at the refrigerator with spoon in hand—I've done it many times), after digesting that food, ninety-seven of those calories go straight to your fattest body part. In my case, it would be my stomach. But what if you ate a hundred calories' worth of nonfat pretzels instead? Only about seventy-five to eighty of those calories would be available for fat storage (20 to 25 percent has been burned up in the digestion process).

So you can see why if your goal is to lose your excess body fat, the only intelligent thing to do is to maintain a low daily intake of fat. Later you'll be able to indulge in any foods you wish once a week. But first you must reach your fitness goal. (I'll explain this in Chapter 7.)

Is It Percentage or Grams? How Do You Figure Out How Much Fat You Can Eat in a Day?

Good news here. Although I've been explaining fat consumption in terms of percentage, I rely on a system that allows you not to have to think about percentage. What do I have against percentage? Nothing, except that figuring percentage is too much work, and from the letters I get, I'm not the only one who feels this way. Most people I know forgot the small amount of math they learned in school. In fact, just thinking about figuring out percentages drives them to eat! With this in mind, I've simplified the whole thing for you by asking only that you do some addition.

In order to be sure that you're eating within the allowed 12 to 15 percent daily fat allowance, all you have to do is add up the fat grams you consume in a day and make sure that you don't go over twenty to twenty-five grams a day. On a bad day, I'll allow you to eat an extra five grams of fat, giving you a grand total of thirty grams. That would still keep you well within the fat-loss range.

Now that the FDA has required that all food labels list the fat grams per serving, your job of counting daily fat gram intake has been made delightfully easy. For the foods that come fresh, such as poultry or fish, you can refer to Chapter 7 or look them up in any fat gram counter (you can find a variety of them in any bookstore).

"98 Percent Fat Free" Can Be Misleading

When you see a food label that says "98% fat free" or some other seemingly impressive percentage, don't be fooled. The food may still contain a good deal more fat than is worth your expenditure.

Let me give you an example. I recently got a letter from a woman who sent me the label for Irish cream coffee. It said that the coffee was 98 percent fat free, but it had three fat grams per serving. She told me that she likes to have three or four cups a day. That would add up to nine to twelve grams of fat—half of her daily fat intake. Ridiculous! Why waste *any* fat grams on coffee, and who cares if it is 98 percent fat free? (And by the way, any regular or decaffeinated coffee without cream or sugar has zero fat grams.)

Is It Okay to Eat "Good Fat" (Polyunsaturated), the Kind That Does Not Clog Your Arteries?

No. Even though polyunsaturated fat is better for your health than saturated fat, it has the same amount of calories per gram as any fat, and will indeed make you just as fat.

For your information, saturated fats are found in animal products such as beef, pork, lamb, full-fat milk, cheese, and butter—and in addition, the vegetable products palm, palm kernel, and coconut oil. Except for the vegetable oils, all saturated fats become solid at room temperature. These fats cause elevated cholesterol levels, which in turn build up a solid material in your arteries, plaque, which in turn serves as a roadblock to your blood circulation. The result: heart attack.

And don't be fooled by "trans fatty acids," which are often billed as being good for your health. They can keep you just as chubby. These fatty acids are found in hydrogenated and partially hydrogenated oils contained in items such as potato chips, crackers, cookies, granola bars, and margarine. They tend to function in the body as saturated fats and can also clog your arteries.

Polyunsaturated fats (they come from vegetables, seeds, and nuts) are different. They are in liquid form and when consumed do not contribute to arteriosclerosis.

Is Cholesterol Fat?

No. Cholesterol is not fat, but a waxy, fatlike substance. It is found in nonfatty foods such as shrimp, eel, and squid and other seafood, and in fatty foods, such as red meats.

Like fat, cholesterol is not all bad. In fact, cholesterol is essential for life. Our cell membranes and nerve linings, brain, liver, and blood contain cholesterol, and cholesterol helps to form adrenal and sex hormones, bile, and vitamin D. It travels to body tissues in the bloodstream in lipoprotein—tiny droplets surrounded with a thin coating or shell-like material. These droplets transport cholesterol to and from body tissues. Cholesterol is naturally produced by your liver; you don't have to go out of your way to consume it.

Good Cholesterol, Bad Cholesterol

While we're on the subject of cholesterol, let's clear up the matter of "good" (HDL) and "bad" (LDL) cholesterol. Bad cholesterol tends to deposit itself on the arterial walls, forming the plaque that clogs arter-

ies and prevents blood from flowing to the heart, causing heart problems that may lead to death.

Interestingly "good" cholesterol does the exact opposite of "bad" cholesterol. It helps to unclog the arteries by removing "bad" cholesterol from the bloodstream and transporting it out of the cells and into the bile and intestines, where it leaves the body through excretion.

But how do you know if you have too much of the wrong kind of cholesterol? You must take a fractionated cholesterol test. This test will give you what is called a cholesterol index. The lower your index, the lower your bad cholesterol and the lower your risk of heart attack. An index of four or lower is considered safe and healthy.

Just in case you're interested, an index is determined by dividing your total cholesterol by your good cholesterol (HDL). Let me give you an example. If your total cholesterol level is 200 and your HDL is 50, since 50 goes into 200 four times, your index is four.

Where's the Fat?

Okay. Now that you know what you know about fat, it's time to face up to the fact that until you get to your goal, certain foods are out of the question. They are:

All fried foods

Butter, margarine, lard, chicken fat, or oil (except very small amounts of olive or canola oil)

Mayonnaise with fat, and any fat-containing salad dressing

Peanut butter

Any ice cream, sour cream, cream cheese, and cheese that is not fat free

Milk, cottage cheese, or yogurt with more than 1 percent fat

Nuts, seeds, or any kind of "chips" (potato, corn, etc.)

Doughnuts, chocolate, croissants

Beef, bacon, lamb, or veal

Olives, avocados

Why such a long list? Anything on this list would be far too costly to your allowance of twenty to twenty-five grams of fat a day. You just can't afford them and stay within your budget. Let me give you some examples so you can see for yourself.

Food Product	Fat Grams
Fast-Food Hamburgers	
Burger King Whopper	36
Burger King Whopper with Cheese	45
Burger King Double Whopper	52
Burger King Double Whopper with Cheese	62
McDonald's Big Mac	36
Wendy's Single Plain Burger	15
Carls Jr. Country Fried Steak	33
Other Fast-Food Beef	
Arby's club sandwich	30
Arby's super roast beef sandwich	28
McDonald's Sausage McMuffin with egg	27.4
Arby's turkey sandwich	24
Burger King ham-and-cheese sandwich	24
Hot dog	15
Fast-Food Fried Chicken	
4-ounce thigh	19
4-ounce drumstick	16
4-ounce breast	15
Fast-Food Fish	
Arthur Treacher's fried fish	19.7
Arthur Treacher's fish sandwich	19.2
Croissant Foods	
Croissant	11
Burger King Croissan'wich with meat, egg, and cheese	24
Fast-Food Mexican Food	
Corn dog	16
Jack in the Box super taco	17
Taco Bell burrito	20
4 ounces refried beans with sausage	32
Fast-Food Potato Dishes	
Burger King french fries	22
Wendy's baked potato with cheese	24
Fast-Food Dessert Products	
Dairy Queen banana split	15
Large Dairy Queen ice cream dipped in chocolate	20

1 Ounce Cheese (One Slice)

Cheddar	9.4
American	8.9
Roquefort	8.7
Munster	8.5
Edam	7.9
Swiss	7.8
Limburger	7.7
Provolone	7.6
Mozzarella	6.1

You might be thinking that, compared to a Whopper hamburger, cheese doesn't seem so bad. But it is. It wouldn't be so terrible if you were willing to sacrifice the six to nine grams of fat for one slice of cheese as long as you kept within your daily twenty-five-fat-gram limit. The problem is, one slice of cheese never satisfied anyone I know. Eat one slice and the cheese starts calling you: "Just one more tiny morsel." Finally you give in and decide, "I'll just have a half." Then you promptly eat the whole slice, and then another, and then another. So forget about it. Stay away from cheese until you reach your goal. Then, once a week, you can have it.

What about low-fat cheeses? I think they are still too high in fat. The lowest of low-fat cheeses have one or two grams of fat per slice (ounce), and the highest nearly five grams per slice. What about nonfat cheese? Okay. But be careful. Calories count too if you overdo it. More about that in Chapter 7.

Ask Questions and Read Your Labels Carefully

Sometimes innocent foods such as granola, a cup of dried noodles (the kind you add water to), a salad, or even pasta can contain more fat than you ever imagined. For example, who would believe that Quaker 100% Natural granola cereal has ten grams of fat in a meager half-cup serving? Most oatmeals have no more than one or two grams of fat per serving. A one-serving container of cup-of-noodle type foods often contains up to twelve grams of fat, and sometimes more! A seemingly innocent chef's salad at Jack in the Box has nineteen grams of fat and, worse, a taco salad at Taco Bell has sixty-one grams of fat. A simple serving of what should be a very-low-fat dish, pasta, at Shoney's, will cost you a whopping sixteen grams of fat. Be a fat investigator. Ask before you eat. Fortunately, most of these fast-food establishments now serve wonderful low-fat alternatives.

What about Pizza?

Pizza that is not dripping in cheese but is heavier on the veggies is the least of all evils when it comes to fast or fatty foods. At least you're getting your nutrition's worth when you eat it—and in addition, it's filling. You won't feel as hungry after you eat a veggie pizza that's light on the cheese as you will with, say, two slices of cheese that contain even more fat.

If you are in an emergency and no other food is available, it's okay to eat a slice of pizza. One medium slice of my favorite pizza from Pizza Hut has ten grams of fat. You could get away with a slice if you watched your fat intake for the rest of the day and made sure you didn't go over your twenty-five grams. You could also blot the pizza with a napkin before eating to get rid of some of the melted fat.

What Do Sugar and Refined Carbohydrates Have to Do with Fat?

Sugar and refined carbohydrates, such as white bread, sourdough bread, fruit juices, sugar candy, jams and jellies, etc., can hinder the fat-burning process. How so? They cause the glucose to travel through your system so quickly that your insulin level rises. When this occurs, the enzyme (hormone-sensitive lipase) responsible for pulling fat from your cells is hindered. Fat is then trapped in your cells, and your body is forced to burn more carbohydrates and less fat. In addition, the rise in insulin stimulates your appetite. So keep your sugar and refined carbohydrates to a minimum (see p. 134).

Drinking Water Can Help Keep Fat off Your Body!

First and foremost, drinking plenty of water will help to calm down your appetite. It will also insure that you're not eating because your body is really dehydrated and craving the water in the food you will eat (foods are made up of at least 50 percent water).

In addition, water helps the body to metabolize its stored fat. Studies have revealed that when water intake is greatly decreased, fat deposits are increased. On the other hand, when water intake is increased, fat deposits are decreased. It works something like this: In order to function properly, the kidneys require a certain amount of water. When deprived of this water, they don't work to capacity, and the liver takes over their job. One of the main functions of the liver is to metabolize fat. However, since the liver is busy doing the work of the kidneys,

it can't devote its full attention to metabolizing fat, and *it metabolizes less fat*. This fat remains stored in the body. I now drink at least eight eight-ounce glasses of water a day.

Where Is Your Main Fat Storage Bin?

For women, the major part of fat is stored in the hips/buttocks, thighs, and abdominals (stomach). But which specific area of your body stores the most fat? Each woman is different. You can determine where you store the majority of your fat by looking in the mirror. Which body part *looks* the fattest? Is it your hips/buttocks area, your thighs, or your stomach? Another way to test where your first storage place for fat is to be aware of where the excess pounds show up first when you start to gain weight. Even when you are in near-perfect shape, it is this area that will hold on to those last few pounds of fat. I get letters from women all the time: "Your workout is great. But I still have one problem. My lower stomach . . ."

In order to get rid of that last bit of fat, you will have to keep your weight-loss eating plan very strict and bomb away at that body part with extra exercises. You'll be doing both if you follow this book exactly as written.

Body Fat Percentage

Some women have a body fat percentage as high as 65 percent. The average American woman has about half that amount, 33 percent Medical authorities seem to agree that a fit woman should have a body fat percentage of about 22 to 23 percent. Interestingly, my body fat is about 22 percent—not as low as you would think! Do I care? Not at all. The only reason I had my body fat measured in the first place was to answer the question so my fans who said, "I'll bet your body fat percentage is about ten percent." For me, that will never happen. Part of it is genetic, and part of it is that I love to eat.

The way I see it, I look good enough the way I am. I want to enjoy my life, and eating happens to be one of the things I enjoy. At my age, I'm not planning on winning a beauty contest or becoming a model, and there's no reason for me to be bone thin. (Anyway, I don't think I would have won such a prize at any age, or have been qualified as a model—I'm too short, not to mention other things.) If you take a close look at my photos, you will notice that I do carry some excess body fat on my stomach and hips/buttocks. I do care, but not enough to give up eating altogether! I love food.

What Is Brown Fat?

You may have heard of something called brown fat, as opposed to regular or yellow fat. It is found in blood vessels that lead to the heart, near the spine, and in the chest, in grapelike clusters. In the 1980s there was a great interest in this type of fat because it was discovered that such fat behaves like fat-burning furnace. In other words, people who have a proper supply of brown fat can get away with an occasional binge without the consequence of weight gain.

I can just imagine what you're thinking: "Tell me, tell me, how can I get this brown fat?" Until now, we don't know exactly how people get it, but we do know who has it, and those are the people who seem to need it the least: athletes who are already in shape. So why am I telling you this? If you follow this workout and get yourself in shape, and better yet, if you do the optional aerobics and follow through with a weight-training program for the rest of your body, you are likely to have more brown fat.

If brown fat really does what it is reputed to do, I think we should change its name to something other than fat. Why? To get fat, all you have to do is eat fat. But to get brown fat, you can't eat fat. In fact, you have to do something quite different. You have to work out and eventually be in the condition of an athlete.

Two Women: Same Height, Weight, Bone Structure—Yet One Looks So Much Fatter!

Just the other day I approached a woman in the gym who seemed to be my height and bone structure. She had just stepped off the scale, and I noticed that it said 116 pounds. As she gathered her gym bag, I weighed myself. I also weighed 116 pounds. But she looked much fatter than I did. On the way out of the gym, I asked her to guess my weight. "A hundred and five pounds," she said. "Nope. I'm a hundred and sixteen," I replied. She was amazed. I asked her what size dress she wears and she said, "Nine." I wear a three to five!

What followed was a discussion like the one in the following paragraphs. Muscle weighs more than fat but takes up less space. I have more muscle on my body than she does, and her feathery or spongelike lightweight fat is wider and bigger than my heavyweight, lean, dense muscle.

Do I make my point? Forget the scale and look in the mirror. As you put muscle on your body you'll see greater changes in the mirror than you will on the scale. You may lose five pounds of fat, but you may also

be increasing muscle, so the scale may show little or no drop. But in the meantime you look and feel much leaner (I mean your body will literally feel harder). Please. I beg you. Let the scale be just a curiosity. Don't use it as a gauge to measure whether or not you are getting in shape. Let the mirror and the way your body feels be your guides.

How Can You Implant within Yourself a Fat-Burning Furnace that Operates Twenty-four Hours a Day?

Muscle is a permanent fat-burning furnace. How so? Muscle raises your basal metabolism—the minimum quantity of energy you use even when resting in order to sustain your life.

When you develop muscles on your body, you will use more energy (use up more calories and burn more excess fat) than you used to while doing the same activities. For example, if you used to burn sixty calories an hour sleeping, you will now burn about 20 percent more, say, seventy-two calories per hour. The more muscle you put on your body, the more you raise your basal metabolism, and the more fat you burn twenty-four hours a day. Champion bodybuilders burn at least twice as much or more fat twenty-four hours a day than average people—and in fact must eat twice as much or more than ordinary people in order to sustain their bodies. You can see why, if you love to eat, having muscles is a good idea!

How Can You Convince Your Discouraged Self that Once and for All You Can Get Rid of the Excess Body Fat?

You can get with the program. You can stop berating yourself for past failures and begin today. You can, by an act of will after reading this book, take the first step by placing the book on the floor, opening to the first exercises, and then "just doing it." That's right. One stroke at a time. One day a time. That's all it takes to begin a new life. And if you need extra encouragement, read my book *Look In, Look Up, Look Out: Be the Person You Were Meant to Be* (see Bibliography)—especially the chapter called "Motivate Yourself: Your Personal Bag of Tricks." That'll get you going for sure.

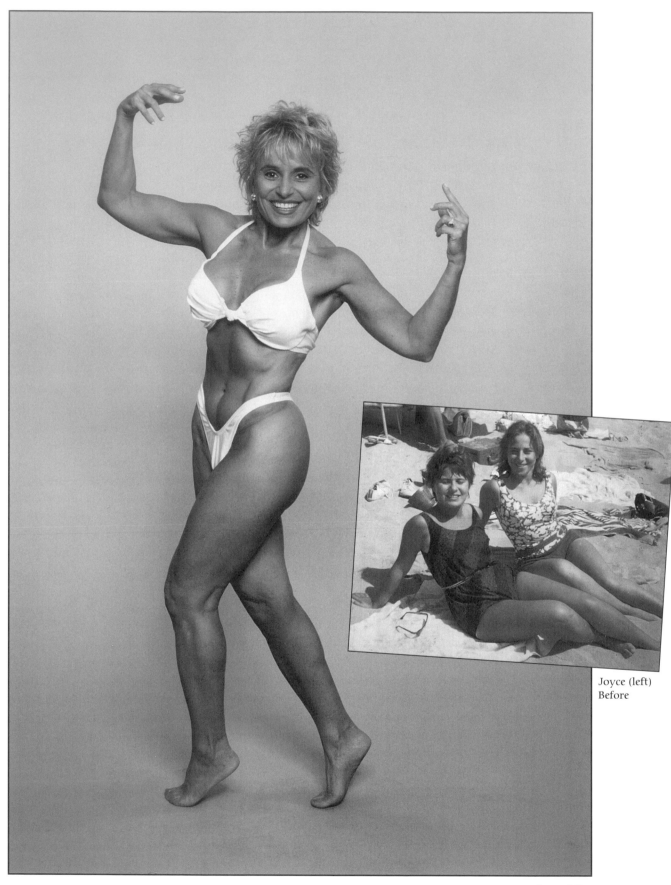

Joyce (left)
Before

Joyce After

BEFORE AND AFTER

Before and after! We all want results. That's what it's all about. The bottom line is, What can I expect to see as a result of this workout? In this chapter you will meet five women who did the Bathing Suit Workout and achieved a wonderful result. But first let's take a look at my before-and-after photos.

I finally dug up an old "fat" photo of myself when I was nineteen years old. I had gone from a "skinny" ninety-eight pounds to a fat 131—and then I stopped weighing myself. After that I went on many diets and, as discussed in my other books, I yo-yoed up and down over the years—but even when I lost the weight I was a "skinny-fat." It was only after learning the secrets contained in this (and other books I've written) that I was able to get in shape.

I've been doing the Bathing Suit Workout for my hip-butt-thigh and stomach area for the past year now and—Wow! I've never had a better "bathing suit body" in my life! In fact, I'm showing you my butt in a "thong" for the first time ever—and you are looking at a fifty-five-year-old butt! I would never do this before (show you a photo of myself in a thong), but I'll make the supreme sacrifice to make the point. (See p. 41 rear-anatomy shot for the photo of me in the thong.)

Now let's talk about the other "before-and-after" women.

Ivonne: Size 20 Before—Size 7 after Thirty Workout Hours

Look at Ivonne. She did the regular Bathing Suit Workout six days a week—and look at the results after thirty workout hours. It took her about twenty-six weeks. She did my Bottoms Up! Workout and, later, used *Definition* for the rest of her body.

"The first time I picked up your book, I hated your guts. What guts! Look at the body that that hussy has! *Wham!* Across the room you went. But finally—I went through many stages, it's a long story—I got started, and the rest is history.

"This past summer I vacationed in Cancún for two weeks. They were the happiest weeks of my life. Why? Because when I was younger, I was given nicknames such as Bon-Bon, which meant marshmallow. My brothers could not get enough of calling me Fatso. I missed out on a great deal, like proms, dates, and parties because of my weight. But thanks to you, now, at thirty-four, I look and feel my best, and I'm no longer ashamed of my body. I am now realizing my dreams—not just in looking good but in achieving goals and fulfilling my potential. I love you, Joyce Vedral—you're a very real person."

Ivonne Before, Size 20

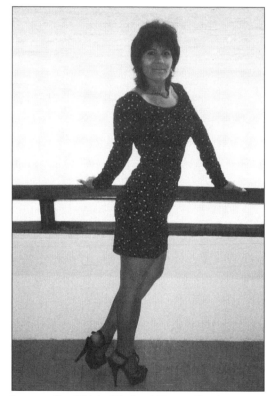

Ivonne after Thirty Workout Hours, Size 7

Chris: Size 16 Before—Size 8 after Thirty Workout Hours

Chris did the regular Bathing Suit Workout—ten minutes a day, four days a week—for forty-five weeks (thirty Bathing Suit Workout hours in all), and look at her now! She did the Fat-Burning Workout for the rest of her body.

"I've never felt so good in my life," says Chris. "It was fun buying

Chris Before, Size 16

Chris after Thirty Workout Hours, Size 8

new clothes, going down the size rack—first a 16, then a 14—all the way down to size 8! I can't begin to tell you how many people I have told about this workout. Most of them don't believe me until I show them a 'before' picture. I get compliments all the time. I am constantly showing my muscles to people. So many people began doing what I'm doing—one girl at work lost over forty pounds. Thank you much, Joyce."

If Chris, who is forty-two years old, has two children, twelve and nine, and works full time as a legal secretary (she is a single mom), can do it, so can you. "I'm really busy, but I always find time to work out because I want to look good. I know that I'm old enough that if I let my body go and I don't start taking care of it, I'm going to be in big trouble. Also, I feel much better when I work out—as if I've accomplished something."

Anita: Size 13 Before—Size 9 after Thirty Workout Hours

Anita did the regular Bathing Suit Workout six days a week for thirty weeks and my Definition Workout for the rest of her body, and look at her now!

"I'm so pleased with the way I look. I never looked like this, even when I was a teenager. Every one I know, including the members of my family, agree. I get compliments all the time. I feel and look—well, people tell me I look—thirty-two, but I'm forty-five years old."

Anita told me that her whole life has changed for the better now that she doesn't have to worry about her body.

Anita Before, Size 13

Anita after Thirty Workout Hours, Size 9

Michelle: Size 12 Before—Size 9 after Twelve Workout Hours

Michelle first wrote to me when she had gone down from a size 22 to 24 to a size 14 in twenty-six weeks after using my book *The Fat Burning Workout*. She later switched to my books *Bottoms Up!* and *Definition*, and got down to a size 12 after another twelve weeks. That's how you see her in the before photo, a size 12.

I told Michelle that she looked fine the way she was, but she said,

"What about my middle? I feel I still need some special work there." So I sent her the manuscript to a new book I was working on—this book, *The Bathing Suit Workout*—and look what she did in twelve workout hours!

Michelle did the Titanium Woman workout from this book, fifteen minutes a day, three days a week. It took her sixteen weeks! She continues to switch back and forth between my other workouts for the rest of her body, among them Definition, the Fat-Burning Workout, and Bottoms Up! and the 12-Minute Total-Body Workout.

Michelle is thirty years old and has a four-year-old son. She also works as a data processor, so she is very busy and does not have a lot of time to work out. "I did my workout at my lunch hour with my friend. I've got a whole lot of people doing your workout now.

"In spite of my hectic schedule, I always find time to do it. At first it seemed like a lot of work, but in a week you get familiar with the exercises and you don't have to read how to do them anymore—and I love the tear-out wall charts.

"I can see my middle body, my stomach and my hip-butt-thigh area. They are a lot tighter and the jigglyness is completely gone."

Michelle Before, Size 12

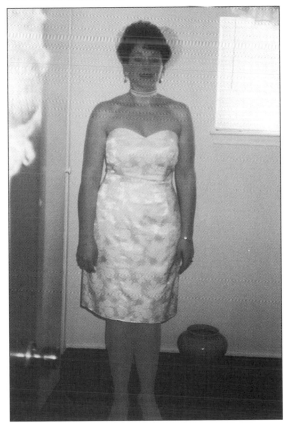

Michelle after Twelve Workout Hours, Size 9

Kelley: Size 8 Before—Size 6 after Six Workout Hours

Kelley is thrilled with her results. She used my Fat-Burning Workout to get down from a size 16 to a size 8 in twelve weeks (sixteen workout hours). Then she used *The Bathing Suit Workout*, doing the maximum plan: the Titanium Woman workout three days a week for eight weeks (six workout hours), and look at her now!

Kelley says, "I'm a landscaper. I'm used to lifting fifty-pound bags—and you see how I looked in my before photo. So what was wrong with this picture? Why wasn't I in shape? Well guess what: It's not how much you're lifting or working, it's how you're working. Once I learned what to do, I got results so fast people don't believe me. And if you think I have time to spend hours working out, forget it. I'm thirty-six and I have three children—ten, thirteen, and fourteen! I get my workout done and out of the way. I used to go to a health club but I dropped it. It wasn't working. I can do this with so little effort. Not only do I look better, but I feel so much better too—stronger, more energy."

Kelley after Six Workout Hours
(Eight Weeks) of the Bathing Suit
Workout, Size 6

Kelly Before, Size 16

Kelley after Sixteen Workout
Hours (Twelve Weeks) of the
Fat-Burning Workout, Size 8

Small wonder. The stomach or midsection, as you may know, is the center of strength. I asked Kelley what she's doing now in the way of a workout. She said, "I devised my own plan—switching back and forth using all of your books in cycles of six weeks for the rest of my body. I'll use *The Fat Burning Workout* for six weeks, then switch to *Definition* for six weeks, then use *Bottoms Up!* or *Now or Never*. I even use (and love) *Top Shape* and *Gut Busters* for six weeks, and so on. I do this to challenge my muscles—so they won't get bored." Kelley tells me that she has all of her friends working out!

What About You?

Now that you've read the inspirational stories of other women, what about you? If it can happen to me and if it can happen to them, it can happen to you. You are not the exception to the rule. That is a lie you tell yourself because of your past false starts. This is not a false start. Begin today by taking a before photo of yourself and pasting it in the space below. Then finish reading this book, underlining text and making comments in the margins (this is the best way to really absorb the book). Then set a start date and go! Begin a workout that will change your life for the better in every way, shape, and form—not just physically but psychologically as well.

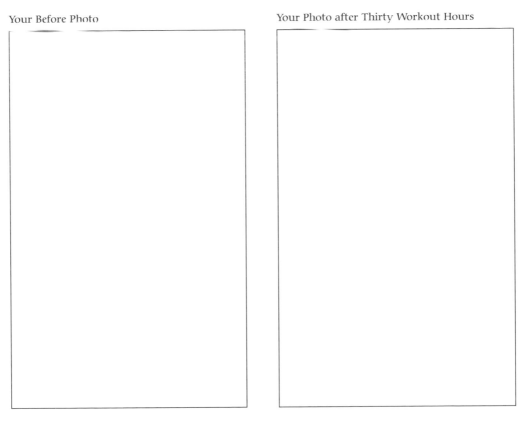

Your Before Photo

Your Photo after Thirty Workout Hours

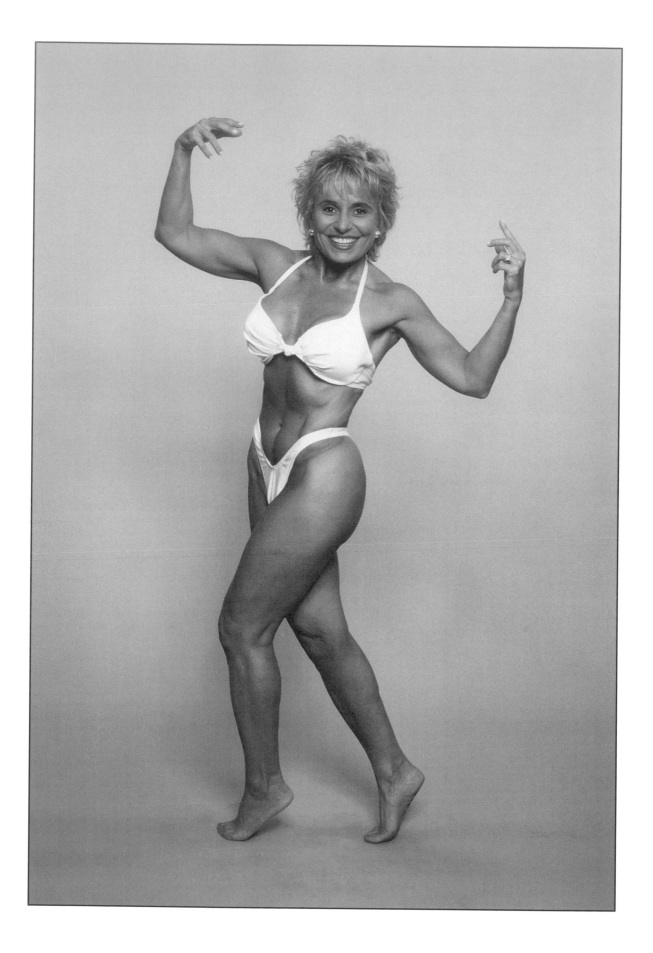

4

WHAT YOU NEED TO KNOW, WHAT YOU NEED TO FORGET!

In order to succeed at any workout, there are certain basic things you must know before you start. In addition to what you must learn, there are things you must forget! There are certain preconceived ideas based upon misinformation and preconditioning that must be removed from your thinking before you start the workout, so that your progress will not be hindered.

In the following paragraphs you will find basic operating information, which will help you to "clear the slate" of your mind so that you can start fresh and begin a workout that will, once and for all, end the problem you've had all of your adult life. No longer will your hips, buttocks, thighs, and stomach represent a vicious circle of frustration for you.

Exercise Information

An **exercise** is a specified movement for a given muscle, designed to encourage that muscle to become stronger, harder, shapelier, and more defined. For example, the knee-raised oblique crunch is an exercise designed to tighten, tone, and define the upper abdominal area.

A **repetition**, or rep, is one complete movement of an exercise, from start, to midpoint, to endpoint (which is really back to start). For example, one repetition of the saddlebag stripper involves lying on your side and raising your leg as high as possible (midpoint) and lowering your leg back to the original position (endpoint).

A **set** is a given number of repetitions of a specific exercise that are performed without a rest. In this workout one set will consist of fifteen repetitions. This will apply to all exercises in the workout.

A **superset** is the performance of two exercises without taking a rest. You can superset within body parts by doing two exercises for the same body part before you take a rest, or you can superset between body parts by doing two exercises for two different body parts before taking a rest. The superset is not used in this workout, but you will need to understand the term when thinking about the workouts described in Chapter 10.

A **speed superset** is a combined set of two exercises for the same body part, without taking a rest between supersets. In other words, you do all three sets for two exercises before you take a rest. The speed superset is not used in this workout, but you will need to know this term in order to understand the workouts described in Chapter 10.

The **speed set** is combined set of all sets of a given exercise, where the exercise stops only long enough to pick up the next weight. For example, if you were to choose to do your chest routine with speed sets rather than combining the flat bench press and the flat bench flye, you would perform all five sets of your flat bench press without resting. Then you would take a short rest and perform all five sets of your flat bench flye. The speed set is not used in this workout, but you will need to know the term in order to understand the workouts described in Chapter 10.

A **giant set** is a combination of three compatible exercises for the same body part without taking a rest. The giant set is not used in this routine, but you will need to know the term in order to understand other workouts, discussed in Chapter 10.

A **tri-set** is a combination of three compatible exercises for different body parts that are done without taking a rest. This entire workout will be based upon tri-sets of hips/buttocks, thigh, and abdominal exercises. Only after one set of exercises has been performed for each of those three body parts can a fifteen-second rest be taken.

The **speed tri-set** is the performance of one tri-set after another without taking advantage of the allowed fifteen-second rest. The advantage of this method is twofold: (1) you save time, and (2) you burn more fat. Note: It is only after you have become very adept at the workout that you can use the speed tri-set.

The **true or "regular" pyramid system** is the adding of weight to each set with a simultaneous reduction of repetitions until a peak is achieved, and then the reduction of weight on each set with a simultaneous addition of repetitions until the starting amount of weight and repetitions is once again achieved.

For example, in this workout, beginning exercisers would use the following pyramid:

Set 1: Twelve repetitions at one pound

Set 2: Ten repetitions at two pounds

Set 3: Eight repetitions at three pounds

Set 4: Ten repetitions at two pounds

Set 5: Twelve repetitions at one pound

The **modified pyramid system** is the adding of weight to each set at the expense of a few repetitions only until the peak of the pyramid is reached. For example:

Set 1: Twelve repetitions at one pound

Set 2: Ten repetitions at two pounds

Set 3: Eight repetitions at three pounds

Since for the most part no weights are used with this workout, neither the modified or true pyramid system is required. You can opt to use the modified pyramid system with your thigh routine. For absolute maximum results, I recommend that you use weights and the modified pyramid system for thighs. You will also need to be familiar with these terms in order to understand the information regarding other workouts in Chapter 10.

A **rest** is a pause between sets or exercises. The function of a rest is to allow the working muscle time to recover so that it can cope with the next set of exercise. As mentioned above, in this workout you will take a fifteen-second rest only after you have performed three exercises—one each for hips/buttocks, thighs, and abdominals. Your muscles can cope very well without resting for three sets because you are not exercising the same body part for three sets in a row. Indeed, you are exercising three different body parts. While one body part is working, the others are resting. But since you are still on the move, you continue to burn fat.

Breathing naturally while you exercise means to inhale and exhale unconsciously in an instinctive, as opposed to a thoughtful, manner and not to hold your breath. When performing a new or challeng-

ing exercise, many people tend to hold their breath. It's an unnecessary "survival instinct" tactic. You will notice that from time to time in the exercise instructions, I remind you to not hold your breath and ask you to breathe naturally.

Some experts believe that you should breathe out (exhale) on the flex part of the exercise, and breathe (inhale) in on the stretch part of the exercise. This would be necessary if you were lifting heavy weights, such as powerlifters do. For our purposes, it's better not to think about your breath at all. Focus all of your attention on your working muscles.

A **routine** is the specific combination of exercises prescribed for a certain body part. For example, in this workout your regular hips/buttocks routine consists of seven exercises: the saddlebag stripper, the lower butt curl, the lower butt crunch, the lower butt side kick, the floor feather kick-up, the lying butt lift, and the one-leg prone butt lift. The Iron Woman workout adds the standing butt squeeze. The Steel Woman workout adds the reverse-lunge lift, and the Titanium Woman workout adds the straight-leg kick-up. In this workout you will perform your abdominal routine in combination with your thighs and abdominals.

A **workout** includes all the exercises to be performed by the exerciser on a given day. For example, in this workout, you will perform seven tri-sets consisting of a hips/buttocks, thigh, and abdominal exercise for the regular workout, eight tri-sets for the Iron Woman workout, nine tri-sets for the Steel Woman workout, and ten tri-sets for the Titanium Woman workout.

The term **weight** refers to resistance, or the heaviness of the dumbbell used in a given exercise. In this workout, except for rare occasions, no weight is used for hips/buttocks or abdominal exercises, and graduated dumbbells can be used for all thigh exercises. (You will raise your weights as you get stronger.)

A muscle is **flexed** when the muscle fibers are shortened as the muscle is squeezed together. For example, your quadriceps (front thigh muscle) is flexed when you return to the start position from a regular squatting position. In this workout, I ask you to add to that natural flex by willfully squeezing your muscle as it flexes, adding to the force of the flex. You can help yourself to flex a muscle by imagining that someone is about to punch you hard in that muscle. Your natural reaction will be to contract or flex that muscle in defense.

A muscle is **stretched** when the muscle fibers are elongated. For example, your quadriceps (front thigh muscle) is stretched when you lower yourself to the squatting position. In the exercise instructions, I ask you to "feel the stretch" in various muscles.

Muscle isolation is the method of exercising each muscle completely and independently of other body parts. Muscle isolation is necessary in order to insure maximum muscle growth, development, and definition. Although this workout combines three exercises, the principle of muscle isolation is not violated because you are not working muscles at random. You are asked to perform three exercises in rapid sequence, and to return quickly to the previous muscle groups and repeat the cycle. The rest time between the exercising of your specific muscles is not long enough to hinder progress. On the other hand, if you skipped around at random, working various muscles on your body at will and taking your time, your muscles would rest too long and would not respond effectively to the challenge of the exercises.

Progression refers to the periodic adding of weight to specific exercises when the weight being used is no longer enough of a challenge. For example, in about four weeks you may feel that you are ready to use ten-pound dumbbells for your thigh exercises. Two months after that, you may see that you can use fifteen-pound dumbbells, and in another six months you may be able to advance to twenty pounds. But where does it end? Will you eventually be lifting fifty-, seventy-five-, and one-hundred-pound dumbells? Of course not. You will eventually reach a "plateau" where you will say to yourself, "I like what I see. I don't want to get bigger muscles." At this point you will keep the same weights forever.

Target date is the date you set for your visualized body to arrive! The date must be realistic. Then mark that date on the calendar and continually picture your body evolving into its ideal form by your target date.

A **plateau** refers to a weight ceiling where the exerciser can either remain or attempt to break through. Most people reach their weight training plateau in about a year. At that time you may choose to remain at that plateau or go higher.

Technique Information: Altering the Effect of Your Exercises

An exercise routine becomes **aerobic** when it causes your pulse to reach 60 to 80 percent of its capacity, and to stay that way for a certain length of time. (Some authorities insist that in order to achieve an "aerobic effect," one must work for twenty minutes uninterrupted. However, more and more exercise specialists are beginning to agree that one achieves an aerobic effect in as short a time as ten minutes.)

You can figure out your maximum pulse rate by subtracting your age from 220 and then multiplying the result by 80 percent. You can find your minimum aerobic pulse by multiplying that number by 60

percent. If you follow this workout exactly as prescribed, taking the minimum number of rests, you will be well within the aerobic range. You don't have to check your pulse continually. If you break into a sweat after about seven minutes, rest assured that you are in the aerobic range. This workout is aerobic if you do not take advantage of the fifteen-second rest after each tri-set. But even if you do choose to rest the fifteen seconds, you get a significant fat-burning effect.

Intensity is the degree of difficulty or challenge of the exercise program you are following. Intensity can be increased by adding to the number of repetitions, increasing the load of weight, reducing the rest periods allowed between sets and between exercises, or using continual pressure. This is a very high-intensity workout because you are asked to do three exercises of fifteen repetitions each before you are allowed to take a rest. If you wish, you could increase the repetitions from fifteen to twenty-five, but frankly, the workout is already intense enough. I do only fifteen repetitions each.

Dynamic tension is the willful force exerted on a muscle as it is being stretched or elongated. In a normal situation when a muscle elongates, no pressure is exerted on the muscle. However, one can deliberately and consciously exert pressure on the muscle even as it elongates.

Isometric pressure is the willful force exerted on a muscle as it is being flexed or shortened, above and beyond the normal force used when flexing a muscle.

Continual pressure involves willfully squeezing (flexing) the muscle as hard as possible on the contraction part of the movement, and continuing to keep pressure on the muscle by deliberately using as much dynamic tension on the muscle as possible on the stretch part of the movement. Continual pressure is a combination of dynamic tension and isometric pressure. You will try to use continual pressure as much as possible as you do the Bathing Suit Workout.

Concentration is mentally focusing on the specific muscle you are exercising by watching, touching, and/or thinking about that muscle as you perform your repetitions, and by picturing that muscle becoming firm, strong, shaped, and defined. Concentration also involves actively "telling" the muscle to grow and be reshaped. (This helps the unconscious mind to go into action.)

Visualization is the picturing in your mind of what you want to have happen to your body. As you are working out, imagine the body part you are working being reshaped into the form you have in mind.

The **unconscious mind** can be used to help you to reach your fitness goal. Your conscious mind (you) "tells" your unconscious mind to get you to your goal in a certain, reasonable amount of time. For example, you've read this book and you're determined to get in shape. In

order to employ your unconscious mind's help, stand in the mirror and "tell" your body to become reshaped by a certain reasonable date, and picture your body evolving into that shape. Your unconscious mind will begin to cooperate and alert you when you are tempted to skip a workout, do a lazy workout, or overeat. I often compare the unconscious mind to a homing torpedo or a Scud missile that zigzags its way toward its target once programmed because that's just what it does. It gets you to your goal on the target date, sometimes seemingly miraculously.

Details Concerning Muscles

Muscle mass is the specific size of a given muscle. In order to experience muscle growth, you must consistently challenge the muscle. Muscle mass is developed, shaped, and sculpted by the particular work or exercise it is being asked to do. For example, your front thigh muscles will become firm as a muscle is formed under the skin, replacing the fat (you will lose this as you follow the low-fat eating plan). Your front thigh muscles will also be sculpted into an appealing form and defined so as to look athletic and sexy.

Muscularity is a comparative term. It depicts the quantity of muscle on your body as opposed to fat. As you continue to do the Bathing Suit Workout and to follow the low-fat eating plan, your muscle-to-fat ratio will increase—that is to say, you will have a higher and higher percentage of muscle and a lower percentage of fat on your hips/buttocks, thighs, and abdominals.

Definition is the clearly delineated lines that separate muscles from each other and divide muscles themselves, and make them appear sculpted and separated. Well-placed definition can also help to give the body a more balanced, symmetrical look. For example, definition in the obliques (side abdominal muscles) draws attention away from a large waistline and causes the waist to appear smaller. The diagonal lines cause the waist to appear to slant in and look less boxy. My waist is twenty-seven inches—that's my bone structure. No matter how thin I get, my waist will never be smaller. Yet because of my definition in that area, most people think my waist is much smaller.

When one has extreme definition, one is considered to be **ripped**. After doing this routine for about six months, assuming that you have lost your excess body fat by following the low-fat eating plan, your abdominal muscles will appear to be ripped. They may in fact have what is called the beer-can look, so called for the six-pack of muscles inscribed on the stomach. (Quite the opposite of the beer-belly look.)

Density is the hardness of a muscle. A muscle is most dense when it has little intramuscular fat. The Bathing Suit Workout will eventually

force the fat not only from under your skin where most of it resides, but from the muscle itself. When muscle density increases, muscles feel more firm to the touch.

Total body **symmetry** refers to the balance and proportion of all the muscles on your body in relation to all the other muscles on your body. In order to achieve total body symmetry, you will want to choose one of my full workout books and do exercises for the other six body parts: chest, shoulders, biceps, triceps, back, and calves. See Chapter 10 and the Bibliography for information on this.

The **forty-eight-hour recovery principle** is the allowing of forty-eight hours (or a day of rest) before rechallenging a muscle with a weight-training workout in order to allow the muscle optimum growth and to prevent overtraining and muscle attrition (wearing down). Traditionally, the only muscle that is an exception to this rule has been the abdominal area, because it is not exercised with weights. However, the buttocks are also not exercised with weights and can also be exercised day after day. In this workout, we will bend the rules and allow you to exercise your thighs consecutively because you will be using very light weights for your thighs. Later, when you get close to your size goal and you have increased the weights for your thigh exercises, you should do your Bathing Suit Workout every other day.

Split-routine is the exercising of a given number of body parts on workout day one, resting, or working on a different given number of body parts on workout day two, and so on.

The purpose and the necessity of the split routine is to allow the exercised muscle forty-eight hours' recovery time before it is challenged again. If you are using significant weights and do not allow this amount of rest time, a muscle may become exhausted from overtraining, and development will be slowed down or even reversed.

Sticking points are periods of time when, although you are working out regularly, no apparent improvement is visible. At such times progress *is* being made, only it is under the surface. Think of it as a seed in the ground. You don't know that anything is happening until the green bud pops through the earth. But in the meantime, a lot was happening under the surface—when you couldn't see a thing.

The body grows and changes in spurts. You can see this in children. No one ever sees a child grow. Yet from one year to the next, if the child is measured, there is progress. Your body will grow and change at its own pace. You may see something right away and then nothing for a few weeks or even a month or more. Then suddenly you see progress. Each body is different. The key is not to let your sticking points fool you into thinking nothing is happening. In fact, it is all happening when you

see nothing. It's only that it isn't showing up yet. If you stop now, you'll never know what you would have seen. Don't fall into that trap.

Muscle soreness occurs when you have exercised muscles that were previously neglected. It is the result of microscopic tears in the fibers of the ligaments and tendons connecting the muscles, and the slight internal swelling that accompanies these tears. The tears usually occur when you are doing the "elongating" or stretching part of the exercise, when the muscle fibers are lengthening, yet at the same time trying to contract in order to deal with the work being required of them.

These tears are normal and necessary in working out—and the soreness that comes from them is a good sign. The soreness occurs twenty-four to forty-eight hours after the workout. The amount of soreness depends upon how out of shape your muscles are when you start and how hard you work the first time you work out. For example, some women ignore the break-in-gently system, and the day after their workout they can hardly move. But they live to tell about it, and many do not regret it because they feel they needed a rude awakening to realize how out of shape they were.

Never stop working out in the hope that the soreness will go away and never return. Doing this will create an eternal soreness syndrome. You must not skip a workout, but instead, work through the soreness. After about seven minutes of working out, your muscles will feel less stiff, almost as if they've been massaged, due to blood circulation in the muscles.

Muscle injury is quite different from muscle soreness. Injury causes immediate, often sharp, surges of pain. The most common injuries are stretching and tearing ligaments, tears to the fascia (covering of the muscle), and tendinitis (inflammation of a tendon that causes pain). If you follow the exercise instructions and photographs and remember to read the tips, you will have little chance of injury.

If you feel recurring pain and are wondering if it is an injury, play it safe and see your doctor immediately.

Equipment for This Workout

You won't need any! Unless, of course, you choose the option of using weights with your leg routine. You can do this later if you wish, or you can start out with using only one set of weights, say, five-pound dumbbells. You could then switch to the pyramid system—and purchase a set of three-pound weights and a set of eight or ten pounders. But that would be all you would ever need—three sets of dumbbells graduating in weight (I always mean each dumbbell when I refer to

pounds of dumbbells). The only time you would need to get more weights would be when your lighter weights become too easy. In this case, for example, you would set aside your three pounders and use fives, eights, and tens. Later you would set aside the fives and use, say, eights, tens, and twelves, and so on, until you reach your maximum. Mine is ten, fifteen, and twenty for thighs.

But again, don't feel obligated to use weights in the beginning. You can do this workout without weights—it's just that you get absolute maximum results with the weights for thighs!

A **dumbbell** is a handheld weight. It is a short metal bar (it can also be made of another material) with raised "ball-type shapes" at either end.

Anatomy of Muscles Used in This Workout

Three muscle groups are exercised in this workout: hips/buttocks, thighs, and abdominals. The following paragraphs will provide a clear description of these muscles so that you can find them on your own body. I want you to place your front- and rear-view photographs next to mine and to label your own body. Then I want you to picture your body evolving into its most perfect form.

The muscles are discussed in the order that they are used in the workout: hips/buttocks, thighs, and abdominals.

HIPS/BUTTOCKS: GLUTEUS MAXIMUS, GLUTEUS MEDIUS, AND GLUTEUS MINIMUS

The gluteus maximus is the largest of the gluteus muscles. It originates from the iliac crest of the thighbone and runs down to the tailbone. It functions to extend and rotate the thigh when significant force is required, such as in stair-climbing. The gluteus medius, located just under the gluteus maximus, functions to raise the leg out to the side and to balance the hips as weight is transferred from one foot to the other. The gluteus minimus originates on the iliac crest of the hipbone and performs the same function as the gluteus maximus.

The above muscles constitute the entire buttocks area, including the side buttocks area, which are the hips and upper outer thigh or "saddlebags." You will notice that certain exercises in this workout specifically zone in on the lower butt, while other focus on the side of the butt (hips or saddlebags), while others cover the entire hips/buttocks area.

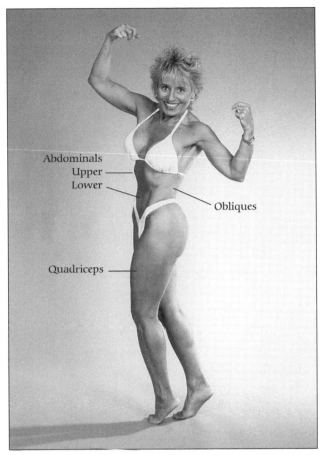

Abdominals
Upper
Lower
Obliques
Quadriceps

Joyce's Front Anatomy

Your Front Anatomy Photo

Gluteus Maximus
Adductor
Sartorius
Hamstrings

Joyce's Rear Anatomy
Note: not touched up!

Your Rear Anatomy Photo

FRONT, INNER, AND BACK THIGH: QUADRICEPS, ADDUCTOR, AND BICEPS FEMORIS OR "HAMSTRINGS"

The front thigh is called the quadriceps muscle. It consists of four muscles, the rectus femoris, and three vasti muscles. These muscles run along the thigh and terminate at the kneecap. These muscles work to extend the leg.

The adductor muscles run along the inner thigh. They originate in the lower pelvic area on the pubic bone and rise to the shaft of the thighbone. This muscle group works in cooperation with other inner thigh muscles to flex, rotate, and pull the legs together from a wide position.

Another inner thigh muscle is the sartorius muscle, the longest muscle in the body. It runs along the inner thigh from the hipbone to the inside of the knee. It functions to rotate the thigh.

The hamstring or biceps femoris muscle group consists of two muscles located on the back thigh. These muscles (the semimembranosus and the semitendinosus) originate in the bony area of the pelvis and terminate at the end of the back of the knee joint. These muscles work to bend the knee.

THE ABDOMINAL MUSCLES: RECTUS ABDOMINAL, EXTERNAL OBLIQUE, AND INTERNAL OBLIQUE

The rectus abdominus is what we call "the abdominals." But really it is one long, powerful muscle that originates from the fifth through seventh ribs and runs vertically across the abdominal wall. Because this muscle is so long, we often refer to it in sections: Upper abdominals are thought of as being located above the waistline and lower abdominals below the waistline. The abdominal muscles are segmented, so that when developed they can be seen in raised ridgelike form. This development is often referred to as "six-pack" abs.

The abdominal muscles work to pull the upper body toward the lower body. For instance, you use them to sit up from a lying or prone position.

You will notice that certain exercises are specifically designed to challenge the upper abdominals, while other exercises are created to challenge the lower abdominals. However, all abdominal exercises have secondary benefits for the entire abdominal area.

The oblique muscles are located on the side of the body. The external oblique muscles originate at the side of the lower ribs and run diagonally to the rectus abdominus. They are attached to a sheath of fibrous tissue that surrounds the rectus abdominus. These muscles work with other muscles to flex and rotate the torso.

The internal oblique muscles run beneath, and at right angles to,

the external oblique muscles. By putting definition in your oblique muscles, you can cause your waist to appear smaller. Once you have lost all excess body fat, the actual size of your waist is determined by the angle of the oblique muscles and cannot be further reduced.

You will notice that certain exercises in this workout are specifically designed to challenge the oblique muscles. As mentioned above, all abdominal exercises have secondary benefits for the entire abdominal area.

Note: Be sure to read each exercise instruction carefully and to be aware of which aspect of the particular muscle is being challenged. Then mentally cooperate by "telling" that aspect of the muscle to do the work and to become tight, toned, developed, and defined.

Workout Plans: Fitting It into Your Real-Life Situation

You have two choices for workout plans: (1) Follow the traditional "split routine" and do this workout every other day, leaving a day of rest between workouts in order to follow the traditional forty-eight-hour recovery principle, or (2) do this workout four to six days a week until you raise your dumbbells for your thigh exercises to fifteen pounds or more, and then go on the split routine. (Note: You can use the split routine using very light weights too!)

You may wonder why I am advising you to ignore the split routine that I have always advocated. First, I must state that only the muscles targeted in this workout can be safely exercised every day. Upper body parts, like the chest, shoulders, biceps, triceps, or back and also the calves, should always be exercised in a split routine. Working them two days in a row could delay your progress and cause muscle atrophy. Why, then, is it okay to break the split routine or forty-eight-hour principle here?

The issue is not the abdominals. You can exercise these muscles two, three, or more days in a row—up to ten days in a row—because the abdominals are not exercised with weights. I never told you this before, but it has always also been okay to exercise the hips/buttocks muscles two or more days in a row because this body part is also not exercised with weights. But it is not absolutely necessary to exercise this area every day. However, if you are in an emergency and want to get into bathing suit shape, you can do it every day.

What about the thigh workout? The thighs are very large muscles and can cope with a daily workout with light weights. If you are using either no weights or very light weights, you can exercise your thighs two or more days in a row. If your goal is to put on significant muscle

and if you advance to heavy weights (over fifteen pounds), you must go on the split routine.

One final point: This is a very challenging workout. If you do it every other day, you'll give yourself a day of recuperation in between, not just physically, but also psychologically. If you find yourself feeling burned out by doing it two or more days in a row and begin to dread the workout, immediately switch to the split routine and avoid, at all costs, giving up! Just make sure you do the workout at least three times a week.

WORKOUT PLANS

Plan A. Do the workout every other day.

Plan B. Do the workout four to six days a week.

It's that simple. Instructions on how to incorporate this workout into a total-body workout will be given in Chapter 10.

Get yourself a wall calendar or a daily planner calendar and write your workout days into your appointment schedule. It is, after all, an appointment. An appointment with the most important person in your life: yourself!

When should you work out? You might want to consider doing it first thing in the morning. This way you know for sure it has been done and the day's events will not interfere with your good intentions. Also, working out gives you a boost of energy to start your day. Finally, working out has a great psychological effect. It makes you feel in control. "I did it," you say to yourself. "I have discipline," you think. "I'm a doer," you say. And you forge ahead with a "can do" attitude.

If you can't do your workout in the morning, the next best thing is to find a space at work and do it at lunchtime or on a break. This workout lends itself to a work situation because you don't need any equipment. Lock your office door and do your workout on a towel on the floor. You don't even need a bench.

Your next option is to work out immediately upon returning from work. Do it like a robot; put on your workout clothing and go. It will be over in a matter of minutes.

The most risky time to do your workout is an hour or two after dinner. First, the later you work out, the more chance there is for someone or something to steal your workout time. In addition, for me at least, it's the laziest time of the day. At that time of the evening the last thing in the world I want to do is work out. However, if it were the only available time I had, I would bite the bullet and do it then. No way would I give up working out just because it's inconvenient.

What You Must Forget!

Okay. Now you know what you must remember. It's time to tell what you must forget. Once and for all.

1. Forget about "devices" or creams that will reshape your thighs, give you a flat "tummy," or melt fat away from your thighs.

Many years ago I bought a device that was supposed to give me thinner thighs. It was an earlier version of one you've seen on TV lately. The instructions said that if I placed the device between my thighs and squeezed, I would get the legs of my dreams. I did exactly as I was told and faithfully worked with the device for the required seven minutes a day. Thirty days later, all I had was a credit card bill; my thighs were as fat, flabby, and shapeless as ever—and every dimple of cellulite was still there.

There are new devices, but the laws of nature have not changed. There are no magical devices that will transform your body. You have to target muscles from a variety of angles with challenging exercises that will eventually reshape, tighten, and define those muscles. No ifs, ands, or buts about it.

The same holds true for thigh fat-remover creams. The creams promise to reduce your thighs by two inches in six weeks. But all they really do is temporarily reduce the size of your thighs by removing excess water weight. The moment you stop applying the cream, your thighs return to their former size. In addition, these creams may well prove dangerous to your health. The skin, as you may already know, is an organ. If you put something on your skin, it is absorbed into your bloodstream.

The bottom line is, creams can't melt fat and make muscle. Only dieting and working out the right way can do that.

2. Forget about the idea that "after a certain age there's nothing you can do."

I am testimony to the fact that you can reshape your body at any age. I was thirty-eight years old and very fat and out of shape. Look at me now. Thousands of women have sent me their before-and-after photos, showing me that as a result of my workouts they have reshaped their bodies. The vast majority of these women are forty, fifty, sixty, and older. In addition, study after study shows that muscles and bones can be developed at any age—without hours of effort, even at the age of ninety. You can do it at *any* age.

3. Forget about the idea that "it's just genetics. Big hips will always be a nightmare, thunder thighs are in the DNA, and I can't escape my grandmother's potbelly"!

While it is true that your bone structure and tendency toward a certain body shape are built into your DNA, it is *not* true that there's nothing you can do about it. Take what you have and make the best of it. For example, if I did not work on my body, I would have a body exactly like my grandmothers, charming women both, but built like tanks. I decided to chisel my body into its present shape by working out the right way. I would bet my life on it—if my grandmother followed my workout and diet, she would look as good as or better than I do.

4. Forget the lie that cellulite is genetic so there's nothing you can do about it.

As mentioned in Chapter 1, while the tendency toward developing cellulite is genetic, there is indeed something you can do about it. Cellulite is merely bunched-up fat, enlarged fat cells that join together and attach themselves to connecting fibrous tissue just beneath the surface of the skin. This gives the skin an "orange peel" look and feel.

With a low-fat diet and appropriate exercise, in time you can get rid of most, if not all, of your cellulite.

5. Forget the delusion that water pills can help to keep you slim.

Water pills are not the solution to your bloated look and feel. They are simply aids to help when your doctor feels that water retention is causing unnecessary discomfort or hazards to your health. As a general rule, I advise you to stay away from them and to allow your body to level off to a natural amount of water retention. More about this in Chapter 7.

6. Forget the idea that you can't spot-reshape.

True. You can't spot-*reduce* by dieting. After all, you can't tell your body where to lose the fat. But you can spot-change. You can tell your body where to change its shape and feel. You can do it by targeting specific exercises to specific areas on the body.

I've said this before, but I think it bears repeating. Here's how it works: As you hit the muscle from every angle, you gradually chisel

the muscle into the desired form. In essence, you completely reshape it, molding it the way a potter works with clay. For example, as you do this workout you will reshape or "spot-change" your hips/buttocks, thighs, and abdominals. This workout will do nothing to reshape your chest, shoulders, biceps, triceps, back, or calves. You would have to do specific exercises for those areas to reshape or spot-change them. So the next time someone says "You can't spot-reduce," tell them you can do more than that. You can completely spot-reshape!

7. Forget fear of failure.

You've tried so many programs and failed. "Why should I succeed this time?" you ask yourself. I remember a lesson I learned in school. The teacher talked about Thomas Edison, and how many times he failed before he finally came up with a working lightbulb. The teacher constantly reminded us never to give up by asking, "What would have happened if he had given up just one try before he broke through?" So I say to you, this time you will make it. This is a new day—and this is a new workout and you *will* make it this time.

8. Forget about the tape measure, scale, and fat caliper or other measuring device.

I'm not a bit impressed with measurements, but I am impressed with what I see in living color—in the mirror or in real life. I'll use myself as an example. Plenty of women have smaller dress sizes, weights, and fat percentage measurements than I do—yet they don't look nearly as toned and shapely. Why is this so?

My experience just the other day helps to answer this question. I got into a conversation with a woman in a fitting room of a department store. I noticed that although she was slim, she looked fat. I wondered if she thought she looked good. I asked her if she works out. "No. I just do aerobics," she said, beaming and bragging that she was down to a size 5 dress and weighed only 105 pounds. (She was about five feet two inches.) But the woman had a pouch of fat on her lower stomach and her butt was quite droopy. Her thighs were quite thin but "mushy" looking. I asked her age and she said, "Forty-two, and my body fat is only seventeen percent." "That's great," I said. "Guess how much I weigh?" She guessed 100 pounds. I told her that I weigh 116 and wear a size 3 to 5 dress. She was surprised. "But you must have a very low body fat percentage," she said. "No. I'm about twenty-three percent," I told her. She was astounded. "What's your secret? You look better than I do but your measurements say the opposite." I told her that my secret

is my workout. End of story. I couldn't care less what any measuring device says.

9. Forget about believing that your stretched-out stomach, cellulite-ridden thunder thighs, and wide-load sagging butt are too far gone for remedy. Nothing is impossible with time and effort.

A picture is worth a thousand words. Look at the before-and-after women in Chapter 2. They got great results after working out—for thirty workout hours. You can do it too. Remember, everything comes in time. Next bathing suit season, but for an act of God, you'll still be here. Either you will have more cellulite and look worse than you do now, or you will look better. It all depends upon what you do during that time. So what's it gonna be?

10. Forget about waiting to lose the weight before you start the workout.

If you wait until you diet down to your weight goal and then start the workout, you will be disgusted with the way your body looks and feels, and you may even be tempted to start eating like a pig again. "I dieted and suffered all this time and this is my reward," you will say. Yes, a flabby, saggy butt, cellulite, loose thighs, and a potbelly. That's what you will have—even at your thinnest—if you don't work out right along with your diet.

Now don't get me wrong. If you do diet first and find yourself a skinny-fat, it is not too late to get the muscle tone to go with your lean body. It is never too late! What I'm saying is that it's quite depressing to see that the diet only reduced your size but did not get you in shape. The answer is clear: The ideal way to go is to do the workout while you are losing the weight! In addition, working out raises your metabolism, so you will actually burn more fat and lose weight faster if you do the workout and develop those muscles (they burn fat twenty-four hours a day, even when you're sleeping).

11. Forget about shaping your thighs, hips, and butt by stair-stepping.

Stair-stepping machines and step aerobics are good for extra fat burning. In short, they are basically aerobic exercises. To try to use them to sculpt and reshape your hips, butt, and thighs is an exercise in foolishness. It just won't work. These activities do help to strengthen

these areas and to build overall endurance, but in order to shape your muscles, you must exercise in a specific manner, in designated "sets" and "repetitions" (and for the thighs, it's a good idea to add weights). In any case, reshaping and defining the body is not a crap shoot where you select an aerobic exercise that seems to target that body part and hope to get lucky. It is a science that has been perfected over the years by champion bodybuilders.

12. Forget about thinking of working out as a punishment.

All of the research agrees. Exercise is not a punishment. If anything, it is a miracle cure. It strengthens the heart, lowers blood pressure, raises HDL (good cholesterol), lowers blood fats, controls insulin, regulates bowel movements, increases endurance, reduces fatigue, improves muscle tone, and improves your state of mind and even your self-esteem. Finally, it lengthens your life. So if exercise is a punishment, lead me to the jail. I'll glady serve a life sentence!

5

HOW TO DO
THE BATHING SUIT
WORKOUT

This workout is very simple to learn. In fact, it's the easiest to learn and do of any workout I've invented! You do fifteen repetitions for every single set of every single exercise. You never have to think, "How many reps am I doing now?" In addition, for most exercises, you don't use weights, and for the ones you do, you use only one set of dumbbells (unless you opt to use the pyramid system)—you don't have to worry about switching weights from one set to the next.

In this chapter I'll teach you how to work in tri-sets, the basis for the Bathing Suit Workout. You'll learn the difference between the regular, Iron Woman, Steel Woman, and Titanium Woman workouts. I'll also explain how you can make the workout completely aerobic by eliminating all rests, and how you can make the workout easier and less intense by adding to and/or lengthening the rests.

For those of you who have back or knee problems and/or are extremely overweight and cannot do certain exercises in the workout, I'll tell you how to work out so that you get the full benefit. I'll also discuss how to use the exercise instructions to maximum advantage. Finally, I'll give you a break-in-gently plan, which will take into consideration your present fitness status!

The Regular Bathing Suit Workout

There are seven tri-sets in the regular Bathing Suit Workout. Each tri-set consists of one exercise each for hips/buttocks, thighs, and abdominals. They are:

HIPS/BUTTOCKS	THIGHS	ABDOMINALS
1. Saddlebag stripper crunch	Lying inner thigh lift	Knee-raised oblique
2. Lower butt curl	Leg curl	Bent-knee sewn lift
3. Lower butt crunch	Chair position firmer	Knee-raised crunch
4. Lower butt side kick	Straddle squat	Side oblique crunch
5. Floor feather kick-up	Front squat	Ceiling sewn lift
6. Lying butt lift	Lunge	Toe-reach crunch
7. One-leg prone butt lift	Regular squat	Ceiling oblique reach

How to Do the Bathing Suit Workout: Working in Tri-Sets

A tri-set is a combination of three compatible exercises that is done without taking a rest. Only after one set of exercise has been performed for each of those three body parts can a fifteen-second rest be taken.

REPETITIONS AND SETS

You will do fifteen repetitions for each set of every single exercise in this workout. It's that simple. But there's a catch, albeit an easy one. Instead of working in normal sets where you rest after each set, you will work in triple sets or tri-sets, where you do a set for three different exercises before you take a rest.

WEIGHTS

You have the option of using a set of five-pound dumbbells for thigh exercises only. You will be reminded of this in the exercise instructions. In time, as the five-pound dumbbells become too easy, raise your weights to eight or ten pounds. When those weights get too easy, go to twelve or fifteen pounds—even twenty! If you choose to do so, you could "pyramid" your thighs, using the modified pyramid system described on pp. 32–33. In this case you will need three sets of dumbbells: threes, fives, and tens. You may also use an optional three- or five-pound dumbbell for any appropriate abdominal exercise.

STRETCHING

If you wish, do one to three relaxed repetitions of each exercise in the entire workout before you start or do your favorite set of stretches.

HOW DO THE TRI-SETS WORK?

Let's take a look at exactly how it works by looking at the first tri-set of the workout.

HIPS/BUTTOCKS	THIGHS	ABDOMINALS
1. Saddlebag stripper	Lying inner thigh lift	Knee-raised oblique crunch

Here's how you proceed:

You do one set of fifteen repetitions of the first hips/buttocks exercise, the saddlebag stripper. Without resting, you do one set of fifteen repetitions of the first thigh exercise, the lying inner thigh lift. Again, without resting, you do one set of fifteen repetitions the first abdominal exercise, the knee-raised oblique crunch.

Whew. Now you take a fifteen-second rest.

Back to work. You repeat exactly what you just did one more time.

Now you can take another hard-earned fifteen-second rest. Now move to the third and final set. You repeat exactly what you did your third and final time.

Now you take a fifteen-second rest, and move to your second tri-set.

HIPS/BUTTOCKS	THIGHS	ABDOMINALS
2. Lower butt curl	Leg curl	Bent-knee sewn lift

You do one set of fifteen repetitions of the second hips/buttocks exercise, the lower butt curl. Without resting, you do one set of fifteen repetitions of the second thigh exercise, the leg curl. Again, without resting, you do one set of fifteen repetitions of the second abdominal exercise, the bent-knee sewn lift.

Now you can take a fifteen-second rest.

Back to work. You repeat exactly what you just did one more time.

Take another fifteen-second rest. Then move to the final set and repeat exactly what you did before for the last time.

Take a fifteen-second rest and move to your third group of exercises.

HIPS/BUTTOCKS	THIGHS	ABDOMINALS
3. Lower butt crunch	Chair position firmer	Knee-raised crunch

You do one set of fifteen repetitions of the third hips/buttocks exercise, the lower butt crunch. Without resting, you do one set of fifteen repetitions of the third thigh exercise, chair position firmer. Again, without resting, you do one set of fifteen repetitions the third abdominal exercise, the knee-raised crunch.

Now you can take a fifteen-second rest.

Back to work. You repeat exactly what you just did one more time.

Take another fifteen-second rest. Then move to the third and final tri-set and repeat exactly what you did before for the last time.

Take a fifteen-second rest and move to your fourth group of exercises. Continue to work as above until you have completed all seven tri-sets.

SETS, REPETITIONS, AND RESTS IN ABBREVIATED FORM

Now let's take a look at the sets, repetitions, and rests as they will apply to all tri-sets in this workout.

Tri-Set 1: Fifteen repetitions each without resting: hips/buttocks exercise, thigh exercise, abdominal exercise. Rest fifteen seconds.

Tri-Set 2: Fifteen repetitions each without resting: hips/buttocks exercise, thigh exercise, abdominal exercise. Rest fifteen seconds.

Tri-Set 3: Fifteen repetitions each without resting: hips/buttocks exercise, thigh exercise, abdominal exercise. Rest fifteen seconds.

Move to the next tri-set. Repeat as above until all seven tri-sets are completed.

The Iron Woman Workout

You work exactly as above. The only difference is that instead of stopping after you've done your seven tri-sets, you do an eighth tri-set. Your workout will look like this.

HIPS/BUTTOCKS	THIGHS	ABDOMINALS
1. Saddlebag stripper	Lying inner thigh lift	Knee-raised oblique crunch
2. Lower butt curl	Leg curl	Bent-knee sewn lift
3. Lower butt crunch	Chair position firmer	Knee-raised crunch
4. Lower butt side kick	Straddle squat	Side oblique crunch
5. Floor feather kick-up	Front squat	Ceiling sewn lift
6. Lying butt lift	Lunge	Toe-reach crunch
7. One-leg prone butt lift	Regular squat	Ceiling oblique reach
8. Standing butt squeeze	Hack squat	Knee-in

The Steel Woman Workout

You work exactly as above. The only difference is that, instead of stopping after you've done eight tri-sets, you do a ninth tri-set. Your workout will look like this:

HIPS/BUTTOCKS	THIGHS	ABDOMINALS
1. Saddlebag stripper	Lying inner thigh lift	Knee-raised oblique crunch
2. Lower butt curl	Leg curl	Bent-knee sewn lift
3. Lower butt crunch	Chair position firmer	Knee-raised crunch
4. Lower butt side kick	Straddle squat	Side oblique crunch
5. Floor feather kick-up	Front squat	Ceiling sewn lift
6. Lying butt lift	Lunge	Toe-reach crunch
7. One-leg prone butt lift	Regular squat	Ceiling oblique reach
8. Standing butt squeeze	Hack squat	Knee-in
9. Reverse-lunge lift	Bent-knee deadlift	Sit-up

The Titanium Woman Workout

You work exactly as above. The only difference is that, instead of stopping after you've done nine tri-sets, you do a tenth tri-set. Your workout will look like this:

HIPS/BUTTOCKS	THIGHS	ABDOMINALS
1. Saddlebag stripper	Lying inner thigh lift	Knee-raised oblique crunch
2. Lower butt curl	Leg curl	Bent-knee sewn lift
3. Lower butt crunch	Chair position firmer	Knee-raised crunch
4. Lower butt side kick	Straddle squat	Side oblique crunch
5. Floor feather kick-up	Front squat	Ceiling sewn lift
6. Lying butt lift	Lunge	Toe-reach crunch
7. One-leg prone butt lift	Regular squat	Ceiling oblique reach
8. Standing butt squeeze	Hack squat	Knee-in
9. Reverse-lunge lift	Bent-knee deadlift	Sit-up
10. Straight leg kick-up	Sissy squat	Leg raise

Review

Whether you are doing the regular, Iron Woman, Steel Woman, or Titanium Woman workout, you work in the same manner. You do one set of three different exercises for three different body parts before you take a rest: hips/buttocks, thighs, and abdominals. You can get an overview of your particular workout by looking at the above lists. If you look across the numbers horizontally, you will clearly see your tri-sets.

Don't worry. You don't have to remember anything. I lead you along in the exercise section. Each exercise is placed after the other, in the order that they are done. And so you won't have to keep turning pages, you can use the handy tear-out wall chart on pp. 209–230. This chart shows you a mini-overview of all of your exercises in reduced photographs.

Make the Workout Completely Aerobic by Eliminating All the Rests

After you've been doing the workout for a while, you may find that you can skip most or all of the rests. If you do that, you will have a completely aerobic workout. In addition, you will save time.

Make the Workout Easier and Less Intense by Adding and/or Lengthening Rests

This is a very demanding workout. Even after breaking in gently, you may feel that the workout is too much for you and may be tempted to quit. Don't do it! Instead, add one or more of the following techniques.

1. Take a fifteen-second rest after *each set*. This means that, instead of doing strict tri-sets where you don't rest until you've completed one set for each of three exercises, you would do gentle tri-sets where you rest fifteen seconds after each set. This would triple your rest periods. The workout would take longer, but it may enable you to go on, whereas before you might have given up in discouragement. If you work this way, you will still get the full body-sculpting, muscle-defining benefit. All you will lose will be some of the aerobic effect.

If that's not enough you can add in #2.

2. Do as above, only double the rest time. Take thirty-second rests between each set. If that's not enough you can add in #3.

3. Do as described in 1 and 2, only reduce the number of tri-sets. Pick out the four tri-sets that are easiest for you to do, and do only those tri-sets.

If you choose one of the above plans, in time you may or may not decide to shorten your rests and eliminate some of them, and add exercises, so that you will eventually be doing the full-force workout. If not, you will still derive a great deal of benefit from the workout.

If You Are Extremely Overweight, Out of Shape, or Cannot Do Certain, Even Many, Exercises

Some of you may open the book with all good intentions, but after trying a certain exercise say to yourselves, "Forget it. I'll never be able to do this." Instead of quitting outright, go through the workout and see which exercises you *can* do. Do only those exercises by substituting them for exercises you can't do. All you have to do is remember to pick

an exercise from the same body part and double up. Let me explain.

Suppose you have zipped through your first three groups of exercises. You've done the saddlebag stripper, the lying inner thigh lift, and the knee-raised oblique crunch; the lower butt curl, the leg curl, and the bent-knee sewn lift; and the lower butt crunch, the chair position firmer, and the knee-raised crunch. You are up to your fourth group of exercises. You do the first exercise in that tri-set, the lower butt side kick. But when you come to your second exercise, the straddle squat, you can't do it because you have bad knees. You can't squat at all. Simple. Look back at all the exercises for that body part, in this case the thighs, and pick an exercise from that body part that you can do and do it in place of the difficult exercise. For example, you may have found the lying inner thigh lift that you did in tri-set number one manageable. So do it again, in place of the straddle squat.

Let's continue the example. Now you're going along in your workout, but soon you get to the lunge. You can't do that. Okay. Pick another thigh exercise that you could do. Maybe the leg curl. You continue on, and sure enough, there's another exercise you can't do. The front frog squat. So you double up on the chair position firmer. And so on.

This will hold true with any exercise. If you can't do it, the rule of thumb is to pick one from the same body part and double up on it. You have ten exercises to choose from.

If your knees or back are really bad, you may find yourself tripling up on some exercises. There may be only four that you can cope with. Fine. You'll still get the major benefit of the workout. You just won't be hitting the muscle from as many angles, that's all.

How to Take Full Advantage of the Exercise Instructions

The first thing you'll see in the exercise instructions is the number of the tri-set and the names of the three exercises in that tri-set. Next you'll see the name of the particular exercise that you will do, and a description of the muscles that will be shaped and defined by that exercise.

Next you'll see the word "Position." Here you'll get a detailed description of how to place yourself in order to start the workout. However, a picture is worth a thousand words, so look at the "Start" photograph first and then as you study the photograph, read the "Position" instructions to be sure that you don't miss anything. For example, you may note that I tell you to press your back into the mat, or to raise your head slightly off the floor, and so on. This may not be obviously visible in the photographs until it is pointed out.

Next you'll see the heading "Movement." The finish photograph de-

picts where you will have "moved to." Look at that first and then read the "Movement" instructions. They tell you exactly how to execute the exercise. You'll want to look at both the start and finish photographs as you read this section and imagine yourself doing the exercise. Go through it in your mind exactly as if you are doing it.

Next comes "Tips." This is very important section. I know the tendencies of beginning exercisers to make certain mistakes, and I've made a special effort to head you off before you fall into the common traps. For example, I remind you not to pull on your neck when doing a crunch, or to stretch gently into a side oblique crunch rather than force it, or to keep your mind riveted on a working muscle, or not to hold your breath, and so on.

Finally, there is the "Machines, etc." section. Here you will be given alternatives. Sometimes I'll suggest a barbell, other times a machine, and other times an alternative exercise. You could completely ignore this section if you want to, or you can use it for variety.

Before you actually start your workout, it's a good idea to read through the exercise instructions, looking at the photographs and trying to do one repetition of each exercise. Do this just to feel it out in your mind, on a day when you are going through the book in a relaxed mood. This is also a great way to precondition yourself for the actual workout. Then set a date to start the break-in-gently system.

Breaking In Gently if You Are in Aerobic Shape and Have Been Doing One of My Other Workouts

Good news. You can do the full regular workout if you can cope with it. If not, switch to one of the other break-in-gently plans.

Week 1. Full Regular Workout.

If you are planning to do the Iron Woman, Steel Woman, or Titanium Woman workouts, add them in one week at a time!

Breaking In Gently if You Are in Aerobic Shape but Have Never Done One of My Workouts

Week 1. One tri-set of the first seven exercises (the regular workout). Do only as many of the fifteen repetitions for each set as you can do.

Week 2. Two tri-sets of the first seven exercises (the regular workout). Do only as many of the fifteen repetitions for each set as you can do.

Week 3. Three tri-sets of the first seven exercises (the regular workout). Do only as many of the fifteen repetitions for each set as you can do.

Weeks 4–6 or more. Now you are on the full program. Keep working until you can do three sets of fifteen repetitions for all three exercises of all seven tri-sets. Then, if you wish, you can add the Iron, Steel, and/or Titanium Woman workouts to your schedule, one week at a time.

Breaking In Gently if You Have Done One of My Workouts Before but You Are Not in Aerobic Shape

Week 1. Do one tri-set of each of the first seven exercises, only "cheat" by taking a fifteen-second rest after each set.

Week 2. Do one tri-set of the first seven exercises without cheating.

Week 3. Try to do two tri-sets of the first seven exercises without cheating, but take an extra rest when you must.

Week 4. Do two tri-sets of the first seven exercises without cheating.

Week 5. Try to do all three sets of the first seven exercises without cheating, but take an extra rest when you must.

Weeks 6–8 or more. Do all three tri-sets of the first seven exercises without cheating. Wait until you are doing full fifteen-repetition tri-sets and then, if you wish, one week at a time, add on exercises until you are doing the Titanium Woman workout.

Note: Don't hold yourself back. Advance more quickly if you can. This is just a guideline.

Breaking In Gently if You Are Extremely Overweight and/or Out of Shape Period

You're in bad shape. You're very out of shape and/or very fat, very weak, and extremely out of breath when you try to do the workout.

You think, "Forget it. I'll never be able to do this." Think again. Here's the way to go.

Look at the exercise photographs and pick out any tri-set that you can do. Then pick another and another, until you have made up four tri-sets. If you can't do it that way, re-create the tri-sets by picking out all the hips/buttocks exercises you can do, all the thigh exercises you can do, and all the abdominal exercises you can do. Then arrange those exercises into new tri-sets that suit you. If you are short on one exercise for a tri-set, double up as described above. Once you have your four tri-sets, you may want to photocopy the photographs and arrange them in the order that you will be doing them.

Now here's how to proceed:

Week 1. Sets one to three of one tri-set, three repetitions each. Cheat and rest between each tri-set.

Week 2. Sets one to three of one tri-set, six repetitions each. Cheat and rest between each tri-set.

Week 3. Sets one to three of one tri-set, nine repetitions each. Cheat and rest between each tri-set.

Week 4. Sets one to three of one tri-set, twelve repetitions each. Cheat and rest between each tri-set.

Week 5. Sets one to three of one tri-set, fifteen repetitions each. Cheat and rest between each tri-set.

Week 6. Sets one to three of one tri-set, fifteen repetitions each. No cheating

Week 7—on. You will add your second tri-set slowly, exactly as above. In six more weeks you will be doing two full tri-sets. You will now have been working out for twelve weeks. Then you will add in your third tri-set, exactly as above. In eighteen weeks you will be doing three full tri-sets. Again, you will add in your fourth tri-set exactly as above. In twenty-four weeks you will be doing four full tri-sets. Just keep going in the same manner as above until you are on the full program and I suspect you will!

You may find that you can advance more quickly than the above schedule. If so, fine. Go at your own pace. In addition, you may find that indeed you can now do some of the exercises that previously seemed impossible. Great. Add them in. If you persist, in time you will be able to do seven full tri-sets.

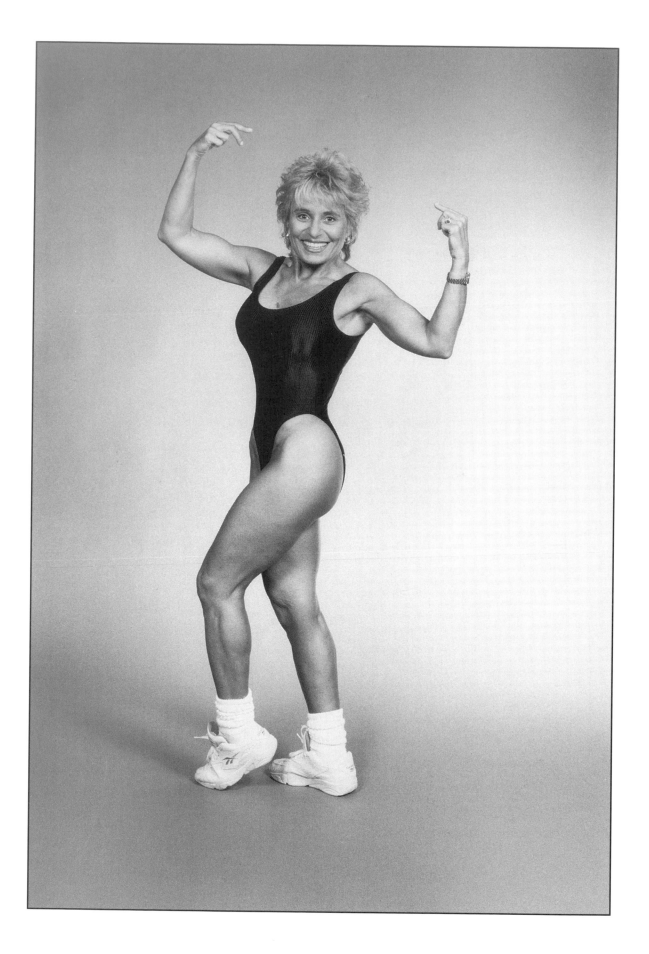

6

THE BATHING SUIT WORKOUT

Now you are ready to do the workout. Remember, you do fifteen repetitions for each set of each exercise. The only exercises that will allow optional weights are most of the thigh exercises, in which case you will use five-pound dumbbells (or less or more weight, depending upon how strong you are and if you decide to pyramid), and one hips/buttocks exercise. All other exercises are done without weights.

You will be exercising in tri-sets, busting the bulge that circles your middle and transforming it into a triangle of tight, toned muscle. You will always start with hips/buttocks, then move to thighs, and end with abdominals. Then you'll take an optional fifteen-second rest and move to the next tri-set.

If you are doing the regular workout, you'll do the first seven tri-sets. If you're performing the Iron Woman workout, you'll work through the first eight tri-sets. If you're conquering the Steel Woman workout, you'll continue through the first nine cycles. If you are challenging yourself with the ultimate conquest, the Titanium Woman workout, you'll complete all ten tri-sets.

If you want to do all ten cycles but find that some of the exercises are too difficult, as mentioned before, choose any exercise from the same body part that you *can* do, and simply substitute that exercise for the one you can't do.

This is not a game. It's not for people who want to make themselves think they have worked out but in reality have done little more than move around a bit. It's a surefire system to get rid of the fat and produce definition and muscle. It *is* work, but you can't put a price on the permanent prize you will get for your effort!

SADDLEBAG STRIPPER, LYING INNER THIGH LIFT, AND KNEE-RAISED OBLIQUE CRUNCH

HIPS/BUTTOCKS: SADDLEBAG STRIPPER SLIMS AND TONES THE "SADDLEBAG" HIP AREA.

POSITION Lie on the floor on your side supporting yourself with your elbow, your hand behind your head. Cross your other arm in front of you and place the palm of that hand on the floor, in front of your chest, as a brace. Bend your lower (nonworking) leg. One side of your body will be completely aligned on the floor.

MOVEMENT With your hips aligned and keeping your working knee facing front, flexing your working hip/buttock area as you go, raise your upper leg as high as possible. Return to the start position and repeat the movement until you have finished your set. Perform the set for the other side of your body. Without resting, move to the next exercise in this tri-set, the lying inner thigh lift.

TIPS Keep your hips aligned as you work. Don't let your body tilt over to the back or the front. Your hips should be "stacked," one lying on the top of the other. Don't hold or think about your breath. Breathe naturally.

MACHINES, ETC. You may substitute this exercise for any hip abductor machine at twenty pounds.

THE BATHING SUIT WORKOUT | 65

THIGHS: LYING INNER THIGH LIFT TIGHTENS, TONES, STRENGTHENS, AND DEFINES THE INNER THIGH MUSCLES AND HELPS TO TIGHTEN AND TONE THE ENTIRE FRONT THIGH MUSCLE.

NOTE: THIS EXERCISE HAS BEEN CALLED "SIDE LEG LIFT" IN OTHER WORKOUTS. I HAVE CHANGED THE NAME TO MAKE IT MORE DESCRIPTIVE OF THE ACTUAL EXERCISE.

POSITION Lie on the floor on your side, supporting yourself with your elbow. Bend your upper (nonworking) leg at the knee and place the sole of that foot on the ground. One side of your body should be completely aligned on the floor. Extend your lower (working) leg and place a dumbbell in the middle of your thigh area. Hold it there with your free hand as you work.

MOVEMENT Keeping your working leg extended and holding the weight on your thigh, flex your inner thigh as you lift your entire leg off the ground until you cannot go any higher. Keeping the pressure on your working inner thigh muscle, return to the start position, and repeat the movement until you have completed your set. Repeat the set for the other side of your body. Without resting, move to the final exercise in this tri-set, the knee-raised oblique crunch.

TIPS Flex your working inner thigh muscle as hard as possible as you raise and lower your leg.

MACHINES, ETC. You may perform this exercise on any hip adductor machine at twenty pounds.

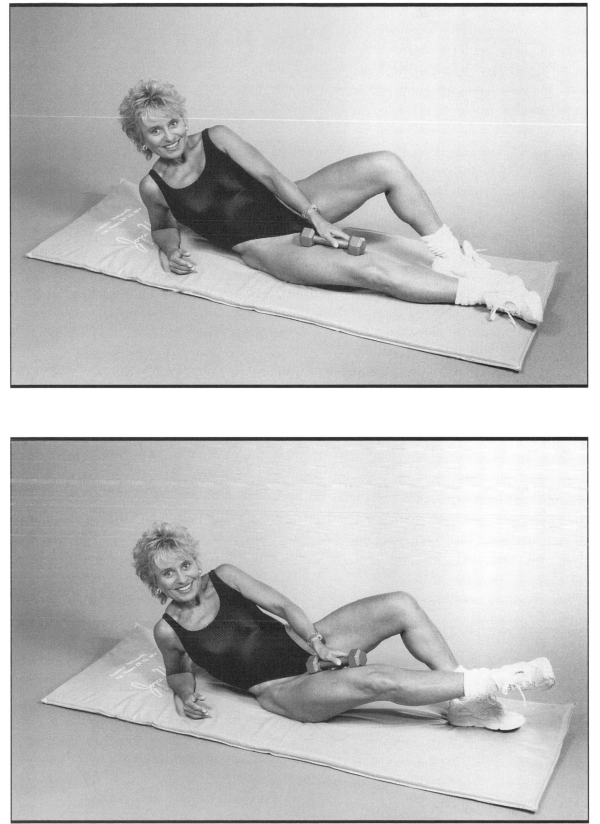

ABDOMINALS: KNEE-RAISED OBLIQUE CRUNCH STRENGTHENS, TIGHTENS, TONES, AND DEFINES THE OBLIQUE AND UPPER ABDOMINAL MUSCLES, AND HELPS TO TIGHTEN THE LOWER ABDOMINAL AREA.

POSITION — Lie flat on the floor with your knees raised and your legs crossed at the ankles. Place your hands behind your head.

MOVEMENT — Leading with your chin, raise your left shoulder off the floor while at the same time bringing your right elbow to your right inner knee, all the time flexing your abdominal muscles. In full control, return to the start position and repeat the movement for the other side of your body. Continue this alternating twisting-crunch movement until you have completed your set. Rest an optional fifteen seconds and do another tri-set of this combination. Again, take an optional fifteen-second rest and perform the third and final tri-set of this combination. Rest an optional fifteen seconds more and proceed to the first exercise of the next tri-set, the lower butt curl.

TIPS — Don't jerk your body as you try to get your elbow to reach the opposite inner-knee area. Feel the flex in your oblique muscles as you go into the oblique crunch position, and enjoy the stretch on the back-to-start position.

MACHINES, ETC. — You may perform this exercise on any rotary torso machine.

Now that you can do all three exercises, let's get down to business.

WHAT TO DO: TRI-SETS, REPETITIONS, WEIGHTS — Set 1: Fifteen repetitions each: saddlebag stripper, lying inner thigh lift, knee-raised oblique crunch. Optional fifteen-second rest.
Set 2: Fifteen repetitions each: saddlebag stripper, lying inner thigh lift, knee-raised oblique crunch. Optional fifteen-second rest.
Set 3: Fifteen repetitions each: saddlebag stripper, lying inner thigh lift, knee-raised oblique crunch. Optional fifteen-second rest.

NOTE: — You can use five-pound dumbbells for lying inner thigh lift, or you can pyramid. No weights used for other exercises. If you choose to use the modified pyramid system for thigh work, see pp. 32–33 for a review.

THE BATHING SUIT WORKOUT | **69**

2

LOWER BUTT CURL, LEG CURL, AND BENT-KNEE SEWN LIFT

HIPS/BUTTOCKS: LOWER BUTT CURL TIGHTENS, TONES, LIFTS, AND SHAPES THE LOWER BUTT AREA AND HELPS TO REDUCE SADDLEBAGS.

POSITION

Lie on your side with your lower leg bent back and your upper leg extended in line with your body. Your hips should be "stacked," in line with each other. Lean on your lower elbow for support and place that hand behind your head. Cross your upper arm in front of your chest and place the palm of that hand on the floor for support.

MOVEMENT

Without tilting your body (your hips should remain aligned throughout the movement), bending at the knee, curl your upper leg toward your chest as far as you can go. Feel the stretch in your working buttock muscle. Flex your working buttock muscle as you go, and in full control. Return to start. Repeat the movement until you have completed your set. Repeat the set for the other side of your body. Without resting, move to the next exercise in this tri-set, the leg curl.

TIPS

Don't merely go through the motions, sloppily curling your leg in half-hearted movements. Instead, focus on your working buttock muscle and flex as hard as possible on the return movement. Don't hold your breath. Breathe naturally.

MACHINES, ETC.

You may perform this exercise on any butt-curl machine. Set the weight at twenty pounds.

THE BATHING SUIT WORKOUT | 71

THIGHS: LEG CURL TIGHTENS, TONES, SHAPES, AND DEFINES THE BACK THIGH MUSCLES (HAMSTRINGS).

POSITION
With a dumbbell placed between your feet, lie in a prone position on the floor or on a flat exercise bench. Extend your legs straight out behind you and lean on your elbows for support.

MOVEMENT
Bending at the knees and flexing your back thigh muscles as you go, raise your legs until they are perpendicular to the floor. Keeping the pressure on your back thigh muscles as hard as possible, return to the start position and repeat the movement until you have completed your set. Without resting, proceed to the final exercise in this tri-set, the bent-knee sewn lift.

TIPS
If you squeeze your ankles together, you will better be able to keep the pressure on your back thigh muscles. Don't do this exercise without sneakers, and especially not barefoot. You'll hurt your feet—and if you are using a dumbbell, it may slip! Don't swing the dumbbell up and down. Maintain control throughout the movement.

MACHINES, ETC.
You may perform this exercise on any leg-curl machine. Set the weight at twenty pounds.

THE BATHING SUIT WORKOUT | **73**

POSITION Lie on the floor and place your hands behind your head. Raise your legs off the floor, bending at the knee and crossing your feet at the ankles. Push your back into the floor so that there is no "curve" or space in your back.

MOVEMENT Making believe that your belly button is sewn to the ground, lift your buttocks off the floor about two to three inches, while at the same time flexing your lower abdominal muscles as hard as possible. (Remember, you couldn't go much higher even if you tried. Your belly button is sewn to the ground.) Repeat this movement until you have completed your set. Rest an optional fifteen seconds and do another tri-set of this combination. Again, take an optional fifteen-second rest and perform the third and final tri-set of this combination. Rest an optional fifteen seconds more and proceed to the first exercise of the next tri-set, the lower butt crunch.

MACHINES, ETC. You may substitute this exercise for the standard knee-in as demonstrated in my book *Bottoms Up!*

WHAT TO DO: Set 1: Fifteen repetitions each: lower butt curl, leg curl, bent-knee
TRI-SETS, sewn lift. Optional fifteen-second rest.
REPETITIONS, Set 2: Fifteen repetitions each: lower butt curl, leg curl, bent-knee
WEIGHTS sewn lift. Optional fifteen-second rest.
 Set 3: Fifteen repetitions each: lower butt curl, leg curl, bent-knee sewn lift. Optional fifteen-second rest.

NOTE: Use five-pound dumbbells for leg curl (optional). No weights required for other exercises. If you choose to use the modified pyramid system for your thighs, see p. 33 for review.

3

LOWER BUTT CRUNCH, CHAIR POSITION FIRMER, AND KNEE-RAISED CRUNCH

HIPS/BUTTOCKS: LOWER BUTT CRUNCH LIFTS, TIGHTENS, TONES, AND SHAPES THE LOWER BUTT AREA.

POSITION With your hands clasped behind your head, lie flat on your back. Raise your legs so that they are vertical to the floor and flex your feet toward your body. Lift your head and shoulders slightly off the floor (as if you are doing a crunch). Keeping one leg straight, bend the knee of the other leg until the heel of the foot of your bent leg touches your ankle, or at least the ankle area.

MOVEMENT Flexing your working buttock muscle as you go, straighten your bent leg while at the same time bending the other leg in a stair-climbing movement. Flexing as you go, straighten the newly bent leg and bend the other leg. Continue this alternate straightening-bending motion, all the time flexing your working buttock muscles as hard as possible, until you have completed a set for each side of your body. Without resting, move to the next exercise in this tri-set, the chair position firmer.

TIPS Keep your back flat on the floor throughout the movement. Give your working buttock an extra-hard flex at the point where you unbend your leg.

MACHINES, ETC. You may substitute this exercise for a butt curl machine.

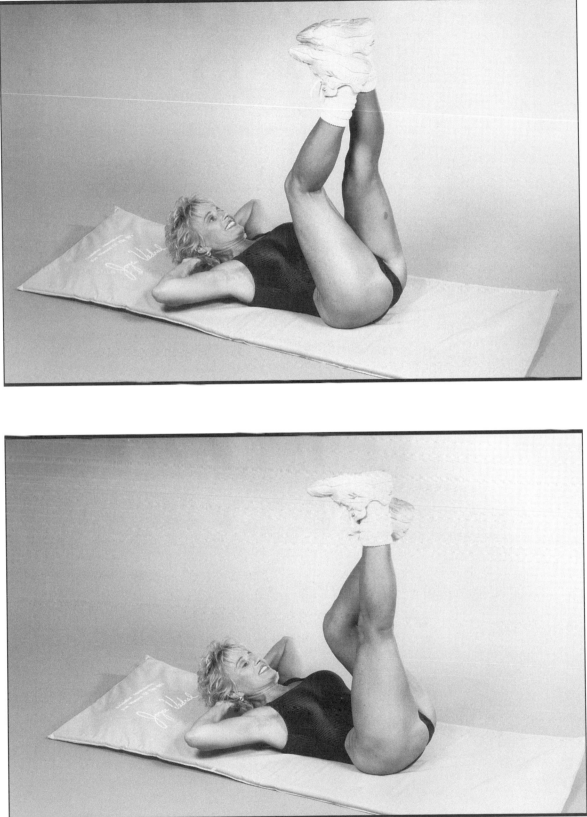

THIGHS: CHAIR POSITION FIRMER TIGHTENS, TONES, AND STRENGTHENS THE FRONT THIGHS AND HIPS.

POSITION

Make believe you are sitting in a chair that is placed against a wall—only do it without a chair! (See photo.) Your back will be flat against the wall, your legs will form a right angle, and your feet will be flat on the floor. Place the optional dumbbells on each knee and gently hold them. If you are not using weights, place your hands on your knees.

MOVEMENT

Good news. Do nothing. Count for fifteen seconds and, without resting, move to the final exercise in this tri-set, the knee-raised crunch.

TIPS

Don't fall into the trap of holding your breath. Breathe naturally. For additional benefit, flex your front thighs as hard as possible for the full fifteen seconds. Also, if you wish, later you can raise the amount of time to as long as a full minute! This is completely optional.

MACHINES, ETC.

You may substitute this exercise for an exercise done on any hips/buttocks machine. Choose a comfortable starting weight. Machines vary, so you'll have to experiment.

ABDOMINALS: KNEE-RAISED CRUNCH DEVELOPS, SHAPES, STRENGTHENS, AND DEFINES THE ENTIRE UPPER ABDOMINAL AREA AND HELPS TO STRENGTHEN THE LOWER ABDOMINAL AREA.

POSITION

Lie flat on your back on the floor, pull your knees up until your legs form an **L**, and cross your feet at the ankles. Place your hands behind your head.

MOVEMENT

Flexing your entire abdominal area as you go, raise your shoulders off the floor in a curling movement until your shoulders are completely off the floor, all the time keeping your knees raised so that your legs are still in an approximate **L** shape. Keeping the pressure on your abdominal muscles, return to start, and repeat the movement until you have completed your set. Rest an optional fifteen seconds and do another tri-set of this combination. Again, take an optional fifteen-second rest and perform the third and final tri-set of this combination. Rest an optional fifteen seconds and proceed to the first exercise of the next tri-set, the lower butt side kick.

TIPS

Don't allow yourself to use your hands behind your head to pull yourself up. You'll hurt your neck. Instead, let your upper abdominals do the work.

MACHINES, ETC.

You may substitute this exercise with any crunch machine, or with the standard sit-up as demonstrated in my book *Gut Busters*.

WHAT TO DO:
TRI-SETS,
REPETITIONS,
WEIGHTS

Set 1: Fifteen repetitions each: lower butt crunch, chair position firmer, knee-raised crunch. Optional fifteen-second rest.
Set 2: Fifteen repetitions each: lower butt crunch, chair position firmer, knee-raised crunch. Optional fifteen-second rest.
Set 3: Fifteen repetitions each: lower butt crunch, chair position firmer, knee-raised crunch. Optional fifteen-second rest.

NOTE:

You may place an optional five-pound dumbbell on each knee for the chair position firmer. No weights used for other exercises. If you choose to use the modified pyramid system for thigh work, see pp. 32–33 for review.

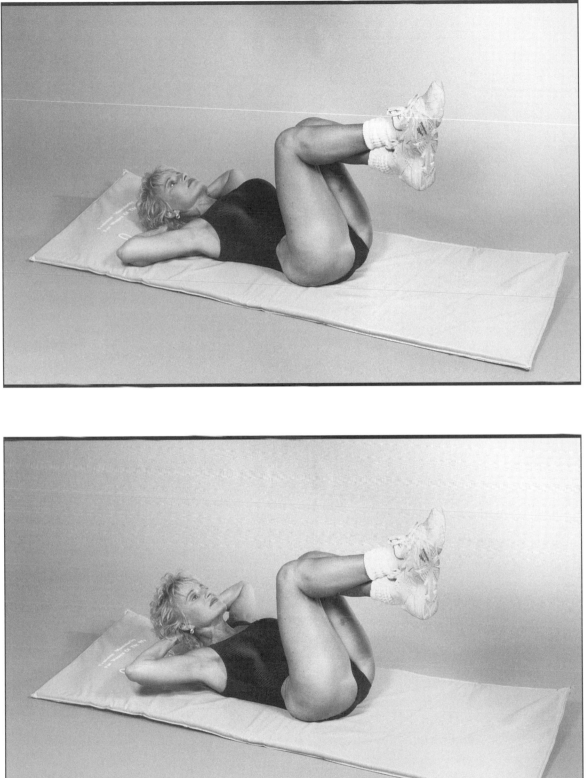

THE BATHING SUIT WORKOUT | **81**

4

LOWER BUTT SIDE KICK,
STRADDLE SQUAT,
AND SIDE OBLIQUE CRUNCH

HIPS/BUTTOCKS: LOWER BUTT SIDE KICK SLIMS, FIRMS, SHAPES, AND LIFTS THE ENTIRE LOWER BUTTOCKS AREA.

POSITION Lie on your side with your lower leg bent back on the floor. Your hips should be in line with each other ("stacked"). Support yourself with your lower elbow and place the palm of that hand behind your head. Bring your other arm in front of your chest and place your hand on the floor for support. Bend your leg at the knee and bring it as close to your chest as possible. Flex your toes.

MOVEMENT Keeping your hips in line with each other ("stacked") and leading with your heel, kick your leg out as far as possible and, flexing your buttock as hard as possible, return to the start position. Repeat the movement until you have completed your set. Repeat the set for the other side of your body. Without resting, move to the next exercise in this tri-set, the straddle squat.

TIPS Keep your floor leg bent back in the **L** position and your hips "stacked" throughout the movement for proper support. Be sure to flex your buttocks as hard as possible every time your working leg is extended. Don't hold your breath. Breathe naturally.

MACHINES, ETC. You may substitute this exercise for any exercise done on a rotary butt machine. Set the weight at a comfortable starting weight. Machines vary so you'll have to experiment.

THE BATHING SUIT WORKOUT | 83

THIGHS: STRADDLE SQUAT DEVELOPS, SHAPES, STRENGTHENS, AND DEFINES THE FRONT THIGH MUSCLE AND HELPS TO TIGHTEN AND TONE THE BUTTOCKS.

POSITION With an optional dumbbell held at each end, palms facing your body, stand with your feet about three to five inches wider than shoulder width apart and your toes pointed slightly outward. Let your arms hang down at your sides. Keep your back erect and your eyes straight ahead.

MOVEMENT Feeling the stretch in your front thigh muscles as you go, descend to an approximate forty-five-degree bend in your knees. Flexing your quadriceps as you go, return to the start position. Willfully flex your quadriceps and repeat the movement until you have completed your set. Without resting, move to the final exercise in this tri-set, the side oblique crunch.

TIPS You may not be able to descend the full distance. Go only as far as possible.

MACHINES, ETC. You may do this exercise with a twenty-pound barbell on your shoulders. You may also do this exercise at any squat machine. Set the weight at a comfortable starting weight. Machines vary, so you'll have to experiment.

FINISH

ABDOMINALS: SIDE OBLIQUE CRUNCH TIGHTENS, TONES, SHAPES, AND DEFINES THE OBLIQUE MUSCLES.

POSITION
Lie flat on your back with one hand behind your head and your knees bent, the soles of your feet flat on the floor. Extend your other arm down at your side.

MOVEMENT
Supporting your head with your hand, reach toward your ankle with the extended arm, flexing your working oblique muscles as hard as possible as you go. Go as far toward your ankle as possible and return to the start position. Feel the stretch in your working oblique muscles and repeat the movement until you have completed your set. Repeat the set for the other side of your body. Rest an optional fifteen seconds and do another tri-set of this combination. Again, take an optional fifteen-second rest and perform the third and final tri-set of this combination. Rest an optional fifteen seconds and proceed to the first exercise of the next tri-set, the floor feather kick-up.

TIPS
Gently stretch into the hand-to-ankle position. Don't force it. Feel the flex in your oblique muscles as you reach the low position. You may raise your head slightly as you work, supporting your neck with your hand.

MACHINES, ETC.
You may perform this exercise on any rotary torso machine. Set the weight at twenty pounds.

WHAT TO DO:
TRI-SETS,
REPETITIONS,
WEIGHTS
Set 1: Fifteen repetitions each: lower butt side kick, straddle squat, and side oblique crunch. Optional fifteen-second rest.
Set 2: Fifteen repetitions each: lower butt side kick, straddle squat, and side oblique crunch. Optional fifteen-second rest.
Set 3: Fifteen repetitions each: lower butt side kick, straddle squat, and side oblique crunch. Optional fifteen-second rest.

NOTE:
Use five-pound dumbbells for straddle squat (optional). No weights required for other exercises. If you choose to use the modified pyramid system for thigh work, see pp. 32–33.

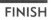

THE BATHING SUIT WORKOUT | **87**

FLOOR FEATHER KICK-UP, FRONT SQUAT, AND CEILING SEWN LIFT

HIPS/BUTTOCKS: FLOOR FEATHER KICK-UP SHAPES, TIGHTENS, TONES, AND LIFTS THE ENTIRE HIPS/BUTTOCKS AREA AND HELPS TO FIRM THE BACK THIGH MUSCLE.

POSITION Place yourself in an all-fours position on the floor.

MOVEMENT Flexing your working foot forward, extend your working leg up and behind you until you cannot go any higher. Your knee should be completely unbent and your extended leg at an approximate ninety-degree angle. In this position, flex your working buttock as hard as possible and, in full control, return to the start position. Repeat the movement until you have completed your set. Repeat the set for the other side of your body. Without resting, move to the next exercise in this tri-set, the front squat.

TIPS Don't fall into the trap of swinging your leg up and down. Use controlled movements at all times. Flex hard on the up movement and feel the stretch on the down movement. You may perform this exercise by extending your working leg to a parallel-to-the-floor position instead of a ninety-degree angle.

MACHINES, ETC. You may substitute this exercise for an exercise performed on any hips/buttocks machine. Set the weight at a comfortable starting weight. Machines vary, so you'll have to experiment.

THE BATHING SUIT WORKOUT | 89

THIGHS: FRONT SQUAT DEVELOPS, SHAPES, TONES, AND DEFINES THE FRONT THIGH MUSCLE.

POSITION — Stand with your feet a natural width apart and angle your toes out slightly. Hold an optional dumbbell in each hand and cross your arms above your chest. The ends of the dumbbells will be touching your shoulders. Look straight ahead and keep your back straight. Note: If you are not using dumbbells, simply take the position you see in the photo—only without dumbbells.

MOVEMENT — Keeping your upper body straight, feel the stretch in your front thighs as you descend to the squat position (descend until your thighs are parallel to the floor or slightly higher). Flex your front thighs as you return to the start position. Give your front thighs an extra-hard flex and repeat the movement until you have completed your set. Without resting, move to the final exercise in this tri-set, the ceiling sewn lift.

TIPS — If you find yourself rising up on your toes, try a wider stance!

MACHINES, ETC. — You may balance a twenty-five-pound barbell on your chest instead of using the dumbbells. You may substitute the leg press done on any leg-press machine for this or any other squat. Set the machine at a comfortable starting weight. Machines vary, so you'll have to experiment.

FINISH

ABDOMINALS: CEILING SEWN LIFT TIGHTENS, TONES, STRENGTHENS, AND DEFINES THE ENTIRE LOWER ABDOMINAL AREA AND HELPS TO STRENGTHEN THE LOWER BACK.

POSITION

Lie on the floor and place your hands behind your head. Raise your legs off the floor, extending your legs fully upward and crossing your legs at the ankles. Push your back into the floor so that there is no "curve" in your back.

MOVEMENT

Making believe that your belly button is sewn to the ground, lift your buttocks off the floor about two to three inches while at the same time flexing your lower abdominal muscles as hard as possible. (Remember, you couldn't go much higher even if you tried. Your belly button is sewn to the ground.) Repeat this movement until you have completed your set. Rest an optional fifteen seconds and do another tri-set of this combination. Again, take an optional fifteen-second rest and perform the third and final tri-set of this combination. Rest an optional fifteen seconds more and proceed to the first exercise of the next tri-set, the lying butt lift.

MACHINES, ETC.

You may substitute this exercise for the leg-raise as demonstrated in my book *Bottoms Up!*

WHAT TO DO:
TRI-SETS,
REPETITIONS,
WEIGHTS

Set 1: Fifteen repetitions each: floor feather kick-up, front squat, ceiling sewn lift. Optional fifteen-second rest.
Set 2: Fifteen repetitions each: floor feather kick-up, front squat, ceiling sewn lift. Optional fifteen-second rest.
Set 3: Fifteen repetitions each: floor feather kick-up, front squat, ceiling sewn lift. Optional fifteen-second rest.

NOTE:

Use five-pound dumbbells for the front squat (optional). No weights required for other exercises. If you choose to use the modified pyramid system for your thighs, see pp. 32–33 for review.

THE BATHING SUIT WORKOUT | 93

6

LYING BUTT LIFT, LUNGE, AND TOE-REACH CRUNCH

HIPS/BUTTOCKS: LYING BUTT LIFT TIGHTENS, TONES, LIFTS, AND SHAPES ENTIRE HIPS/BUTTOCKS AREA.

POSITION Lie on the floor flat on your back with your knees bent and the soles of your feet flat on the floor. Clasp your hands behind your head, or extend your arms out in front of you and place the palms of your hands on the floor.

MOVEMENT Keeping your back and the soles of your feet flat against the floor and squeezing your entire hips/buttocks area as hard as possible, raise your hips/buttocks off the floor. (You will be raising only about three inches.) On the high position, give your hips/buttocks area an extra-hard flex and return to start. Repeat the movement until you have completed your set. Without resting, move to the next exercise in this tri-set, the lunge.

TIPS Don't be fooled by the small amount of movement in this exercise. If you flex hard on the up movement, it is extremely effective. Don't fall into the trap of getting your back involved in the movement and jerking your entire buttocks off the floor. Maintain intensity by forcing your back and the soles of your feet to remain flat on the floor throughout the movement.

MACHINES, ETC. You may substitute this exercise for any exercise done on a hips/buttocks machine. Set the weight at a comfortable starting weight. Machines vary, so you'll have to experiment.

THE BATHING SUIT WORKOUT | 95

THIGHS: LUNGE DEVELOPS, SHAPES, TONES, AND DEFINES THE ENTIRE FRONT THIGH AREA AND HELPS TO LIFT AND SHAPE THE BUTTOCKS.

POSITION Stand with your feet approximately shoulder width apart, keeping your back straight and looking straight ahead of you. Hold an optional dumbbell in each hand, palms facing your body, with your arms straight down at your sides. (If you are not using weights, simply assume the position in the photograph—without the dumbbells.)

MOVEMENT Keeping your knee aligned with your toe, bending at the knee, step forward with one foot (about two feet) until you can just about see your toes. (If you cannot see your toes, you have stepped too far.) Feel the flex in your stepping front thigh muscle, and the stretch in your nonstepping front thigh muscle. In full control, return to the start position and give both thighs an extra-hard flex. Repeat the movement for the other leg. Continue this alternate lunging movement until you have completed your set. Without resting, move to the final exercise in this tri-set, the toe-reach crunch.

TIPS If you're not accustomed to lunges, at first you will be tempted to call yourself uncoordinated, clumsy, and worse. Don't believe it. Ninety-five percent of the people I've worked with stumble about for the first few weeks, then learn balance and love this exercise. Be patient. Everything in time. Don't bounce as you work. Be in full control. As an alternative, you may work one leg at a time, doing one set of lunges for one leg and then the other until all three sets are completed.

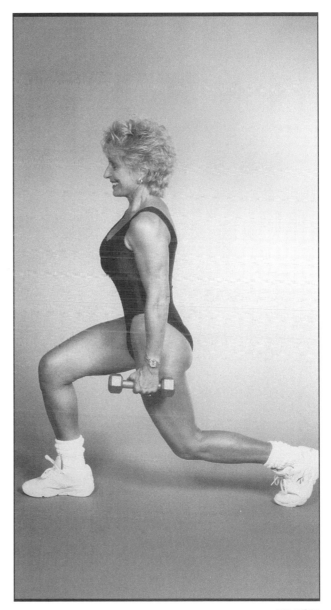

THE BATHING SUIT WORKOUT | 97

ABDOMINALS: TOE-REACH CRUNCH TIGHTENS, TONES, SHAPES, AND DEFINES THE ENTIRE ABDOMINAL AREA.

POSITION

Lie flat on your back on the floor, extending your legs straight up until your knees are only very slightly bent. Extend your arms straight out behind you.

MOVEMENT

Keeping your legs as straight as possible, partially sit up as you extend your arms forward in an attempt to reach for your toes and to touch them with your fingertips (you will not be able to do so), all the while flexing your entire abdominal area. In the highest position, give your abdominal area an extra-hard flex and return to the start position. Without resting, repeat the movement until you have completed your set. Rest an optional fifteen seconds and do another tri-set of this combination. Again, take an optional fifteen-second rest and perform the third and final tri-set of this combination. Rest an optional fifteen seconds more and proceed to the first exercise of the next tri-set, the one-leg prone butt lift.

TIPS

An easier version of this exercise is: Lie with your buttocks against a wall and your legs extended straight up, leaning against the wall. Then perform the movement as described above.

WHAT TO DO: TRI-SETS, REPETITIONS, WEIGHTS

Set 1: Fifteen repetitions each: lying butt lift, lunge, and toe-reach crunch. Optional fifteen-second rest.
Set 2: Fifteen repetitions each: lying butt lift, lunge, and toe-reach crunch. Optional fifteen-second rest.
Set 3: Fifteen repetitions each: lying butt lift, lunge, and toe-reach crunch. Optional fifteen-second rest.

NOTE:

Use five-pound dumbbells for the lunge (optional). No weights are required for other exercises. If you choose to use the modified pyramid system for your thighs, see pp. 32–33 for review.

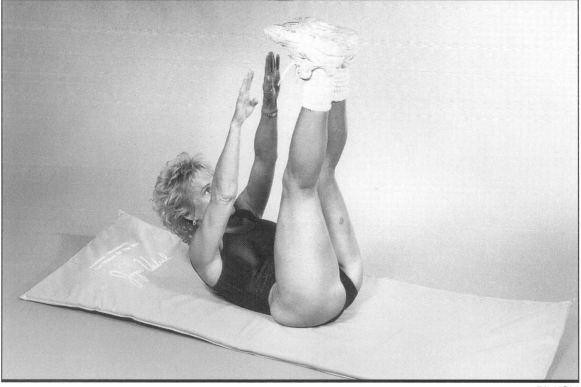

THE BATHING SUIT WORKOUT | **99**

ONE-LEG PRONE BUTT LIFT, REGULAR SQUAT, AND CEILING OBLIQUE REACH

HIPS/BUTTOCKS: ONE-LEG PRONE BUTT LIFT TIGHTENS, TONES, LIFTS, AND SHAPES THE ENTIRE HIPS/BUTTOCKS AREA, AND HELPS TO TONE THE BACK THIGH MUSCLE.

POSITION
Lie on the floor on your stomach, resting your head on the floor or folding your arms and resting your head on your hands. Extend your legs and point your toes, keeping your feet about twelve inches apart.

MOVEMENT
Flexing your hips/buttocks muscles as you go and keeping your knees as locked as possible, lift one leg until you cannot go any higher. Keeping the flex in your working buttock, return to the start position and relax that buttock. Without resting, repeat the movement for the other side of your body. Continue this alternate movement until you have completed your set. Without resting, move to the next exercise in this tri-set, the regular squat.

TIPS
Don't tense your lower back. Relax as you work.

MACHINES, ETC.
You may substitute this exercise for any exercise performed on a hips/buttocks machine. Set the weight at a comfortable starting weight. Machines vary, so you'll have to experiment.

THE BATHING SUIT WORKOUT | 101

THIGHS: REGULAR SQUAT DEVELOPS, SHAPES, TONES, AND DEFINES THE ENTIRE FRONT THIGH MUSCLE.

POSITION Holding a dumbbell in each hand (optional), palms facing your body, stand with your feet about shoulder width apart and point your toes very slightly outward. Extend your arms down at your sides. Keep your back straight and look straight ahead.

MOVEMENT Feeling the stretch in your front thigh muscles as you go, descend to an approximately forty-five-degree bend in your knees. Flexing your quadriceps as you go, return to the start position. Give your quadriceps an extra-hard flex and repeat the movement until you have completed your set. Without resting, move to the final exercise in this tri-set, the ceiling oblique reach.

TIPS You may not be able to descend the full amount. Go only as far as possible. You may find that you rise on your toes as you descend. If so, adopt a wider stance.

MACHINES, ETC. You may do this exercise with a twenty-pound barbell held on your shoulders. You may also do this exercise at any squat machine. Set the weight at a comfortable starting weight. Machines vary, so you'll have to experiment.

THE BATHING SUIT WORKOUT | 103

ABDOMINALS: CEILING OBLIQUE REACH TIGHTENS, TONES, DEVELOPS, AND DEFINES THE ENTIRE ABDOMINAL AREA, ESPECIALLY THE OBLIQUE AND UPPER ABDOMINAL MUSCLES.

POSITION

Lie with your back flat on the floor and your legs extended straight up. Place your hands behind your head.

MOVEMENT

Keeping your legs straight up in the air at all times and flexing your working oblique and abdominal muscles as you go, bring your elbow to your opposite knee (or as far as you can go toward the knee). Then extend your arm fully outward. Give your oblique and abdominal muscles an extra-hard flex and, in full control, return to the start position. Without resting, repeat the movement for the other side of your body. Continue this alternating movement until you have completed your set. Rest an optional fifteen seconds and do another tri-set of this combination. Again, take an optional fifteen-second rest and perform the third and final tri-set of this combination. If you are on the regular workout, stop here. Congratulations! You have completed the Bathing Suit Workout. If you are on the Iron, Steel, or Titanium Woman workouts, rest an optional fifteen seconds and proceed to the first exercise of the next tri-set, the standing butt squeeze.

TIPS

Don't fall into the trap of lurching forward as you attempt to touch your elbow to your opposite knee. Maintain control and go only as far as you can go. Beware of the temptation to pull on your head. Use your hands only as *support* for your head.

WHAT TO DO: TRI-SETS, REPETITIONS, WEIGHTS

Set 1: Fifteen repetitions each: one-leg prone butt lift, regular squat, ceiling oblique reach. Optional fifteen-second rest.
Set 2: Fifteen repetitions each: one-leg prone butt lift, regular squat, ceiling oblique reach. Optional fifteen-second rest.
Set 3: Fifteen repetitions each: one-leg prone butt lift, regular squat, ceiling oblique reach. Optional fifteen-second rest.

NOTE:

Use optional five-pound dumbbells for the regular squat. No weights are required for other exercises. If you choose to use the modified pyramid system for your thighs, see pp. 32–33 for review.

FINISH

STANDING BUTT SQUEEZE, HACK SQUAT, AND KNEE-IN

(FOR IRON WOMAN, STEEL WOMAN, AND TITANIUM WOMAN WORKOUTS)

HIPS/BUTTOCKS: STANDING BUTT SQUEEZE TIGHTENS, TONES, LIFTS, AND SHAPES THE ENTIRE HIPS/BUTTOCKS AREA.

POSITION Holding an optional dumbbell in each hand, palms facing your body and arms straight at your side, stand with your feet a natural width apart with your back straight. Bend at the knees slightly, so that your body is about four inches lower to the ground.

MOVEMENT Flexing your entire hips/buttocks area as hard as possible, slowly rise to a full standing position. When you reach the highest point, give your hips/buttocks area an extra-hard flex. Repeat the movement until you have completed your set. Without resting, move to the next exercise in this tri-set, the hack squat.

TIPS Don't do this in front of the opposite sex! I won't be responsible.

THIGHS: HACK SQUAT TIGHTENS, TONES, STRENGTHENS, AND DEFINES THE ENTIRE FRONT THIGH MUSCLE AND HELPS TO DEVELOP AND TONE THE BACK THIGH MUSCLE AND TO REMOVE SADDLEBAGS.

POSITION
Stand with your feet a natural width apart. Hold an optional dumbbell in each hand, behind your back and in line with each buttock and back thigh. Your palms will be facing away from your body.

MOVEMENT
Keeping the dumbbells in position as you go, bend at the knee until you are in a full squat or as far as your knees will allow. Feel the stretch in your front thigh muscles. Flexing your front thigh muscles as you go and keeping the dumbbells in line with your buttocks and back thighs, return to the start position. Give your front thighs an extra-hard flex and repeat the movement until you have completed your set. Without resting, move to the third and final exercise in this tri-set, the knee-in.

TIPS
If you rise up on your toes, take a wider stance.

THE BATHING SUIT WORKOUT | **109**

ABDOMINALS: KNEE-IN TIGHTENS, TONES, STRENGTHENS, AND DEFINES THE ENTIRE LOWER ABDOMINAL AREA.

POSITION Lie flat on your back on the floor and extend your legs out in front of you with your knees very slightly bent.

MOVEMENT Flexing your lower abdominal muscles as you go and keeping your knees together and your back flat on the floor, pull your knees toward your chest until you cannot go any farther. Keeping the tension on your lower abdominal muscles, return to the start position and repeat the movement until you have completed your set. Rest an optional fifteen seconds and do another tri-set of this combination. Again, take an optional fifteen-second rest and perform the third and final tri-set of this combination. If you are on the Iron Woman workout, stop here. Congratulations! You have completed your Bathing Suit Workout. If you are on the Steel Woman workout or the Titanium Woman workout, rest an optional fifteen seconds and proceed to the first exercise of the next tri-set, the reverse-lunge lift.

TIPS Don't jerk your knees toward your chest. Use controlled movements, and remember to keep the pressure on your abdominals throughout the movement.

WHAT TO DO: Set 1: Fifteen repetitions each: standing butt squeeze, hack squat, *TRI-SETS,* knee-in. Optional fifteen-second rest.
REPETITIONS, Set 2: Fifteen repetitions each: standing butt squeeze, hack squat, *WEIGHTS* knee-in. Optional fifteen-second rest.
 Set 3: Fifteen repetitions each: standing butt squeeze, hack squat, knee-in. Optional fifteen-second rest.

NOTE: Hold five-pound dumbbells in each hand for the standing butt squeeze as for an anchor (optional), and use five-pound dumbbells for the hack squat (also optional). No weights are required for other exercises. If you choose to use the modified pyramid system for thighs, see pp. 32–33 for review. There is no need to pyramid when doing butt work. The weights are used only as an anchor.

9

REVERSE-LUNGE LIFT, BENT-KNEE DEADLIFT, AND SIT-UP

(FOR STEEL WOMAN AND TITANIUM WOMAN WORKOUTS)

HIPS/BUTTOCKS: REVERSE-LUNGE LIFT TIGHTENS, TONES, SHAPES, AND LIFTS THE ENTIRE HIPS/BUTTOCKS AREA.

POSITION Stand with your left leg forward, bent at the knee, and your right leg nearly straight and about two feet behind your left leg. Extend your left arm back and your right arm forward. (You will be in a lunge position.)

MOVEMENT Keeping your left leg in place, bending your right knee, and swinging your right arm back and your left arm forward, move your right leg forward, bending at the knee until you cannot go any higher. Return to the start position and repeat the movement until you have completed your set. (Note: Whichever leg is back, that arm is forward!) Repeat the set for the other side of your body.

TIPS This is not a thigh exercise—it's a hips/buttocks exercise. Remember to flex your buttocks as hard as possible each time you reach the straight-leg position.

MACHINES, ETC. You may substitute this exercise for any exercise done on a hips/buttocks machine. Set the weight at a comfortable starting weight. Machines vary, so you'll have to experiment.

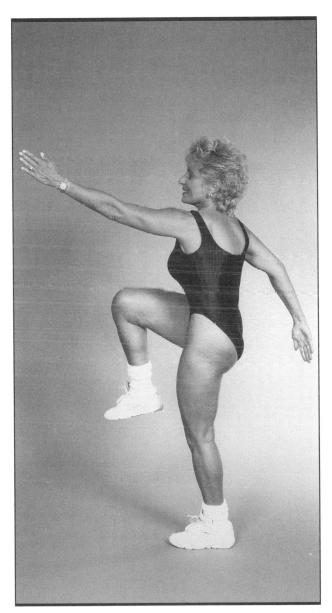

THE BATHING SUIT WORKOUT | 113

THIGHS: BENT-KNEE DEADLIFT TIGHTENS, TONES, STRENGTHENS, AND SHAPES THE BACK THIGH AREA AND HELPS TO STRENGTHEN THE BACK.

POSITION With an optional dumbbell in each hand, palms facing your body, stand with your feet a natural width apart and bend at the knees while holding a dumbbell in front of each knee. If you are not using weights, simply assume the position you see in the photograph—only without dumbbells.

MOVEMENT Flexing your back thigh and buttocks muscles as you go, rise to a standing position and squeeze your butt and back thigh muscles as hard as possible. Without resting, repeat the movement until you have completed your set. Without resting, move the final exercise in this tri-set, the sit-up.

TIPS The effectiveness of this exercise depends upon strict performance and intense flexing.

MACHINES, ETC. You may perform this exercise with a twenty-pound barbell.

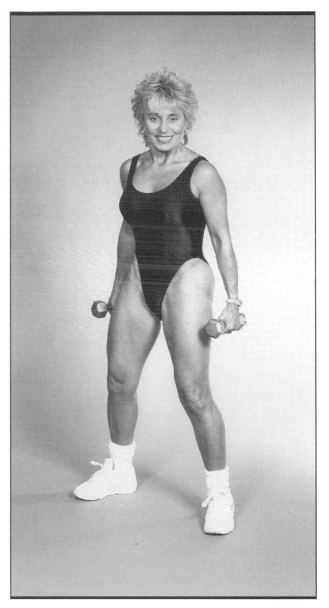

FINISH

ABDOMINALS: SIT-UP TIGHTENS, TONES, STRENGTHENS, AND DEFINES THE UPPER ABDOMINAL AREA.

POSITION Lie flat on your back on the floor and bend your knees so that the soles of your feet are touching the floor. Place your hands behind your head or cross them in front of you on your stomach or chest.

MOVEMENT Flexing your upper abdominals as you go, raise yourself off the floor until you are in a nearly perpendicular position. In full control, lower yourself to the start position and repeat the movement until you have completed your set. Rest an optional fifteen seconds and do another tri-set of this combination. Again, take an optional fifteen-second rest and perform your third and final tri-set of this combination. If you are on the Steel Woman workout, stop here. Congratulations! You have completed your Bathing Suit Workout. If you are on the Titanium Woman workout, rest an optional fifteen seconds more and proceed to the first exercise of the next tri-set, the straight leg kick-up.

TIPS Don't jerk up, but rather curl to the up position. If necessary, you may cross your ankles for leverage, or place your ankles under a piece of furniture.

WHAT TO DO: Set 1: Fifteen repetitions each: reverse-lunge lift, bent-knee
TRI-SETS, deadlift, sit-up. Optional fifteen-second rest.
REPETITIONS, Set 2: Fifteen repetitions each: reverse-lunge lift, bent-knee
WEIGHTS deadlift, sit-up. Optional fifteen-second rest.
 Set 3: Fifteen repetitions each: reverse-lunge lift, bent-knee deadlift, sit-up. Optional fifteen-second rest.

NOTE: Use five-pound dumbbells for the bent-knee deadlift (optional). No weights are used for other exercises. If you choose to use the modified pyramid system for your thighs, see pp. 32–33 for review.

THE BATHING SUIT WORKOUT | 117

10

STRAIGHT-LEG KICK-UP, SISSY SQUAT, AND LEG RAISE

(FOR TITANIUM WOMAN WORKOUT)

HIPS/BUTTOCKS, STRAIGHT-LEG KICK-UP TIGHTENS, TONES, LIFTS, AND SHAPES THE ENTIRE BUTTOCKS AREA AND HELPS TO REMOVE "SADDLEBAGS."

POSITION Take an all-fours position on the floor. Extend one leg straight out behind you, in line with your body, and flex the foot of that leg forward.

MOVEMENT Flexing your working buttock as hard as possible as you move, raise your extended leg until it is parallel to your body. Give your working buttock an extra-hard flex and, continuing to keep the pressure on your buttock muscle, return to the start position. Repeat the movement until you have completed your set. Repeat the set for the other side of your body. Without resting, move to the next exercise in this tri-set, the sissy squat.

MACHINES, ETC. You may substitute this exercise for any exercise done on a hips/buttocks machine. Set the weight at a comfortable starting weight. Machines vary, so you'll have to experiment. You may perform a variation of this exercise with your toes pointed back and by raising your leg as high as possible.

THE BATHING SUIT WORKOUT | 119

THIGH: SISSY SQUAT TIGHTENS, TONES, STRENGTHENS, AND DEFINES THE FRONT THIGH MUSCLE, GIVES DEFINITION TO THE INNER THIGH, HELPS TO LIFT THE BUTTOCKS AND TONE THE BACK THIGH MUSCLE.

POSITION

Stand with your feet about five inches apart and your toes pointed slightly outward. Place one hand on a stable object for support. Note: Even if you are taking advantage of the optional weights, no weights are used with this thigh exercise.

MOVEMENT

Applying tension to your front, inner, and back thigh muscles as you go, raise yourself on your toes. At the same time, lean your upper body back as far as you can go and squeeze your buttocks as hard as possible. You will be completely up on your toes at this point and you will feel an extreme stretch in your front thigh muscles. Be sure that your hips are in line with your ankles as you work. Continuing to keep the pressure on your thigh and buttocks muscles, return to the start position and repeat the movement until you have completed your set. Without resting, move to the final exercise in this tri-set, the leg raise.

TIPS

At first this exercise will seem awkward, especially if you try to follow the words and not the photographs. Look at the picture and imitate what I do. In time you'll appreciate this weightless exercise for its ability to stretch and define your front thighs fully. Advanced bodybuilders perform this exercise with a weight-belt attached to their waists.

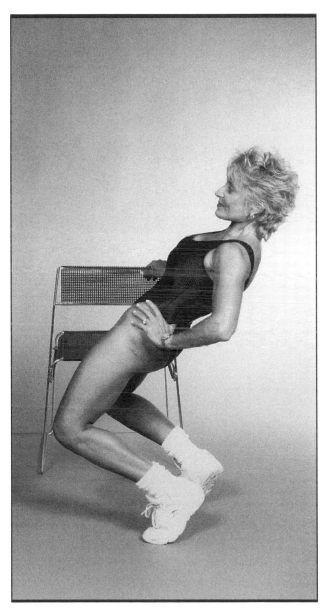

ABDOMINALS: LEG RAISE TIGHTENS, TONES, STRENGTHENS, AND DEFINES THE LOWER ABDOMINAL AREA.

POSITION Lie flat on your back and place your hands behind your head or at the sides of a bench. Bend at the knees and keep your shoulders and back grounded as you work.

MOVEMENT Flexing your lower abdominal muscles as you go and, keeping your knees moderately bent, raise your legs until they are perpendicular to the floor. Give your lower abdominals an extra-hard flex and, in full control, return to the start position—but do not touch the ground with your feet. Without resting, repeat the movement until you have completed your set. Rest an optional fifteen seconds and do another tri-set of this combination. Again, take an optional fifteen-second rest and perform the third and final tri-set of this combination. Congratulations! You have completed the Bathing Suit Titanium Woman workout.

TIPS Don't arch your back as you work. Keep it flat on the floor. Be sure to keep your knees and ankles together throughout the movement.

MACHINES, ETC. You may perform this exercise on any Roman chair by extending your legs until they are parallel to the floor.

WHAT TO DO:
TRI-SETS,
REPETITIONS,
WEIGHTS
Set 1: Fifteen repetitions each: straight-leg kick-up, sissy squat, leg raise. Optional fifteen-second rest.
Set 2: Fifteen repetitions each: straight-leg kick-up, sissy squat, leg raise. Optional fifteen-second rest.
Set 3: Fifteen repetitions each: straight-leg kick-up, sissy squat, leg raise. Optional fifteen-second rest.

NOTE: No weights are used for any exercise in this tri-set, not even thighs!

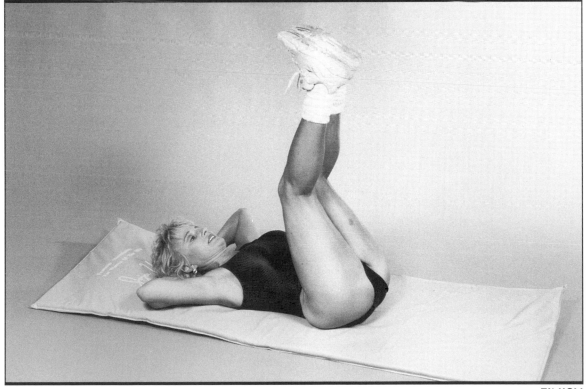

THE BATHING SUIT WORKOUT | 123

Review of Exercises Found in This Workout

HIPS/BUTTOCKS	THIGHS	ABDOMINALS
1. Saddlebag stripper	Lying inner thigh lift	Knee-raised oblique crunch
2. Lower butt curl	Leg curl	Bent-knee sewn lift
3. Lower butt crunch	Chair position firmer	Knee-raised crunch
4. Lower butt side kick	Straddle squat	Side oblique crunch
5. Floor feather kick-up	Front squat	Ceiling sewn lift
6. Lying butt lift	Lunge	Toe-reach crunch
7. One-leg prone butt lift	Regular squat	Ceiling oblique reach
8. Standing butt squeeze (Iron, Steel, and Titanium Woman workouts)	Hack squat	Knee-in
9. Reverse-lunge lift (Steel and Titanium Woman workouts)	Bent-knee deadlift	Sit-up
10. Straight-leg knee-up (Titanium Woman workout)	Sissy squat	Leg raise

Marthe, Joyce's daughter, who also loves to eat!

7

THE
BATHING SUIT DIET

You know what to do for exercise; now you must learn about the other half of your fitness program: what to eat! Diet (meaning what you eat on a daily basis) is the key to showing off your hard-earned hard body! Without the diet, your fat would cover the muscles. You would feel firmer, but you wouldn't look sleek and shapely.

But what about if you're not overweight to begin with—in fact, you may even be a bit too thin—but your body is soft and mushy? Do you have to follow this eating plan? No. You can continue to eat your regular fare—assuming it is a healthy diet. You and your doctor can decide upon that. For the rest of us poor souls, we must follow the diet and thank God that we have the knowledge that will allow us to eat plenty of food and still lose our excess body fat.

A Balanced, Low-Fat—Not Nonfat—Diet is the Key

As mentioned in Chapter 2, the three macronutrients, carbohydrates, protein, and fats, are needed by the body in a certain balance in order to maintain good health and to keep the body lean and fit. We've already gone into details about fat, which is needed in a lower percentage by the body than the carbohydrates, and in about an equal percentage to protein. In this chapter you'll learn the details about protein and carbohydrate, and how to balance them along with fat in your diet so that day by day you will lose your excess body fat. The percentages of the three food elements you will eat are not exact, but to round it off, you'll be consuming about 15 percent fat, 15 percent protein, and 70 percent carbohydrates.

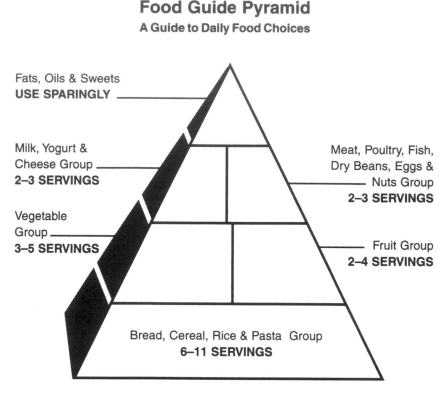

Food Guide Pyramid

A Guide to Daily Food Choices

Fats, Oils & Sweets
USE SPARINGLY

Milk, Yogurt &
Cheese Group
2–3 SERVINGS

Meat, Poultry, Fish,
Dry Beans, Eggs &
Nuts Group
2–3 SERVINGS

Vegetable
Group
3–5 SERVINGS

Fruit Group
2–4 SERVINGS

Bread, Cereal, Rice & Pasta Group
6–11 SERVINGS

Source: U.S. Department of Agriculture

The USDA has come out with a "food pyramid" that outlines what is considered by health and nutrition experts to be a balanced diet. Here it is:

The bare minimum of fats and refined simple carbohydrates

2–3 servings of protein

6–11 servings starches (breads, grains, rice, pasta, cereal)

3–5 servings of vegetables (unlimited complex carbohydrates)

2–4 fruits

1–2 servings of dairy products

I have based the diet plan in this chapter on the food pyramid. However, I've changed the maximum number of the "starches" group to ten servings. I've also renamed that category and called it "limited complex carbohydrates." In addition, I must advise you that if you want to lose your excess body fat at the quickest possible pace, except

for "unlimited complex carbohydrates" keep to the lower end of the food allowances. ("Unlimited complex carbohydrates" work in reverse. The more you eat of them, the faster you will lose your excess body fat. You'll understand why as you read this chapter.) Finally, I've given you food lists from which to choose your food portions, in order to insure that your diet remains low-fat and at the same time nutritious.

Protein

If you read Chapter 2, you already know that you are not allowed to eat pure fat in any form (butter, margarine, etc.). You must rely on the other two food sources to get your fat! Protein will be your main source of fat, specifically, low-fat sources of protein.

Only about 15 percent of your food intake will be protein. You will get your 15 percent protein simply by eating two to three portions (listed below) of protein per day. You don't have to calculate anything. I've done it for you.

Protein has a strange characteristic. It can only be used productively by your body in small amounts at a time. If you eat it in large portions, it ends up getting stored on your body as fat. (Note: For some people, 15 percent of protein is too much. If you feel this way, you can increase your carbohydrate intake and lower your protein intake. Simply reduce the portions of protein to four ounces and have only two portions instead of three.)

Protein is considered to be the "building block" of the body because it is responsible for the major content of muscle, skin, hair, nails, blood, and internal organs. It is also responsible for body repair, water balance, and hormone production that controls metabolism, growth, and sexual development, and regulates the acid-alkaline balance of the blood and tissues.

In other books, I've stated that the ideal amount of protein consumption if you work out with weights is about 1/2 gram of protein per day for each pound of body weight. (Bodybuilders often consume double that amount.) For example, if you weigh 120 pounds, you could consume sixty grams of protein in a day. I stand by that figure here; however, I will modify it to say that you could consume much less if you wish. The bare minimum would be forty-four grams a day for women.

But where will you get your protein? There are approximately five grams of protein per ounce of poultry, and six grams per ounce of fish. So if you wish to consume the smaller portion of four ounces of fish instead of six ounces, you will have had twenty-four grams of protein in

a serving. Later in the day you might consume four ounces of chicken—twenty grams of protein. That adds up to forty-four grams of protein. You're allowed another portion of protein (you are allowed two to three portions a day) but if you don't feel like having any more protein, that's okay. You have consumed your minimum required amount for good health.

Low-Fat Sources of Protein

All poultry is without skin and cooked without fat! I'm listing the fat grams for your convenience.

Poultry (4 oz. cooked)	Grams of Fat	Grams of Protein
Turkey breast	1	34
Turkey drumstick	4.5	33
Turkey thigh	5	31
Chicken breast	4.5	35
Chicken drumstick	6.8	37
Chicken thigh	5	31

Fish (4 oz.)	Grams of Fat	Grams of Protein
Mahi-mahi (dolphin fish)	0.8	20.8
Haddock	1	23
Cod	1	26
Abalone	1	16
Sole	1	19
Pike	1	25
Scallops	1	26
Tuna in water	1	34
Squid	1.8	20
Flounder	2.3	34
Red snapper	2.3	26
Sea bass	3.4	25
Halibut	4	31
Trout	4	30

Other Sources of Protein

Food Product	Grams of Fat	Grams of Protein
4 ounces low-fat yogurt	2	6
4 ounces nonfat yogurt	0	7
8 ounces 1 percent milk	3	8
8 ounces skim milk	1	8
4 ounces (1/2 cup) 1% cottage cheese	1	14
4 ounces (1/2 cup) full-fat cottage cheese	5	14
3 egg whites	2	9
1/2 cup beans	1	9
1/2 cup soft tofu	6	10
1/2 cup firm tofu	11	19

YOU WILL GET MUCH OF YOUR FAT ALLOTMENT FROM PROTEIN

You will notice that I've included the fat grams in the above calculations. That is because you will get a major part of your 15 percent or twenty to twenty-five grams of fat from your protein allotment. The rest will come from limited complex carbohydrates (sometimes called starches). You don't have to count the traces of fat found in unlimited complex carbohydrates and fresh fruit.

Carbohydrates

Most of your food intake (70 percent) should come from carbohydrates—they are the energy food for both body and mind. If you deprive your body of them, you feel enervated and irritable!

Carbohydrates are divided into two categories. The first is simple carbohydrates or sugars, which itself divides into two categories: refined (sugars found in candy, cake, doughnuts, white flour, etc.) and unrefined (sugars found in fruit). The second category is complex carbohydrates, which consist of vegetables, grains, and fiber.

You get an immediate shot of energy from simple carbohydrates. Complex carbohydrates, on the other hand, supply gradually released energy. The majority of your carbohydrate consumption will come from the latter group. We'll discuss the carbohydrates in order, from most consumed to least consumed in the ideal diet.

COMPLEX CARBOHYDRATES: YOUR MAIN FOOD SOURCE

As mentioned above, complex carbohydrates include all vegetables, grains, and fiber. But there are two types of complex carbohydrates: low caloric density and high caloric density. (Caloric density is the number of calories per weight of a particular food.) It is better to eat foods low in caloric density—foods that weigh more but have fewer calories—than foods in high caloric density—foods that weigh less and have more calories. Why?

If you're anything like me, you like to eat until you feel full. Since your calories are limited, you can't eat enough of the lighter-weight foods and still feel satisfied. Since your stomach can only hold about two pounds of food, it's better to eat two pounds of vegetables than two pounds of bread, even if that bread is whole-wheat bread. The bread would cost you too many calories.

Complex carbohydrates that are low in caloric density include all vegetables, pasta, rice, and hot cereals. Of course this doesn't mean you must eliminate healthful low-caloric-density foods such as wheat bread, cold cereals, rice cakes, etc. It just means that, if you want to feel full without eating too much, you're better off filling up on the high-caloric-density foods.

BEWARE: SOME CARBOHYDRATES CAN HINDER FAT BURNING

Processed carbohydrates, such as all forms of sugar and white breads, rice, and pasta can hinder fat burning. Why? When such foods are consumed, large amounts of glucose are released to the bloodstream, causing your body to produce high levels of insulin, which in turn inhibits hormone-sensitive lipase—the enzyme that is responsible for draining fat from the cells! A simple rule of thumb is: sugar very rarely, and brown is better than white!

6–10 SERVINGS OF LIMITED COMPLEX CARBOHYDRATES
(STARCHES)

This group of complex carbohydrates includes bread, cereal, rice, pasta, and all grains, plus two high-starch vegetables.

One Serving Equals	Fat Grams
1 slice whole-wheat bread	.5
1/2 bagel	.6
1/2 English or bran muffin	.6
1/2 cup cooked hot cereal	1

One Serving Equals	Fat Grams
1 cup dry cold cereal	1
1/2 cup cooked pasta or rice	.5
1 ounce pretzels	0–1
4 low-fat medium-sized crackers or 2 rice cakes	.6
1 large potato or 1 medium-sized yam or sweet potato	.1
1 cup corn or 1 large corn on the cob	.9

You will have a minimum of six servings and a maximum of ten servings for the day—and still lose weight. The less weight you have to lose, the closer you will have to go to the minimum number!

3–12 OR MORE SERVINGS OF VEGETABLES: UNLIMITED COMPLEX CARBOHYDRATES

You can and should eat as much as you please of these vegetables. In fact, it is mandatory for good health that you have at least three servings per day. However, for our purposes, three servings is not enough. If you keep to the bare minimum, you will probably feel hungry all the time. Why? Your other foods are very limited. Once you use up your allotment of those foods, you'll have two choices. Either feel hungry or eat vegetables!

1 Serving of Unlimited Complex Carbohydrates Equals:

1/2 cup cooked or 1 cup raw equals a serving.

Asparagus	Leeks
Broccoli	Lettuce
Brussels sprouts	Mushrooms
Cabbage, Chinese cabbage	Okra
Carrots	Onions
Cauliflower	Peppers, green or red
Celery	Radishes
Chicory	Rutabagas
Collard greens	Shallots
Cucumber	Sprouts
Eggplant	Squash (summer or zucchini)
Endive	Tomatoes
Escarole	Turnips
Kale	

Note: One tomato, cucumber, or pepper counts as a serving. As mentioned above, you don't have to count the fat grams in the unlimited vegetables or fruits.

SIMPLE CARBOHYDRATES: FRUIT

Both fruit and fruit juice are simple unrefined carbohydrates (sugars), but fruit is much better for you than juice because, as mentioned in Chapter 2, fruit juices function as do pure sugar or refined carbohydrates: They cause your insulin level to rise, which in turn can cause hunger and hinder fat burning. In addition, when you drink juice instead of eating the real fruit, you deprive yourself of the nutritious fiber and bulk of the fruit—and the opportunity to feel full!

2–4 SIMPLE CARBOHYDRATES (FRUIT) PER DAY

One Serving of Fruit Equals:
One medium to large piece of any fruit: apple, orange, pear, banana, etc.
1 cup berries of any kind or papaya
1 1/2 cups strawberries, watermelon
1/2 cantaloupe, grapefruit, large plantain
15 cherries
20 grapes
3 persimmons, kumquats,
fresh prunes
*1/2 cup juice
1/4 honeydew or pineapple
2 plums or tangerines
1 serving of nonfat cake, cookies, candy, jam, jelly, etc. (You will have this no more than twice a week. A serving is whatever is designated on the package as a serving.)

*Note: It is always better to have fruit rather than fruit juce. Fruit adds fiber to your diet and fills up your stomach. Juice may trigger a hunger response.

SIMPLE REFINED CARBOHYDRATES

Since simple refined carbohydrates can hinder your fat-burning process and must be kept to a minimum in your diet. So, except for a small amount, leave them out of your diet. However, when you do indulge, you will of course choose the low-fat, or better, the nonfat variety. As noted in your fruit food list, you can have a simple refined carbohydrate in place of a fruit. Later, you will be given an opportunity to have a simple refined carbohydrate in place of a dairy product (like nonfat sugar-containing ice cream).

WHAT ABOUT DAIRY?

2–3 DAIRY FOODS PER DAY

One Serving Equals:
1 glass of skim or 1 percent milk
8 oz. nonfat or 1 percent yogurt
4 oz. nonfat or 1 percent cottage cheese
2 tbsp. nonfat cream cheese
11/2 slices (ounces) nonfat cheese
1/2 cup nonfat ice cream, no more than twice a week

WHAT ABOUT FIBER AND WHERE IS IT FOUND?

Fiber is found in vegetables and fruit. Your daily fiber intake should be at least thirty grams, but you won't have to count fiber grams because if you follow this eating plan, you'll automatically get more than your bare minimum!

Fiber helps to prevent all kinds of diseases, helps to move fat out of your system, and helps you to eliminate foods (through bowel movement).

WHY IS FIBER GOOD FOR YOUR HEALTH?

There are two types of fiber. First, there is **soluble fiber**, which is found in oat bran, psyllium, fresh fruits and vegetables, and legumes. It can be digested by the body when consumed, and helps to lower blood sugar and cholesterol levels.

Insoluble fiber, which is found in whole wheat, whole grains, celery, corn, corn bran, green beans, green leafy vegetables, potato skins, and brown rice, cannot be digested by the body. Because of this, when you consume it, insoluble fiber does not register as calories—and in fact, the foods that contain them are automatically 15 percent lower in calories than they appear to be. Insoluble fiber also acts as a fat vacuum because when insoluble fiber exists in the body, some of the fat in your digestive system clings to the rough surface of the fiber and exits right along with it.

In addition, insoluble fiber gives the stool needed volume and helps to prevent constipation and possibly eventual colon and rectal cancer.

How Do You Know You're Not Consuming Too Many Calories?

If you keep to the lower or even the middle of the food allowances, I promise you that you will not be consuming too many calories. Depending upon your present weight, height, and metabolism, the higher end may be too high for you. To be on the safe side, try to stick to the middle or lower end of the food allowances until you reach your fitness goal.

Caffeine

When it comes to caffeine, it's up to you. It all depends upon your medical condition and your ability to tolerate caffeine. Caffeine's reputation varies from year to year. Some studies claim that in moderation, it increases energy and is good for your heart. Other studies claim that it's bad for your heart and causes a host of problems from fibrocystic breast disease to raised cholesterol levels. You should discuss your particular situation with your doctor.

I used to be able to drink two to three cups of regular coffee a day. Lately, I find that drinking that amount of coffee makes me jumpy, so I've switched to the "light" coffee with half the amount of caffeine. I can still have my two to three cups, and I no longer feel "hyper." You'll have to pay attention to your body to see if caffeine is friendly to your body, and in what amounts.

Alcohol

Although many studies indicate that up to two glasses of wine a day can in fact be beneficial to your health, I would not drink every day. Why? If nothing else, alcohol consumption, even light alcohol, such as wine or light beer, temporarily slows down your metabolism, and you burn less fat.

If you're going to indulge, save it for the weekend and have one to two drinks one day, or the most, two drinks two days. Such drinking will not retard your fat loss, even if you are on the strictest regimen. But remember to indulge only in the low-calorie nonmixed drinks such as white or red wine, light beer, or liquor with plain soda, water, or, at worst, fruit juice. You may count each drink as a fruit, but remember, you're not getting the nutrition of a fruit.

Salt or Sodium

The human body needs a certain amount of sodium for good health, but not nearly as much as most people consume. The minimum daily requirement for sodium is between 1,500 and 2,400 milligrams, but most people consume as much as double that amount. How so? One serving of full-sodium soup has about 1,000 grams per serving. All full-sodium canned vegetables also have that amount, and most frozen dinners are just as bad. Other high-sodium foods are Chinese food, smoked foods, and all pickled foods—including, of course, my favorite: pickles!

Sodium will not make you fat. It will just make you feel fat and indeed look fatter in the mirror. Why? Sodium holds up to fifty times its weight in water. When you indulge in high-sodium foods you will temporarily retain water—which will make your scale weight go up one to even ten pounds.

But what about health? My motto is, if possible, "Everything in moderation." However, if you don't have a health problem such as high blood pressure, like me, with your doctor's permission you may occasionally want to indulge in high-sodium low-fat foods such as pickles, full-sodium soups, and so on. The way I see it, if it's going to prevent me from eating full-fat cream cheese, I'd rather eat pickles! In fact, I've devised a great sandwich that makes me feel as if I've had a feast. I take a bagel, cut it in half, and load it with sliced pickle, tomato, and onion. Then I go to town. Even now, as I write this, my mouth is watering for such a treat. And you know what? It only has about one gram of fat! Sure, I pay the price of being bloated for a day or two, but once I go back to moderate sodium intake, in a few days the bloat goes down.

The point is you can't get fat by eating high-sodium foods—you can only look fat, but that will go away in a few days from the time you lower your sodium intake!

Calcium

Calcium is the most important mineral when it comes to the maintenance of bones. Most doctors agree that 1,500 milligrams of calcium daily is a healthy minimum amount for women of every age, and especially for women over thirty. The following foods are perfect for natural calcium consumption.

Food Item	Serving	Calcium Content
Yogurt, plain, nonfat	1 cup	452
Yogurt, plain, low fat	1 cup	415
Milk, skim	1 cup	302
Milk, 1 percent	1 cup	300
Mozzarella cheese, part skim	1 oz.	207
Ricotta cheese, part skim	4 oz.	335
Cottage cheese, 1 percent	4 oz.	69
Broccoli	1 cup	100
Collard greens	1 cup	300
Turnip greens	1 cup	200
Kale	1 cup	206
Swiss chard	1 cup	128
Orange juice, calcium fortified	1 cup	300
Soybeans	1 cup	131
Tofu, soft	4 oz.	108
Sardines with bones	3 oz.	372
Lima or kidney beans	1/2 cup	48
Ocean perch	4 oz.	156

Note: Cottage cheese is not considered as good a calcium source as other dairy products.

Get a copy of my book *Bone Building Body Shaping Workout* (see Bibliography) for a list of many other sources of calcium. If you are not sure that you're getting enough calcium in your diet, see your doctor about taking a supplement. But remember, it's always better to get your calcium from food. I never took a calcium supplement in my life, and my bone thickness was measured at 219.3—almost double the thickness of "normal" women my age, and thicker than an average twenty-five-year-old's. Why are my bones so thick? I do my own workouts, and I get my calcium from natural sources.

Drinking Water Helps You Not to Retain Water!

In Chapter 2 we discussed water in the context of its importance in allowing the kidneys the freedom to do their fat-processing work. Now we will see how drinking lots of water actually helps you to flush out excess water from your system.

When your body gets less water than it needs, it goes into a survival mode and begins to retain any bit of water it does get, even the water from foods. This water is stored in the extracellular spaces (out-

side of the cells) and can actually be seen in your hands, feet, and legs (they will appear swollen). Taking "water pills" (diuretics) is absolutely not the answer because the body goes on red alert and feels that it is being robbed of its life-sustaining water. Then the moment you stop taking the water pills, your body retains every bit of water it can—and you have to wait about a week for it to level off. (It levels off only if you don't eat high-sodium foods.)

So what's the answer? Drink lots of water. But how does water help to flush water out of your system? As the water passes through the kidneys, it takes any excess sodium—and water—with it!

If you drink lots of water, you will also look and feel better. Your skin won't look saggy; it will look firm and healthy. But more than that, water helps to flush out waste from your system and relieve constipation!

How much water should you drink? Six eight-ounce glasses a day would be just fine, even eight if you can swing it. I know it isn't easy—and you'll probably be finding yourself going to the bathroom a lot—but it's well worth it.

Eat Often!

You'll lose more weight if you eat five small meals a day, even if those meals add up to more calories than one big meal! Why? When you break up your eating, you give your body the energy it needs to function, and it does not go into the "survival" stage and slow down your metabolism—which in turn causes you, all things being equal, to burn less calories.

The only way to lose weight and keep it off is to prevent the body from feeling deprived. You must gently coax your body into letting go of its excess fat by giving it food all day long. The trick is, instead of giving it fatty foods, you give it nutritious low-fat foods in a well-balanced diet (as listed above). Your body will cooperate with you fully because it was created to eat a well-balanced diet.

If, on the other hand, you try to go against nature and punish your body for being fat, telling it "You will not eat all day, you fat pig," and then at the end of the day give it some food, your body will rebel and sabotage you and force you to eat much more than you had planned. Clearly, then, for two reasons, slowed metabolism and sabotage, you must eat often. Five or more times a day is ideal, but three is the bare, bare minimum.

Once You Reach Your Goal, Eat Anything You Want One Day a Week!

There's a pot of gold at the end of the rainbow! Once you reach your goal, you can eat anything you want, all day long, once a week. "But how could this work?" you might ask. By consuming a well-balanced low-fat diet all week long, you make room for the additional fat intake on the free day. In other words, it evens out! But how can you be sure that you won't gain weight if you do that? Think of it logically. For six days you are eating a low-fat diet. One day you eat high fat. Yes. It's one step forward and one step back, which leads you right to where you are now: maintenance of what you have, in other words.

The fact is, if you continued to follow the low-fat, balanced eating plan in this chapter for the rest of your life, never taking a free eating day even when you reached your ideal body weight, you would eventually lose too much weight and you would begin to appear too thin.

When I first tried this out, I planned my eating day all week. Every time I thought of a goody that I was missing, I would write it down, and then when I was in the supermarket, I would purchase the item: Cheez-Its, Tootsie Rolls, full-fat ice cream, full-fat cream cheese, lox, a juicy red steak, and so on. Then when my free eating day came, I got up early in the morning and started my day with a fatty lox and cream cheese bagel. I continued to eat all day, and was in fact annoyed that at times I was too stuffed to eat—and even felt slightly nauseous. By the end of the day, or should I say night, I was upset that I couldn't fit in those last few full-fat gingerbread cookies!

The next day I'd feel horrible. I had a headache, a stomachache, and even a backache. I ate well all week, and when the next week came, I just ate what I pleased instead of going out of my way to "get it all in."

Why did I tell you this? I wanted you to know that it is okay to go through your crazy stage. Don't worry. Your own body will help to level you off. And the beauty of it is that, with this plan, you soon lose your sense of depression. You realize that there's no emergency. If you don't get to eat that goody you've been craving this week, you can always have it next week.

A free eating day! What a wonderful gift. If I didn't have it, I don't think I would be motivated to keep to a low-fat eating plan, knowing that for the rest of my life I would have no reward coming to me.

But what happens if you slip and start taking two or more free eating days—and, say, you start gaining weight? Fine. Just go back on the

full low-fat eating plan until you are again at your goal. Then take your free eating day once a week again. In order to prevent weight gain, a good rule of thumb is, any free eating day over one a week will cost you an extra week of not taking a free eating day. In other words, if you pig out on the holidays for five days in a row, then don't take a free eating day for five weeks. It's that simple—and it works. (For other options for free eating, like having one small goody a day, see my diet book *Eat to Trim* in Bibliography.)

In Summary: The Basic Food Rules to Follow

1. Eat your minimum for the day: 2–3 servings of protein; 6–10 servings of limited complex carbohydrates; 3–12 or more servings of vegetables; 2–4 fruits; 1–2 servings of dairy. (Except for the vegetable category, which works in reverse, the closer you keep to the lower allotment, the faster you will lose your excess fat.)

2. Eat often—five times a day or more. Never go more than four hours without eating!

3. Drink lots of water. Drink six to eight glasses of water a day. You can have a glass first thing in the morning, one before each meal, and one during or after exercising.

4. When you reach your fitness goal, eat anything you want once a week.

5. High-fat foods are public enemy number one, but high-sugar foods are potential menaces to fat loss. High-sodium foods will not make you fat—they will make you *look* fat for a short time! Be aware.

Make Your Own Meal Plans

Using the above guide, here is a sample meal plan:

Breakfast	Fat Grams	Calories
1/2 cup hot cereal (1cc #1) with 1 cup 1% milk (d #1)	2 milk, 1 cereal	150 cereal 100 milk
1 orange (f #1) No-calorie drink	0 orange	69

Snack	Fat Grams	Calories
4 oz. nonfat cottage cheese (d #2)	0 cottage cheese	80

Lunch

	Fat Grams	Calories
6 oz. flounder (p #1)	3.2 flounder	120
and 1 cup rice (1cc #2 and 3)	1 rice	200
large tossed lettuce and tomato salad (v #2,3,4)	0 salad	50

Snack

	Fat Grams	Calories
4 low-fat crackers (lcc #4)	1 cracker	48
1/2 grapefruit (f #2)	0 grapefruit	46

Dinner

	Fat Grams	Calories
6 oz. broiled chicken (p #2)	7.5 chicken	192
1 cup broccoli and cauliflower (v #5 and 6)	0 vegetables	50
2/3 cup pasta, with 1/2 cup low-fat tomato sauce (lcc #5 and 6)	1 pasta, 6 tomato sauce	200 50

Snack

	Fat Grams	Calories
2 cups brussels sprouts and carrots (v #7–10)	0 vegetables	130

Note: The code for each nutritional requirement is in parentheses. v = vegetables; lcc = limited complex carbohydrates; f = fruit; p = protein; and d = dairy.

Now let's count it up and see if we have filled the bill for a nutritionally healthy diet, and, at the same time, a low-fat diet.

3–12 or more servings of vegetables

6–10 servings of limited complex carbohydrates

2–4 fruits

2–3 servings of protein

2–3 servings of dairy

You've consumed twenty-three grams of fat—under your maximum—and only 1,485 calories, and look at all the food you ate. You had two servings of protein, opting for the six-ounce servings instead of the four-ounce, but keeping to the two instead of the three servings. You had six limited complex carbohydrates—the lower end of the allowance—and two fruits—again the lower end of the allowance. You had two dairys—the higher end of the allowance—and you had ten servings of vegetables, a good amount more than the bare minimum—exactly what I want you to do. But what if you were still hungry?

You would have two options: (1) eat more vegetables from the unlimited complex carbohydrate group; or (2) go closer to the higher end of your food allowance. It is much better to use option number one if your goal is to lose the most weight in the least amount of time. If you choose to eat toward the higher end of your food allowance, you will still lose weight in time, but it will take a little longer. But so what? I don't want you to feel deprived. Better to keep to the higher end than to blow your diet and start eating fatty foods in rebellion, in which case, in time, you'll only be fatter!

Note: For a much more complete diet with a whole month's worth of meal plans (three meals and two snacks a day—easy recipes, and you never repeat a meal), send for a copy of *Eat to Trim*. See Bibliography.

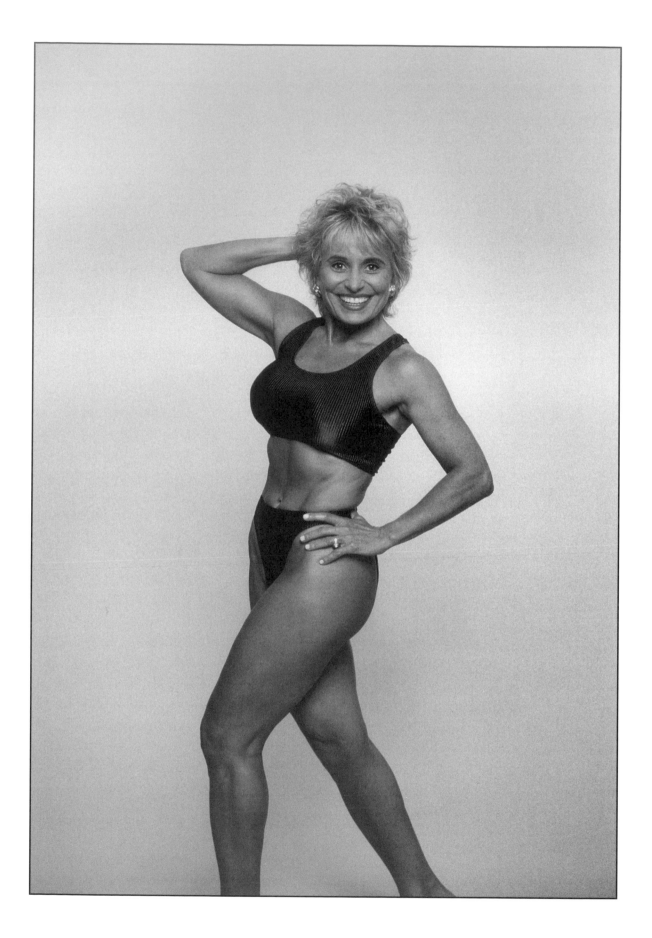

8

EXTRA
FAT-BURNING
TECHNIQUES

Y ou can't burn enough fat. You probably feel that way, at least if you love to eat as much as I do! In this chapter, I'll share some of my additional fat-burning techniques, methods I've discovered that help to burn extra calories during a given day, so that you can eat more than you would otherwise be able to eat—and still stay lean and sexy. First we'll talk about aerobics in general, and the amount of fat that can be burned doing various activities for a given amount of time. Then we'll discuss specific aerobic activities, detailing the advantages of each and describing the specific muscles utilized. Finally, we'll talk about simple ways to stimulate the metabolism during a typical day so that yet more fat can be burned in a relatively painless way.

Aerobic Activities

First of all, I must point out that in order to burn fat, an exercise does not have to be aerobic. As long as you are alive, you are using calories and burning fat. However, if you were going to depend upon just breathing to burn fat, your fat-burning rate would be very slow—because most people burn only about forty to sixty calories an hour just breathing. So what's the most time-efficient way of burning fat? Although it will not sculpt your body, aerobic exercise will burn the most calories in the shortest amount of time.

But what is aerobic? Literally, the word means "with oxygen." Although all exercise, indeed all life, requires oxygen, exercise is considered aerobic when it causes your pulse to reach a rate of 60 to 85 percent of its capacity, and to maintain that elevated rate for a certain length of time, usually twenty or more minutes. In the following para-

graphs you will find a description of various aerobic exercises in order of most fat-burning to least fat-burning.

I can guess what you may be thinking. "Great. I'll just look at the top of the chart and pick the most fat-burning of all the activities." That may or may not be a good idea! It's much better to pick an exercise that you enjoy so you will look forward to working out. If you don't enjoy your exercise, you'll probably feel defeated; you won't want to work out, and you may find that even the thought of the exercise robs you of your will to live, much less work out. I know that feeling—believe me!

In other words, while one fat-burning activity may be more "aerobic" than another (burn more fat in a given period of time) and although you may be perfectly capable of performing that activity, if you hate it, you are setting yourself up for failure. It's just not worth it.

Before we begin our discussion of aerobic workouts, I want to point out that the Bathing Suit Workout is aerobic if you don't take your optional rests—and even if you do, it is partially aerobic. If you only have limited time and have to choose "either/or"—that is to say, the Bathing Suit Workout or one of the aerobic workouts listed in this chapter—by all means, choose the Bathing Suit Workout! However, if you have the time (and I hope you *make* the time) it's a good idea to perform additional fat-burning aerobic activities.

As mentioned in Chapter 4, when performing a fat-burning aerobic activity, the goal is to get your heart rate up to between 60 and 70 percent of its capacity. You could go higher—as high as 80 to 85 percent of capacity. However, most fitness experts agree that the ideal fat-burning range is the lower range of 60 to 70 percent of capacity. In addition, working at this lower heart rate enables most people to work out for longer periods of time if they choose to do so—and in the end, burn more fat.

By way of review, in order to tell whether you are in the fat-burning range, subtract your age from the number 220 and then multiply that by 60 percent. This will be your basement fat-burning range. To calculate the higher ranges, simply multiply the 220 figure by 65 percent, 70 percent, and so on.

I'll use myself as an example. I'm fifty-five years old. If I subtract 55 from 220, I get 165. Now I multiply that number by 60 percent. The answer is 99.0. So when I measure my pulse rate for one minute after doing a given exercise for at least seven minutes and my pulse beats 99 times, I know that I am in my fat-burning range of about 60 percent. If my pulse beats, say, 115 times in a minute, I'm in the 70 percent range (70 percent of 165 is 115.5).

All well and good. But how do you find *your* pulse, and then how do you calculate *your* percentage? Luckily, you don't have to count your pulse for an entire minute. You can do it for fifteen seconds and multi-

ply the number by four instead. Place your fingers on your wrist and feel around until you can feel a pulse. Then set a stopwatch or look at the second hand of your watch for fifteen seconds while you count the beats. When you get a final figure, multiply it by four. For example, if my fifteen-second rate were 26 and I multiplied it by 4, I would have a total of 104. I would know that I was working at 60 percent of my capacity. If it were higher, say 30, the total would be 120—and I would know that I was in the 70 percent range.

If you get a headache just thinking about all this calculating and monitoring, you can do what I do. Instead of counting, just notice whether you are breaking into a mild sweat after about seven minutes. If you are, you are in the fat-burning range. If you're not, work a little harder. Move faster, flex your muscles—whatever it takes to give it that extra bit of effort.

Aerobic Fat-Burning Chart

Aerobic Activity	Calories Burned per 20 Minutes
Running an eight-minute mile (outdoors or on a treadmill)	230
Running a nine-minute mile (outdoors or on a treadmill)	220
Cross-country skiing	220
Swimming	210
Box aerobics (Boxercise)	200
Step aerobics	200
Stair-stepping	200
Rope jumping	200
Low-impact aerobics (aerobic dance)	200
NordicTrack machine	165
Trampoline jumping	165
Racewalking	160
Hiking (hills)	160
Rowing machine	150
Jogging at a slow pace (outdoors or on a treadmill)	145
Bicycle riding (stationary or moving at moderate pace)	140
Pool aerobics and water walking	140
Dancing at quick pace	120
Walking at a quick pace (outdoors or on a treadmill)	110

The above chart is a generalization for people of medium height and weight. If you are a big person, you will burn more calories than above. If you are a small person, you may burn a little less than the chart above, but you can compensate for that by moving faster and flexing your muscles as you work.

How Many Minutes Should You Work Out?

The ideal time is twenty to forty-five minutes. Can you go shorter or longer? Of course. Most fitness experts agree that even eight to ten minutes of aerobics is a lot better than nothing. But what about going longer—say, an hour?

I don't think it's a good idea as a general rule. If you try to do aerobics for sixty minutes at a session, you may overtrain your body and become fatigued. In addition, you will probably find yourself dreading the next aerobic workout. Remember, you're in this for the long term. It's much better to do short, enjoyable aerobic activities over a sustained period of time than to do one or two killer workouts that destroy your morale.

When I do aerobics, I work out from twenty to forty-five minutes, depending upon how strenuous the exercise. When I'm leisurely riding the exercise bike, I'll do up to forty-five minutes. But when I'm running, I run for about twenty minutes. If I walk, on the other hand, I can go for a full hour.

What? Didn't I just contradict myself? No. You see, since walking at a brisk pace is the least strenuous aerobic activity (in fact it is considered by some to be near-aerobic, not strictly aerobic) you can do it longer than other aerobic activities without becoming exhausted.

How Many Days a Week Should You Do Aerobics?

If possible, in addition to your Bathing Suit Workout and/or other weight-training workout, you should do aerobics four to five days a week. If you want to do less, three days is fine. If you want to do more, take a day off after six to ten days—preferably after six days.

You can do your aerobics on the same days you do your Bathing Suit Workout and/or other weight-training workout (you'll have to do that if you are doing aerobics more than three days a week), or you can do your aerobics on the days you don't do your Bathing Suit Workout and/or other weight-training workout.

When Should You Do Aerobics—Before or after Your Bathing Suit Workout or Other Weight-Training Workout?

In other books, I've always said, "Do your aerobic activity when it suits you best. It doesn't really matter." But after careful experimentation, I must tell you that if your schedule allows, it's always better to do your aerobics first, and your weight-training workout immediately after. The aerobic activity seems to provide an energy burst that lasts for about forty minutes, so why not take advantage of that energy and use it to do your Bathing Suit Workout and/or other weight-training-type workout?

But wait a minute. I'm still wary about encouraging you to do your aerobics first. Why? It is the Bathing Suit Workout that is most important. I'm afraid that you may say to yourself, "Well, I did my aerobics—and I just don't have time to invest in my Bathing Suit Workout (and/or other weight-training-type workout)." That would be the biggest mistake you could make. So if it comes down to either/or and you are pressed for time, do your Bathing Suit Workout first.

The best idea is to get used to your Bathing Suit Workout first. Make it an essential part of your life, like brushing your teeth or taking a shower. After you've established the workout habit, then, if you choose to do your aerobics first, I'm not worried that you'll be tempted to cut out the most important workout.

How Can You Break In to Aerobics if You've Never Done Aerobics Before?

The following schedule applies to all aerobic activities except brisk walking, which can be done ten to twenty minutes a day for the first week, and then adding ten to twenty minutes a week until you reach your goal. For all other aerobic activities, the following chart applies.

Week 1: Three to five minutes

Week 2: Five to seven minutes

Week 3: Seven to ten minutes

Week 4: Ten to fifteen minutes

Week 5: Fifteen to twenty minutes

Week 6: Twenty to twenty-five minutes

Week 7: Twenty-five to thirty minutes

Week 8: Thirty to thirty-five minutes

Week 9: Thirty-five to forty minutes

Week 10: Forty to forty-five minutes

Can you build up to your maximum amount more quickly than the above chart? Yes. With your doctor's permission, you can probably double your time, but be sure to check with him or her.

In any case, begin at the lower end of each week's range and work your way upward, so at the end of the week you are doing the higher number. For example, if you're jumping rope, on the first day of Week 1 you will jump rope for three minutes. The second time you jump rope that week, you will go for four minutes. The last few times you jump rope, you will go for five minutes.

Breaking In to a New Aerobic Activity if You're Already in Aerobic Shape with Another Aerobic Activity

What if you are already in aerobic shape for, say, using the stair machine, but now you want to try rope jumping? You are used to using the stair machine for twenty minutes with no problem. So you think, "I'll just jump rope today for twenty minutes." But after three minutes you are shocked to see that you are out of breath. "What's wrong with me?" you wonder. Perhaps rope jumping is much harder than stair-stepping.

Wrong. Had you been a rope-jumper and tried to switch to stair-stepping, you would probably have felt the same way. One aerobic activity is different from another, because different muscles are emphasized. For example, when you stair-step, you use your lower body muscles in a pumping motion, whereas when you jump rope, you use lower body muscles in a springing motion. In addition, in rope-jumping your upper body comes into play.

No matter which aerobic activity you are switching to, it takes a little while to make the transition. How much time? It all depends upon you. Happily, it will not take nearly as long as the regular break-in-gently program if you are already in aerobic shape. Here is a guideline. As above, you may break in twice as fast if you are able to do so and, of course, with your doctor's permission.

Week 1: Five to ten minutes

Week 2: Ten to fifteen minutes

Week 3: Fifteen to twenty-five minutes

Week 4: Twenty-five to forty-five minutes

Specific Aerobic Activities

Which aerobic exercise you choose will depend upon your particular interest and ability. For example, I hate the water, so I would never choose swimming. I love running but my joints hurt, so I can only do that twice a week at the most. So what I like is not always what I can do. My second choice for aerobics is either riding the stationary bike or doing the stair-stepper or, better yet, walking at a brisk pace.

The ideal thing is to switch around and do various aerobic activities in a given week. For example, if I'm going to do aerobics five times a week, I run twice, ride the bike twice, and do the stair-stepper once. I may do that for a few weeks and then replace the running with jumping rope. A few weeks later I may replace the bike with trampoline jumping. On weeks when I have a swing dance lesson, I use the sixty-minute lesson as one aerobic session.

What if you want to do the same aerobic activity every day? Fine with me. You'll still burn fat and get your heart and lungs in shape. Bear in mind, however, that after a while your body might appreciate some variety. It will give other muscles a chance to be involved and will round out your overall endurance.

No matter which aerobic activity you choose, remember that the key is to enjoy yourself and at the same time burn excess fat and get your heart and lungs into top shape. If you find yourself dreading your aerobic activity, give yourself a break and take the time to explore others. If you're a creature of habit, in the beginning you may fight the idea, thinking "I may not get as much out of it" or "This will be too hard." But you'll be surprised to see that after a week or two you'll feel as if you've been doing the activity forever.

RUNNING OUTDOORS OR ON A TREADMILL

For me, running outdoors is one of the most enjoyable ways of exercising. You breathe fresh air and at the same time watch the scenes of nature as you go. After the first few minutes, you find yourself thinking, solving problems, or just letting your mind run free. In addition, running seems to give the highest of natural highs. I tell you, it is almost impossible to remain sad or depressed after having a great run.

Unfortunately, running outdoors can put a strain on your joints

and eventually cause problems. For example, I started running about fifteen years ago. In the beginning I overdid it, trying to use running as a way to get in shape (before I knew what I know now). I ended up with shin splints and knee problems. Later I purchased the proper running shoes and began running mainly on grass or dirt—and cut my running time to thirty minutes instead of an hour. But still, in time, the running became a problem. At night my knee and hip joints would ache; I would feel a grinding sensation. So I experimented by cutting out running for three months. Sure enough, the pain went away. "I'll see what happens if I run only twice a week," I said. And I did and it worked fine.

But I didn't leave it at that. I decided to see what would happen if I ran three or four days a week again. Sure enough, in two months the pain was back. Again I stopped for three months. After that I made it a rule: Never, no matter what, run more than two days a week—and I'm fine. No problem.

What about running on a treadmill? Is it the same as running outdoors? Yes and no. If you raise your feet off the ground and "spring" the way you must do on the real ground, it is the same. However, if you move as quickly as you would if you were running but take advantage of the sliding surface of the treadmill and don't spring off the ground, you save your joints from the shock of the bounce.

Running on a treadmill has another advantage. You can adjust the speed and incline of the "floor," making the run harder or easier depending upon your needs. In addition, most treadmills have monitors that will tell you, depending upon your weight, sex, age, and height, exactly how many calories you are burning for a given time period.

Why don't I switch to the treadmill? I hate it! To me it's boring, even if you put flying country scenes on a screen in front of me. Also, I can't help but feeling like the proverbial rat on a wheel, scurrying madly and going nowhere. But don't let my feelingsg stop you. I have many friends who love the treadmill and in fact use it as their main aerobic activity, burning much fat and getting their hearts and lungs in top shape.

CROSS-COUNTRY SKIING

If you don't mind cold weather and love the snow, cross-country skiing can be a wonderful aerobic activity. Unlike downhill skiing where once you glide down the hill you must stop and wait to ascend the hill on a lift, in cross-country or Nordic skiing, you are continually on the move. What's more, depending upon where you live, cross-country skiing can be done right outside your door. In fact, I've seen

cross-country skiers in the streets of Manhattan—yes, Manhattan—during winters when there have been continual heavy snowstorms.

With this activity, you use not only your lower-body muscles—calves, thighs, hips, buttocks, and abdominals—but your upper-body muscles as well—back, chest, shoulders, and arms.

SWIMMING

The most body-gentle aerobic activity is swimming. When you swim, you put almost no pressure at all on your bones or joints. In fact, when an athlete sustains an injury and wishes to remain in shape, the first thing most doctors will recommend is swimming. In fact, years ago, when I used to be a judo player, I tore the cartilage in my knee. After about six weeks of complete layoff, my knee was still not in condition to even walk more than the minimum amount, much less run. My doctor recommended swimming

As much as I hate the water, I dragged myself to the pool every day. At the time I was teaching in a high school where there was a pool. I would arrive every day at 6 A.M. and swim back and forth from one end of the shallow side to the other. (I have a fear of deep water and finally realized that swimming alone was not the way to overcome it.)

I thought that in time I would come to love the water. But in spite of the fact that I was forced to swim for four months, I'll never forget the first long walk I took without pain! I felt as if my life were given back to me. I never went near the water again! I'm just not a water person.

Notwithstanding my personal preferences, swimming is excellent exercise. It involves all the muscles in the body, but there is a greater emphasis on upper-body muscles—back, chest, shoulders, and arms are involved—and in fact even the neck comes into play. Of course you also use your thighs and hips/buttocks area. The calves are hardly involved at all.

BOX AEROBICS (BOXERCISE)

Box aerobics or boxercise can be great fun, and at the same time it provides an outlet for stress, aggression, and anger. In addition, this exercise can increase ability in self-defense and, with it, self-confidence and even self-esteem. The workout consists of a jumping movement with punches and jabs, and sometimes includes the punching of a "heavybag," and a little rope jumping. Women who engage in this exercise tell me that every time they boxercise they leave the exercise room feeling transformed.

Boxercise works all of the upper-body muscles—back, chest, shoulders, arms—as well as the lower-body muscles—calves, thighs, hips/buttocks, and abdominals. You gain muscle strength, coordination, and skill in self-defense, all at the same time. I love this exercise.

STEP AEROBICS

If you are fairly coordinated and enjoy working out with people, step aerobics can be fun. You get to key into the energy of the group, especially the step-aerobics leader, who usually has enough energy to fuel a battleship!

The one drawback I find with step aerobics is that you must "learn" something. In other words, unlike simply getting on a treadmill or paddling away in the water (assuming you know how to swim), you must learn the sometimes complicated steps the instructor is doing. Most step-aerobics teachers provide classes for beginners so that newcomers don't become discouraged from the start. In time, most people surprise themselves and are able to keep up with even the most advanced step-aerobics sessions. I don't like step aerobics. To me, no matter how many fancy steps they throw in, it's tedious. But to each her own. I know women who live for this exercise.

Step aerobics provides most of its work for the lower body, specifically the calves, thighs, and hips/buttock area, as well as the abdominals. Can you reshape these body parts with step aerobics? Not in a million years. What you will do is strengthen them by the repeated motion. In order to do ultimate reshaping, you must work in sets and repetitions and, ideally, with graduated weights.

STAIR-STEPPING

There are a variety of stair-stepping machines ranging from the kind featuring elaborate devices that enable you to increase the incline and the tension of the "climb" to those with no high-tech controls at all.

If you choose to do stair-stepping, you don't need the fancy devices. But make sure you do break into a sweat after about seven minutes. I've seen people on these machines working out for forty-five minutes and not break into a sweat. The watch TV or read a book and barely move their legs, all the time thinking, "I'm really working out."

To avoid this pitfall, when stair stepping, pump hard and make sure you don't shorten the "stepping" movement to just two or three inches. Go the full range (six to ten inches), and flex your thighs and/or hips/buttocks muscles as you go. If you squeeze your working buttock on each descent, you will put more emphasis on that area. On the other hand, if you flex your working thigh muscle with each down move-

ment, you'll put more emphasis there. And if you flex both your thighs and your hips/buttock muscles as you go, you'll get the most aerobic workout for your exercise time. It isn't easy—you'll find yourself wanting to just forget about flexing and enjoy yourself. You can do that as long as you are sweating. But if you're not, you'll have to put in the extra effort.

Stair-stepping works mainly your lower body: calves, thighs, hips/buttocks, and abdominals. The upper-body muscles are not really involved, except for a little lower-back work.

ROPE JUMPING

Rope jumping can be lots of fun. You can do it at home while watching TV, or out in your backyard while gazing at the birds, flowers, trees, sun, and sky. You can also use rope jumping as an aerobic activity in your hotel room while on vacation or on a business trip. I do it whenever I'm on the road. In fact, rope jumping saves me the time and effort of waiting for a free exercise bike if there is a workout room, or of walking or running around a strange neighborhood early in the morning—something I'm not always in the mood to do. Knowing that I can do my aerobic workout in the privacy of my own room helps me to look forward to getting up in the morning instead of dreading the ring of that telephone wake-up call.

Rope jumping involves both lower- and upper-body muscles. You use your calves, thighs, hips, and buttocks, as well as your abdominal muscles, as you jump. At the same time, you use your back, chest, shoulders, and arms as you swing the rope around with every step. If you like rope jumping, after a while you can begin to vary your steps, doing fancy quick combinations the way fighters do when they train. In fact, at some health spas they have rope-jumping classes where you can really learn to get fancy. But you don't have to go to that extreme. I find that just the basic jump gives me quite a workout.

LOW-IMPACT AEROBICS (AEROBIC DANCE)

If you love music and have rhythm, aerobic dance can be the most painless aerobic activity in the world. When you do it to great music with a reasonable instructor who keeps it simple enough for you to follow, you lose track of time. Before you know it, twenty or more minutes have flown by and the session is over. You can't believe your workout is finished.

If you do aerobic dance, you'll find that if you choose a class where the music suits your temperament, you'll be much more motivated to move. For example, if I go to a class where they're playing disco-type

music, which offends my sensibilities, I find myself slugging away, watching the clock and wishing it were over with. On the other hand, if I choose a class that features jazz-type music, or music from the fifties, I work out with so much enthusiasm and energy that I'm actually surprised and disappointed when the class ends. What's more, I'm in such a great mood when it's over that I can't help but start conversations with the next five people I meet.

Aerobic dance involves the entire body. You're using your lower body to propel you—calves, thighs, hips/buttocks, and abdominals—and at the same time you're using your upper body—back, chest, shoulders, and arms—in rhythm to the music. It's a great total-body workout.

Note: Be sure to choose "low-impact" aerobic dance as opposed to "high-impact," where you leap off the ground and land hard. This can cause eventual damage to your bones and joints.

NORDICTRACK MACHINE AND OTHER SIMILAR MACHINES

The NordicTrack machine can provide an excellent total-body workout. While it of course can't reshape any body part, it can help you to increase your overall body strength and endurance. The great thing about this machine is that it can be purchased at a reasonable price and kept in the corner of a room at home. You can do it while watching TV listening to music, or just thinking. If you don't want to purchase such a machine, you can find one in most fitness centers.

This machine mimics the motion of cross-country skiing, which is handy if you live in a climate with no snow. It allows you to use both lower- and upper-body muscles in a challenging way. Your calves, thighs, hips/buttocks, and abdominals are working as you perform the skilike motion, while at the same time your back, chest, shoulders, and arms are being challenged as you simulate the movement you would make with ski poles.

TRAMPOLINE JUMPING

Trampoline jumping can be lots of fun if you do it to music. It's a real gift for those who would like to jump rope but can't do so because they live in an apartment building and would disturb neighbors by jumping directly on the floor. What's more, trampolines come in small sizes now and can be stored under a bed or behind a piece of furniture.

When you jump on a trampoline, make up your own routines. March for a while, then just plain jump high with both feet, then do a skipping motion, and so on. Try to use your arms. You can move them up and down the way you would if you were walking at a fast pace,

punch into the air as if you were boxing an imaginary opponent, or clap them over your head as if you were doing jumping jacks.

Depending upon how you work, the trampoline can exercise your entire body. No matter what you do, you will be exercising your calves, thighs, hips/buttocks, and abdominals. If you employ the above upper-body techniques, you'll also be using your back, chest, shoulders, and arms.

RACEWALKING

If you love to run but can't do it for health reasons, racewalking is your second-best bet—and it's quite a challenge. In order for your activity to be considered true racewalking, you must move very fast—almost as fast as a runner—but without springing off the ground the way runners do. Experienced racewalkers can in fact outpace some runners.

If racewalking has any disadvantage, I would say it's the way people look when they do it. I've never seen a racewalker who in my eyes, didn't look, well, foolish! They seem to be jerking forward in an unnatural, almost robotic, way. Why do they look this way? In order to racewalk properly, you must maintain high muscle tension and an as-rapid-as-possible pace. In addition, at the same time you must move your arms back and forth with each step in a rigid marchlike motion.

If I liked to racewalk, I wouldn't let the way I looked stop me. Who cares what people think? If they're not paying your rent, I say forget about people and enjoy yourself.

If performed properly, this exercise utilizes all the muscles in the body: calves, thighs, hips/buttocks, abdominals, back, chest, shoulders, and arms.

HIKING (HILLS)

Hiking is one of my favorite activities because it is done out of doors and you can lose yourself in nature. In fact, when I hike, I don't know I'm working out at all, and I can do it for hours at a time. I especially love hiking in Arizona, where I can take in the view of the cacti and the canyons. It fills my soul with joy and I remember it for months afterwards. Also, hiking is an activity that you can do either by yourself or with others. I like to hike with a group of people. Often I find that we don't speak for long periods of time, each of us absorbed in experiencing nature. Yet we seem to be communicating anyway, because when we do speak, we seem to start in the middle of a conversation, yet no one is confused. Apparently we were all tuned in to nature and on the same wavelength.

If you're going to hike, be sure that you do it where the ground is not always completely flat because you won't get as much out of it. Find a place where there are hilly spots as well as flat terrain. If you can't find hilly spots, then walk faster and try to flex your muscles as you go.

Hiking utilizes both lower- and upper-body muscles if you do it right. You use your calves, thighs, hips/buttocks, and abdominals as you propel yourself along, and you use your back, chest, shoulders, and arms if you make a conscious effort to do so.

ROWING MACHINE

The rowing machine does exactly what its name states: It simulates the rowing motion. In fact, if you've ever rowed a boat, you'll recognize the feeling as soon as you begin the workout. It isn't easy at first, but once you get used to it you'll surprise yourself with how quickly you build endurance. I remember the first time I tried it. I only lasted seven minutes. But the next time I doubled my workout. By the end of the week, after a fourth try, I was rowing for thirty minutes! Of course, I was already in aerobic shape from other exercises.

Naturally, the rowing machine stresses mainly upper-body muscles: back, chest, shoulders, and arms. You can build a nice amount of upper-body strength doing this exercise. I must remind you, however, that you cannot hope to reshape an upper-body part with this aerobic exercise. You must work out with weights the right way in order to do that! The machine is set up in such a way that your hips, buttocks, and legs are doing a small amount of work, but not enough to build any lower-body strength. The calves are completely left out of the workout.

JOGGING AT A SLOW PACE

Years ago, when running first became popular, whether people ran or jogged they called it "jogging." But over time, the term *jogging* came to mean running at a slow or leisurely pace.

Jogging can be a very relaxing, enjoyable exercise. In fact, it is so relaxing that the people who do it often appear to be half asleep! Every time I see a jogger padding by I have to bite my tongue because I feel like quipping, "Now don't strain yourself." In fact, if you want to know whether you're jogging or running, think of that image. If someone were to see you, would they be tempted to say that to you?

Jogging is the halfway point between walking and running, yet notice that you don't burn as many calories doing it as you would racewalking. Why? When you racewalk, even though your feet don't

spring off the ground, you really push it. You're straining every muscle in your body to propel yourself along as quickly as possible without catapulting yourself off the ground. In addition, you're using a marching movement, swinging your bent arms back and forth and flexing your muscles all the time. When you jog, on the other hand, speed is not the issue. Even though you do spring off the ground with each step, you spring in a very leisurely manner. In addition, when you jog, instead of making your arms work as hard as possible, you simply use them naturally.

Jogging employs mainly the lower-body muscles: calves, thighs, hips/buttocks, and abdominals. You do exercise your upper body—back, chest, shoulders and arms—but very lightly. If you have trouble with your bones and joints, just as in running, you will have to keep jogging to a limit, although jogging will provide slightly less stress on bones and joints than running because you are going slowly and not landing as hard. I am too impatient to jog. I'd rather run or walk at a quick pace.

BICYCLE RIDING (STATIONARY OR MOVING AT A MODERATE PACE)

I find riding the stationary bike while watching TV and keeping up with the current talk shows to be a painless way of burning off some excess fat! I keep the tension low and pedal fast. (High tension may wear down hard-earned muscle.) I do it for about double the time I would do a more strenuous aerobic activity. To me it's worth the extra bike-riding time to burn off the same amount of calories because it's so relaxing. (I'll ride for forty minutes whereas if I ran, I would run for only twenty minutes.)

There are many fancy stationary bicycles available. They have monitoring devices that will tell you exactly how many calories you burned in a given time period, what your heart condition is for your age, and whether or not you defeated the computer "competitor." Such devices can be fun and can help the time to go by more quickly. From time to time I like to try them.

Many stationary bicycles have upper-body devices that allow you to move your arms along with your legs, giving you an upper-body workout along with your lower body. If you are already working your upper body with weights, like me, you may find that this addition is superfluous.

Riding the bicycle outdoors provides basically the same exercise as does the stationary bike; however, outdoor riding cannot be as consistent as the stationary bike. When you are outdoors you may have to

stop for pedestrians, dogs, traffic lights, obstacles in the road, and so on. On the other hand, outdoor riding can be more pleasurable. You get to breathe in the fresh air and fill your eyes with the wonders of nature. In addition, it can be more challenging, especially if your route includes hills.

Unless you are using the upper-body attachment on a stationary bike, bicycle riding exercises mainly the lower-body muscles, thighs and hips/buttocks, with a little exercise of the calves and abdominals. If you use the upper-body device on a stationary bicycle, you are also working your back, chest, shoulders, and arms.

POOL AEROBICS AND WATER WALKING

Pool aerobics and water walking are done in a group and can be lots of fun if you like the water. Some of the exercises are done in standing or lying positions (on the stomach or back). Others are done walking in the water. Pressure of the water against the working muscle provides the resistance for the workout. This type of exercise is very gentle on your joints, and is ideal for people who have arthritis or injuries and want to work out.

If you don't mind feeling a bit waterlogged and if you like working out in a group, this exercise can be a welcome change of pace. It provides a total-body workout, depending, of course, on the emphasis of the group leader. Back, chest, shoulders, arms, calves, thighs, hips/buttocks, and abdominals should all come into play.

DANCING AT A QUICK PACE

In order to count dancing as an aerobic activity, you'll have to keep it moving. In other words, if you go out socially to dance, you can't sit down—even for one number—until, say, twenty minutes are up. Since I take ballroom dance lessons that are one hour long and we don't stop moving for a minute, I can count my dancing as aerobic. However, I can do so only because the dances I do are quick paced. I do the fox-trot, tango, the peabody, the quick-step, swing, the samba, the mambo, the cha-cha, and the merengue—all fast-paced dances. But even the waltz, when done with fancy steps and energy, can be considered a quick-paced dance.

Most people don't do ballroom dancing, but rather "freestyle" or country and western dances. Freestyle dancing can be perfect for an aerobic workout because you are in complete control of your pace. Your partner is not connected to you. He or she is dancing nearby doing his or her own thing. You can move as quickly and as vigorously as you choose. You can leap up or, if you dare, even go down to the floor—or

do anything you please—and get the amount of calorie burning you choose.

Country and western dance is also perfect for quick-paced dancing that burns calories. If you do the two-step with energy or engage in any of the line dances, you are sure to burn a decent amount of fat.

Dancing provides a total-body workout. The lower-body muscles are employed with each step—calves, thighs, hips/buttocks, and abdominals—and the upper-body muscles—back, chest, shoulders, and arms—are moving to the rhythm of the music. And dancing is fun. You don't even think of it as a workout.

WALKING AT A QUICK PACE

Walking is by far the most convenient of all aerobic workouts. You do it anyway, so all you have to do is do it longer and more briskly, and you've got yourself a workout. In addition, you can do it anywhere, and in any clothing. And perhaps the best part is that, when you do it, nobody has to know you're exercising because you look as if you're just walking like anybody else, only you're moving at a brisk pace as if you have business to attend to.

I love to walk. That's when I do some of my best thinking. Whenever possible, I go early in the morning, at the crack of dawn. I smell the freshly cut grass and the fragrance of the flowers and trees and look at the cloud formations in the sky. And no matter where I am, I marvel at the wonder of God's creation. Whether I'm looking at the tall palm trees waving in the breeze or the barren, snow-covered branches of East Coast trees stripped of their foliage for the winter, I feel as if I'm in the middle of energy and life, and I'm revitalized. I often use this time to look up to God and say, "How am I doing?" And I try to center myself on the path that I should go.

Whether or not you are as philosophically inclined as I am, walking will provide you with a total-body workout—and without stress on your bones and joints. You'll work your lower body—calves, thighs, hips/buttocks, and abdominals—and your upper body—back, chest, shoulders, and arms. And you'll never feel as if you've strained yourself.

Additional Ways to Burn Fat

SPORTS

One of the most painless ways to burn additional fat is engaging in a favorite sport. You become absorbed in the competition of the game

(either with yourself or your partner) and before you know it, you've worked out for an hour or more. But there's one important thing to remember when it comes to using a sport as a part of your fitness regimen: Sports cannot reshape your body and they are rarely equivalent to an aerobic workout. Why?

When you perform a sport, you exercise a particular body part in a certain manner, as is required by the sport. For example, golfers exercise their shoulders and arms, but only at one or two angles. In fact, even though golfers do a lot of shoulder–arm work, I've never seen one who, unless he or she also works out with weights, has beautifully shaped shoulders or arms. The same holds true in any sport. Tennis players have one developed forearm, swimmers have broad backs, and soccer players have developed thighs and calves. But yet even these body parts are not developed and shaped to the best form. Other body parts are completely neglected.

But what about the aerobic effect of sports? Since a sport is rarely done at a continual pace (there are too many stop-and-goes), sports are not usually considered to be strictly aerobic. In addition, most people do not engage in their sport three or more times a week, the recommended amount of aerobic sessions for additional fat burning.

So then, what part do sports play in your fat-burning life? If you enjoy sports, then they should play a major role. I want you to pick a sport or two or even more, and play it as much as your schedule allows. The more you play, the more fat you will burn. However, don't fool yourself into believing that your sport is all that is required to be in shape.

For your information, here is a chart that shows approximately how many calories are burned after playing certain sports for one hour. This, of course, assumes that no breaks are taken.

Sport	Calories Burned per 60 Minutes
Walleyball	600
Racquetball	600
Handball	600
Squash	600
In-line skating	600
Basketball	570
Waterskiing	540
Downhill skiing	540
Rowing	540
Canoeing	540
Roller-skating	540

Sport	Calories Burned per 60 Minutes
Ice-skating	540
Tennis (singles)	480
Tennis (doubles)	420
Volleyball	420
Frisbee	420
Golf	315
Tai chi	300
Yoga	270

Keep in mind that the sport or activity must be done vigorously and nonstop in order to burn the amount of calories in the chart. If you're half asleep, don't expect to reap the same benefit. In other words, if you're anything like me in volleyball and duck every time the ball comes near you, face it, you're not really even in the game! Also note that the chart is a generalization for people of medium height and weight. If you are a big person you will burn more calories than above. If you are a very small person, you may burn a little less than the chart above, but you can compensate for that by putting more energy into your movements.

When it comes to your sport, a general rule is, If you want to burn maximum fat, the goal is to keep on the move and to put everything you have into your moves! In other words, don't stand around in a re-laxed manner, even when waiting for the ball. Your body should be tensed from start to finish. Every muscle in your body should be flexed and on the alert. If this ruins the joy of your sport, don't force it. You'll still burn some fat if you play just for enjoyment, but not as much as you would otherwise.

HOUSEHOLD ACTIVITIES

You can burn more fat vacuuming the house than you can sitting on the couch and watching TV! With this in mind, perhaps you can mo-tivate yourself to clean the house more often. For example, if you sit and watch TV for a half an hour, you burn about fifty calories. If you vacuum the house, on the other hand, for the same amount of time, you burn about 105 calories. (Why do you burn any calories sitting and watching TV? Remember, we burn calories twenty-four hours a day—even while sleeping. Breathing itself requires the expenditure of energy. It takes about 2/3 of a calorie to one calorie a minute just to breathe as you sleep!)

But what if you're lazy and just the thought of spending a half

hour cleaning or doing other work around the house makes you want to go to the refrigerator and eat? Then just do the chore for ten minutes. You'll still burn some fat. Here is a chart of common household chores and the fat you will burn in ten minutes of work.

Household Activity	Calories Burned Per 10 Minutes
Shoveling snow	125
Washing the walls	100
Painting the walls	90
Washing the car	90
Mowing the lawn	85
Washing the dog	65
Trimming the hedges	50
Weeding the garden	48
Cleaning the windows	40
Mopping the floor	38
Polishing the furniture	38
Vacuuming	35
Raking	35
Dusting	30

DURING THE DAY AT HOME OR OFFICE

You can also burn additional calories during a normal given day. Whether you are at home or in the office, try to do following:

1. Never sit still for more than one hour. If you find yourself sitting at the kitchen table, on the couch, or at a desk, get up and walk around. If possible, stay on your feet five to ten minutes before you sit again.

2. Take a ten-minute walk after each meal! You don't have to do it the moment you finish eating, but within fifteen minutes of the end of your meal, begin your walk. You don't have to walk at a brisk pace. Walk at a leisurely tempo and enjoy yourself, but get moving for that ten minutes. It makes a difference. You'll have to think ahead if you're going to do this at your lunch break at work—and allow the time. Instead of sitting down for the entire hour, get up ten minutes earlier and walk! If you're home and have young children who can't be left, then walk around the house for ten minutes or ride the stationary exercise bike.

3. When talking on the telephone, stand half the time you would ordinarily sit. In other words, if you are used to sitting for ten minutes while talking to your mother on the telephone, sit the

first five minutes and then stand up. After another five minutes, you can sit again. Does this sound crazy? In a way it is, but then so is the whole business of keeping fat off your body in the sedentary world we live in.

4. If you live in an apartment building or work in an office where there are stairs and you feel it is safe, take the stairs rather than the elevator. If you take the subway or bus to work and if your job requires that you sit all day, refuse a seat and stand. Also, when taking the subway, never use the escalator. Take the stairs.

5. When parking your car in a mall, etc., instead of driving around for ten minutes looking for the spot closest to your destination, take a spot that has fewer cars (you may even avoid a fender-bender) and walk the extra distance.

6. In general, remember: It's better to move than be stagnant. It's better to sit up and watch TV than to lie down. It's better to stand up and talk on the telephone than to sit. It's better to walk around the room while talking on the phone than to stand still. It's better to walk quickly from one part of the house to another than to drag along.

7. Remember, in order to burn up one pound of fat, you must use up 3,500 calories. The more active you are, the more calories you burn. Instead of using this information to torture yourself, try to precondition yourself to think action rather than stagnation. Then you'll find yourself automatically choosing the movement mode rather than the vegetation mode. In time it will pay off and you won't think you had to suffer for it.

8. Take your dog on an *extra* walk each day.

But new habits must be established before they become automatic and comfortable. In the beginning you'll be self-conscious about forcing yourself to be more active, and you may resent it. Realize that this too shall pass, and before you know it, you'll be a more energetic person, and it will be more natural for you to move than to be still! Soon people will ask you, "Where do you get all that energy?"

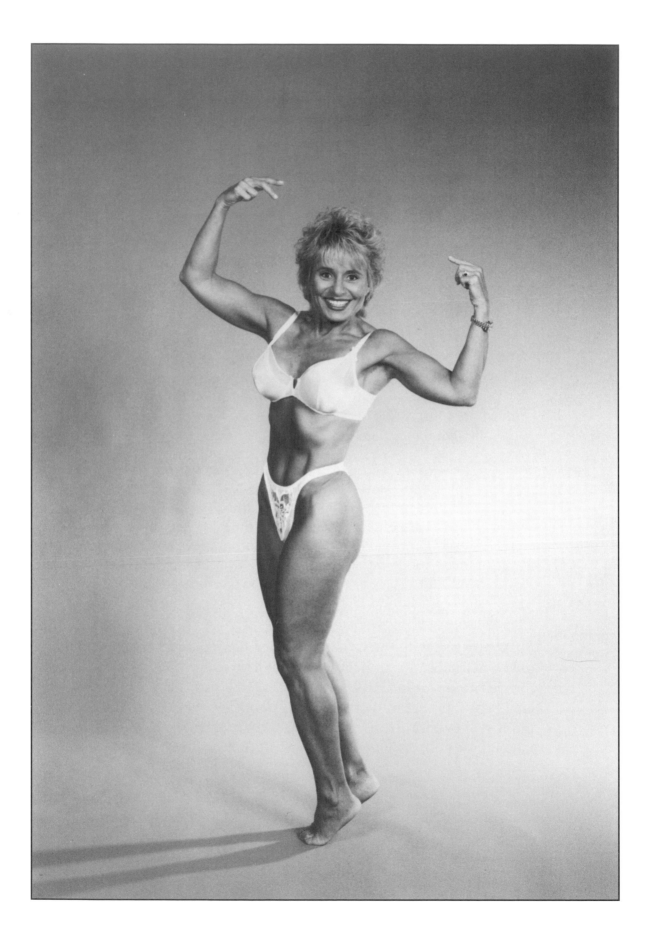

9

COSMETIC SURGERY AND FAT

If it were possible to get your body in shape with cosmetic surgery, every wealthy woman in the world would have the most beautiful figure possible. Think about it for a moment! Cosmetic surgery is obviously available, and the only thing stopping a person (short of the normal fear of any surgery) is money. With that out of the way, why not do it?

The truth is that many women do it—and not just those with money to spare. Many women go so far as to go into debt in order to get cosmetic surgery in the hope of finally having the body of their dreams. But instead of ending up with the body of their dreams, most of these women are sadly disappointed. There's just no way around it: In order to have a tight, toned, defined, beautifully shaped body at any age, you must work out a certain way. What you've learned in this book so far, and what you will learn in Chapter 10, will give you that body. Cosmetic surgery alone simply can't do it!

What? Am I saying that I am 100 percent against all cosmetic surgery when it comes to the body? No. I am saying that even with cosmetic surgery, you will still have to work out (as all reputable cosmetic surgeons will agree) if you want to be tight and toned—to have firm, defined muscles and to have a beautiful, shapely body. If this is the case, then who should get cosmetic surgery for the body? In my view, very few people. In the following paragraphs you'll find out who they are.

First we'll talk about the most popular form of body cosmetic surgery: liposuction. Then we'll discuss tummy tucks and all sorts of "lifts." In the end you will know what cosmetic surgery can and cannot do for your body.

One more thing. I must say that I am absolutely not against cosmetic surgery for the face, eyes, chin, and neck. Contrary to what you may have heard, these areas cannot be improved by exercise, and must be treated by surgery.

From time to time I get letters from readers asking me if facial and neck exercises can make them look younger. My answer is always no. In fact, the way I see it, facial and neck exercise can cause more lines on the face and neck! How so? When you exercise you not only get muscle, but you get "definition." And what is definition if it is not lines or delineation? The last thing you want on your face, neck, or chin are lines of delineation. And as for muscles on the face, neck, or chin, thankfully, it is very difficult to build them. I say thankfully because if you did build your facial muscles with exercise, you would have a chipmunk-looking face, a wrestler's thick neck, and a hulky, muscular double chin!

The same would go for eyes and brow. You could exercise these areas from now until next New Year's and, at best, nothing would happen. At worst, you would get "definition" or, to put it another way, more lines around your eyes and brow. The truth is that when it comes to the neck and above, unless you want to let those areas age gently with time, the cosmetic surgeon is your best bet. As for me, when the time comes, I shall visit the cosmetic surgeon for facial work without hesitation and age gently with time—only a little more slowly than I would otherwise.

Liposuction: Fat Removal from the Hips, Buttocks, Thighs, or Abdominal Area

Liposuction has been billed as the magic formula for getting rid of excess body fat! The technical terms for this procedure are *suction lipectomy* or *suction-assisted lipectomy*. It is an operation that permanently removes fat cells from specific areas of the body by sucking them out with small tubes. Depending upon how much fat is to be removed and how many areas are involved, the operation can take up to two hours. It is done most safely with an overnight stay in a hospital, and most comfortably, and safely, in my opinion, under general anesthesia. However, it can be done under local anesthesia with sedation in a doctor's office if only a very small area is to be suctioned.

Complete recovery takes about two weeks, although most doctors will suggest that you wait at least three weeks before you start to exercise.

HOW IT IS PERFORMED

The operation is performed by making tiny incisions (about an inch long) in the areas to be suctioned. A small tube is placed in the incision area and moved around in a back-and-forth motion to loosen the fat. The fat is then vacuumed out through the tube. The procedure is made easier and less painful by the injection of large volumes of cold saline water into the fatty tissue. (The water distends the area, making the fat suction more easily and more quickly.)

DO YOU REALLY NEED IT?

Cosmetic surgeons claim that the advantage of liposuction is that it removes a bulge of fat that stubbornly refuses to diminish, even after diet and exercise. But the question is, What kind of dieting and exercise has the potential liposuction patient done before she gives up? My experience with women who were about to get liposuction for thighs, hips, buttocks, and/or stomach tells me that, nine times out of ten—or more—while they may have dieted themselves down to the low-fat ideal body weight, they did not do the proper exercises. Most of them have tried endless aerobics and/or lengthy abdominal and/or hips-butt-thighs classes where they do a series of exercises for these body parts that are not the most effective way to sculpt the body.

When I encourage these women to work out in the way described in this and my other books, they come back in six months to a year and tell me, "I never would have believed it. I was about to get liposuction and now my thighs are firm and defined—and most of the cellulite is gone," or "My stomach is finally getting tight and toned—and I see definition all over. I'm going to keep doing your workout instead of getting surgery," or "Thank God I didn't get liposuction on my buttocks. All I needed was your hips/butt and thigh workout." (Some thigh exercises also lift and shape the buttocks.)

Am I saying that liposuction is an unnecessary operation, period, and in every case it can be eliminated by diet and exercise? No. The truth is that, while in most cases if you follow my workout plan to a T, in time your body will look better than it would had you had liposuction and not exercised, there are certain cases where, after all is said and done, there will still be a small, annoying pocket of fat that stubbornly remains. But even in such cases, often it is only because the person needs to lose those last few pounds of fat.

For example, if I didn't know better, I would think that I needed liposuction on my lower stomach. Why? In spite of all my exercise, when I am even a pound or two overweight, my lower belly protrudes!

However, when I diet down and get rid of that last pound of excess fat, my lower belly is absolutely flat. So I would never get liposuction.

WHAT LIPOSUCTION CAN AND CANNOT DO

But what if even after you've done the workout as prescribed in my books and dieted down to that last pound of excess fat, you still have a pocket or two of unsightly fat on your body? Should you get liposuction or should you just live with it? The choice is yours. I would live with it. But if you do decide upon liposuction, remember one thing: Liposuction cannot make your body firm, nor can it give you definition. You must still work out in order to do that. (Only muscle makes the body firm and defined. Liposuction simply removes fat. It cannot create muscle.)

THE IDEAL TIME TO GET LIPOSUCTION

For optimum results, you must get it when you are already dieted down to your ideal weight. Why? The operation is limited to the amount of tissue that can be removed at one time safely. (Fat cells do not multiply when you gain weight; they merely get bigger.) When you are at your thinnest, your fat cells are at their smallest in size and the surgeon can remove the greatest number of cells. (If, on the other hand, you were at your fattest, your fat cells would be larger in size and the surgeon would only be able to remove a certain amount of tissue safely and would be forced to leave behind many fat cells. This would mean that you would remain partially fat, or need another operation.)

WHEN YOU GAIN A FEW POUNDS THE FAT HAS TO GO SOMEWHERE!

There's a big problem when it comes to getting liposuction. If you gain weight at any time in your life, even a few pounds (and if you are human, trust me, you will), since the fat can never return to the area from which the fat cells were removed, it must go somewhere else—and you never know where it will go. Let me explain.

Suppose you had liposuction on your butt. Years ago, before I started working out, I was thinking of getting my butt made smaller by liposuction. But then I read that the fat cells would go somewhere else if I gained weight. I already knew that my last bit of fat tends to go to my lower stomach. I pictured yet more fat landing on that area—and I envisioned myself looking pregnant twelve months of the year. So I decided not to do it. Later, after working out, my butt was lifted and shaped by the workout and I'm delighted with it.

You could think positive and believe that if you gain weight, the fat will go where you want it to go—for example, to your breasts and nowhere else. But while this could happen, it's as likely as winning the lottery. You could think another way and say, "Okay. I'll beat the system. I'll have liposuction on my butt, my hips, my thighs, and my stomach. This way the fat can never return to any of those areas." Fine. But as mentioned above, if you gain weight, you will store excess body fat somewhere. The fat may go to your neck, your ankles, your knees, or it may form itself in a jelly roll around your lower back. In any case, it *will* appear and, chances are, in a most inconvenient place. You may find yourself wishing that you'd never had the liposuction; at least this way, when you gained weight, you would not have to worry about looking misshapen.

Don't mind me. I'm a pessimist when it comes to cosmetic surgery to shape the body! I'm sure you could have a positive experience. But I do want you to keep in mind the very real issues when it comes to this decision.

WHAT ABOUT CELLULITE?

Finally, can liposuction remove cellulite? Until recently, no! When the excess fat was removed by liposuction, the craterlike appearance of the skin remained. However, some cosmetic surgeons claim that recent advances in the process of fat removal now allow the surgeon to break the fibrous bridges that cause the dimpled look of cellulite. Not every cosmetic surgeon is aware of this procedure, however. It was discovered by Brazilian and Italian surgeons.

Once again, I must emphasize that by proper diet and correct working out, you can get rid of most, if not all, of your cellulite. As you diet, the fat diminishes. As you work out, you create a muscle under the skin. In time, this muscle creates a smooth area and the skin over it is no longer dimpled and craterlike. (See pp. 3–4 for a review of this subject.)

One more point. Depending upon how much fat you've had removed, the body part that had liposuction may sag down and need further surgery, a "lift," to get rid of the excess skin. For example, you may need a tummy tuck, a mini tummy tuck, a thigh or butt lift, and so on. A competent surgeon will help you to avoid this problem by giving you an accurate evaluation in the first place so that you can get what is needed done at the same time and not have to go back for further surgery.

BEWARE: YOUR SKIN CAN BECOME DISCOLORED

Even if you have the best surgeon available anywhere, you may have permanent skin discoloration in the areas where you've had liposuction. In other words, you may have patches of blotchy brown coloration on your stomach, hips, buttocks, thighs—anywhere where fat was sucked from your skin. Your doctor will speak to you to find out what your odds are of having this problem; however, he or she cannot tell for sure. It is always a risk.

Full and Mini Tummy Tucks

A full tummy tuck is the most drastic surgery discussed in this chapter. The technical name for it is *abdominal lipectomy with repair of diastasis recti, resection of lipocutaneous excess, and repair of umbilical or abdominal hernia.* The operation involves the removal of excess body fat around the entire upper and lower abdominal area, the sewing up of loose muscle to tighten that area, the removal of excess skin, and the necessary repositioning of the navel. The operation takes two to three hours and is always performed in a hospital. It usually requires a two-to-three-day stay in the hospital.

The healing process is about four to six weeks. You should wait at least six to eight weeks before you resume your full exercise program.

HOW IT IS PERFORMED

The operation is performed by first removing the excess fat around the entire abdominal area, just as is done by liposuction described above. Next, the deep layer of fat is separated from the abdominal muscle, from the top of the muscle down to the navel. The skin is then freed from the navel and the surrounding area, all the way to the ribs. Now, with a clear field to work on the abdominal muscles, the surgeon pulls the stretched muscle together by stitching it down the middle from the ribs to the pubic bone. After that, excess skin is pulled tight and removed.

You will have a scar in the lower abdominal area that may remain lumpy, firm, and red for up to eighteen months. The scar is in the best possible of places, just above the pubic bone and running across to either side of your body. Even in a skimpy bikini, no one would see it!

DO YOU REALLY NEED IT?

In my opinion, women who may need this operation are those who, through many pregnancies, have damaged muscles to the point

where they are unable to respond to exercise. You will know whether or not this applies to you if you have dieted down to your proper weight and, in addition, have done the workout in this book or that found in *Gut Busters* or in my *Bottoms Up Workout: Middle Body* video for one year, with little or no results. (Chances of this happening are very slim—98 percent of the women who've written to me thinking that they fall into this category find out to their delight that after working out for a year, they see major improvement and opt to keep going with the exercise.)

WHAT A FULL TUMMY TUCK CAN AND CANNOT DO

A full tummy tuck can remove vast amounts of excess fat from your entire abdominal area and flatten that area to some extent, but it cannot give you a completely flat abdominal area, nor can it give you definition. Don't even dream that a tummy tuck can give you "washboard abs." For that you will have to do exercises after your stomach heals enough so that you can exercise. (Note that all surgeons agree that in order to obtain a firm, defined stomach, it is also necessary to begin a regular exercise regimen for the stomach and to continue that regimen for life!)

THE IDEAL TIME TO GET A FULL TUMMY TUCK

If you are going to get a tummy tuck, it's most important that you wait until you are finished with pregnancies. Otherwise, your repaired muscles may stretch again and you'll have to undergo more surgery. In addition, it's important that you try to shape up your stomach muscles as much as possible before the operation. If you do this, you will heal in less time than you would otherwise heal and will be able to exercise more quickly after surgery.

BEWARE: IF YOU GET REALLY FAT, YOU COULD AGAIN STRETCH
OUT YOUR MUSCLES

We've already discussed what may happen if you get pregnant again after a tummy tuck, but gaining a lot of weight (fifty or more pounds) can be just as damaging. You can stretch out your muscles once again and have to go through the surgery all over. The truth is, if you're not planning to go into a lifetime diet and exercise program, it's not a good idea to get a tummy tuck.

MINI TUMMY TUCK

A mini tummy tuck is much less drastic than a full tummy tuck. In essence, it is a tummy tuck for the area below the waistline only. The technical name for it is *modified abdominal sipectom with repair of inferior diastasis rectus and resection of lipocutaneous excess*. In this operation, excess fat is removed from the lower abdominal area, the lower abdominal muscles are sewn and tightened, and excess skin is removed.

The operation takes one to two hours and, in my opinion, it should always be done with at least an overnight stay in a hospital and under general anesthesia, although some doctors will perform it in an office using local sedation. It takes about four to six weeks before you can return to your normal activities.

HOW IT IS PERFORMED

The fat is suctioned from your lower stomach area in the same way as is done with liposuction. The rest of the operation follows the same procedures as a full tummy tuck, only instead of pulling the skin away from both the upper and lower abdominal area, sewing up the entire abdominal muscle, and cutting a volume of skin, the surgeon works only on the lower abdominal area, and there is less trauma to the body. The result is a much smaller scarring area; however, just as in a regular tummy tuck, your scarred area may remain lumpy, firm, and red for up to eighteen months. The scar runs horizontally across the pubic bone area. The navel is not moved in this operation.

DO YOU REALLY NEED IT?

If your lower stomach protrudes no matter how much exercise you do—and if you've followed this workout, *Gut Busters*, or *The Bottoms Up Workout: Middle Body* video for a year—and have dieted down to your ideal weight and if you have a small pot on your lower belly along with a pocket of skin sagging above your pubic bone, you may want to consider this operation. Frankly, I've encouraged many women to take up my challenge and give it a year of following my workout. The result is that the only women who ended up getting surgery were those who told me flat out that they didn't have the patience to wait a year to see what would happen. Since they had the money and the inclination, they decided that they would get the operation and then do the workout.

WHAT A MINI TUMMY TUCK CAN AND CANNOT DO

This operation will give you a somewhat flatter, tighter lower abdominal area. It will in no way affect your upper abdominals. However, the operation will not give you a lower abdominal area that is flat as a board, nor will it produce defined muscle. It only tightens your existing muscle.

THE IDEAL TIME TO GET A MINI TUMMY TUCK

As with a full tummy tuck, you should wait until you are finished with pregnancies before undergoing this operation, otherwise your repaired muscles and tucked skin may stretch again, and you'll have to get more surgery. Also as with the full tummy tuck, be sure that you don't gain a great deal of weight again—or your hard-earned money and investment of precious time and energy in this operation may be wasted.

Hip, Thigh, and Butt Lifts

The technical term for this operation is *resection of lipocutaneous excess of hips, thighs, and buttocks,* or *body contouring of hips, thighs, and buttocks.* The operation is designed to tighten loose and/or "hanging" skin on these areas. The operation is always done in a hospital (the stay is one to two nights) under general anesthesia.

Complete recovery takes about two weeks, although most doctors will suggest that you wait three to four weeks before you resume a full exercise program.

HOW IT IS PERFORMED

The body part being "lifted" has been premarked either the night before or an hour before surgery. The surgeon then makes incisions in the marked areas and injects a dilute epinephrine (adrenaline) into them to limit excessive bleeding. Then, following the markings, the surgeon removes the excess skin down to the muscle and, along with it, usually a thick layer of fat under the skin. If it is your thigh that is being lifted, your thigh skin is raised as high as possible on your leg. The excess skin is later cut off and the wound is sewn up. The same is done for the buttocks or hips: Excess skin is pulled down or aside, and later cut off and the wound sewn up.

DO YOU REALLY NEED IT?

The "lift" type of cosmetic surgery on the hips, thighs, and butt is in my opinion, the least necessary cosmetic surgery available. Working out, particularly with weights, is a far more effective remedy to sagging flesh than any cosmetic surgery.

I have never seen a woman using one of my exercise routines who has not been able to lift her thighs, hips, or buttocks. If you have thighs that sag significantly, you may have to use heavier weights than the five-pound dumbbells suggested in this book. In fact, you may want to switch to my book *Now or Never*, or *Top Shape*, at least for thigh work—and use a barbell and a squat rack for heavier thigh work. If you do this, in time, not only will you have performed a wonderful thigh lift (without any stitches), but your thighs will gain a beautiful shape that no surgical process could ever duplicate. It will take six months to a year to complete this "operation."

The same holds true for the hips and buttocks, and in fact, it is the same exercises—squats and lunges done with heavy weights—that lift the skin on the hips/buttocks area. So if your thighs, hips, or buttocks have hanging skin and you find that the *Bathing Suit Workout* or the workouts with lighter weights don't do it, go to *Now or Never* and follow the heavy-duty thigh workout there—with the goal of gradually building up to the heavier weights—and you will solve your problem.

Am I saying that thigh, hip, and butt lifts are never needed? No. In cases where medical reasons prevent an individual from working out with weights, then the surgery is the only way to lift the sagging skin. But in such cases you must realize that you cannot hope to get the same results you would get through working out.

WHAT HIP, BUTTOCK, AND THIGH LIFTS CAN AND CANNOT DO

As described above, surgical "lifts" can raise sagging skin so that it no longer hangs down in an unsightly manner. However, lifts can never make your body feel firm, nor can lifts give the lifted body part a pretty shape or definition. After all, lifts do not create muscles. In order to re-shape your thighs, hips, or buttocks, for example, the surgeon would have to use muscle implants. There has been some experimentation in these areas, but little success. And in any case, if they do perfect a way to implant muscle all over the body, we could be walking around with our own skeletons and a whole body of artificial muscle. I don't think the human body would stand for such a thing, do you? So I guess we'd better resign ourselves to shaping our bodies the way Nature intended—by exercising them, making muscles naturally—and keeping ourselves strong and healthy.

If you got your hip, butt, or thigh lift in the hope of showing off your new, "tight" body part, you may be sadly disappointed if you're not lucky when it comes to scarring. Even if your doctor is highly skilled in making sure that your scars are placed in the least noticeable areas, your scars can widen or shift. In addition, should you get an infection while in the healing process, the scars could become permanently lumpy. Can you imagine yourself wearing a bathing suit with ribbonlike scars under your buttocks and on your upper thighs? Not everyone will have this problem, but it's something to think about.

Making the Decision: To Do or Not to Do

Before you make the decision to get cosmetic surgery on your body, ask yourself the following questions and answer them honestly:

1. Does my medical doctor agree that I am physically incapable of working out with weights as described in my workout book? If he or she does not agree and says that you should try exercise, then:

2. Have I tried the workout for this body part for at least a year? If so, have I followed the workout exactly as written? Have I gradually raised my weights in order to create a muscle that would lift the skin? If you are still not satisfied with the results, then:

3. Is it important enough for me to spend the money that will be required for the operation? If you think it is, then ask yourself:

4. Am I willing to take the risks involved with the operation (scarring, discoloration, fat going to other places, future sagging if excessive weight is regained and then lost again, etc.)?

If after all of the above thinking you still want to get cosmetic surgery on your body, it is your choice. You have every right to do what you want to do. After all, it's your money, your body, and your life. No one should make your decisions for you.

Finding a Reputable Cosmetic Surgeon

First, if you are seriously thinking of cosmetic surgery, I suggest that you read the book *The Complete Book of Cosmetic Surgery*, or another complete guide to the cosmetic surgery of your choosing. Such a book

will give you a much more detailed understanding of what is involved in the operation you are considering. It will also give more particulars than I will give here on how to find a competent surgeon to perform the operation.

In the following paragraphs, I'll offer a brief outline of the "musts" to keep in mind before agreeing to an operation with a given doctor.

As shocking as it may seem, any doctor, as long as he or she is licensed by a given state to practice medicine, can call him- or herself a "cosmetic," or "plastic," surgeon. This doctor may have a general degree with no specialization in cosmetic surgery. For this reason, you must be sure that the doctor you choose is "board certified." But board certified by whom? The surgeon must be certified by a board approved by the American Academy of Facial Plastic and Reconstructive Surgery. If the doctor has such certification, you can be sure that he or she has spent many years studying and practicing specifically in the field of cosmetic surgery—and is not just a general doctor who happens to think he or she is talented in cosmetic surgery.

One of the best ways to find a cosmetic surgeon is by recommendation of someone who has had success with that surgeon. If you are lucky enough to know such a person, however, don't forget to ask the doctor if he or she is board certified as above—and, in fact, to ask to see his or her certification, which should certainly be hanging on the wall, prominently displayed.

If you really want to be sure of your surgeon's history, ask to see what is called his or her curriculum vitae. It will give a full report on his or her schooling, medical practice experience, etc. You can then count the years he or she has spent specifically studying cosmetic surgery, as well as the years he or she has spent practicing his or her art. (And cosmetic surgery is indeed an art! The way I see it, this doctor is really an artist, sculpting your face or body. In fact, I think talent, as well as skill, is needed.)

If you don't know where to find a doctor, call your county medical society. They will be happy to supply a list of qualified, board-certified surgeons in the area where you are considering surgery.

Another way to go is to get hold of a copy of *The Directory of Medical Specialists*, which is available at most libraries or on the Internet. It lists all board-certified surgeons according to their specialties and the area where they live. The book comes in a few volumes and can be intimidating. If you have trouble, don't hesitate to ask your librarian to help you. Librarians are wonderful people who delight in doing just that!

A Final Word about Cosmetic Surgery on the Body

Cosmetic surgery can lift skin and cut away the excess. It can suck out the fat cells from a given area. It can even, in some cases, sew together a loose muscle, tightening that muscle. But cosmetic surgery can never create muscles on your body, and it can never make you physically stronger. Only exercise can do that. Finally, cosmetic surgery cannot sculpt and shape your muscles into their most perfect form. So even if you do get cosmetic surgery, plan on working out. There's simply no substitute.

Joyce Vedral—the little chunky one—getting ready to snatch the ball!

10

KEEP IT OFF!
THIS MEANS THE FLAB!

You've taken the first step. You're in shape. What? How dare I say that getting in shape is only "the first step" after all the work you've done? Haven't you taken all the steps you need to take? No. *Getting in shape is only the initial step to a beautiful, fit, low-fat body for the rest of your life.* Steps two, three, four, five, and all the way to infinity are to follow as you heed the advice in this chapter.

In the following paragraphs, you will learn not only how to keep the beautiful body you have achieved, but also how to improve on that body. You'll discover ways to sculpt your physique so that not only your hips/butt, thigh, and abdominal areas look great, but your other body parts as well: chest, shoulders, back, biceps, triceps, and calves. But your goal will be not only to work out in order to get the rest of your body looking beautiful. It will also be to add muscle to your overall body, muscle that will create for you a fat-burning furnace that allows you to eat more without putting on weight. And don't worry. I'm not talking about hulking, masculine muscles. I'm referring to the petite, sexy, shapely muscles that give the body its best form. And speaking of form, look at my form at two years old! I'm the one eyeing the ball.

In addition, you'll want to work with weights so that you have an insurance policy against future bone thinning (osteoporosis). As mentioned in Chapter 7, my bones are almost double the density of women my age—and more dense than in-shape twenty-five-year-olds. So let's get started. First we'll talk about diet and then we'll discuss how to incorporate this workout with other weight-training workouts or how to switch to a different workout completely—for the sake of variety, for a lifetime of fitness.

Diet: Maintaining Your Low-Fat Body

Thankfully, as discussed in Chapter 7, once you've eliminated your excess body fat and like what you see in the mirror, you can eat anything you want once a week. But what if, for some reason, you throw all caution to the wind and eat what you will for months at a time—and find yourself carrying five, ten, or more pounds of fat on your body?

All is not lost. In fact, you are better off than you were when you started. At least now you have learned that gaining and losing body fat is not based upon luck and chance but is instead a very reliable science. Just as surely as the tide comes in and goes out again, when you eat more calories than you burn, you add body fat. When you burn more calories than you eat, you lose body fat. It's an immutable law of nature. It won't change no matter what you do.

It's an Emotional Issue

For most of us, weight gain is an emotional issue. When we cannot zip up our jeans, or when that form-fitting dress rides up around our hips, we don't just logically say to ourselves, "Oh well. I've eaten more calories than I've burned and I've stored some fat. I guess I'll have to reverse the process and start losing the stored fat." Instead we panic and imagine that not only will we never get rid of the fat, but we will continue to get fatter and fatter, no matter what we do.

We also imagine that no matter what we do the fat will never come off! It is our guilt that makes us feel this way. We condemn ourselves for not having been more alert, blame ourselves for not exercising more self-control. Instead of acknowledging the fact that overeating is both normal and human, we become angry with ourselves. We look at ourselves in repulsion and hatred. "You're disgusting," we think. "You have neither self-discipline nor self-respect," we accuse. These feelings and thoughts depress us. And when we feel depressed, we try to make ourselves feel better by—you guessed it—eating more.

Break the Cycle by Changing Your Thinking!

It's a vicious circle. But it can be stopped by changing our thought process, by getting back to logic and not psychological voodoo that dooms us to failure. Gaining weight is based upon very predictable laws of science.

Think about it. If you fill a glass beyond its capacity, the water flows over the rim. There is no chance that one day things are going to change and suddenly when you fill a glass beyond its capacity, the water is going to start piling itself up in the air. Ridiculous! Right? The same way, when you sip away at a drink of water, the water level goes down and down. As you use up the water, there is less in the glass. There is no way that one day while you're sipping a glass of water, you will suddenly be able to sip away forever and the water level will not go down and the water will eventually not be consumed.

So it is with excess body fat. There are scientific, unchanging laws that apply. You gained the weight according to the laws of nature, and you will lose the weight the same way. Don't panic. Talk to yourself. Realize that just as you gained the excess fat, slowly, consistently, over time, you will lose it. Go back to the eating plan in Chapter 7 until you reach your goal, then once again you can eat anything you want once a week. And if you've stopped working out, start up again. Which brings me to my next point.

Never Stop Working Out!

When it comes to working out, people ask me, "Will I have to do this for the rest of my life?" They say it as if they're being condemned to lifetime imprisonment. Their attitude is all wrong. Dreading exercise is like dreading getting out of bed every day. Regardless of how much you like to sleep, you've already resigned yourself to that necessity. If you remained in bed forever, you would get bedsores, your muscles would atrophy, your bones would thin. Your entire body would eventually deteriorate. The same attitude should apply to exercise.

Of course you must do it every day—or at least almost every day. Why? Most of us don't do enough exercise naturally and we need a regular exercise regimen to make up for that. We must incorporate a workout regimen into our daily life. So instead of looking at exercise as a life sentence, think of it as necessary maintenance—like brushing your teeth, taking a shower, and even eating.

It Doesn't Have to Be Boring

Even though your exercise regimens will become as natural as your daily hygienic routines, thankfully you can incorporate more variety into them than you can into brushing your teeth or taking a shower! (There are only so many ways to brush your teeth, and only so many varieties of bath and shower soaps, oils, perfumes, and sponges you can try.)

In the following paragraphs you'll find various workouts that you can switch to from time to time, for the rest of your life, so that you can stay in top shape and at the same time never be bored with your workout. But first I must point out that no matter which routines you decide to follow, it's important that eventually you add exercises for the body parts that are not working in your Bathing Suit Workout—otherwise your middle body will look tight, toned, sexy, and defined, but your upper body will look sad in contrast.

Adding the Rest of the Body Parts to Your Bathing Suit Workout

It's easy to make your workout complete. Just select one of the books listed below and add in the body parts you are not exercising in the Bathing Suit Workout, leaving out the hips/buttocks, thigh, and abdominal workout for that routine and continuing to do your Bathing Suit Workout for those body parts. Later, when you get bored with the Bathing Suit Workout, you can stop doing that routine and do any of the total-body workouts (they are all total-body workouts) listed below. Then later, if you choose, you can again go back to the Bathing Suit Workout and continue doing the rest of your body parts with one of the routines in this chapter.

The closest system to your Bathing Suit routine, and the one that will net you the highest muscle quality for your time investment, is the upper-body workout in the book *Bottoms Up!*, or *Definition* or *The Fat-Burning Workout*.

Both of these routines employ the method of the superset or "twin set." It is exactly the same method as you use in *The Bathing Suit Workout*, except instead of exercising three different body parts before you take a rest, you exercise only two body parts. For example, in *Bottoms Up!*, you do one set of chest exercises and one set of shoulder exercises. Then you take a fifteen-second rest and repeat the sequence until you have finished those two exercises. You then move to the next two exercises for chest and shoulders, and so on, until you have completed your entire chest-shoulder routine. You then move to the next combination, arms—and you "twin-set" biceps and triceps. Finally, you combine back and calves (yes, the one lower body part that makes me a liar! You are not really working only upper body, but calves were left out of your Bathing Suit Workout, and they are paired with the back in *Bottoms Up!*).

If you are doing the Bathing Suit Workout, you will of course leave out the lower- and middle-body routine of *Bottoms Up!* It is an excellent

routine and a welcome change to your Bathing Suit Workout, and after, say, three months, you may want to switch completely to that workout. But for now, simply add in the six missing body parts as mentioned above: chest/shoulders, biceps/triceps, and back and calves.

If you choose to do the workout in *Definition*, you will be using the same method—supersetting—but within the same body part, and your combinations will be different, and some of the exercises will also be different. In addition, instead of doing three sets per body part, you'll be doing five. If you choose to do the Fat-Burning Workout, you'll be doing the giant set but with different exercises and different combinations. Review Chapter 2 and see which workouts the before-and-after women did for the upper body.

I advise you to pick one or the other immediately and add it to your Bathing Suit routine. Along with your Bathing Suit routine, do that for three to six months. Then stop doing your Bathing Suit routine and do the total body workout in that book. If you want an intense workout for your hips/buttocks, thigh, and abdominal areas, do the entire workout in *Bottoms Up!* If you want a less intense but yet very effective workout for those areas, do the entire workout found in workout level 4 of *Weight Training Made Easy*, or use my book *Definition*.

What to Do as Time Goes By!

Okay. Fine. But what do you do as the years go by? Do you have to keep up that same old routine, doing your Bathing Suit Workout but adding the missing body parts from either of the above books and from time to time stopping the Bathing Suit Workout and doing the entire workout from one of the above books? No. Thankfully, you have a choice of many other effective workouts that will not only give you the feeling of variety, but in addition will help to perfect your body still further and provide a workout that will suit your specific life situation. At any time, you can do the Bathing Suit Workout for hips/buttocks, thighs, and abdominals and add in the routines for the missing body parts—chest, shoulders, biceps, triceps, and calves—found in any of the books listed below, or you can stop doing the Bathing Suit Workout and do the total-body workout found in any of the books listed below.

From Shortest to Longest—From Least Muscle to Most Muscle

Except for *Weight Training Made Easy*, which is presented last, the workouts presented below are given in the order of least time consuming to most time consuming—and from the least muscle yielding to the most muscle yielding. For intensity or difficulty, see the particular descriptions. Note that the three specialized workouts are discussed separately.

THE 12-MINUTE TOTAL-BODY WORKOUT

The 12-Minute Total-Body Workout is the least intimidating of all of my workout books. It allows you to become acquainted with exercising the rest of your body with weights without asking you to commit a whole lot of time. All you need is twelve minutes a day.

You need only one set of three-pound dumbbells in order to do the workout and, in fact, since you create your own force by flexing your muscles hard (isometric pressure), you could actually do the workout with no weights. For this reason, it is also ideal for traveling.

Although this workout does not increase muscle size at all unless you have very underdeveloped muscles, it does produce what all women want: firmness or "muscle hardness." And it is so simple to perform that you wonder how it could be so effective.

You exercise each body part individually, doing two exercises for each body part—three sets each. You do ten repetitions for each set. But in order to make up for the fact that you are using very light weights, you must create your own "work" by using "dynamic tension" and "isometric pressure." In other words, you continually put force on the working muscle by flexing and tensing it throughout the movement. Because of the continual flexing and tensing, every muscle fiber participates in each movement—and, in turn, your muscles become more firm.

If you want to begin a total-body workout and you feel a bit intimidated about starting, this would be the ideal place to begin. I do it myself for weeks at a time when I am burned out and feel like having an easier workout. I also use it when I'm on the road and don't have access to weights. As mentioned above, you could either add this to your Bathing Suit Workout, leaving out the hips/buttocks, thighs, and abdominals, or you could stop doing the Bathing Suit Workout for a while and simply do the entire 12-Minute Total-Body Workout.

DEFINITION: SHAPE WITHOUT BULK IN FIFTEEN MINUTES A DAY

Definition does exactly what it says: It gives you paramount definition and muscle shaping without adding much muscle size. You burn maximum fat while working out—and in fact, if you don't take your optional rests, the workout is completely aerobic. You go so fast that you can do it in fifteen minutes a day. What's more, if you choose you can double up with this workout and do your entire body in one day. Your time investment of thirty minutes will allow you to work out only three days a week. Other than *Top Shape*, which allows men to do this only if they are not exercising their legs, it's the only other book I've written that allows only three days of working out.

Use *Definition* if you're looking for a greater challenge than *The 12-Minute Total Body Workout* and you want to burn the utmost amount of fat and get more delineation.

For this workout, you do five sets of each exercise as you utilize the workout principal called the full pyramid system. With this method, you add weight to each of your first three sets, then decrease the weight for your last two sets, until you return to your original weight, for a total of five sets. (This is the only one of my books that utilizes the full pyramid system.) You use three sets of very light dumbbells, perhaps ones, twos, and threes (heavier if you are strong enough). You work in "speed supersets," doing one set each of two different exercises for the same body part and then, without resting, raising your weight and repeating the sequence, and so on, until all five supersets (ten sets in all) have been completed.

Since there are five sets per body part, only two exercises per body part provide a complete and intense workout. However, an optional two exercises per body part are given for those who wish to be Wonder Women or Dragon Ladies.

THE FAT-BURNING WORKOUT

The Fat-Burning Workout takes twenty minutes to do (there are optional "intensity" and "insanity" workouts that add ten minutes each to the workout). This workout allows for more muscle development than *Definition*, yet it still allows you to burn maximum fat. You do the workout by using what is called the giant set. Here, you do one set each of three different exercises for the same body part before taking a fifteen-second rest. You will notice that you did something similar in your Bathing Suit Workout. You did one set each of three different exercises before taking a fifteen-second rest, only you did one set each of

three different exercises for three different body parts: hips/buttocks, thighs, and abdominals. In *The Fat-Burning Workout*, you work within the body part. (For example, you would do one set each of three different exercises for thighs before taking a fifteen-second rest.)

This workout utilizes the modified pyramid system. It requires that you go up the pyramid, adding weight to each of your first three sets. Then you stop. By way of contrast, with *Definition*, you were required to do the full pyramid system, where you not only ascend the pyramid but also descend it. (In that workout, you are asked to go down the pyramid, doing two additional sets by decreasing the weight until you return to your original weight.)

The Fat-Burning Workout is less intense than *Definition*. You are allowed to rest after three sets rather than after ten sets! In *Definition*, not only are you using the "true pyramid," which requires that you do five sets before you take a rest, but you are also speed-supersetting two exercises (see above) so with that workout, you are actually doing ten sets before you take a rest.

The Fat-Burning Workout asks you to use three-, five-, and eight-pound dumbbells, but you don't have to go that high. You can start with dumbbells as light as one, two, and three pounds and gradually increase your weights. Also, as with any other of my workouts, over time you can increase your weights still further.

With this workout, you can get more muscle than with either *The 12-Minute Total-Body Workout* or *Definition*—but don't worry, not the bulky kind, but sexy, defined, taut muscle.

If you decide to do this workout, it's very important that you get and read the book first, even though you can also purchase this workout in video! There are many important tips in the book, and the book provides motivational talk.

The video is no longer available in stores, so you can order it by writing to me at my P.O. box. Volume I is a forty-minute video that has only the regular workout. (You will not do forty minutes a day, but twenty minutes for upper body on workout day one, and the other twenty minutes for lower body on workout day two, and so on.) Volume II is an eighty-minute video that has the intensity and insanity workouts. (Again, you will not do an eighty-minute workout in one day, but will divide your workout into days one and two.)

If you have gone past the regular workout, you won't need Volume I—just Volume II. See p. 199 for prices and ordering information.

THE COLLEGE DORM WORKOUT

You don't have to go to college to do it! The College Dorm Workout takes only twenty minutes to do! It is very similar to The Fat-Burning Workout, only even less complicated, and you get slightly less muscle and definition than you do with The Fat-Burning Workout. You never have to raise your weight (you don't use the pyramid system, or even the modified pyramid system). You use one set of five-pound dumbbells for sets of all exercises. What's more, you don't even need an exercise bench. The workout was designed for people with a small workout area. All you need is a chair, the floor, yourself, the dumbbells, and a five-by-six-foot space!

For this workout, you do three exercises for each body part—ten repetitions each. You "giant set," just as in *The Fat-Burning Workout*, doing one set each of three different exercises for a given body part before you take a rest. Only, as stated above, instead of doing your next set with a higher weight, you continue to work with the same weight. But in order to compensate for the lack of added weight, you are asked to squeeze your working muscle as hard as possible throughout the movement, utilizing the principles of "dynamic tension" and "isometric pressure" as is used in *The 12-Minute Total-Body Workout*.

In addition, the book provides handy tips on eating in difficult situations. What is described for college-life eating scenarios—parties, cafeterias with limited offerings, etc.—can be applied to other situations—restaurants, eating dinner at people's homes, etc. Except for *Gut Busters*, the book is smaller, less expensive, and less intimidating than any of my other books.

BOTTOMS UP!

Bottoms Up! takes twenty minutes to do if you don't take your optional rests; otherwise it takes about thirty minutes, unless you choose the optional Wild Woman and Terminator workouts, which add ten minutes each to the workout. This workout allows for more muscle development than any of the above workouts—yet, because you are rarely resting, it allows you to burn maximum fat. (You can't build hulky muscles with this or any of my workouts. I'm talking about firm, sexy muscles here!)

You are able to develop more muscle with this workout because of the way you work out. Instead of bombing away at one body part with multiple sets, you are constantly switching back and forth between two body parts. You are not stopping your workout by taking rests but, on the other hand, you are allowing certain body parts to rest: While one

body part is working, another body part is resting. As mentioned above, it is most similar to your Bathing Suit Workout, only here you are exercising two body parts at a time, whereas in the Bathing Suit Workout you exercise three body parts at a time.

This workout requires that you work in twin sets, where you do one set of, say, a hips/buttocks exercise and then, without resting, one set of a thigh exercise, and so on. But *Bottoms Up!* provides a more intense workout for the lower and middle body than for the upper body. Seven twin sets are required for lower, five for middle, and three for upper (although Wild Woman and Terminator options are given, to extend the upper-body challenge).

The workout utilizes the modified pyramid system (the same as is used in *The Fat-Burning Workout*). You gradually increase your weight for the first three sets, using three-, five-, and ten-pound dumbbells. (Of course you can start with lower weights and work your way up, eventually to as high as ten-, fifteen-, and twenty-pound dumbbells.)

Even if you love the Bathing Suit Workout, after a while it's a good idea to switch to the entire *Bottoms Up!* workout, *The Fat-Burning Workout*, or *Definition*. You'll be hitting your hips/buttocks, thighs, and abdominals from different angles and, in time, improving your shape even more—because muscles need a change to be challenged.

In addition to being in book form, this workout is on video on three volumes: *The Bottoms Up Workout: Lower Body; The Bottoms Up Workout: Middle Body;* and *The Bottoms Up Workout: Upper Body.* But don't just get the videos. You must first read the book for motivation, the diet, and other important information. You can purchase the videos by writing to me at my P.O. box. See p. 199.

TOP SHAPE

Top Shape is billed as a men's book. In fact, the byline reads, "Now Joyce shows men what to do." Yet the book is a women's workout as well as a man's workout! The reason I addressed the book to men is that there are some things that men do differently than women. First, they don't have to exercise their hips/buttocks area the way we do. They get enough of a butt workout when they do thigh exercises such as squats and lunges. Also, since men can eat more than women and still lose body fat, there is a special diet just for men in this book. Other than that, women can follow the book. This book allows you to build more muscle than any book yet discussed.

Since *Top Shape* is my only book that has a machine workout using a home gym machine (as well as a dumbbell workout, of course), you may find this book very helpful if you have a home gym machine and

wish to do the machine substitutes listed in all of my books. In addition, *Top Shape* has a regular dumbbell workout that allows more rests than any of the above workouts—and in this sense it is the least exhausting.

The workout takes thirty minutes and is done four to six days a week. It allows you to rest fifteen seconds after each and every set of exercises. It utilizes the modified pyramid system as is used in *The Fat-Burning Workout* and *Bottoms Up!*, where you add weight to each of three sets. Men begin with three-, five-, and ten-pound dumbbells or higher, depending on their beginning strength, and work their way up to as high as twenty-five, thirty, or thirty-five pounds or higher. Women begin at the same weight or lighter, and usually work up to no higher than ten-, fifteen-, and twenty-pound dumbbells. (If you are using machines, you will follow the specific machine-weight advice.)

The workout is similar to the next book I'll talk about, *Now or Never*, but with different exercises, and this is an excellent book to switch to if you are doing *Now or Never* and want to continue to build muscle but are getting bored with the exercises. Keep in mind, however, that if you switch to *Top Shape* you will have to add in a hips/buttocks routine from one of my other workouts, and that for women the thigh routine is not optional! (Many men feel that they don't want to use weights to exercise their legs since their lower body is rarely seen in public and they run or play a sport that, at least to some extent, exercises their legs. Therefore, I've made the lower-body workout optional for the men!)

NOW OR NEVER

Like *Top Shape*, *Now or Never* is a less intense workout than *Definition*, *The Fat-Burning Workout*, or *Bottoms Up!* But it allows you to develop more of a muscle base than any other workout yet discussed (except *Top Shape*, which allows an equal amount or more of muscle building).

The workout takes forty minutes if you shorten the thirty-second rests to fifteen seconds. Otherwise, it takes a full hour. You begin working with three-, five-, and ten-pound dumbbells and work your way up to ten-, fifteen-, and twenty-pound dumbbells—or higher, depending upon how much of a muscle base you wish to create.

Like *The Fat-Burning Workout*, *Bottoms Up!*, and *Top Shape*, the workout utilizes the modified pyramid system, where you add weight to each of three sets at the expense of a few repetitions.

Now or Never features a machine workout photographed at a fitness center using various machines. If you want to incorporate machines into your workout, you can use this book to get a clear idea about how to use them.

How will you know if it is time to switch to *Now or Never*? Take a hard look at your body and ask yourself if you need more of a muscle base. If your triceps have improved somewhat but are still slightly waving in the wind even after doing one of my other workouts, switch to *Now or Never*, at least for that body part, for six months to a year or more. If you are an older woman and you notice that after you have lost your excess body fat, your front thigh muscle is sagging and hanging over your knee, you should switch to the thigh workout in *Now or Never*. In fact, you would probably be doing yourself a real favor if you switched to *Now or Never* for your total body workout for at least six months to a year!

WEIGHT TRAINING MADE EASY: TRANSFORM YOUR BODY IN FOUR SIMPLE STEPS

This book does exactly what the title says it does: It makes things simple and brings you along step by step. Nothing is assumed; everything is explained clearly and simply. You are taken from workout level 1 (the easiest) through workout level 4, the most challenging. Each workout takes approximately twenty to thirty minutes, four to six days a week. The workouts include: Level 1: Learning the Moves; Level 2: Establishing a Muscle Base; Level 3: Sculpting and Defining the Muscles; and Level 4: The Finishing Touch. Each workout level requires a little more effort and a little more thinking, but the graduated levels are done in such a manner that by the time you reach level 4 you are truly an expert. In many ways, this book is four books in one, but much less intimidating than four books would be.

Weight Training Made Easy pulls the whole idea of weight training all together! Not only does it gently lead the reader along from one stage to the next in a nonintimidating way, but it also provides a clear, photographed explanation of how to substitute barbells and machines for dumbbells if you so desire. In addition, everything in that book is simplified, even the diet. I wrote the book because of popular demand. Many of my readers were writing and asking me to write one book that pulls it all together for them. This is the book!

Specialized Workouts

GUT BUSTERS

There is a special book I've written just for stomach work: *Gut Busters*. Although it is addressed to men, women do exactly the same

workout. It contains the seven exercises most used by champion body-builders and, in fact, this is how most of them get their amazing mid-sections. If you are tired of doing the stomach work in the Bathing Suit Workout, or if you switch to another book but still want to bomb away at your stomach only with different exercises than are found in *The Bathing Suit Workout*, switch to *Gut Busters*.

Once you get used to the workout, it takes only fifteen minutes a day. Since no weights are used with the workout, you do not use the pyramid system or the modified pyramid system. You simply do fifteen to twenty-five repetitions per set of exercises, doing three sets for each body part with a fifteen-second rest between each set. It is very simple to follow.

BONE BUILDING BODY SHAPING WORKOUT

This is a specialized book featuring a routine that can be done in eight minutes a day for a minimum workout—up to thirty-two minutes a day for a maximum workout. It includes body-shaping and bone-building exercises specifically organized for women most interested in protecting themselves against future problems with fractures. The skeleton is featured and each bone being enhanced by each exercise is clearly shown, as well as each muscle that is being reshaped. The diet in the book is especially geared not only to weight loss, but also to calcium-rich foods. The workout gives tone and shape—and definition—all the while, building bone from every angle.

THE BOTTOMS UP WORKOUT: MIDDLE BODY VIDEO

There is yet another special stomach workout on video, *The Bottoms Up Workout: Middle Body*. It takes the stomach work from the book *Bottoms Up!* but greatly expands the workout, giving ten instead of six abdominal exercises and changing some of the exercises so that people with problem backs can also do them.

If you want to use *The Bottoms Up Workout: Middle Body* video, you can either use it to replace the stomach workout in the book you are using or you can alternate it with the stomach workout contained in the book!

Another way to use either of the specialized stomach workouts, *Gut Busters* or *The Bottoms Up Workout: Middle Body*, is to do one workout one day and the other workout the next day, six days a week and alternating days—one day *Gut Busters* and the next day *The Bottoms Up Workout: Middle Body*.

Finally, you can do the stomach workout contained in the book you are using, and on alternate days do either *Gut Busters* or *The Bottoms Up*

Workout: Middle Body, for a three-day routine, and then repeat the sequence. On the seventh day, give your stomach muscles a break from working out.

When Should You Change Workouts?

As a general rule, you should not switch workouts for about six weeks. However, the 12-Minute Total-Body Workout may be used as just a break-in to weight training or as a vacation for you, and you may want to use it for only a few weeks.

With all the other workouts, however, it's a good idea to allow six to twelve weeks to really see what the workout can do for you. If you like what you are seeing and want more of it, stick with your workout for another three months. You can even remain with a workout as long as a year or more, though it is really better to switch after about a year to shock your body into further development.

How to Decide Which Workout You Should Do Next

Your decision about which workout to do next will depend upon two things: what you see in the mirror and how much time and energy you have to invest.

Suppose, for example, you have been doing the Fat-Burning Workout along with the Bathing Suit Workout, but you feel that you need more muscle on your upper body and, in addition, you are bored with the Bathing Suit Workout. The ideal thing to do is to switch to workouts in *Bottoms Up!*, *Now or Never,* or *Top Shape.* Each of these workouts will give you more of a muscle base. In addition, both give a total-body workout, although *Bottoms Up!* gives more work for hips/butt, thighs, and stomach than does *Now or Never* or *Top Shape.*

Now let's take a different scenario. Suppose you took my advice in the earlier paragraphs of this book. You added *Bottoms Up!* to your Bathing Suit Workout for a total-body workout (leaving out hips/butt, thigh, and abdominal work from *Bottoms Up!*, of course, because you are already doing that with your Bathing Suit Workout). After a few months you look in the mirror and think, "I want more definition. Also, I want a shorter workout." Perfect. Switch to *Definition.* You'll get maximum cuts, burn more fat, and, in addition, you'll shorten your workout to fifteen minutes a day! If that workout is just a bit too intense and you have the extra five minutes to spare, instead go to *The Fat-Burning Workout* or *The College Dorm Workout.*

Now let's take a third scenario. Suppose you've been doing *Now or Never* because you've felt a need for more of a muscle base. But now you're burned out on working out and you really feel like taking a three-month vacation from it all. Don't do it. Instead, switch to *The 12-Minute Total-Body Workout*. As the title indicates, you'll only have to work out twelve minutes a day, but the return for your efforts will be worth hours a day because this workout will maintain your hard-earned muscles and when you are ready to go back to one of my longer workouts, you will not have to go through much muscle soreness—perhaps none at all. This workout provides enough of a challenge to your muscles to keep them "at the ready."

My Prescription: If You Don't Want to Think about It

If you want to make sure your body enjoys the benefit of a wide variety of exercise, pick any of my workouts, do it for three months, and then switch to another.

What order should you take? It won't matter in the long run. Over time, as long as you do all of my workouts, your body will have gorgeous muscles, sexy definition, and it will be tight, toned, and shaped to the hilt. It's inevitable. How so? In time, you would be taking advantage of all of the basic body-shaping principles invented by champion bodybuilders, techniques that, like the law of gravity, cannot fail to reshape and define your body over time.

In review, here is the list of my exercise books according to length of workout, from shortest to longest, from least muscle building to most muscle building:

1. *The 12-Minute Total Body Workout*—Twelve minutes every day

2. *Definition*—Fifteen minutes six days a week, or thirty minutes three days a week

3. *The College Dorm Workout*—Twenty minutes five to six days a week

4. *The Fat-Burning Workout*—Twenty minutes four to six days a week

5. *Bottoms Up!*—Twenty to thirty minutes four to six days a week

6. *Top Shape*—Thirty to forty minutes four to six days a week

7. *Now or Never*—Forty to sixty minutes four to six days a week

8. *Weight Training Made Easy*—Twelve to thirty minutes four to seven days a week (depending upon which of the four levels you are doing)

Specialized Workouts

9. *Gut Busters*—Fifteen minutes four to six days a week

10. *Bone Building Body Shaping Workout*—Eight to thirty-two minutes two to six days a week

11. *The Bottoms Up Workout: Middle Body* (Video)—Twenty to thirty minutes three to six days a week

Note: Books are available in all major bookstores. Videos can be ordered through me. See pp. 199–200 for further details.

Taking Time Off from Working Out with Weights

The most time you should take off is one week every six months to a year. This adds up to a total of no more than two weeks off a year from working out with weights. Why take a break at all? The human body is not much different from the human mind when it comes to boredom. It simply needs a change! If you tried never to take time off from working out with weights, after a while your body would rebel and would refuse to cooperate with you. Every workout would become a struggle. You would have to fight yourself with each repetition. You'd be tempted to quit in the middle of a workout.

The bottom line is, you can't fool mother nature. So don't try to behave as if your body were a machine. It's not. It's human, and made of flesh and bone. So think ahead and take time off—at least one week a year. Don't worry. You don't have to vegetate completely during that time. You can still walk, engage in sports, or even do a favorite aerobic activity. Just stay away from the weights for a week.

The Lifetime Guarantee

If you make up your mind to incorporate a weight-training workout into your daily routine (well, at least four days a week) and, better, if you do aerobics at least three times a week in addition (this will give you an exercise regimen for each day of the week), I promise that even if you do overeat and gain some weight, you will never go back to being as out of shape as you were before you started. In addition, I

promise that it will be relatively easy to get back in shape once you start again. All you will have to do is to follow, once again, the low-fat eating plan in any of my fitness books, or a doctor-approved, low-fat, balanced diet of your own choosing.

Why does this work? Your hard-earned muscles and the beautiful definition will be there waiting for you under the fat, whereas had you completely stopped working out, your muscles would have slowly atrophied. You would now have soft flab under the fat, and would have double the trouble getting back in shape.

But even if you did the wrong thing and stopped working out in addition to pigging out, there's good news. Muscles remember! Yes, every muscle you build is like putting muscle in the permanent memory bank. Once you start working out again, it takes only one third the time it took you originally to get the muscles. In other words, say you worked out for a year and got in shape. Then you stopped working out for a year. It takes only four months to get back what it took you a year to get the first time. (And by the way, it takes as long as you took to get the muscles to lose them. In other words, it takes a whole year to lose muscles you built for a year, two years to lose all the muscles you build after working out for two years, and so on.)

So the bottom line is that you've got nothing to lose and everything to gain from working out with weights—even if you do let yourself go. But the key is not to let yourself go. Incorporate working out into your daily life plan for now and forever!

A Final Note

If you wish to write me to make a comment or ask a question or to send me your "before-and-after"s, please include a stamped, self-addressed envelope and I will personally reply. See p. 199 for address.

News Flash

I'm having a special cruise for fun and fitness. If you're interested, call Gotta Go Cruises at the toll free number: 888-446-8824.

BIBLIOGRAPHY

Videos by Joyce Vedral

Vedral, Joyce. *The Bottoms Up Workout: Upper Body*. New York: Good Times Video, 1995. $14.98. (See below to order.)

Vedral, Joyce. *The Bottoms Up Workout: Middle Body*. New York: Good Times Video, 1995. $14.98. (See below to order.)

Vedral, Joyce. *The Bottoms Up Workout: Lower Body*. New York: Good Times Video, 1995. $14.98. (See below to order.) Note: $39.98 if you buy all three.

Vedral, Joyce. *The Fat-Burning Workout: Volume I*. Regular Workout. (20 minutes a day). New York: Time-Life Video, 1993. $21.98. (See below to order.)

Vedral, Joyce. *The Fat-Burning Workout: Volume II*. Intensity and Insanity Workout. (40 minutes a day). New York: Time-Life Video, 1993. $21.98. (See below to order.)

To order, add $3.95 for each item for shipping and handling. Send a check or money order to:

> Joyce L. Vedral
> P.O. Box 7433
> Wantagh, NY 11793-7433

Note: if you order the Bottoms Up Series, all three, you need send only $3.95. Also, if you order Volumes II and III of *The Fat Burning Workout*, you need send only $3.95.

Books by Joyce Vedral

Vedral, Joyce, Ph.D. *Bone-Building Body-Shaping Workout.* New York: Simon & Schuster, 1998. $14.00.

Vedral, Joyce, Ph.D. *Weight Training Made Easy: Transform Your Body in Four Simple Steps.* New York: Warner Books, 1997. $14.99.

Vedral, Joyce, Ph.D. *Eat to Trim: Get It Off and Keep It Off.* New York: Warner Books, 1997. $15.98.

Vedral, Joyce, Ph.D. *Look In, Look Up, Look Out: Be the Person You Were Meant to Be.* New York: Warner Books, 1996. $12.98.

(Ask about personally autographed discount hardcover when you write to me.)

Vedral, Joyce, Ph.D. *Definition: Shape Without Bulk in Fifteen Minutes a Day.* New York: Warner Books, 1995. $14.99.

Vedral, Joyce, Ph.D. *Top Shape.* New York: Warner Books, 1995. $14.98.

Vedral, Marthe S., and Joyce L. Vedral. *The College Dorm Workout.* New York: Warner Books, 1994. $8.95.

Vedral, Joyce, Ph.D. *Bottoms Up!* New York: Warner Books, 1993. $12.98.

Vedral, Joyce, Ph.D. *Get Rid of Him!* New York: Warner Books, 1993. $8.95.

Vedral, Joyce, Ph.D. *Gut Busters.* New York: Warner Books, 1992. $8.95.

Vedral, Joyce, Ph.D. *The Fat-Burning Workout.* New York: Warner Books, 1991. $14.98.

Vedral, Joyce, Ph.D. *The 12-Minute Total-Body Workout.* New York: Warner Books, 1989. $12.98.

Vedral, Joyce, Ph.D. *Now or Never.* New York: Warner Books, 1986. $12.98.

If you cannot find any book, please write to me. The address is on p.199. Send list price plus $3.95 each, for shipping and handling. I will personally autograph the book to you. Note: I have copies of both *Eat to Trim* and *Look In, Look Up, Look Out* in hardcover—at the above discounted prices.

INDEX

Page numbers of illustrations appear in italics

ABOUT THE AUTHOR

We'll never forget the day in 1991, when Joyce Vedral appeared on the *Sally Jessy Raphael Show*. It was a quiet July morning and Joyce had been invited on the program to promote her new book, *The Fat-Burning Workout*. With a built-in flair for the dramatic, Joyce decided to appear on camera in a provocative gold bikini that showed off her toned, enviable forty-eight-year-old figure to best effect.

If we told you that all hell broke loose a mere five minutes into the broadcast, it wouldn't begin to describe the pandemonium that followed as viewers all over the country raced out to find copies of Joyce's workout. "If she can do it, I can do it too," they cried to bookstore owners, the Warner switchboard, and to anyone who would listen. In no time, Joyce was a recognized fitness guru, well on her way to the *New York Times* bestseller list.

If anyone ever tells you that lightning does not strike twice, don't believe them. Joyce did it again. She appeared on the *Montel Williams Show* and had an even greater reaction to her book *Bottoms Up!* For the week of January 1, 1994, her book beat all books in print in America, including books by Howard Stern, Rush Limbaugh, and Michael Crichton—making number one on the *USA Today* list for that week. That same book, *Bottoms Up!*, reached number one on the *New York Times* bestseller list.

Today, at a fit and classy fifty-five, Joyce's fitness library combines for an in-print total of well over one million copies. The reason books like *Bottoms Up! Top Shape, Definition, Gutbusters, The 12-Minute Total-Body Workout, Now or Never, Eat to Trim*, and *Weight Training Made Easy* have sold so well is simple: They achieve the promised results.

But there's another reason for Joyce's success: Joyce, with her trademark upbeat voice, is a real person who convinces people in lectures and on television shows all over the country that "if I can do it, so can you." She isn't shy about the before picture of herself, fat at twenty-six, nor is she afraid to poke fun at her "bad genetics." "I come from a Russian heritage," she says. "My whole family look like boxes on wheels."

When Joyce gives a lecture, people are mesmerized. She has a way of relating to an audience as if she knows each and every one personally, and a gift for getting right down to the level of each eager listener. In the words of Paul Adamo of The Learning Annex in New York City, "In all the years of my having lecturers I have never seen anything like this in my

life. She arrests the audience and keeps each and every one of them in the palm of her hand throughout. People walk away with love in their eyes. No one can have a Joyce Vedral 'experience' without being touched."

Joyce is a frequent guest on *Oprah*, the *Today* show, *Sally Jessy Raphael*, and CNN, and has been written up in the *New York Times*, the *Daily News*, and the *Post*. She is a sought-after speaker in women's groups, fitness centers, and shopping malls across the country.

Perhaps what makes Joyce most interesting is her unusual background. Unlike so many other fitness experts who are one-dimensional, Joyce earned her Ph.D. in English literature from New York University. Her knowledge of fitness came after years of teaching high school and college English, getting "fat and out of shape," and by luck, landing freelance assignments to *Muscle and Fitness* and *Shape* magazines, where she became acquainted with the techniques that now fill her books and lectures. Joyce says, "My mission is to help others who lead busy lives and are interested in getting healthy and in shape in minutes rather than hours a day."

Always a women's advocate, and concerned with women's issues, Joyce is, in addition, the author of *Bone-Building Body-Shaping Workout* and the international best-seller, with Warner Books, *Get Rid of Him!*, a book that helps women build their self-esteem, discover their inner strength, and move on when it's time—and to find the right man—and her new self-help book, *Look In, Look Up, Look Out!*

APPENDIX

THE BATHING SUIT WORKOUT
Tear-Out Wall Chart

Once you learn the Bathing Suit Workout, you can use the convenient tear-out wall chart on the following pages. If you paste the pages together, you will have an overview of the entire workout in the order in which it is done.

TRI-SET #1

HIPS/BUTTOCKS: SADDLEBAG STRIPPER

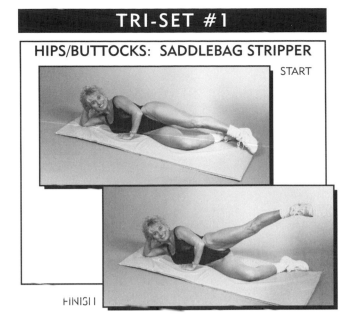

START

FINISH

THIGHS: LYING INNER THIGH LIFT

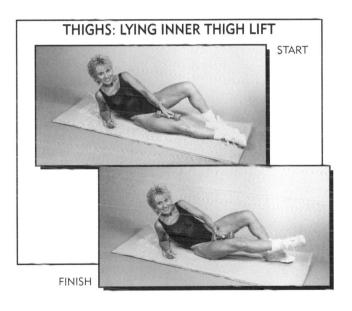

START

FINISH

ABDOMINALS: KNEE-RAISED OBLIQUE CRUNCH

START

FINISH

TRI-SET #2

HIPS/BUTTOCKS: LOWER BUTT CURL

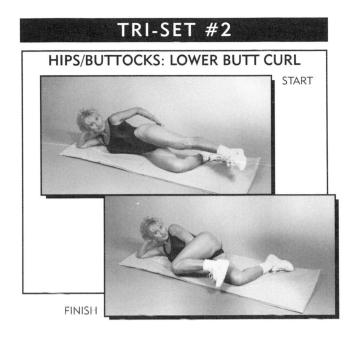

START

FINISH

THIGHS: LEG CURL

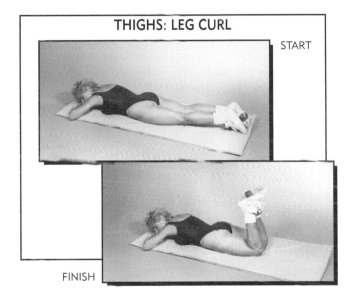

START

FINISH

ABDOMINALS: BENT-KNEE SEWN LIFT

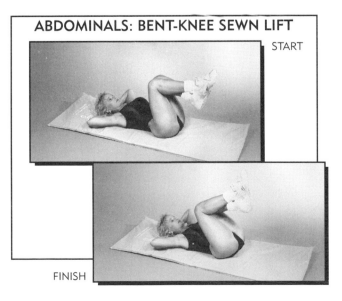

START

FINISH

TRI-SET #3

HIPS/BUTTOCKS: LOWER BUTT CRUNCH

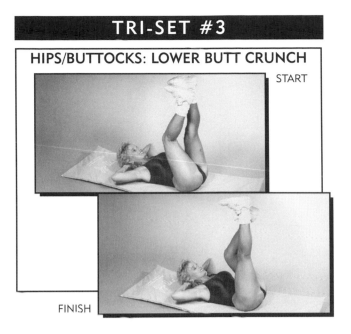

START

FINISH

THIGHS: CHAIR POSITION FIRMER

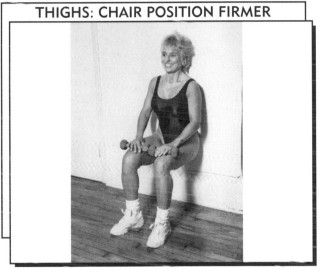

START FINISH

ABDOMINALS: KNEE-RAISED CRUNCH

START

FINISH

TRI-SET #4

HIPS/BUTTOCKS: LOWER BUTT SIDE KICK

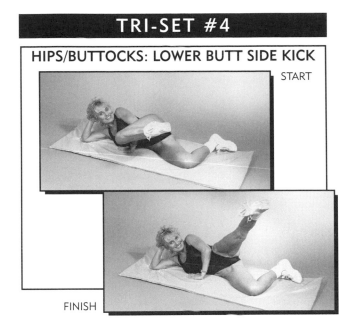

START

FINISH

THIGHS: STRADDLE SQUAT

START

FINISH

ABDOMINALS: SIDE OBLIQUE CRUNCH

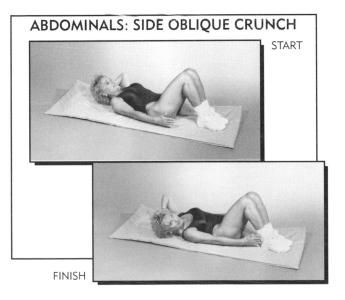

START

FINISH

TRI-SET #5

HIPS/BUTTOCKS: FLOOR FEATHER KICK-UP

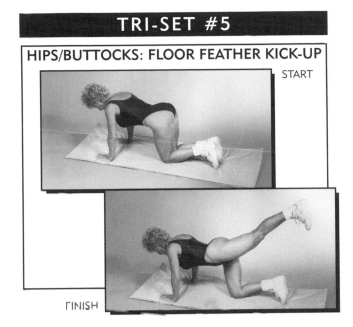

START

FINISH

THIGHS: FRONT SQUAT

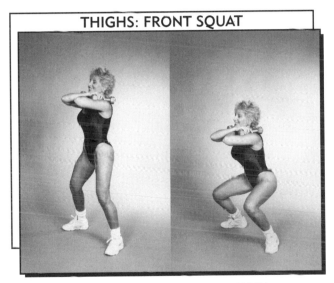

START · · · · · · · · · · · · FINISH

ABDOMINALS: CEILING SEWN LIFT

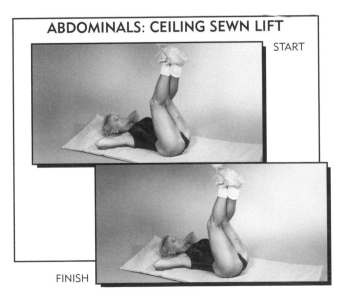

START

FINISH

TRI-SET #6

HIPS/BUTTOCKS: LYING BUTT LIFT

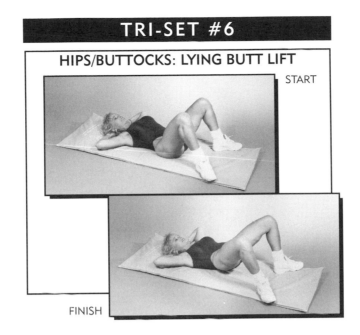

START

FINISH

THIGHS: LUNGE

START FINISH

ABDOMINALS: TOE-REACH CRUNCH

START

FINISH

TRI-SET #7

HIPS/BUTTOCKS: ONE-LEG PRONE BUTT LIFT

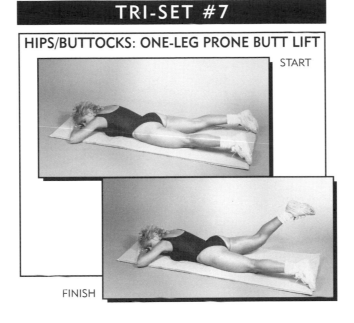

START

FINISH

THIGHS: REGULAR SQUAT

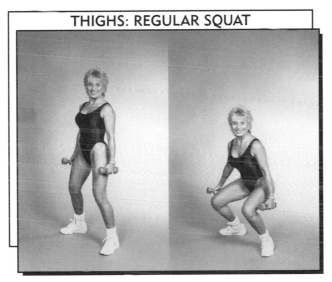

START　　　　　　　　FINISH

ABDOMINALS: CEILING OBLIQUE REACH

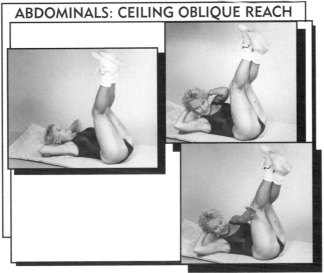

START　　　　　　　　FINISH

TRI-SET #8

HIPS/BUTTOCKS: STANDING BUTT SQUEEZE

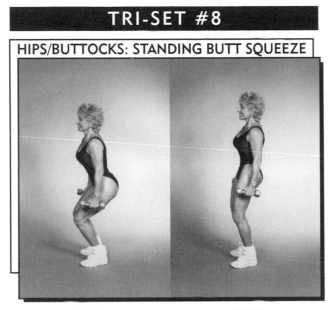

START FINISH

THIGHS: HACK SQUAT

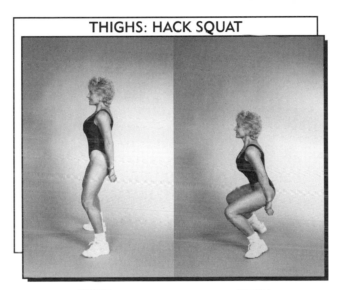

START FINISH

ABDOMINALS: KNEE-IN

START

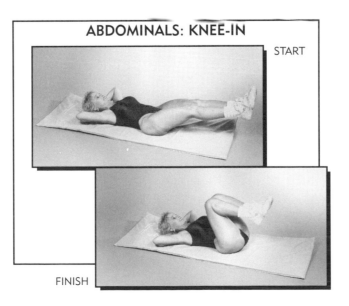

FINISH

TRI-SET #9

HIPS/BUTTOCKS: REVERSE LUNGE LIFT

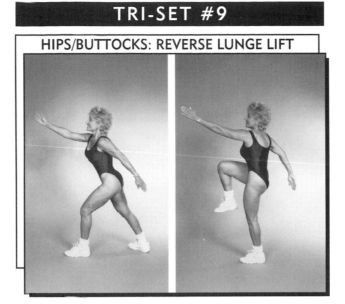

START FINISH

THIGHS: BENT-KNEE DEADLIFT

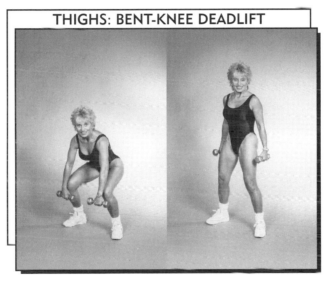

START FINISH

ABDOMINALS: SIT-UP

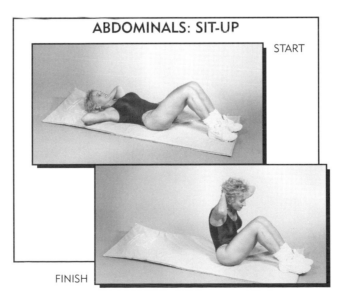

START

FINISH

TRI-SET #10

HIPS/BUTTOCKS: STRAIGHT-LEG KICK-UP

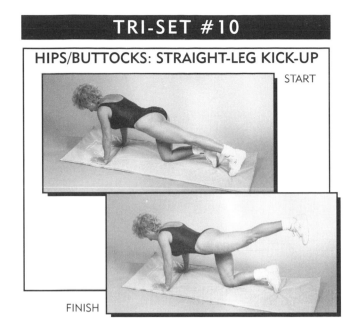

START

FINISH

THIGHS: SISSY SQUAT

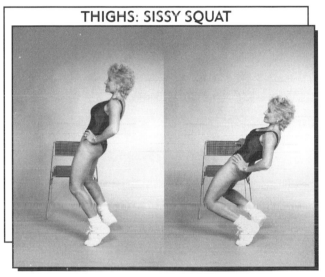

START FINISH

ABDOMINALS: LEG RAISE

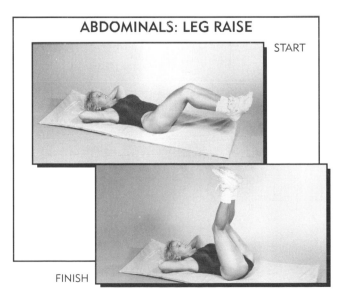

START

FINISH